For Jerry, Jim,
Pam, and Scott

Magazine Writers Nonfiction Guidelines

Magazine Writers Nonfiction Guidelines

Over 200 Periodical Editors' Instructions Reproduced

compiled and edited by
Judy Mandell

McFarland & Company, Inc., Publishers
Jefferson, North Carolina, and London

Library of Congress Cataloguing-in-Publication Data

Magazine writers nonfiction guidelines.

Includes index.
1. Authorship—Handbooks, manuals, etc.
2. American periodicals. I. Mandell, Judy, 1939–
PN147.M33   1987   070.5′72′0973   86-43088

ISBN 0-89950-239-3 (acid-free natural paper) ∞

Manufactured in the United States of America.

McFarland & Company, Inc., Publishers
Box 611, Jefferson, North Carolina 28640

Table of Contents

**Magazines That Accept Freelance
Contributions But Have No
Writer's Guidelines**

Preface

Magazine Writer's Guidelines includes the official writer's guidelines for over two hundred magazines, as well as comments from the editors of thirty additional publications that do not provide guidelines but do accept freelance contributions. The book should be a useful tool for novice and professional freelance writers, students, scholars, and teachers of writing. It also provides a behind-the-scenes look at the editorial policies of magazines.

The compilation includes magazines found on large and comprehensive newsstands, popular periodicals sold on a subscription basis only, and airline magazines.

Nearly 65,000 magazines are published in North America. Magazines abound for every imaginable (and some unimaginable) special interest groups, hobbies, and professions. Magazines are geared toward age, gender, race, and religion. There are city magazines, state magazines, regional magazines, and magazines for and about airlines, buses, boats, and trains, as well as those with an emphasis on physical and mental health, science, computers, arts, leisure, women's interests, men's interests, and prurient interests. Magazines are produced to entertain, to teach, and to titillate. If an idea exists, a magazine exists to cover it.

Two years ago, while planning to submit an article, I realized that magazine freelancers needed a book of guidelines. Requesting writer's guidelines was a nuisance, taking energy, money, and most important, time. And when the guidelines finally arrived (sometimes in six weeks) my idea had become stale, if not out of date. Yet it's very important for a writer to use these guidelines in order to prepare an article properly.

This book should help the writer who is uncertain about where to send the piece he or she has written as well as the writer who already has a periodical in mind but doesn't quite know his or her angle. Even if the author has thoroughly read the magazine and thinks he's figures out its tone, style, content, and readership, he's better off knowing exactly what the magazine's editors have to say about what they want from freelancers.

I wish to thank the hundreds of magazine editors who encouraged me in this project, and sent me their writer's guidelines for publication in this book.

I'm equally grateful to the editors of magazines that do not provide guidelines (but do accept freelance contributions), whose interviews provided valuable material for the readers of this compilation.

And a special thanks to Jerry, who egged me on.

Judy Mandell
Earlysville, Virginia

The Guidelines

american baby

575 LEXINGTON AVENUE   NEW YORK, N.Y. 10022   212 752-0775

EDITORIAL GUIDELINES FOR AMERICAN BABY MAGAZINE

Article Content:

Readership is composed of women in late pregnancy (6-9 months) and early new motherhood (baby age 1-6 months). Most readers are first-time parents; some have older children (age 2-4 years). Fathers also read the publication.

Articles should either give "how to" information on some aspect of pregnancy or child care; should cover some common problem of child raising, along with solutions; should discuss some personal experience which is universal (though not in diary type fashion); or should give advice to the mother on some psychological or practical subject.

Medical subjects are acceptable as long as some doctor or medical authority is mentioned. Interviews with experts in a related field are also acceptable.

Article Style:

A simple, straightforward, clear approach is mandatory. No "hearts and flowers" or fantasy pieces are accepted. Focus on the reality, the humor, and the delight of child rearing, but not on its "mystical" or "magical" qualities.

Article Length:

Full-length articles run between 1500-2000 words.

Fillers or short articles run between 500-1500 words.

Article Payment:

Between $100 and $400, depending on article length, is paid upon publication.

Article Submission:

Submit all manuscripts with a self-addressed, stamped envelope to: Editor, AMERICAN BABY Magazine, 575 Lexington Avenue, New York, New York 10022.

For a sample copy of AMERICAN BABY Magazine, send a 9" X 12" self-addressed envelope, stamped with 85¢ postage, to the above address.

American Baby ● The First Year of Life ● Childbirth '84 ● Childbirth Educator ● American Baby TV Show

AMERICAN FILM INSTITUTE

AMERICAN FILM
MAGAZINE

WRITER'S GUIDELINES

ALL AUTHORS SHOULD BE ACQUAINTED WITH THE CONTENTS OF RECENT

ISSUES OF AMERICAN FILM BEFORE SUBMITTING LETTERS OF QUERY

AND/OR MANUSCRIPTS FOR POSSIBLE PUBLICATION.

QUERY LETTERS

* Editors prefer to receive query letters. They should
be concise, clearly stated queries, explaining the story
idea. The proposed approach and the theme should be
well-defined.

* A short selection of writing samples and/or published
clips can accompany the query letter.

MANUSCRIPTS

To submit a manuscript for publication, the following guidelines
are standard procedure:

* Manuscript should be double-spaced with 1½-inch margins
on all sides.

* 1500-1700 words - for a column
2500-3000 words - for a feature

* A cover letter should accompany the manuscript with your
name, address, and date in the upper right-hand corner.
The title should be clearly defined in the cover letter.

* Enclose a stamped, self-addressed envelope and clips
(if you have any) with the manuscript.

American Health
80 Fifth Avenue
New York, NY 10011

REVISED 11/14/83

Information for contributors

AMERICAN HEALTH: Fitness of Body and Mind is a lively general-interest publication about health and everything that affects it. As of May 1984, it is a monthly magazine, sold primarily by subscription. Its guaranteed circulation is 650,000.

We cover both the scientific and the "lifestyle" aspects of health, including laboratory research, clinical advances, fitness, holistic healing and nutrition. Whether an article is about developments inside or outside the medical establishment, our commitment is to high-quality information with a minimum of bias and a maximum of perspective and data. We look for readable, jargon-free articles that present a subject with the excitement it deserves.

We want information that's new, that's authoritative, and that's helpful to readers. When we cover research advances, for example, we do so with an eye towards how they affect the individual. Psychological and political articles, to work for us, must show a solid understanding of health and physiology.

Our approach admits humor, offbeat subjects (if covered with a critical intelligence), and an occasional first-person anecdotal report that gives an unusual view of health issues or appreciation of the body.

In each issue, we run several feature articles of 1,000 to 3,000 words and 35 to 45 shorter news reports (100 to 750 words). A lively, informative style is important to both types of article. We believe that a magazine about health can be serious without being solemn, and we believe that some of the most important stories are brief.

The best way to help us decide on an assignment is with a story proposal in writing. Please submit ideas for news and feature articles in two paragraphs (or less) that offer the best possible sample of your writing style and approach to the material, as well as describe the value of the story and its basic facts. You can include a resume and one or two clips. **We can accept only queries accompanied by a self-addressed stamped envelope. We do not read unsolicited manuscripts. We do not take responsibility for the return of any material sent without an SASE.** Please address all queries to: Editorial, American Health Magazine, 80 Fifth Avenue, Suite 302, New York, NY 10011.

Writers are paid on acceptance of an article, and AMERICAN HEALTH generally buys all rights, except that the author retains the right to use material from an article in any book project. AMERICAN HEALTH articles are often reprinted in other magazines and newspapers, and may soon be used in a network of international publications. Reprint of an article in any publication automatically entails additional payment to the writer.

Features generally range from 1,000 to 3,000 words, for which we pay $600 (kill fee $150) to $2,000 ($500). Articles that are commissioned unusually long, require especially difficult research, or are requested on a crash basis merit a fee bonus.

More than most magazines, we seek to break stories into sidebars whenever they provide the best way to give readers access to a range of material. We consider the sidebars as important as the central text. Occasionally we commission sidebars to accompany articles written by another author; such sidebars are paid at the same rate as short items.

News. The magazine has a well-developed array of news sections that cover a wide range of health topics concisely. The 35 to 45 short items per issue are grouped thematically into six or seven sections. The sections include: Medical News, our general news round-up; The Fitness Report; The Nutrition Report; Lifestyles, which focuses on personal and cultural beliefs in health care; Consumer Alert, which focuses on the consumer side of health; plus tooth matters, skin, scent and hair, and occasional other topics.

Writers are paid by the assigned manuscript page (250 words per page) as follows: 1 page—$125 ($35 kill fee); 2 pages—$250 ($65); 3 pages—$375 ($100).

AMERICAN HEALTH has no full-time staff writers; we have chosen to rely on outside contributors for almost all our articles. The magazine needs good ideas, and good articles, from professional journalists, health educators, researchers and clinicians. We look forward to hearing from you.

AMERICAN HERITAGE PUBLISHING CO., INC.
10 ROCKEFELLER PLAZA · NEW YORK. NEW YORK 10020
(212) 399-8900

AMERICAN HERITAGE, The Magazine of History, 10 Rockefeller Plaza
New York, New York 10020. Editor: Byron Dobell. Our subject
is the American experience -- what makes life here different from
life anywhere else. Our topics range from serious concerns to
colorful sidelights, from powerful institutions to ordinary men
and women, but our treatment of them is always informed by the
knowledge of our national past. We try to use the past to illuminate the present.

We welcome the contributions of free-lancers, but suggest that ideas
for articles be submitted -- in some detail -- to our editors in
advance. We also suggest that prospective contributors consult our
indexes before suggesting a topic. We publish excerpts from non-
fiction books. We do not publish fiction or poetry.

A study of past issues of AMERICAN HERITAGE will help you with
regard to length and manner of treatment. If we decide to buy
your article, we will ask you to annotate all quotations and factual
statements. We would also like to have a very brief biographical
note about yourself.

We pay on acceptance; our rates depend on the length of the piece
and the nature of the subject. Maximum length is 6,000 words, but
we are also interested in shorter pieces.

We regret that we are unable to send out sample copies. Any suggestion or submitted manuscript should be accompanied by a self-
addressed, stamped envelope.

Historical Times, Inc.
2245 Kohn Road/Box 8200
Harrisburg, PA 17105
(717) 657-9555

American History Illustrated
British Heritage
Civil War Times
Country Journal
Early American Life
Fly Fisherman
Opus
The New England Skiers' Guide
The Original New England Guide

Museum Editions Limited
Historical Times Travel

AMERICAN HISTORY ILLUSTRATED

GENERAL GUIDELINES FOR CONTRIBUTORS

American History Illustrated is a magazine of cultural, social, political,
and military history published for a general audience. With more than
120,000 subscribers throughout the United States and abroad, it has a
readership ranging from young people of high school age to college graduates
and senior citizens. The magazine is published monthly except in July and
August, and it is sold on newsstands as well as by subscription.

American History Illustrated seeks to bring history to life through
accurate but lively articles on significant and interesting persons,
events, issues, and places from the American past. We regard our "typical
reader" as being an intelligent and well-educated individual who--while
having no connection with the history profession--happens to have a deep
interest in various aspects of our nation's heritage. We anticipate that
our subscribers read the magazine for enjoyment as well as for information.

Material in American History Illustrated is presented on a popular rather
than scholarly level. Key prerequisites for publication in the magazine
are thorough research and accurate presentation, precise English usage and
sound organization, a lively style, and a high level of human interest.

We are strong advocates of simple, clear writing; at the same time we ask
that you do not oversimplify events or issues. For an excellent guide to
clear communication, we recommend On Writing Well: An Informal Guide to
Writing Nonfiction by William Zinsser (Harper and Row, 1980).

* * *

Articles appearing in American History Illustrated fall into several
well-defined categories, and specific information on each appears on
the following pages. The following general guidelines apply to all
submissions:

* As a first step toward becoming a contributor, we suggest that you
   read one or more recent issues of American History Illustrated to
   become familiar with our style and format.

*PLEASE NOTE WE ARE NOT RESPONSIBLE FOR RETURN OF MATERIALS NOT ACCOMPANIED BY SASE.

* We encourage you to query us before submitting a manuscript. It is possible that your topic has been previously covered in the magazine, or we may already have something on it "in the works." Unsolicited manuscripts will be considered for publication, however.

* Query letters should be limited to a concise one- or two-page proposal defining your article, with an emphasis on its unique qualities. Please also give us an idea of your qualifications for handling this topic, and a brief summary of your previous writing experience.

* Be sure to enclose a stamped, self-addressed return envelope (or adequate return postage) with your materials.

* When submitting a manuscript, please send us your original typed copy. Use a clean typewriter ribbon, double-space the lines, number the pages, and leave adequate margins for editing. Enclose a cover letter with your manuscript. Retain a second copy of the manuscript for your own reference.

* Please provide us with a list of your basic sources and references. And along the left margin of your manuscript, opposite key quotations, dates, and figures, pencil in brief annotations (author and page) directing us to the correct references. These will be used by our staff researchers to confirm the information prior to publication.

* If your manuscript draws on quotes from sources not commonly available (i.e., locally or privately published materials, unpublished manuscripts, dissertations, or old newspapers), enclose photocopies of the revelant pages from these sources.

* Your narrative will possess power and human interest in proportion to your ability to bring your characters to life. However, avoid supplying conversations or thoughts of characters that cannot be supported by memoirs or other sound evidence. Fictionalization is unacceptable.

* Questions of punctuation, capitalization, and style should be handled in accordance with The Chicago Manual of Style (University of Chicago Press), the generally-accepted reference for such matters.

* Good illustrations are a key ingredient of articles appearing in American History Illustrated. If you are aware of appropriate illustrations for your article, please tell us about them. Photocopies are especially helpful.

* Multiple submissions will not be considered.

* * *

We will endeavor to respond to query letters within ten weeks of receipt, and to manuscript submissions within sixteen weeks.

All materials are considered on speculation, with no obligation to buy.

We purchase all publication rights to accepted manuscripts.

A contract is forwarded to the author upon acceptance of a manuscript, and payment is normally made within ten days after return of the signed contract.

We reserve the right to edit manuscripts as we see fit. Whenever possible, however, we provide authors with galley proofs of their articles prior to publication.

* * *

SPECIFIC GUIDELINES

FEATURE ARTICLES

Major essays on significant individuals and events from the American past. These run from six to eight pages in the magazine. All periods from 1492 to the Vietnam conflict are appropriate for coverage.

These articles are the heart of American History Illustrated. Interesting topics, thorough research, good organization, clear writing, accuracy, and an engaging style are keys to successful submissions.

Manuscripts should be between 2,500 and 3,500 words in length.

Payment: $250 to $350 (may vary in some cases).

* * *

"PORTFOLIO"   (continuing series)

Pictorial feature on notable American artists, sculptors, and photographers, and on other topics having a strong graphic theme. Portfolios run six to eight pages in the magazine.

Manuscripts should be about 1,500 words in length.

Payment: $150 (may vary in some cases).

* * *

"GLIMPSES INTO THE EVERYDAY PAST"   (continuing series)

Essays describing once-routine but now-unfamiliar trades, activities, and ways of life from various eras in the American past. Two to six magazine pages.

Many details of American life that in their time were common knowledge are generally forgotten today--casualties of inevitably changing lifestyles and technologies. This series focuses on seemingly ordinary things--skills, crafts, tools, and associated minutia--that through their very unfamiliarity to us become fascinating.

Representative themes: life in Jamestown in 1607, the printer's trade in 1775, plantation life in 1830, a day on the Oregon Trail in 1843, a doctor's work in 1860, travel on the transcontinental railroad in 1870, life in a Northwest logging camp in 1895.

Three key requirements for contributing to this series are (1) a detailed knowledge of the subject, (2) clarity and accuracy in describing skills and activities, and (3) the ability to breathe life and interest into these descriptions.

Manuscripts should be between 1,000 and 2,500 words in length.

Payment: $100 to $250.

                            * * *

"ARTIFACTS"   (continuing series)

Human interest stories behind objects from the American past. Two magazine pages.

Each feature consists of (1) a photograph of an artifact, (2) an interesting description of the object, and (3) a concise and lively account of the historical events that give the item significance.

Appropriate subjects could range from an object as small as a spent bullet to something as massive as a restored aircraft. The object itself can be innocuous in nature, but the story behind it must be full of human interest.

Because the success of this feature depends so crucially on how well the story is told, style, organization, and development of the theme are of special importance. Particular attention should be given to construction of the opening and closing paragraphs.

Manuscripts should be about 1,100 words in length.

Payment: $100.

"TESTAMENTS TO THE PAST"   (continuing series)

Articles on noteworthy historical sites. (Articles on major historical re-enactments are also appropriate.) Two to six magazine pages.

Each article consists of two main elements: (1) a tour-in-words of the present-day landmark, and (2) a concise overview of the historical events and circumstances that gave the place significance.

This series is generally limited to historical sites that have been preserved, restored, or re-created to the extent that they provide the visitor with a realistic illusion of stepping back through time.   The landmark should be one that the author can personally visit so as to develop an accurate, vivid description based on first-hand observation.

Manuscripts should be between 1,000 and 2,500 words in length.

Present-day photographs of the historical site--preferably in color-- are an integral part of each article. Photography provided by the author will be useful but is not a requirement.

Payment: $100 to $250.

* * *

"PAGES FROM AN AMERICAN ALBUM"   (continuing series)

Compact, lively profiles of lesser-known but interesting figures from the American past. Two magazine pages.

Manuscripts should be 1,100 words in length. Because of the specific graphic format required, profiles should not deviate from this standard by more than 100 words.

In spite of (or more accurately because of) its short length, this feature presents special challenges to the writer. Precise organization, a careful choice of words and selection of pertinent facts, and a lively style are all required. Particular attention should be given to construction of the opening and closing paragraphs. This is, in effect, a demanding exercise in short-story writing.

The subject should be someone of general interest, but not of such importance as to merit treatment in a major article. He or she must be someone for whom an excellent photographic or artist's likeness can be found.

Payment: $100.

* * *

P.O. BOX 1055 · INDIANAPOLIS, INDIANA 46206-1055 · (317) 635-8411

WRITER'S GUIDELINES

The American Legion Magazine, a recognized leader among national general-interest publications, is published monthly by The American Legion for its 2.5 million members. These military service veterans, working through 16,000 community-level posts, dedicate themselves to God and country and traditional American values; a strong national security; adequate and compassionate care for veterans, their widows and orphans; community service, and the wholesome development of our nation's youth.

We publish articles reflective of these aims and values to inform our membership and their families of significant current issues affecting our nation, the Free World and the way we live. The American Legion Magazine's primary focus is in the areas of national security, foreign affairs and contemporary problems and trends of national importance. However, we also report on a wide range of other subject matter including, but not limited to, analyses of key events in American history that have lessons for today; incidents that occurred in the wars of the 20th Century, and areas of general concern to all people, such as sports, hobbies, medicine and health, ethics and the arts.

We will consider purchasing interviews conducted with prominent national and world figures who address topics of current concern to our readership.

We place a premium on good taste, objectivity, accuracy, and tight and dynamic writing. Ground rules include no exposes, no partisan politics and no articles that ridicule the opinions, appearance or activities of any individuals or groups. We address only the issues, not the partisans involved.

Format and Style

Articles published in The American Legion Magazine generally adhere to a three-part editorial format: (1) statement of the problem, (2) explanation of the impact of the problem, (3) solutions. We like to see these points summarized early in an article, then expanded as needed to include vivid examples, facts and expert opinion needed to report the story in a dynamic, interesting manner.

Articles should be "three dimensional" in that each should cover a topic's breadth in terms of its relationship to other areas; depth in terms of basic significance and ways the subject matter affects people and the nation, and time in terms of putting it into perspective with present and future events.

- 2 -

Outline Required

Before being assigned an article, writers will be required to submit an outline showing the general thrust of the proposed article. The outline need not be long, but it must be thorough and it must demonstrate a writer's firm understanding of the proposed topic and the particular slant being recommended.

Documentation

When articles are submitted, writers are required to include appropriate documentation of pertinent facts and, whenever possible, citations verifying that key persons quoted in the article have reviewed quoted material for accuracy. This is especially important when quoting people whose professional reputations could be damaged if misquoted or quoted out of context. Before the purchase of an article is authorized, a writer may be required to submit additional documentation and clearances as required by either the editor or the Legion's legal counsel.

Rights Purchased

We purchase First North American serial rights, unless otherwise negotiated.

Payment, Length, Queries

We generally pay from $250 to $1,200 depending on the complexity of subject matter and on our current needs. Kill fees and reimbursement of expenses are negotiable with writers working on assignment.

The minimum manuscript length is from 750 to 1,200 words for material written for specific departments; 1,500 to 1,800 words for general features, and up to 2,500 words for major, analytical features.

We report on queries within six weeks. Although we prefer queries, we will consider unsolicited manuscripts. Written queries are preferred to telephone calls.

Return Of Materials

Queries, unsolicited manuscripts and art must be accompanied by a self-addressed, stamped envelope if the submitter desires that they be returned. We will not return submissions without a SASE. We cannot assume any financial liability for the loss of any submissions, whether requested or not.

Samples

The best way to get a feel for our type of article is to read several issues of the magazine. Sample available for $1.50 to cover postage and handling.

AMERICAN SURVIVAL GUIDE MAGAZINE

A McMullen Publishing publication, 2145 West La Palma Avenue, Anaheim, CA 92801 (714) 635-9040

American Survival Guide Writer Guidelines

American Survival Guide magazine is for independent, self-reliant people concerned with protection of individual life and property and with preservation of the United States of America as a nation. Readers are interested in learning about human and natural forces posing threats in day-to-day American life as well as possible threats in the future: terrorism, crime, conventional and nuclear/biological/chemical warfare, disease, accidental injury, toxic wastes and other pollution, earthquakes, tornados, floods, hurricanes and other environmental disasters, poisonous plants and animals, etc. Readers want to acquire the "how to" of survival to enable them to succeed and prosper in their daily lives as well as in any number of possible future situations. They expect to succeed through knowledge of self defense, medicine and health, communications, transportation and other aspects of survival. American Survival Guide presents the knowledge, technology, hardware (including weapons), problems, practice, tactics, strategies, attitudes and philosophy for survival in a wide range of situations and scenarios.

Subject matter of high interest to readers includes identification of threats, preparedness, instruction in self reliance, food production and storage, self defense and weapons (especially firearms, cutlery and archery), tools and specialized equipment, retreats, shelters, caches, field medicine, health and fitness, home and group defensive tactics and mental wellbeing. Natural and manmade environmental disasters such as earthquakes, hurricanes and nuclear/ biological/chemical warfare and pollution dangers are also subjects of interest.

Each submission to American Survival Guide should be a complete package. That is, text and photos or other illustrations should be present as a unit. Editors WILL NOT accept text without photos and vice versa. Articles should be typewritten and double spaced on one side of 8½ x 11 white bond paper or a similar arrangement on computer printer paper. Photos and other illustrations must be accompanied by captions. Text, photos and other illustrations should be accompanied by a self-addressed, stamped envelope.

Illustrations can be black and white photos, minimum size 5 x 7, or color TRANSPARENCIES, i.e., slide film, NOT color negative film. In some cases, color prints of high quality may be accepted. Editors prefer that both black and white prints or other illustrations and color slides be submitted with each article if possible. Professional quality line drawings, charts, graphs, engineering drawings and sketches are highly acceptable. Pen and ink drawings are preferred.

Queries in written form are preferred to telephone queries with regard to possible articles. Preferred article length is 1,500 to 2,000 words. Shorter, tighter articles of interest are also purchased. A good selection of artwork is desired. Photo model releases are MANDATORY for ALL persons appearing in ALL photos submitted. Photos involving copyrighted material MUST be accompanied by written permission to use the photos from the copyright holder. American Survival Guide buys First North American Rights to text and illustrations for publication. Authors may request release and reassignment authorization. Payment is $70 per page in the magazine, on publication. Special rates may apply in some instances.

Jim Benson, Managing Editor - American Survival Guide   January 1, 1986

Publishers of:
POPULAR CARS • VW TRENDS • TRUCKIN' • HOT BIKE
STREET RODDER • STREET RODDING ILLUSTRATED
ALL ABOUT BEER • CAMARO TRANS AM • KIT CAR ILLUSTRATED
4WD ACTION • and a variety of Specialty Publications

Revised 3/85

American Way

WRITER GUIDELINES

American Way is published every other week by American Airlines. A copy is kept throughout the month in each of the approximately 45,000 seatpockets in the AA and American Eagle fleets for the use of airline passengers.

Magazine content is very nearly all written by free lances who also supply the great majority of assigned article ideas. We think that much of our success is attributable to the broad spectrum of the resulting articles. Thus, we have a hearty respect for free lances and endeavor to treat them courteously and pay them promptly and competitively. But we are demanding.

We have a very small editorial staff. We do not have the research and "blue dot" personnel of a Time or a National Geographic to verify every fact. This responsibility rests with the free lance, and, while we acknowledge human frailties and certainly have our own, we do not do further business with a free lance whose misspelled proper name or error of fact gets into print. We also tend to think that a writer who is careless with spelling or article organization also will be careless with facts.

We shy away from single-source articles or those based primarily on published material. Good writing first involves good reporting, touching base with friends and adversaries of an article subject, or with business associates and competitors.

With very few exceptions we do not accept articles written by persons significantly involved in the subject matter. While the information supplied by a public-relations person or company can be very useful to an independent writer, we never use articles prepared by a PR company or department.

We don't publish poetry nor are we currently accepting essays developing the writer's point of view.

And before turning to those article areas in which we are interested, a few words about procedural and technical points:

QUOTES

We assume that direct quotes were spoken by the subject to the writer. It is mandatory for a writer who uses quotes arising otherwise to indicate the source. It is the writer's responsibility to obtain permission to use extensive quotes from a published work or any quotes from lyrics of a musical work not in the public domain.

STYLE

We will go for nearly any style that is readable, interesting, and conforms to conventional rules of sentence and paragraph structure. Consistency is important; we tend, for example, to furrow brows when a writer bounces back and forth

- 2 -

between tenses. And while we don't think you should concern yourself too much about this, The Random House Dictionary (unabridged edition), the University of Chicago Press A Manual of Style, and the Rand McNally Premier World Atlas are our basic checkpoints.

LENGTH

Major articles generally run from about 1,500 to 1,750 words. Items for "American Observer" in the front of the magazine run from one paragraph to 700 words. Time permitting we return extensively edited articles to the writer for checking; we do not return galleys from routinely edited manuscripts.

DEADLINES

Production time is two months. Manuscripts used in a given issue must have been in hand a minimum of 2¼ months prior to the date of publication. We always try to adjust deadlines to the writers' convenience. While we do not always publish an article in the first possible issue after a deadline, we still want deadlines followed so that we can always count on having enough articles on hand from which to pick and choose so as to give each issue a well-balanced selection of subjects.

Delay in publication will not delay payment as we pay upon acceptance and endeavor to reach an acceptance decision within four weeks following manuscript receipt. If we hold an article for an unusually long period after acceptance, we will ask the author to check and update anything that might have changed in the interim, paying him or her for this added work.

PAYMENT

We pay upon acceptance. Major-article rates start at about $400. Short items start at about $100. A factor in negotiating an article fee are the rights a writer is willing to sell. We prefer exclusive world rights, and if we have them we negotiate the best possible reprint fee and split it 50:50 with the author. If we don't hold such rights we simply refer reprint requesters to the author's last known address.

PHOTOS & ARTWORK

Our art director, in consultation with the writer, usually will assign a photographer and/or illustrator or buy art from a stock house. We will, however, pay $50 for each published photo made by a writer incidental to researching an article. (We do not pay for artwork supplied by public relations offices or, ordinarily, by sources.) Writers who consider themselves to be professional photographers and wish to have a photo as well as writing assignment should communicate that fact at the outset. Such persons will be referred to our art director who will make the decision on whether to authorize such additional services and negotiate fees.

SUBMISSIONS

We prefer to see a query first but will review unsolicited manuscripts. First-time queries should be accompanied by writing samples, which will not be re-

- 3 -

turned unless clearly so requested. (We give ordinary care to all unsolicited materials but do not guarantee the safe return of any.) If we are not familiar with a writer's work we usually will ask to see an initial submission on speculation. Unless time is of the essense -- i.e. a key element of a proposed article is to occur within two weeks -- we will not consider phone queries; we simply do not have a large enough staff to do so.

It is not always possible to reply to each query with a personal letter, and we do not go into detail about our reasons for declining a suggestion. However, every query gets careful consideration. All assignments are made in writing in memos of agreement satisfactory to both parties.

Please enclose a stamped, self-addressed envelope with queries or unsolicited manuscripts.

And now to what interest us:

SUBJECTS

We are amenable to almost any subject that would be interesting, entertaining, or useful to a passenger on American Airlines. Most are businesspersons who are well educated, affluent, and have broad interests. We do not talk down to them. Because they are, in a sense, "guests in our house," we are less likely than a conventional consumer magazine to schedule an article that may raise their blood pressures. Articles involving current controversies are rarely scheduled. However, we are not Pollyannaish. We can and do publish thoughtful articles on serious subjects.

Most of our articles fall into one or more of the following categories:

Business

Because many readers are businesspersons -- a growing proportion of them women -- there are many opportunities for in-depth business coverage. A sampling of recent articles includes: how business-furniture placement affects performance, women managers, merging U.S. and Japanese auto-making techniques, and odd-ball stock indicators.

The Arts and Entertainment

We are interested in all the arts, lively or static. We like to spot and report on new trends and faces. A recent sampling: fair and festival performers, actor Robert Guillaume, Indian-art-dealer Charles Eagle Plume, and Broadway librettists.

Sports

We are interested in all spectator and participatory sports. Recent subjects: darts, golfer Hal Sutton, conditioning an Olympic volleyball team, jockey Willie Shoemaker, and jousting.

- 4 -

Personalities

These should be about persons who are interesting for reasons other than their popularity. A string of glib quotes isn't enough. However, quotes that provide good insights can sell a personality story. The writer must try to "get into the subject's head" so that the reader will have a better idea of why and how the subject has achieved success. Successful articles in this area almost always have comments from associates or competitors of the subject. Recent subjects (this area spills over into Arts and Entertainment): Mandy Patinkin, George Wein, cartoonist Gary Larson, actor John Hillerman, and Commodore Grace Murray Hopper.

Science & Medicine

Writers who can find a topic that hasn't been overworked and cover it in readable style will find us receptive. We have bought articles on whether heart bypasses are overprescribed, use of high temperature to fight cancer, better ways to administer medicine, and handicapped physicians.

Travel

Perhaps surprisingly, we are not the best of markets for travel articles. We rarely use travelogue-type pieces on what to see and do. We prefer to tell about an area through the eyes and words of its residents. For example, we published an article on the London of Charles Dickens, the writer having been guided by Dickens's great-grandson. Other winners involved touring Barbados in a Rolls-Royce, with chauffering and commentary by the wife of a Barbadian soccer hero, and a trip from San Juan to Ponce via Publico. We do use at least one destination article in each issue, almost without exception about a place or an area served by American Airlines.

Books

A contributing editor for books has locks on reviews but not on author profiles or the publishing industry.

Humor

We love it but see almost none we consider usable.

Other

Try us; we've published articles on trivia contests, a writing-improvement missionary, home vegetable gardening, genealogy tips, photographing sunsets, using humor in police work, and arson detection.

Good luck!

THE EDITORS

American West

3033 N. Campbell Ave. • Tucson, Arizona • 85719
(602) 881-5850

Guide for Contributors

AMERICAN WEST is a bimonthly magazine devoted to the living traditions as well as the history of the West from the Mississippi to the Pacific. We strive to connect what the West was with what it is likely to become. Top-quality writing is a requisite for publication. We seek dynamic articles with strong appeal to the intelligent general reader, rather than academic treatises. Writing should reflect good research and thoughtful organization of historical details around a central story line.

The best guide for contributors is the magazine itself, available at most libraries. Query letters are required. All queries and manuscripts should be accompanied by a stamped, self-addressed envelope and sent to the managing editor. Payment is upon acceptance and ranges from $200 to $800 depending on the article.

FEATURES

Examples: "A Gathering of Grizzlies" (November/December 1984), "Building a Dream--Hoover Dam" (July/August 1984), "Rubber Rafting Western Rivers" (March/April 1984), "Hairy Partners" (November/December 1983), "The Blood of Abel" (May/June 1983). Major features generally run about 2,500 to 3,000 words, skillfully capturing and consistently maintaining the reader's interest. Illustrations are important. Short features of about 950 words are also welcome.

PICTORIALS

Examples: "Living Portrait of the North American Cowboy" (September/October 1983), "Will James--Inevitable Cowboy" (January/February 1983), "Nicolai Fechin" (May/June 1982). Pictorials typically present the works of an outstanding Western painter or photographer with an accompanying text.

HIDDEN INNS & LOST TRAILS

Examples: "The Peck House" (January/February 1985), "Steamboat Inn on the North Umpqua" (July/August 1984), "On the Trail of Chief Joseph" (May/June 1984), "Cochise Stronghold" (September/October 1983). This feature reveals the history behind Western landmarks. The text of about 800-850 words should be free of promotional jargon.

GOURMET & GRUB

Examples: "Stone Stew for Depression Menus" (January/February 1985), "Down-Home Molasses" (May/June 1984), "Tortillas: The Emperor's Spoons" (January/February 1984). The text of about 900-950 words (including recipes) should describe a particular Western food in its historical/cultural context. Include an old-fashioned recipe and a photograph or illustration.

Note: Submissions to our Western Snapshots Yesterday, Western Snapshots Today and Western Lore are also welcome. We seek old photographs that tell stories of bygone times and contemporary photos that link the present to the past.$25.

Because of heavy demand for sample issues, AMERICAN WEST has found it necessary to discontinue the practice of supplying complimentary copies to potential contributors.

AMTRAK EXPRESS
P.O. Box O
Huntington, NY 11743

WRITERS' GUIDELINES

Amtrak Express is a general interest magazine, distributed on board
Amtrak trains nationwide. Circulation: 160,000. Readers are business
and professional people as well as leisure travellers.

Contents

No fiction, poetry or politics. Otherwise, topics range widely, but
can be loosely described as people, places, events and things. Regular departments are Business, Health, Sports, Money. General interest topics may be entertainment, lifestyles, profiles or interviews,
travel (within Amtrak territory), art, oddities.

This is not a complete list. Our most popular recent articles included one on Faberge art objects and another about a custom bicycle maker.
We would rather add a new category than lose a good article. We look
for a fresh outlook or information on a topic of interest to a broad
audience. Well-written, well-organized material is a must. Closest
thing we have to a style book is The Elements of Style by Strunk and
White. If more writers used it, how much happier editors' lives would
be! Obviously, however, we are not rigid stylists.

Photo features and cartoons are also of interest.

Basics

Editorial is about 85% free lance. We expect to buy 80 to 90 stories
this coming year. Most of these will be first North American serial
rights, but second rights will also be considered. Seasonal and holi-
day material should be submitted at least 4 months in advance. Simultaneous queries are okay, but should be accompanied by SASE. Manuscripts are welcomed; should be clean copy, word processors letter
quality, not dot matrix; SASE included. Sample copies, $2 and SASE
(average postage $1.20). Photos (color or b&w), art (illustrations
or ideas) accompnying scripts are a plus. We pay for all art and
photos we use. Replies to scripts and queries 3-4 weeks.

Humor is welcomed but should be in good taste and in keeping with
these guidelines. As the new publisher, we have moved away from heavy
emphasis on business toward more general interest articles, although
business topics still play an important part. We also plan to include
one article per issue on technology or science.

Rates

Departments: (Health, Business, Sports, Money, Books). Submit script
or query with published clips. Length: 1200 to 2100 words. Rates average $250 to $500.

General Interest Features: As outlined in Contents above; length 1500
to 3500 words. Rates average $300 to $700.

With writers with whom we have had little or no experience, we expect
manuscripts to be submitted on "spec" and final acceptance subject to
discussion of rates.

Photos: State availability or submit with script. $25-75 for b&w
prints, 5 x 7 or 8 x 10 preferred. $35-150 for color (tranparencies
5x7 or 35mm.) Identification of subjects essential.

AUTHOR'S GUIDELINES FOR ANTIQUE MONTHLY

I. Antique Monthly's editorial content includes:

   A. Antique Shows
   B. Decorative arts exhibitions (excluding contemporary objects)
   C. Art exhibitions (excluding contemporary paintings)
   D. Major auctions
   E. Dealers and shops
   F. Historic landmarks--restored areas and homes open to the public
   G. Private collectors
   H. Museums, administrators and curators
   I. Market analyses--prices, popularity; buying and care tips

II. General rules:

   A. To query

      1. Queries by mail are required
      2. Include a short biography and clippings of previously published material
      3. List complete information about suggested article

   B. To submit material on speculation

      1. Send a self-addressed stamped envelope
      2. The author will be informed of acceptance or rejection within a month
      3. Rejected manuscripts will be returned in 5 or 6 weeks
      4. Each manuscript should be based on original work not published elsewhere
      5. It is the author's responsibility to inform ANTIQUE MONTHLY if the article has been submitted for publication elsewhere

   C. Manuscripts

      1. Manuscripts must be doubled spaced
      2. Length is usually 1,000-1,500 words
      3. ANTIQUE MONTHLY uses modified newspaper style based on the Associated Press stylebook
      4. Authors provide photographs; ANTIQUE MONTHLY rarely pays for such All color slides and transparencies will be returned; black and white photographs are returned if requested
      5. Deadlines are usually the first of the month for the following month's issue (i.e. September 1 deadline for the October issue)
      6. All manuscripts are subject to editing
      7. The editorial staff may direct that certain portions be rewritten or cut

   D. Payment

      1. Upon publication
      2. Some minor expenses are allowed (i.e. telephone, film); these should not exceed $25 and if they do, previous agreement is required
      3. Usual rate is $100 per article; negotiable

Please direct all questions regarding policy in writing to:

Cindy Graff Hobson
Senior Editor
Antique Monthly
P.O. Drawer 2
Tuscaloosa, AL 35402

Writer's Guidelines

Arizona Highways Magazine for six decades has attempted to
carry out its mandate, "to promote travel to and through the State
of Arizona." State owned and operated, the magazine over the years
pioneered many ideas and technologies ahead of its time. The
December, 1947, issue was the first magazine, ever, printed in
four-color lithography on every page. In addition to emerging as
the premier state sponsored book of high quality photography, the
magazine also has attracted Western writers of first rank: Irvin S.
Cobb, J. Frank Dobie, Mary Kidder Rak, Ernie Pyle, Clarence Budington
Kelland, Ross Santee, Frank Lloyd Wright, Frank Waters, Jonreed
Lauritzen, David Lavender, Wallace Stegner, and many others.

So for America's favorite (500,000 average circulation)
regional picture book, there thrives also the tradition of good
writing.

Subject matter: Arizona and environs (including Mexico) travel,
obviously, but beyond the narrow dimension of "I went there and did
this." Text should be well researched, sprinkled with anecdote,
historical reference, and dialog. We also buy adventure, history,
personality, nature, (quality) arts and crafts, humor, life-style,
art profile, nostalgia, archeology, and Western nonfiction romance--
all with an Arizona slant.

Approach: Informal yet polished, with a readable, literary
quality. We do not want choppy, topical, shallow Sunday supplement
treatments. First person, okay. Present tense, fine. Vignette,
flashback, quotation, diary, direct address, and personal involvement
are desirable alternatives to the standard third-person past tense
essay. Above all use strong verbs. Avoid over use of the "to be"
verb in all its forms.

Read back issues of our magazine. Also Strunk and White's
Elements of Style, and Zinser's On Writing Well. Keep in mind that
85 percent of our readership is outside Arizona. Address a national
and international audience.

Over-the-transom. Ours is a small staff. We prefer to see
written queries (see attached example) instead of finished unsolicited
manuscripts. Telephone queries out of the blue are difficult for
everybody. But, of course, there are exceptions, and we'll listen.

Contract and rights: For commissioned works we require an
executed contract. We buy one-time North American serial rights,
and expect original work.

Writer's Guidelines - con't.

Research: We require our writers to get things right the first time. Abandon assumption. Adopt a dedication to checking and double-checking facts, dates, directions, distances, heights, names, quotes, and historical record.

Lead time and deadline: The magazine normally is planned about 10 months in advance. Deadlines are set four to five months before the month of issue.

Manuscript length: We think our readers want 2000-2500 words in a major piece. Once or twice a year we will run a 5000-worder. Many sidebars are done in 300-1000 words.

Copy style: We generally follow the University of Chicago A Manual of Style and Webster's Third, unabridged.

Payment: Immediately on acceptance, within the terms of the contract.

DOs

--Type manuscript double-spaced on 8½-by-11-inch nonerasable paper.

--Set line length at 55 characters.

--Head first page with your name (as you want it to appear in the byline), address, and daytime telephone. Put your last name and page number in the top right corner of each following page.

--Provide 1-inch margins at top and bottom.

--Begin text halfway down the first page.

--Submit a list of your sources, including names, addresses, and phone numbers. We use it for verification and to send out complimentary copies when possible.

--Submit any maps, charts, or specifications for possible incorporation in the layout.

--Check and double-check spellings of names and businesses, titles, addresses, phone numbers, dates and times of events, and foreign and technical terms. Assume nothing: ask the individual for the correct spelling, since friends and relatives aren't always right. Put a small check mark (✓) in ink over names, addresses, phone numbers, dates, times, etc. (first occurrence only), so that we know you have verified them beyond a doubt.

Writer's Guidelines - con't.

<u>DON'Ts</u>

--Don't break words at the end of lines. No hyphens! It's better
  to go beyond 55 characters.

--Don't underline headings or subheadings.

--Don't type headings and subheadings in all caps. Use caps and
  lower case.

--Don't forget to check and double-check all your information.

<u>ON THE SAFE SIDE</u>

--Always keep a copy of your article. It's possible your manuscript
  may get lost in the mail or in our offices.

--If you want an immediate response, submit a self-addressed, stamped
  post card with your manuscript, and we'll confirm receipt.

--Always check and double-check your information.

A WINNING QUERY NEED NOT BE LONG. THIS IS AN ACTUAL QUERY WHICH SOLD A MAJOR NATIONAL MARKET.

BRAILLE TRAILS: America's Gift to the Handicapped

Until recent times, one American in six generally was deprived a priceless national heritage: the parks and playgrounds so cherished by the young and healthy. The tragedy was that 35 million blind and crippled citizens could not enjoy an outdoor or scenic adventure.

Today there has come into being a nationwide network of braille trails, hikes for the handicapped and basic facilities for people of limited abilities.

Nearly all of these improvements have derived support from one of the nation's little-known source of funds--the Land & Water Conservation grants. To date, some 20,000 national, state and local parks, ranging from the deepest wilderness to the neighborhood downtown, have derived support totaling more than $2 billion.

And where does this vast amount of money come from? From the leasing of oil and gas tracts off the shores of America. A story about the Land & Water Conservation Fund truthfully could offset much of the unfair and unreasonable opposition to energy exploration off our coastlines.

Suggested illustration: send a top photographer to a braille trail park, and show blind visitors experiencing the joys of nature.

THE ARTIST'S MAGAZINE

Writer's Guidelines

The Artist's Magazine is a monthly publication dedicated to helping the beginning artist, the student artist, and the professional artist succeed at the business of becoming--and of being--an artist. It is a magazine that shows readers how other artists have tackled problems, solved them, and moved ahead successfully in their field.

We are interested in working with writers who can help us reach this special audience of emerging and practicing artists. Here are some specifics on what we need:

THE ARTIST'S LIFE: This department features short items, either newsy or humorous in tone, and sympathetic to the agonies and the ecstasies of the artist's life. Mini-profiles of offbeat artists are of interest here; or profiles of mainstream artists who have an interesting sidelight to share with our readers. Length is 350-500 words, with good black and white prints or 35mm transparencies of the artist at work required after manuscript is accepted.

We also use light verse, humorous anecdotes, personal experiences that make a point of artistic interest, and seasonal items--such as what to buy an artist for Christmas. Such items can be as short as 50 words, or as long as 500.

Pay for Artist's Life items ranges from $10 to $100; most mini-profiles earn $100, which includes payment for photography. Query on profile subjects in advance, please. Include SASE (self-addressed, stamped envelope).

FEATURES. Our most consistent need is for articles written in the artist's voice ("I"), based on extensive interviewing of the subject and a broad acquaintance with the artist's work. In effect, we are seeking writers who can do the writing, but who will forsake a byline so that the story can be told from the artist's point of view. Our readers identify with this kind of story more readily than they do with a writer's reportage on an artist, and we prefer the intimacy and power of instruction such an "as told to" article conveys.

Articles should range from 1,000 to 1,500 words with an emphasis on the how-to: how the artist works, solves problems, conducts business, and performs distinctively (as opposed to being part of the herd). If the artist has a unique approach, we want to know how she or he arrived at that approach--what lessons were learned during the trial-and-error

-2-

period, what materials proved helpful, and what work was produced with success.

The article must be written from the point of view of a teacher talking to a student. An artist must not talk over the heads of the magazine's audience--if his expertise is in air-brushing, for example, he should assume that while some readers are air-brush practitioners, most know only a little bit about the field, and they are reading this article to find out more. That is the core audience. Aim accordingly. The reader, immediately after finishing your article, should be able to pick up a paintbrush (or whatever) and duplicate the process or technique you or the artist have described. We're after basic, practical, step-by-step instruction.

We also need numerous samples of the artist's work (color slides or transparencies preferred), and at least two "progressives"--that is, demonstrations that show how a painting developed from start to finish, with at least four distinct phases captured on camera along the way. All photography must be professionally done and suitable for magazine reproduction. (Artists usually have professional copies of their own work; these slides can be duplicated, and are usually preferable to taking new photographs.) Slides must be clearly labeled; all artwork must include title and unframed dimensions (in inches, height preceding width: The Mona Lisa, 48x36, for example). All published photos will be accompanied by long captions, written in the first person from the point of view of the artist. These captions are especially important with the "progressives"; each must fully explain the techniques, strategies and processes of moving from one step to the next in the creation of the painting or other artwork. In fact, you can use the captions to tell much--if not most--of your story.

Pay is $100 to $300 for total package of manuscript and artwork.

Query in advance, please. Queries should include:

* The artist's vita.
* If the writer is not the artist, the writer's résumé and credits.
* Three or four sample slides depicting the artist's work.
* A statement of the availability of a good photo of the artist.
* A clear statement of the slant and purpose of the proposed article.
* Samples of the writing style that will be used in the article, preferably a proposed lead and conclusion.
* A statement of the author's continued access to the artist--we may send the writer back for more information, for additional work on photographs (especially in setting up "progressives"), etc.
* SASE.

RANGE OF COVERAGE: While most of The Artist's Magazine will cover painting (in watercolors, oils, etc.), we are open to articles on work in other media--sculpture, for instance. We will also instruct readers on working with commercial art: cartoons, greeting cards, and so on.

(Articles about commercial art can take one or both of two focuses: 1. Mastering the creative techniques that the discipline requires. 2. Breaking into that particular business: how you get started, where you find markets, how to contact and deal with art directors and editors, and other pertinent information.)

We will also discuss such topics as problems with lighting and how to solve them; the mechanics of setting up a studio; creating business cards and promotional brochures; selecting the proper tools; keeping business records; selecting the right art courses for you; experimenting with new media and artforms.

In sum, The Artist's Magazine tells its readers how to succeed. But remember that the definitions of success vary widely. Success can mean mastering a creative technique as simple as a type of brushstroke. Success can mean having one's work displayed in a gallery. Success can mean earning extra money drawing editorial cartoons for a local weekly paper. And success can mean simply being satisfied with, inspired by and in love with being an artist.

OPPORTUNITIES with The Artist's Magazine lie basically with feature articles and with items for The Artist's Life. Most columns (including Young at Art, The Pro's Nest, Artist's Adviser and Artist's Market) are written by Artist's Magazine contributing editors. Special Reports on art supplies and equipment are usually staff-written, but we are interested in short items that show how artists use supplies ingeniously in the field.

We are also interested in developing a corps of correspondents who can cover the art scene in their respective areas and supply us with periodic reports on who is doing what, gallery trends, artists' retreats, etc. as we do national roundup stories. If you have the background and the enthusiasm, write and tell us why you think you can be an effective correspondent and we will give you full consideration. Correspondents go on the masthead, get a free subscription to the magazine, and get our full attention when we need help on a story--or when they have an idea of their own. Pay for published materials is at our usual rates.

SUBMISSION MECHANICS: Manuscripts, queries, and love and hate mail should be typed double-spaced on $8\frac{1}{2}$x11 bond paper, one side only. No erasable paper, please. Type your full name and address on the first page of the manuscript. Include your phone number with all correspondence, too.

In general, we prefer query letters, not unsolicited manuscripts. A query saves us both time--if we don't like the idea, you don't have to write and we don't have to read a complete manuscript. What counts with us is your ability to conceive how the subject will be treated or the idea carried out--and then your ability to write the article. So before you query us, do your groundwork. Let your query demonstrate that you know where you want to go and how to get there. If we like the idea

-4-

you query about, but you haven't written for <u>The Artist's Magazine</u> before, we may ask you for a more detailed query, or possibly request a full outline of the piece you have in mind.

Each query should be presented on a separate sheet of paper, although you can send several ideas at one time. Don't query about a new idea at the bottom of a page of correspondence that discusses an earlier letter or assignment.

Submit 35mm transparencies (which are standard, though we will accept larger-format transparencies) in protective plastic sleeves.

IN CONCLUSION. We will respond to any submissions or correspondence if SASE is enclosed. Submissions that don't include SASE will <u>not</u> be returned. If you are sending a newspaper clipping, do not include SASE, because clippings cannot be acknowledged. We do not pay for market tips.

We look forward to hearing from you. Good luck.

9933 Alliance Road
Cincinnati, Ohio 45242

1/84

9933 Alliance Road
Cincinnati, Ohio 45242
Tel. 513-984-0717

**THE ARTIST'S MAGAZINE
FEATURE ARTICLE THEMES/CONCEPTS**

If you're an artist or writer you should find these guidelines helpful when submitting article ideas. Generally, seventy-five percent of our features fall into categories one through five. All articles should be in the how-to form--first person narrative, step-by-step instruction, very detailed and with a friendly tone. Please, no profiles; stick to art instruction and other topics that will help the amateur artist.

1. <u>"New Mediums</u>." "New," meaning new to our readers, who are beginning and amateur artists. Discuss the necessary tools, their uses, and the basic techniques of mastering a medium. "The Collagraph: The Most Textured Print," by Suzy Farrell, for instance (May, '85).

2. <u>Painting or Drawing a Specific Subject</u>. Many of our readers are interested in birds, skies, trees--objects that fill a landscape, still life or will hold a viewer's attention. Any article that demonstrates and explains the visual structure of a certain subject, and offers various techniques for drawing and/or painting it, will most likely do well.

3. <u>Basic Techniques</u>. Color mixing, perspective, new or traditional means of design, glazing, drybrushing, etc., and how these techniques apply to the different mediums. For instance, color mixing in watercolors, acrylics, oils, caseins, alkyds, etc.

4. <u>Special Effects</u>. These articles cover a new, unique, or time-tested technique in any one medium. For instance, an article on drybrushing in watercolor, glazing in oils, or any other method used to create a stimulating painting.

5. <u>Any Combination of the Above</u>. For instance, a unique spattering technique for rendering birds in acrylics.

6. <u>Business Articles</u>. On any subject that the beginning artist needs to master to become a professional. Recordkeeping, pricing, selling, portfolios, etc.

Page 2

7. <u>New Markets</u>. These cover the scope and potential of a new market category and explain precisely how an artist may break in. For instance, the poster market, its size, basic submission requirements, payment, salable styles, etc.

8. <u>Graphic Arts</u>. An introduction to new or basic techniques, special effects or mechanics of the graphic arts field. For instance, how an artist handles an airbrush to create illustrations.

9. <u>Cartooning</u>. Our readers want to know how to draw them, create characters, use ink washes, etc. (About three manuscripts per year.)

10. <u>An Approach to Art</u>. Take us step-by-step through the creative process an artist uses to get ideas, concepts, and how this reflects in the techniques the artist uses. ("Painting From the Imagination," by Marilyn Phillis, for instance Jan. '85).

11. <u>Genres of Art</u>. This should cover the basic, new or unusual techniques of still life, landscape, portraiture or wildlife painting. For example, ten ways to design, paint or arrange a still life.

12. <u>Techniques of the Masters</u>. Here, you would be doing the research and gathering slides (you'll need to get reproduction permissions) that show how a great artist created his or her works.

The Artist's
MAGAZINE

9933 Alliance Road
Cincinnati, Ohio 45242
Tel. 513-984-0717

"THE ARTIST'S LIFE"
WRITER'S GUIDELINES

The Artist's Magazine's "Artist's Life" section is a place for our readers to relax and get away from it all; a place to get away from our features and columns which stress the more serious side of art. Here, we want the artist to be able to kick off his creative shoes and have a good time without working at it.

Basically, "The Artist's Life" can be broken down into two categories: mini-profiles and fillers. Fillers include poems, anecdotes (especially historical) and technical tips. Pay for fillers ranges from $2-10.

Mini-profiles range in length from 350-600 words and can be of various themes. Pay is $50-100, and good-quality 35mm color slides must accompany the article. Also, the artist's address and telephone number (as well as the author's) must be attached.

Profiles must touch on one or more of the following themes:

-An artist's unusual but insightful reasons, philosophies or concepts for creating art. For an example, see Creative Business in the February 1985 issue.

-Humorous stories or·anecdotes which elucidate the creative life of the artist (see Gag Me With A Whale, February '84).

-A fresh or unusual look at the American art system, or helpful insights into the ways of the system.

-Biographical pieces that bring out an unknown or unusual aspect of famous artists (Itching to Etch, October '84).

-Innovation. How an artist has come up with an unusual application of common materials (Rag Time, October '84); how an artist uses unusual materials to create an interesting artform (Resistance Art, April '85); how an artist has arrived at financial gain through a new or unusual marketing technique (Blueprint For Success, May '85).

-Success. How an artist has followed his or her personal vision in the creation or style of art; how and why an artist has trudged on, despite unacceptance and overcome a problem; how the artist has solved a personal, creative or emotional problem involving art.

Query first for all profiles; send in complete fillers. All manuscripts/queries must be accompanied by SASE if return is desired. Sample copy is available for $2.50.

WRITER'S GUIDELINES

ASTRONOMY MAGAZINE

I. The Readers

A. Mean Age: 35 years

B. Over 60% university or college graduates, or currently attending college

C. Middle/upper-middle class, mostly white collar professionals, about 85% male

D. Assume a beginner's or dilettante's astronomy background. Your reader is not dumb, so don't talk down to him. His interest, however, will not sustain him through a dreary manuscript. He is also a voter and taxpayer, and supports the space program.

II. ASTRONOMY Magazine's Structure

A. Feature Articles

1. *Lead Feature article* — Our profusely illustrated monthly "showpiece." It's written at an elementary level and often features astronomical artwork and photographs that "put you in space." Most are reviews or discussions of well-established topics in astronomy. Normally 2,500-3,500 but sometimes up to 6,000 words.

2. *Second Lead* — A short, simple article often based on pictures or current news items. Often written in-house. 500-1,500 words.

3. *Stellar Frontiers* — Our feature for more advanced "amateur" astronomers; assumes an audience already versed in the basics. Explores current research areas, cosmology, areas of controversy — the frontiers of knowledge. Requires professional astronomer author. 2,000-4,000 words.

B. Hobby Articles

1. *Gazer's Gazette* — What to see and what to do as an active observer, everything from basic constellation identification to occasional advanced projects. Usually elementary. 1,000-3,000 words.

2. *Equipment Atlas* — Telescopes and equipment, what they are, how to use them, how to build them. All levels from elementary through advanced. 1,000-3,000 words.

3. *Photography in Astronomy* — How to, what to do with your camera in astronomy. Basic star trails to sophisticated techniques. 1,000-3,000 words.

4. *Eye on the Sky* — Six pages on naked-eye observing, finding and observing the planets and stars, skylore, reader pictures, and our Star Dome map.

5. *Through the Eyepiece* — Eight pages devoted to telescopic observation of a region, detailing double stars, clusters, galaxies, and other objects of telescopic interest.

C. **News and Opinion**

1. *ASTRONOMY Forum* — Short science articles, interviews, opinion pieces, and speculative essays. The criterion for acceptance is that the material be interesting. Lengths of 500-2,500 words for individual pieces. ASTRONOMY buys only one-time rights.

2. *AstroNews* — Four to eight pages on the latest news in astronomy. Current news and research findings desirable. Pays on a different rate structure.

3. *ASTRONOMY Reviews* — Book reviews must be short and to the point. Most are assigned by ASTRONOMY; contact us if you're interested.

III. **Science**

A. Your logic must be clear, your premises and arguments readily apprehended.

B. Stress the nature of scientific thought; return to observational evidence frequently and label speculative arguments clearly. Stress that models and theories are constrained by observation.

C. Avoid personification. Don't project a world picture where events just happen; avoid phrases such as "given a collapsing gas cloud" that imply events by "fiat." In such an instance, make a reasonable case for the gas cloud's existence.

D. Ask yourself all the obvious questions a non-scientist would; then *be sure* you answer them. (Why, for instance, is it important to know the mean density of a planet?)

E. If there is doubt or conflict in the field, say so. The layman should recognize astronomy as a human activity, with human uncertainties and squabbling.

F. Your manuscript is subject to review by other scientists and revision by ASTRONOMY's editors.

IV. **Writing**

A. Your manuscript must have a solid logical construction.

B. Remember ASTRONOMY is *not* a technical journal. Most of our readers are non-scientists, so avoid technical and formal language. We strive to be conversational, informal, and lively.

C. We will edit for consistent magazine style. Read several issues — recent ones — to gain a sense of this style. If you keep your writing simple, clear, and direct, it will usually be quite close to ASTRONOMY's style.

D. Factual errors may creep in when an editor tries to straighten out a dull or confusing explanation. Keep it lively through use of analogy and "visually vivid" descriptions.

E. Define new terms when they appear. Single sentence and single phrase definitions are often sufficient.

F. Write in the active voice. Don't begin sentences with: There are, It is, We find that, etc. We will mercilessly remove these constructions.

G. If possible, submit your manuscript typed 50 characters per line, 24 lines per page, double spaced. This aids our editorial and production processes.

V. **Working With Us**

A. We do not always assign a deadline. Your article usually cannot appear sooner than 12 weeks after you submit the manuscript, and sometimes the delay is much longer. Articles are normally not assigned to an issue until they are in the Editor's possession.

B. If we *do* assign a deadline, we mean it. This deadline is usually 12 weeks prior to the cover date of the issue in which your article has been scheduled to appear. *If you cannot meet a deadline, let us know immediately.*

C. We will submit a final copy of your article to you for proofreading and checking for errors only if time permits — *so meet your deadline!*

D. We reserve the right to make stylistic changes. Our main concern in submitting a final copy to the author is to ensure scientific accuracy.

E. Please submit a biographic sketch approximately six lines long with your article.

F. After the article appears in print, we'd be pleased to have you critique it for us. We want to know your reactions, and we are concerned that you're happy too.

VI. **Illustration**

A. You may have access to photographs that are new, unique, or simply haven't been published in the popular press before. Don't hesitate to send them. They can help make your article a big success.

B. You may be asked to work closely with us and our artists by phone or letter in developing diagrams and artwork. Remember that 55% of the surface area of an average article is illustrative.

VII. **Payment and Copyright Policy**

A. Payment is determined by individual negotiation with each author. As a rough guideline, we offer between 8 and 10 cents per word for *all rights,* or roughly $200 to $400 for a feature article, $250 for Stellar Frontiers, and $150 for hobby articles. One-time and one-time plus reprint rates are lower. All Forum authors are paid $100 for one-time rights.

B. Payment is made within 30 days of the date of publication.

C. When your article is assigned to a specific issue, and only if we wish to purchase more than one-time rights, we will send you a contract outlining what we are purchasing and what your payment will be. Most often, we will have discussed the terms of this contract before you receive it. No contract is issued for purchase of one-time rights.

D. Manuscripts submitted on speculation must not be submitted to other magazines without the knowledge and consent of ASTRONOMY.

E. Because articles are protected by ASTRONOMY's copyright notice, we do not run author copyright notices on articles.

A SUBSIDIARY OF COMMUNICATION CHANNELS INC
ATLANTA MAGAZINE INC /6285 BARFIELD ROAD/ATLANTA GEORGIA 30328/ 404 256-9800

WRITER'S GUIDELINES

ATLANTA Magazine is a consumer publication of local, state regional and, sometimes, national focus Emphasis is on people, places, issues, trends, goods and services. Subjects and topics include politics, government, travel, leisure, theatre, films, books, music, art, dance, dining, wine, food, interiors/furnishings/decor, sports, fashion and nostalgia. First person opinion pieces are occasionally published, depending on subject matter and general reader interest.

Submitting ideas: In a letter addressed to the Editor, briefly outline idea, summarizing reason to do story, background of story, theme to be developed; point(s) to be made; conclusion(s) to be drawn. Include name, address and telephone number for contact. If this is your first submission to us, please furnish any clippings of previously published work.

Submitting manuscripts: They must be typed, double spaced, on white bond paper. Include cover letter with name, address and telephone number for contact. Also include self-addressed, stamped envelope for return of manuscript if it is not accepted.

The Atlanta Journal
Covers Dixie Like the Dew
★ AND ★
THE ATLANTA CONSTITUTION
The South's Standard Newspaper

P.O. BOX 4689 · ATLANTA, GA. 30302

GUIDELINES

Atlanta Weekly

The Editorial Department of Atlanta Weekly Magazine seldom accepts unsolicited manuscripts. The department is, however, open to receiving query letters outlining ideas for articles that would complement the magazine format.

Prospective freelancers should include a resume and recent tear sheets with the initial inquiry. It is also helpful to include all pertinent information such as current address, telephone number, and social security number.

Response time to freelance queries is generally two to four weeks. In the event an assignment is made it is customarily given on a speculation basis.

Successful query letters should include a brief synopsis of the suggested topic, giving enough information so that a proper editorial decision can be made. Suggestions for artwork and/or photographs could also be included along with a tentative completion date.

Features	Departments		"ETC"
3,000-8,000 words	SOUTHWORDS:	1000 words	80-100 words
	GOOD TIMES:	1000-2500 words	
	GOOD LOOKS:	200 - 400 words	

AUDUBON
The Magazine of the National Audubon Society

GUIDELINES

FOR

FREE-LANCE

WRITERS

Most of our articles are written on assignment. But we are always looking for new voices and fresh ideas. Every story suggestion should be submitted in a brief query letter, accompanied by a stamped, self-addressed envelope. Be sure the query not only outlines the subject matter, but also indicates the approach you would take and how you would handle the material. Please estimate, if possible, approximately how many words you would need to cover the subject. Also, if we don't know your work, please send us some samples of your writing.

AUDUBON's articles are concerned largely with conservation and environmental issues, natural history, ecology, and related subjects. We are looking for good writing, sharp insight, solid reporting, and careful research. We are definitely **not** looking for emotional diatribes, environmental lectures, didactic recitations of fact, or articles that read like rewarmed encyclopedia entries. We'd generally rather show our readers than tell them about something. We do not publish poetry and we seldom publish fiction because we can't find any that's good enough and appropriate to our readership. We don't use articles on the rescue or taming of wild animals, and we rarely use material on bird-watching or attracting birds.

Manuscripts should be typed double-space on one side of the page, with plenty of margin on all four sides (60 characters is a good line length), and please use a reasonably fresh ribbon and paper that isn't see-through flimsy. We don't like photocopies! If you use a word processor, know that our eye-weary editors **hate** manuscripts from dot-matrix printers that produce faint, ugly, hard-to-read characters that do not have descenders on them.

Manuscripts should be accompanied by a stamped, self-addressed envelope of sufficient size. If you are submitting photographs with a manuscript, be sure your submission includes the stiffeners, sufficient postage, and instructions we need to return the photos the way you want them returned.

We are overstocked and understaffed, so it may take a few weeks for us to consider your submission. We pay for articles on acceptance, and our rates vary according to length, the amount of work and thought required, and the quality of the writing. Our lengths vary considerably, from 500-word text blocks accompanying photo essays to articles of considerable length. Generally we are looking for articles that will run to less than 5,000 words, and our greatest needs are for stories that run 2,300 to 3,500 words.

Thanks for your interest in writing for **AUDUBON.**

950 THIRD AVENUE, NEW YORK, N.Y. 10022 (212) 832-3200

185 MADISON AVENUE   NEW YORK, NEW YORK 10016   TELEPHONE (212) 679-4400

WRITER'S GUIDELINES

Enclosed is a copy of BABY TALK that will show you the type and length of articles we buy.

All articles with a by line (including those in our "Opinions," "Budgets" and "Careers" sections) were purchased from among the many submitted to us each month by free lance writers.

We look at all material on a speculation basis. It is not our policy to give assignments or agree to purchase material in advance.

All manuscripts should be accompanied by a stamped, self-addressed envelope.

BACKPACKER MAGAZINE
ONE PARK AVENUE
NEW YORK, NEW YORK 10016

WRITER'S GUIDELINES

Backpacker is written and edited for the informed enthusiast, and
for people just beginning to get involved in the sport. Our
major article categories are how-to, where-to, and with what.
Approximately 60 to 70 percent of each issue deals with outdoor
equipment, reflecting reader interest in knowing what is available
that can make camping and hiking experiences easier and more rewarding.
Technique and destination articles make up the bulk of the rest of
each issue. Every issue contains:

DESTINATION ARTICLES. Trip stories, with emphasis on adventures
readers can duplicate. Domestic destinations much preferred. 35mm
color transparency art necessary. "Daily Log" format discouraged,
in favor of interpreting the trip--planning, unusual occurrences,
lessons learned, discoveries not in guidebooks, etc.

WEEKEND WILDERNESS. Short writeups on desirable hiking and camping
destinations three hours or less from a metropolitan area.

MATERIEL. Discussion of a major component of backpacking equipment--
Cordura, wool, synthetic insulations, and the like.

FIRST EXPOSURE. Wilderness photography tips.

OUTFITTING. Short roundup of a specific equipment category--new
bottled-gas stoves, bivy sacks, packs for cross-country ski-campers.

GEOSPHERE. What we can learn from the earth, as hikers.

BODY LANGUAGE. Health and conditioning.

Most of the rest of the book is staff written or commissioned.
The above list is not comprehensive, and there's always room for the
occasional short technique piece, or well-wrought humorous anecdote,
or point of view. We do not print fiction, nor do we cover exotic
destinations.

Your best guide is our recent issue, and one or two before that.
If you have any further questions, you can reach our Editorial
Department at 212-725-7080. We cannot accept collect calls, unless
prearranged.

BACKPACKER MAGAZINE
ONE PARK AVENUE
NEW YORK, NEW YORK 10016

PHOTOGRAPHY GUIDELINES

<u>Backpacker</u> Magazine welcomes freelance photographers of ability.
If you're planning to send us some of your work, please note
the following requirements:

* All submissions MUST be accompanied by a letter
  of explanation, and a statement of the quantities sent.

* Name, address, and telephone number should be on your
  letterhead. Include your Social Security number, without
  which we cannot process any payments.

* All photography MUST be identified by location and date
  taken.

* If any photos have been published previously, name and
  issue of publications <u>must</u> be supplied.

* All color slides (35 mm, 2¼, 4X5) should be in protective
  plastic sleeves, individually titled.

* Black and white photos should be 5X7 or 8X10 glossy.

* A stamped, self-addressed return envelope should be
  enclosed, for the return of your material.

<u>Backpacker</u> is a magazine of beauty <u>and</u> utility. That means we're
interested in two types of photography: photos that show the
splendor of nature, and photos that show people enjoying it.
Therefore, your submissions should have a nice blend of man and
nature.

* All photos MUST be in sharp focus; soft images get even
  softer when published.

* Color work should be properly exposed, with good color
  saturation and a good balance of light and shadow.

* Color prints are NOT ACCEPTABLE.

* Black and white prints should have good contrast, but
  keep detail in the highlights and shadows.

* Send only photos in good condition. DO NOT send slides
  that are dirty or scratched.

* All photos must look natural, even if staged.

* Compositions should be tight and creative.

We'll treat your work as carefully as possible while we have it,
but <u>Backpacker</u> assumes no responsiblity for materials sent to us
on speculation.

We'll look forward to hearing from you.

Locust at 17th • Des Moines, Iowa 50336 • 515-284-3000

BETTER HOMES AND GARDENS
FREE LANCE FACT SHEET

Some ten to fifteen percent of our editorial material comes
from free lance writers, artists, and photographers; the rest
is produced by staff.

We read all free-lance articles submitted, but much prefer
to see a letter of query rather than a finished manuscript.
The query should be directed to the department where the
story line is strongest. *See appropriate editors and
departments below.

A free lancer's best chances lie in the areas of travel,
education, health, cars, money management and home entertainment.
We do not deal with political subjects or with areas not
connected with the home, community, and family. The best
way to find out what we do use, and to get some idea of
our style, is to study several of our most recent issues.

We buy all rights and pay on acceptance. Rates are based
on our estimate of the length, quality, and importance of
the published article.

*Building	Joan McCloskey
Furnishings	Shirley Van Zante
Foods	Nancy Byal
Crafts	James Williams
Travel	Barbara Humeston
Garden	Doug Jimerson
Outdoor Living	
100's of Ideas	Steven Coulter
New Products	
What's Happening	
Health & Education	Paul Krantz
Money Management	Margaret Daly
Automotive	
Features	
Home Electronics	Kathy Stechert

Publishing Group Meredith CORPORATION

Bicycling Magazine's

Guidelines for Free-Lance Contributors

Like many magazines, *Bicycling* is forced to turn down the overwhelming majority of manuscripts submitted by free-lance writers. This saddens us; we like nothing better than to discover a new contributor whose articles and photographs are ideally suited to our magazine. The purpose of these guidelines is to help you understand our needs so you can do your best to meet them. But first, let us say there is no substitute for knowing the magazine well. If you want to write for us, you should be reading us.

We are a nine-issue per year magazine which is sold both by subscription and on the newsstand. Our quarter-million readers (see also the profile at the end of these guidelines) are very interested in and well-informed about cycling. That's why they read a special interest magazine. Accordingly, some kinds of articles are unpopular with them. These include "my first tour," "how I lost 30 pounds by taking up cycling at 37," and any other article which incorporates a novice's point of view. So we must counsel you against submitting this kind of story.

We cannot use stories that are too local in their appeal, such as a local club tour or a local personality in cycling. The magazine must serve all 50 states and thousands of foreign readers as well.

We do not use fiction and poetry.

Now that we've told you what we don't want, here's what we do want:

— Articles for New Readers. We do publish one or two articles each month intentionally directed at the new reader and novice cyclist. (Please note the difference between an article written *for* a novice and an article written *by* a novice.) Articles for the novice may include riding techniques, maintenance and repair, training tips, and almost anything else. They should be accurate, easy to understand, and very well-illustrated where appropriate. Length should be about 1,000 to 2,000 words. Most of these articles are staff-written, but we welcome outside submissions. We urge you to query us with suggestions of specific topics before submitting a story.

— Touring Features. These are the bread and butter of the magazine, and of some of the books we publish. Most free-lancers we do publish write touring features.

Roughly speaking, there are two kinds of tour articles, and the requirements differ for each:

Adventure Tours are not intended to be "how-to" articles. They are tales brought back from the rim of the world; we've recently published adventure tours from Iceland, Morocco, the Panamanian jungle, the Sahara Desert, and more. Those which have sold with us are first-person articles, written by the cyclist who took the tour. (A very skilled interviewer who knows our publication may be able to capture the excitement of someone else's experience, but it's not easy.)

Route information is unnecessary in such an article, because we doubt many readers will want to follow in your tire tracks. Anecdotes, suspense, a sensitive understanding of the local culture which you are visiting, some local history, the ability to make people in your story come alive, and stunning photographs are what make an adventure tour successful for us. Again, query us first.

Road-Tested Tours are published for other cyclists to try. Most are within the United States and Canada, but we are willing to consider road-tested tours in any country our readers might like to visit. Anecdotes and local cultures are important, as before, but route information, advice on where to camp (or rent a room), good restaurants, road conditions, and best time of year for the tour are essential. If you toured an area during poor weather, don't send us an article decrying the weather; call a meteorologist and find out when the weather is usually best in that area. Tell our readers the worst they can expect and the best they can hope for. Include a legible map with your route indicated on it. The format we use has appeared in *Bicycling* since the March 1981 issue. Your submission should follow this format.

Although we don't always require photos for road-tested tours, we encourage you to send them if you have them.

— Notable Cycling Events. Some cycling events are more than local and they deserve national recognition. For example, we have written about New York City's Five-Boro Bike Tour; San Diego's Five Cities Bike Tour; the *Register*'s Annual Great Bike Ride Across Iowa (RAGBRAI); Davis Double Century; and more. Why these events and not others? These draw participants from all over the country, they are unusually large, and they introduce many new cyclists (and spectators in the general public) to cycling activities. We also cover certain major bike races. We welcome submissions on all such events described above. Especially with this type of story, good photos increase your chances of acceptance. In the writing, anecdotes, local color, and a lively sense of the human beings involved will help to make your story readable.

Because of our long lead-time, merely covering the event is usually not enough. Your story needs a theme to develop or an "angle," since it cannot appear until four or five months after the event has taken place.

We don't cover each event each year. So we don't recommend submissions about an event we covered last year. We do want submissions about major events we haven't yet publicized, especially if they're in parts of the country that haven't been getting enough attention from the cycling press. Query us before attending, or at least before writing your article, as we may already have arranged for coverage.

—Legal and Political Issues. These are very important to cyclists. But they are hard to report on because they often involve a great deal of legal detail, and the answers are frequently tentative and inconclusive. A story that has too limited a perspective — for example, a story about local or state laws which doesn't mention any precedent set for the rest of the country — is unlikely to be usable. If you're an expert in the field, you're probably aware of all the hidden implications of any one incident. Many of our readers, however, aren't so aware. You should spell it out for them.

A story on events or the concerns of bicycle activists is worth national attention if it's precedent-setting or, in some other way, of broad general interest. You should know the issues well enough to write with authority what conclusions can and what conclusions cannot be drawn from that event.

Two topics we've recently accepted articles on should give you a feel for what suits us. One is an article on bicyclists' rights (or lack thereof) to the road, comparing those rights in the best and worst state vehicle codes, and in the provisions of the nationwide Uniform Vehicle Code. Another discusses the role of the bicycle coordinator in state and local government and the bureaucratic problems bicycle coordinators face in trying to enact their programs.

—Equipment Testing. Most of this is done in-house. If you have access to laboratory equipment, special ideas for equipment tests, or exceptional qualifications as an equipment tester, contact us with your suggestions. Remember, however, that we are a newsstand magazine. Lengthy, technical articles are fine if they're of interest to all cyclists. But if they focus on a small problem most cyclists don't care about, they'll drive readers away.

—Fitness and Training Tips. If you have good qualifications in exercise physiology, sports medicine, nutrition, or as a cycling coach, we welcome your expertise. Submissions in this area must be well substantiated by experience and research. Query us with specific topics before writing.

Note in our reader profile the types of bike riding most typical for our audience. Clearly, short-distance touring and fast recreational riding are the chief concerns of readers, while only a small percentage actually race. On the other hand, all readers might benefit from something that racers know. So much depends on how an article is slanted.

Some recent articles include Training for a Century; Avoid Running on Empty — Without Carbohydrates You Can't Perform; Mental Exercises to Tap Your Hidden Potential; and Cycling During Pregnancy.

—Riding Technique. Articles may deal with the cyclist's efficiency on the bike or with interactions with other cyclists. These articles are frequently aimed at newer readers, but there's plenty of information that could help longtime readers fine-tune their skills.

—**Cycling in Traffic.** We seek to educate both newer and older readers in safe, predictable, and correct vehicle-like behavior in traffic with frequent articles on various in-traffic situations. Submissions are welcome. Authors of these articles should have a good knowledge of traffic law and of the state of the art in bicycle safety training.

We publish more articles between and outside these categories. Personality profiles, book reviews, build-it projects, and others appear frequently. If you're in doubt whether a story is suitable, please write with a query. In fact, we urge you always to query first. And consider if it has appeared in the magazine recently, and if readers would find it useful or entertaining? Chances are, if you want to write for us, you are already a subscriber. If not, you should become one. Our most successful writers read every issue.

Photography

Good illustration is essential to our development as a newsstand magazine. In many cases, the manuscript you send us is less important than the photos which come with it. We can always edit your copy, but we can't do much about poor or nonexistent photos.

So if you have photos, send them in at the same time you send your manuscripts. We still use some articles without photographs, but the articles with photographs are given more prominent play in the magazine. And we pay more for well-illustrated articles.

We don't want to scare away amateur photographers with stern-sounding guidelines. A recent favorite cover was taken by an amateur. Please, however, observe the following guidelines:

• Film Specs: 35mm is preferred; 2¼ x 2¼ is acceptable; no 110 film, please. Shoot Kodachrome 64 or 25, if possible. Ektachrome, Fuji, etc. don't separate as well as Kodachrome. Shoot faster color films only if conditions require it. For black and white, Tri-X will be fine.

• Color prints are seldom usable for technical reasons. Any black and white prints you send us should be smooth (glossy) surface, not silk or crystal surface.

• If your article is one which would lend itself to the magazine's black and white sections, send black and white photos. Most color photographs translate poorly into black and white.

• If you make prior arrangements with us, we can process your black and white film for you. But please do not mail unprocessed film unless you have made such arrangements. We can't process color.

• Covers: Shoot vertical. The logo and blurbs run on every cover. These are constant; be aware of their location and what that means while shooting. A large single image that creates a simple cover often works best.

• Riding: While shooting people riding, be aware of the background. Watch out for wires, shadows, or other major distractions. Make sure people are riding in proper positions and on the correct side of the road.

• We often purchase slides for future use as covers, posters, or promotional pieces. We are interested in purchasing exclusive or all rights to photographs; if other purchase rights are involved, specify upon submission of material.

Profile of Bicycling's Readers

Our readership is well-educated (77 percent are college graduates), and most (76 percent) are affluent enough to own their own homes. Median age of readers is 31. The majority are male, yet we also take care not to exclude our female readership.

Here's how subscribers use their bicycles. (Because of multiple answers to our survey, the total adds up to more than 100 percent.)

Short-distance touring—67.3%
Fast recreational riding—59.0%
Commuting—54.0%
Just for fun, occasional use—43.0%
Long-distance touring—33.5%
Racing—12.9%

All submissions should be typed, generously double-spaced on 8½ x 11-inch paper, with 1½-inch margins. Your title, subtitle, and name should be at the top of the first manuscript page. On a cover letter be sure to include your name, address, and a phone number at which you can be reached during working hours.

Length may be from 1,000 to 2,500 words. Most typical is 1,500 to 2,000 words.

Often free-lance contributors will receive an acknowledgement or acceptance of a submitted article and/or photographs and expect to see their material published in the next issue of *Bicycling*. However, our production schedules and procedures make this impossible, unless material has been specially solicited by our editors. We work approximately four to five months in advance of an issue's publication date; for example, articles for our January issue are put into production as early as September of the year before. Please keep our production schedules in mind when submitting material.

We buy all rights to published text and/or photographs, including the right to reuse in other Rodale Press publications, and the right to grant reprint permission, unless otherwise negotiated prior to publication.

Bicycling Magazine has a new format for road-tested tour articles. We
now publish in the magazine "thumbnail sketches" of submitted tours --
tour overviews and highlights of interesting routes and sights. If
readers find they would like more extensive information on these sketched
tours, they will write to Bicycling to receive complete copies of the
author's adventures.

For the use of submitted tours in this manner, we will be paying freelance
contributors between $50 and $150, dependent on the extent of detail
and quality of information provided, and publication of any accompanying
photos.

Bicycling Magazine®

33 East Minor Street, Emmaus, PA 18049

CAT FANCY
DOG FANCY
BIRD TALK
HORSE ILLUSTRATED
magazines

Editorial Offices
P.O. Box 6050
Mission Viejo, California 92690
Telephone (714) 240-6001

WRITER'S GUIDELINES

Thank you for your interest in our publications. We would be pleased to see your material. Below we have listed some of the publication requirements of CAT FANCY, DOG FANCY, HORSE ILLUSTRATED, and BIRD TALK to assist you in preparing submissions.

ARTICLES

CAT FANCY, DOG FANCY, and BIRD TALK are directed at the general pet-owning population and written for an adult audience. HORSE ILLUSTRATED is directed at the amateur competition and pleasure horse owner. We suggest that you read past issues of the magazines to acquaint yourself with the types of material we use. Past issues may be obtained by sending $3.00 to the above address. We need informative articles, limited to 3,000 words or less, on the care and training of cats, dogs, birds, and horses (health, nutrition, training, etc.); photo-essays on historical and current events dealing with cats, dogs, birds, and horses; how-to articles; human interest stories; and good fiction, with the animal as the primary focus of interest. We rarely use stories in which the animals speak as though they were human. We use a breed article in each issue, but these articles are assigned. Please query if you have a breed article in mind.

Manuscripts should be typewritten, double-spaced with wide margins. We prefer that articles be accompanied with appropriate art in the form of professional-quality color tranparencies or black & white photographs (NOT SNAP SHOTS) or professional illustrations. Additional guidelines are available for artists and photographers.

We are always happy to review material on speculation, but with the exception of fiction, the best working procedure is to query before preparing the article. Our usual rate of payment is 3 cents per printed word, (5 cents if accompanied by good quality photographs). Payment is made in the latter part of the cover month in which your article appears, (i.e., if your piece was in the November issue you would be paid in the latter part of November). We buy first American rights only--all other rights revert back to the author.

POETRY--CAT FANCY ONLY

We use a limited number of poems in each issue. Competition is fierce! Payment is $10 and payment is made as it is for articles. We prefer short poems, but we will use longer works that can be illustrated. Payment for longer, special-use poems is $25.

We cannot assume responsibility for material submitted, but we assure you that reasonable care will be taken in handling your work. If you would like a response to your work, PLEASE INCLUDE A SELF-ADDRESSED, STAMPED ENVELOPE.

Blair &
Ketchum's **Country Journal**

PRESENT STAFF OF COUNTRY JOURNAL

Tyler Resch – Editor
David Sleeper – Managing Editor (send queries
                and unsolicited ms. to him)
Patricia McWilliams – Associate Editor
Wanda Shipman – Associate Editor
Lynne S. Welsh – Assistant to the Editor

Ray Maher – Art Director
Ann Kearton – Associate Art Director

Steve Swinburne – Picture Editor

Castle Freeman – Copy Editor

Diane K. Bierly – Editorial Assistant

Editorial Office: P.O. Box 870 · Manchester Center, Vermont 05255 · 802-362-1022

Blair & Ketchum's Country Journal

GUIDELINES FOR WRITERS

We appreciate your interest in contributing to COUNTRY JOURNAL. While we don't have too many hard-and-fast rules, here are some observations that might be helpful.

We don't publish fiction, and we seldom use articles that don't have a reasonably clear connection to country life. We usually avoid history, nostalgia, and reminiscence. Profiles of "typical" country characters are out, although we do use profiles of people who are doing useful and interesting things. We occasionally publish accounts of personal experiences or essays reflecting personal points of view, but we're usually flooded with these, and we can't accept many. Articles on natural history subjects are welcome, but again, we get many more than we can publish. We are always looking for short, practical, how-to pieces, and we are interested in thorough, solid reports on issues that concern country people.

We encourage our writers to keep their articles short; we'd like to get more stories that run about 2,000 words. Articles of about 2,500-3,000 words are average, while occasionally a major feature runs as long as 4,000 words. It's a good idea to send us a query rather than a manuscript. We tend to work closely with our contributors, and we like to be able to offer suggestions as an article develops. Ordinarily we like to have an article in hand four months or more in advance of the publication date.

Generally we don't worry about illustrations until we have an article in hand. Sometimes, of course, an author will be working on a subject that requires him or her to collect photographs or other illustrative material while doing research for the story.

Finally, we pay on acceptance; the amount varies with the length and quality of the manuscript and the importance of the topic. Feature pieces--roughly 2,500 to 3,500 words--are fetching about $400 for first North American serial rights and non-exclusive reprint rights.

A copy of the magazine is available for $2.50 to writers who are unfamiliar with COUNTRY JOURNAL but would like to learn more.

We hope this information is helpful to you.

Editorial Office: P.O. Box 870 · Manchester Center, Vermont 05255 · 802-362-1022

BOX 111, BROAD RUN, VA 22014
703-361-8992

WRITERS & PHOTOGRAPHERS GUIDELINES

Thank you for your interest in Bluegrass Unlimited. We would like
to take a look at your material for possible publication in our magazine.

The following are some guidelines for your information:

*Articles - 500-5000 words in length - typed (double spaced).
We pay 4¢ to 5¢ per word upon publication. We would prefer
to stay away from "fan" style articles and would rather the
material be informational, based on personal experience or
interview with lots of quotes from subject, profile, humor, etc.

*Photographs - Black & white gloss finish preferred. Color slides
or color prints. We usually pay $50.00 for the cover (B & W) and
$125.00 for color (cover) upon publication. Payment for inside
pictures is approximately $20.00 - $40.00 (B & W), $40.00 - $80.00
(color) per printed page.

*Cartoons, tablature and drawings - We publish occasionally.
Payment is usually $15.00 - $25.00 upon publication.

Please enclose a self-addressed stamped envelope with your material.
We will review it and get back to you within 30-60 days. A sample copy of
Bluegrass Unlimited is being sent to you under separate cover.

The Boston Globe

Boston, Massachusetts 02107 Telephone 617-929-2000

Dear Freelance Writer,

The general guidelines for freelance articles submitted to The Boston Globe Magazine are:

1) Freelance articles are accepted on speculation only.

2) The length should be from 2,500 to 4,000 words.

3) Fees are negotiated upon acceptance.

4) No reprints of any kind are accepted.

The magazine works on a six-week lead time which should be taken into consideration when writing articles with a specific time element. All articles and/or query letters and outlines should be addressed to: Ms. Ande Zellman, Editor, Boston Globe Magazine, Boston, MA 02107.

Thank you for your interest in the magazine.

Sincerely,

Ande Zellman, Editor
Boston Globe Magazine

AZ/lh

BOW & ARROW HUNTING

Box HH, 34249 Camino Capistrano,
Capistrano Beach, CA 92624

EDITORIAL REQUIREMENTS

Manuscripts should be typed, double-spaced, on one side of the paper. Typical full length articles, as we use them, run from about six to twelve pages of manuscript. It is not necessary to count the words, since we do not pay by the word.

In preparing your manuscript, we recommend that you make and retain at least one copy for your files. This is against the possibility of loss in the mail or due to some other cause. Each typed page should have the author's name and address in the upper left-hand corner, to ensure payment should the title page become separated from the manuscript. Please include your social security number on the title page. Please include your phone number, and a suggested time you can be reached there, in your covering letter.

We never purchase articles sight-unseen; although, if queried, we often indicate whether we are or are not interested in seeing the article as outlined and described. Accordingly, all manuscripts should be accompanied by return postage. We cannot accept liability for unsolicited manuscripts, photographs or artwork.

The likelihood that we will purchase and use a given article is strongly affected by the amount and quality of artwork accompanying it. Good black and white photographs of high contrast, together with the necessary information for accurate captions, are a decided asset to your manuscript, so far as we are concerned.

Submission of color transparencies for possible cover use is encouraged. Transparencies not selected will be promptly returned when accompanying postage is included. Payment rates depend upon the content and quality of the individual transparencies. Originals accepted only — no copies.

As to the mechanics of preparing your manuscript, we recommend that you review a few copies of BOW & ARROW HUNTING with a view toward absorbing the general writing style customarily employed.

Please note that the primary emphasis must be upon bowhunting. Stories for BOW & ARROW HUNTING should be concerned with various aspects of hunting with details on archery tackle, and the accompanying illustrations should concentrate upon this theme, as well.

As to what we want: Do-it-yourself articles, telling and showing how the reader can make or modify items connected with archery are always of interest to us. Hunting articles are good, both large and small game, but must impart information that will be of interest or benefit to the readers. We tend to put more emphasis upon informing rather than merely entertaining.

We pay upon acceptance and the amount is determined by the length and quality of the manuscript and illustrations as well as, to some extent, the amount of work we have to do on it to make it suitable for our purposes. If it's weak on artwork and we have to shoot additional photos, this will reduce the amount we will pay for that story. As a general guide, payments run from $150 to $250, rarely higher than the latter.

Writing For BYTE

BYTE continues to solicit and publish articles and reviews that keep you informed about what's new and important in microprocessor-based technology, and many of our articles are still written by you, the people directly involved with the field we report on. Details on querying us about article, product-review, and book-review ideas are listed below. We also welcome submissions (typed and double-spaced, please) to our Letters to the Editor column. Please contact us, via the appropriate department at:

> **BYTE**
> POB 372, Hancock, NH 03449
> (603) 924-9281

You may also want to call or write us (send a stamped, self-addressed business envelope) for our current author guidelines.

ARTICLES

Because our editorial needs are very specific and subject to change, we prefer receiving query letters instead of completed articles. A query letter should contain one or two pages explaining the subject to be covered, its importance to the BYTE reader, and the focus of the proposed article. Query letters should be addressed to the features editor.

If you send us a completed article, we need double-spaced printed versions of the main text (up to 25 numbered pages) and all listings, figures, and tables; please label all items and place all captions on a separate page. Photos should be 35 mm (or larger) transparencies or 5- by 7-inch (or larger) prints. If possible, we would also like to receive magnetic copies of the text, listings, and tables on Apple DOS, IBM PC, Kaypro, or 8-inch CP/M disks; we will pay an additional $20 for this. The files should be standard ASCII text files and should not contain any nonprintable characters; we prefer files that use carriage returns *only at the end of each paragraph*. You should also include a stamped, self-addressed return envelope of the appropriate size. Address these to the features editor.

PRODUCT REVIEWS

We frequently need good product reviewers and sometimes accept unsolicited reviews. BYTE product reviews must be fair, accurate, and comprehensive. Reviewers must have considerable experience in the microcomputer field. Writing experience is preferred but not required, and reviewers must have no financial connection to the company whose products are being reviewed. If you are interested in becoming a BYTE reviewer, send a letter to our product-review editor stating what computer products you own, what products you are interested in, and what writing experience you have.

BOOK REVIEWS

BYTE is always looking for qualified book reviewers. Submit queries and proposals accompanied by a resume, writing samples, or a list of computer-related interests and expertise to the book-review editor. Unsolicited book reviews also will be considered.

We pay competitive rates for articles and reviews and offer you the chance to share your expertise with hundreds of thousands of BYTE readers. Your comments and submissions are always welcome.

BYTE

AUTHOR'S GUIDE

Substance

Knowing the reader: Over three-quarters of BYTE's readers are involved professionally with computers as programmers, systems analysts, engineers, or technicians. Most of them are dyed-in-the-wool hobbyists at heart and spend a lot of time with their systems. The majority have college degrees or higher, although we also have many student readers. They are interested in virtually every aspect of personal computing, including high-level language, original hardware designs, reviews of software and hardware (we are especially interested in these), graphics, artificial intelligence, using computers to control the home, games, robots, etc, etc.

Although many of our articles contain highly technical information, we also encourage the submission of lower-level tutorial articles to enable readers to brush up on the basics. BYTE's readers like to have fun with their systems — a fact that should not be overlooked.

Form

•All submissions should be double-spaced and typewritten on 8½- by 11-inch paper, with the narrow dimension horizontal. Double-spacing is important, since proofreader's marks and other additions must be made to the manuscripts.

•Take the time to write complete, descriptive captions for all figures, tables, listings, and photos.

•Schematic diagrams should be neatly drawn, using the schematics in BYTE as a guide. Note that we prefer a certain type of connector designation, and that power connections to integrated circuits are usually listed in a separate power-wiring table rather than being included in the schematic. The direction of flow in a flowchart is assumed to be downward and to the right. No directional arrows should be used unless the flow is contrary to the aforementioned directions. Again, see the magazine for examples.

•We prefer not to typeset listings, but rather to photograph them for the magazine in order to eliminate the possibility of typographical errors. Because of this, we ask authors to submit listings printed on white paper with a dark ribbon (preferably new).

•Photographs can be either color or black and white, but should be as sharp as possible. We prefer color slides to color prints.

•If programs are written in a commonly used language, BASIC, for example, they should be supplied in a standard version such as Microsoft BASIC, Applesoft, or TRS-80 BASIC. Other BASICs often have specialized (and nonstandard) formats which are difficult for readers to implement on their personal computers.

•We acknowledge all manuscripts upon arrival, and make a final determination within 8 to 12 weeks.

Business Matters

We normally purchase all rights to articles appearing in BYTE and normally pay $50 per printed page. After a "purchase" decision is made, a purchase agreement is sent to the author. Until the agreement is signed and returned, we cannot forward a payment check nor begin editing.

Since payment is based upon length of the *published* article, a "down payment" (called a "binder") is made when the signed agreement has been returned and a final payment is made when the length is determined upon actual publication.

It is important that you submit your article to only one publication at a time. If an article has been simultaneously submitted to any other publication or publications, it will be rejected without further consideration. Unsolicited material should be accompanied by full name and address, as well as return postage.

What's Wrong with Technical Writing Today?

Chris Morgan,
Editor in Chief

In going through the scores of articles that cross my desk each month, I've begun to notice that many of them are poorly written. I'm talking here not so much about incompetent writing (although the number of spelling and syntax errors is alarming), but rather about *misguided* writing — that is difficult to read, unclear, or wasteful of the reader's time. The problem is certainly not BYTE's alone. Editors of other magazines have told me much the same story. Thinking about possible solutions to the problem led me to write this editorial.

The quality of technical writing affects all of our readers in one way or another. Whether you program for a living or just for fun, you need to write clear, concise documentation to accompany your programs. And you undoubtedly have to write reports as part of your job or your studies.

There *are* tricks to good technical writing. I'd like to describe some of them here, and list some sources of information that have proved helpful to us in our writing work. I've also included a list of recommended readings at the end of the editorial.

Ask someone on the periphery of our field what the problem is with our prose, and he or she will probably say, "There's too much jargon." Things like: *I/O, ASCII, byte, CPU, compiler, nonvolatile memory, BASIC, NAND gate, modem, macro, Pascal, floppy disk, Z80, 8080, 8086, 6809, 6502, 68000, Z8000, BCD, CP/M, Unix, Xenix, bootstrap, OS, DOS, DMA, CAI, CAD, CAM, vectored interrupt, monitor, RS-232C, S-100 bus, global variable, checksum, NOP, SWI, VOM,* and so on, and so on.

It's a lexical maze for the uninitiated. But is jargon really our downfall? I think not. We need jargon in the same way that doctors and psychologists do — as a convenient form of shorthand. Programmers have traditionally wrestled with the problem of fitting the most program into the least amount of memory space, so it's only natural that their everyday speech has been condensed down to a sort of technical "alphabet soup." Jargon isn't intrinsically bad — it's how you use it that counts.

Knowing Your Audience: The Seesaw Effect

Outside of grammar, syntax, and spelling (all of which I'll deal with later), there is the major consideration of your intended audience.

Imagine your readers to be sitting at irregular intervals along a large seesaw. At one end are the most technically astute members of your audience; at the other, the interested novices. In the middle are people with varying degrees of knowledge in the subject you are writing about. Your job is to keep the seesaw as level as possible by attending to the various groups in proportion. If there are many novices involved, you must "hold up" their side by providing them with a lot of introductory material. But if you go too far in this direction, the experts will get bored, dismount, and leave you hanging with a partial audience. It's a quandary, one that has no simple answer. Some topics are so technical that even the most intelligent novice will be left in your wake. You can't understand the workings of a compiler, for instance, until you know a lot about computer languages in general.

Some seesaws can't be balanced despite the best intentions of the writer. It is the job of the writer to know this. Nevertheless, within limits, a lot can be done to encourage those readers who are interested in your topic, but who may need some extra clarification. This leads me to the first of what I immodestly refer to as *Morgan's Laws of Writing* (not to be confused with DeMorgan's Law):

Morgan's Law #1: *No Writer Ever Got Shot Down for Writing Too Clearly.*

How do you write clearly? A good first step is to buy a copy of *The Elements of Style* by Strunk and White. There is more wisdom contained in this slim volume than in many a three-pound guide to English Usage.

Next, find some good technical writing and study it. I've included a bibiliography of good technical books at the end of this editorial. We can learn a lesson from painters and musicians who take it for granted that good paintings and pieces of music by other artists should be carefully studied. Donald E Knuth's three-part series of books, *The Art of Computer Programming*, contains some of the best writing you're likely to find in our field — and he's funny, too boot!

One of the best hints I've seen in some time about writing comes from Peter Jacobi, a professor of journalism at Northwestern University's Medill School of Journalism:

Read your writing out loud.

How does it sound? Is it awkward, circumlocutory, pedantic? If so, rewrite it. There's something about reading a piece out loud that lays bare its weaknesses. You can be clear without turning off the majority of your audience. See the accompanying text boxes for some Dos and Don'ts of clear writing.

Morgan's Law #2: *The Beginning Is Half the Thing*

Actually, this is an old Roman saying I borrowed. The main point is that the first few paragraphs of an article are crucial to the rest of the text. The chances are you'll win or lose your readers at the beginning. Still, it's the one part of an article that fledgling writers gloss over in their eagerness to write the main body of the text. One very good writer I know told me he spends up to *half* of his article-writing time creating the first few paragraphs!

Morgan's Law #3: *Avoid the Penguin Syndrome.*

A famous story made the rounds a few years ago that involved a publisher of children's books. A copy of one of the company's books about penguins appeared in the publisher's mailbox along with a letter from an eight-year-old girl that read, "Dear Sirs: I am returning your book, because it told me more about penguins than I wanted to know."

The moral? Tell your readers what they need to know, and no more. If you're zealous about a given topic, tell the reader how to get more information by including a comprehensive list of references. Don't waste space.

Morgan's Law #4: *Writing Is Nonlinear.*

Article ideas don't come in an orderly sequence. Be prepared to jot down your ideas as they come, perhaps on index cards, as John McPhee does. McPhee is blessed with a short-term memory that permits near-total recall. Even so, he writes his ideas on index cards and pins them to a bulletin board where he can mix and match them. The actual writing of a piece might not occur until some time later. E B White recommends that writers use scissors and glue to cut and paste their efforts during the first-draft stage. Some of the more advanced word-processing programs can help to do this. Another great writing aid is to use a data-base-handling program that allows you to cross-index ideas and file them away.

Morgan's Law #5: *(Otherwise known as the Three-Foot Rule): Don't Write Anything Unless You Have a Dictionary and a Thesaurus Within Three Feet Of You.*

I know I'm being a little strict here, but it's important. Unless the dictionary is within easy reach, you probably won't bother to use it, and you may make a spelling error. Going without a thesaurus is a further way of handicapping yourself. Both these books are vital to every writer, and I needn't tell you that the average level of spelling accuracy these days is low. *The American Heritage Dictionary* is a good all-round choice because of its excellent usage notes.

There's nothing much I can say about improving grammar and syntax other than to suggest the reference books at the end of the editorial. *The Careful Writer* and *Miss Thistlebottom's Hobglobins* by Theodore Bernstein both help to dispel many of the bugaboos that have haunted our language ever since the well-meaning Victorians got their hands on it. Bernstein correctly points out that it's all right to occasionally split an infinitive, or to use a preposition to end a sentence with. William Sloane's *The Craft of Writing*, although primarily aimed at the fiction writer, contains a valuable chapter on nonfiction. It's a beautifully written book.

Morgan's Law #6: *Don't be Afraid to be Interesting.*

This may be the most important law of all. Involve your reader by being specific. Generalities make for dull reading. Use humor if you can carry it off. Otherwise, don't! Add some personal observations and opinions. The reader will take them in stride.

All of this leads to the general conclusion that you should write about what you know well. William Sloane said "There are no uninteresting subjects, only uninteresting writers."

In closing, I can think of no better quote than the

following one from the same book. (Although Sloane is talking here about nonfiction books, the sentiment applies equally well to technical articles):

If a book has a beginning, it also has an end. Nonfiction develops by increment, builds on its own material, and ends when its material has been completely exploited. If the book fulfills its contract with the reader, the end will complete the book by fulfilling the promises it made at the start. And if the people who read that book feel continuously that they are added to and believe, at the end, that there is more to them than there was before, the work of nonfiction has succeeded. The same can be said of fiction. In both cases, the contract between the writer and the reader has been kept.

Clear Writing: Some Dos

DO: *(1) Tell your audience what you're going to talk about, (2) Talk about it, and (3) Tell them what you talked about. This old saw from your creative-writing class in high school is as valid as ever. Not observing it is a common failing of much technical writing today.*

DO: *Include a theme sentence near the beginning of your writing that concisely sums up what you want to say in the piece.*

DO: *Tell your story in miniature in the captions to figures, photos, tables, listings, and other illustrations. Your readers may not have time to read all of your article: give them a quick summary and they'll thank you for it. Scientific American magazine does this sort of thing very well.*

DO: *Spell out acronyms and abbreviations when they first appear in text. How many times have you been stopped cold by an unfamiliar abbreviation in the middle of an interesting article?*

DO: *Use verbs. Avoid adjectives and adverbs. A verb in an article title can add a lot of spice. (See Electronics magazine for good examples of verbs in titles.) Adjectives and adverbs, to paraphrase Robert Benchley, are the spinach of technical prose. Everybody says they're vital, but few of us would miss them if the majority of them suddenly disappeared tomorrow. John McPhee (perhaps the best nonfiction writer in the country) has written several books on technical subjects (such as The Curve of Binding Energy) that illustrate these principles better than a hundred paragraphs from me.*

DO: *Break up your text into digestible chunks with subheadings.*

DO: *Remember the questions you had when you were first learning the subject.*

Clear Writing: Some Don'ts

DON'T: *Use the passive voice as your primary voice. Many of us were taught to use the passive voice when writing technical reports and the like. But the passive voice lends an air of coldness and formality to writing—the sort of thing you'd expect in technical transactions, but not in an article that's designed to be read. For example, "I ran the program" is more personal than "The program was run." Sometimes you need the passive voice for* variety, but in general, own up: Say I, Me, My, We, Us or You.

DONT: *Make your reader search for information in an article. If you have a list of items in text, perhaps they could be set off in a table. If you have a glossary in your article, tell the reader at the beginning.*

DONT: *Use big words when small words will do. A good example is utilize, a word that can almost always be replaced with use. Another popular word that should be avoided is implement. Don't implement when you can install, design, code, control, enable, connect, build, or operate: your readers will have a better idea of what you are doing.*

DONT: *Use a clever title for an article if it fails to convey the article's content. Imagine that your title is all that reader has to go on in deciding whether or not to read your work.*

DONT: *Use it or other pronouns if the meaning is obscured. Vague pronoun references in an article slow the reader down. What does the it mean?*

Reference Books

Rathbone, Robert R. Communicating Technical Information. *Reading MA: Addison-Wesley, 1972. A good source of information about technical writing.*

Ralston, A, and Meek, C, eds. Encyclopedia of Computer Science. *New York: Petrocelli/Charter, 1976. Although this book is oriented more toward large computers, it contains a wealth of information about high-level languages, assembly language, data processing, and hundreds of other topics, all presented in lucid fashion. Every serious computer science library should have a copy.*

Bernstein, Theodore M. The Careful Writer: A Modern Guide to English Usage. *New York: Atheneum Press, 1977. Highly recommended, along with the author's other book,* Miss Thistlebottom's Hobgoblins.

Burton, Philip E. A Dictionary of Microcomputing. *New York: Garland Publishing Company, 1976. Still the best dictionary in the microcomputing field.*

Turner, R P. Technical Writer's and Editor's Stylebook. *New York: Howard W Sams and Company, 1964.*

Todd, Alden. Finding Facts Fast. *Berkeley CA: Ten Speed Press, 1979. As Alvin Toffler says, "The shortest distance between two facts may well be Alden Todd."*

Even practiced denizens of the library will find information of interest in this book about reference sources.

Sloane, William. The Craft of Writing. *New York: Norton, 1979.*

Some Examples of Good Technical Writing

Knuth, Donald E. The Art of Computer Programming (three volumes). *Reading MA: Addison-Wesley, 1968, 1969, 1973. An indispensible set.*

Papert, Seymour. Mindstorms: Children, Computers, and Powerful Ideas. *New York: Basic Books, 1980. A refreshingly readable text that discusses Piaget's theories about learning and the use of personal computers the classroom.*

Gardner, Martin. The Ambidextrous Universe, *second edition. New York: Scribner's, 1979. This book deals with symmetry in nature, and shows Gardner's remarkable ability to discuss technical subjects in the clearest of terms. He is the author of the monthly "Mathematical Games" column in the* Scientific American *magazine. I recommend all of his books to those interested in good technical writing.*

Hofstadter, Douglas R. Gödel, Escher, Bach: An Eternal Golden Braid. *New York: Basic Books, 1979. This Pulitzer prize-winning work discusses computer science, art, music, philosophy, and physics in a way that is nothing short of wondrous. It is positive proof that a technical book can be artistic, rigorous, and fascinating.*

Swann and Johnson, Prof. E. McSquared's Original, Fantastic, and Highly Edifying Calculus Primer, Joint Edition. *Los Altos, CA: William Kaufmann, Inc, 1975. This colorful offbeat book is actually a cleverly disguised introduction to differential calculus in comic book form. It manages to be witty and rigorous at the same time. Would that there were more books like this one.*

Jacobs, Harold, Mathematics: A Human Endeavor, *and* Geometry. *San Francisco: W S Freeman and Co., 1976, 1978. The art of the textbook at its finest.*

Two other writers should be mentioned for their contributions to good technical writing: Jeremy Bernstein and Philip Morrison. Their book reviews about scientific and mathematical books appear regularly in The New Yorker *and* Scientific American, *respectively, and they are among the best in their field.* ■

CAT FANCY
DOG FANCY
BIRD TALK
HORSE ILLUSTRATED
magazines

Editorial Offices
P.O. Box 6050
Mission Viejo, California 92690
Telephone (714) 240-6001

WRITER'S GUIDELINES

Thank you for your interest in our publications. We would be pleased
to see your material. Below we have listed some of the publication
requirements of CAT FANCY, DOG FANCY, HORSE ILLUSTRATED, and BIRD TALK
to assist you in preparing submissions.

ARTICLES

CAT FANCY, DOG FANCY, and BIRD TALK are directed at the general pet-
owning population and written for an adult audience. HORSE ILLUSTRATED
is directed at the amateur competition and pleasure horse owner. We
suggest that you read past issues of the magazines to acquaint yourself
with the types of material we use. Past issues may be obtained by sending $3.00 to the above address. We need informative articles, limited to
3,000 words or less, on the care and training of cats, dogs, birds, and
horses (health, nutrition, training, etc.); photo-essays on historical
and current events dealing with cats, dogs, birds, and horses; how-to
articles; human interest stories; and good fiction, with the animal
as the primary focus of interest. We rarely use stories in which
the animals speak as though they were human. We use a breed article in
each issue, but these articles are assigned. Please query if you have
a breed article in mind.

Manuscripts should be typewritten, double-spaced with wide margins. We
prefer that articles be accompanied with appropriate art in the form of
professional-quality color tranparencies or black & white photographs
(NOT SNAP SHOTS) or professional illustrations. Additional guidelines are
available for artists and photographers.

We are always happy to review material on speculation, but with the exception of fiction, the best working procedure is to query before preparing the article. Our usual rate of payment is 3 cents per printed
word, (5 cents if accompanied by good quality photographs). Payment is
made in the latter part of the cover month in which your article appears,
(i.e., if your piece was in the November issue you would be paid in the
latter part of November). We buy first American rights only--all other
rights revert back to the author.

POETRY--CAT FANCY ONLY

We use a limited number of poems in each issue. Competition is fierce!
Payment is $10 and payment is made as it is for articles. We prefer
short poems, but we will use longer works that can be illustrated. Payment for longer, special-use poems is $25.

We cannot assume responsibility for material submitted, but we assure you
that reasonable care will be taken in handling your work. If you would
like a response to your work, PLEASE INCLUDE A SELF-ADDRESSED, STAMPED
ENVELOPE.

CHATELAINE ARTICLE AND FICTION REQUIREMENTS:

Chatelaine is a Canadian monthly magazine published in Canada for Canadian women.

Editor: Mildred Istona

GENERAL: Payment for all material is on acceptance. All manuscripts must be accompanied by a self-addressed, stamped envelope (international reply coupons in lieu of Canadian stamps if sent from outside Canada).

ARTICLES: Preferably, submit a page or two outline/query first. Full-length major pieces run from 2,000 to 4,000 words. Payment for an acceptable major article starts at $1,000. Chatelaine buys first North American serial rights in English and French (the latter to cover possible use in Chatelaine's sister French-language edition, edited in Montreal for French Canada).

We look for important national Canadian subjects, examining any and all facets of Canadian life, especially as they concern or interest Canadian women; for example: current issues (Porn: Does It Incite Violence Against Women? September 1983); personalities (Chatelaine's Woman of the Year: Maureen McTeer, January 1984); lifestyles (Baby Boom Women: High Hopes, Uncertain Prospects, August 1983); health (Progesterone: The Answer to Severe PMS?, March 1984); and relationships (Real Women/Real Men: Role-Free At Last?, January 1984). For all serious articles, deep, accurate thorough research and rich detail are required. Send outline/queries to Elizabeth Parr, Senior Editor, Articles.

UPFRONT COLUMNS: 1,000-word stories about relationships, health, nutrition and fitness; 750-word stories about parents & kids. Submit outline first. Payment for an accepted story starts at $350. We also seek 2,000- to 3,000-word personal experience stories with deep emotional impact, $750. Send queries/outlines to Diane Passa, Senior Editor.

FICTION: Length: 3,000 to 4,500. Canadian settings and characters preferred. We look for well-written material with strong human interest, pace, emotional impact, humor, believable characters. The central character should be a contemporary woman in the 25 to 45 age range, dealing with relationships and situations our readers relate to. Stories concerned mainly with men, set in the past, or concentrating on violence, the supernatural, science fiction, explicit sex or old-fashioned romance are not likely to appeal, nor are introspective mood pieces or avant garde experiments. Payment starts at $1,500 for first North American rights. Send manuscripts to Barbara West, Fiction Editor.

OTHER: Features on beauty, food, fashion and home decorating are supplied by staff writers and editors, and unsolicited material is not considered.

Maclean Hunter Building, 777 Bay Street, Toronto, Canada M5W 1A7 Telephone 596-5425. Toronto/Montreal/London, England

LARRY FLYNT PUBLICATIONS

CHIC FICTION/ARTICLE SPECIFICATIONS

All submissions should be written in a simple, straight-
forward style which is easily readable and not academic.
PLEASE: All manuscripts must include a return envelope,
STAMPED AND SELF-ADDRESSES. All others will be destroyed.
Allow six weeks for response.

FICTION

Maximum length: 4500 words   Fee: $500.00

At present we are buying stories with emphasis on erotic
themes. These may be adventure, action, mystery or horror
stories, but the tone and theme must involve sex and eroticism. The main sex scene should be a minimum of one-and-
half pages of length. However, the erotic nature of the
story must not subordinate to the characterizations and
plot; the sex must grow logically from the people and the
plot, not be contrived or forced.

Stories should start fast and continue to move forward,
with a minimum of flashbacks, preferably none at all. The
dialogue should sound authentic and carry the story forward
as well as reveal the story's characters.

We do not buy poetry. Please refrain from stories with
themes about sex with minors, incest, homosexual activity
or blasphemy.

ARTICLES

Maximum length: 4500 words   Fee: $750.00

a. Hard-hitting, documented exposes.
b. Highly readable, well-researched material on all
    social, religious, political and sexual topics.

NOTE: All information, statistics and quotations used in
articles must be verifiable. (Every article is throughly
checked by our Research Department.) Please refrain from
using the first-person singular. Query first.

PROFILE

Maximum length: 4500 words   Fee: $500.00

Up-close and personal looks at well-known or trend-setting
individuals. Absolutely no promotional copy. Please refrain
from using the first person singular. Query first.

SEX LIFE

Maximum length: 1800 words   Fee: $350.00

Informative pieces, written from a well-researched reportorial
stand-point, on sexual mores around the world. Material can
cover cultural pressures, rites of passage, mating rituals,
new trends in sexual medicine, surgery, therapy, etc.

CLOSE-UP

Maximum length: 1000 words   Fee: $300.00

Interesting and unusual interviews with personalities in and
out of the news who have something to say. Most often, people
from off-beat walks of life are featured. Past examples include
prostitutes, heavy-metal females, rock artists, transsexuals,
ex-Moonie, and New York vice cop. The format is question/answer.
Tape of conversation is required for back-up. An accompanying
color photo of the interviewee pays an extra $50. The questions
should be hard-hitting and uncensored.

DOPE

Maximum length: 2000 words   Fee: $350.00

Highly informative, non-advocacy articles about recreational
drugs or the recreational use of other drugs. Frequently
covers one drug and its use and effects, based on interviews
with top experts in that field; any dangers should be included.
Also uses news-inspired articles about drugs, even those
previously covered in other ways. Dope articles should contain
anecodotes whenever possible, especially as the lead, and should
be written in layman's language, never in technical style.
They should never endorse drug use. Complete fact-and-quote
back-up essential.

Chicago® EDITORIAL GUIDELINES

A major magazine that covers a wide metropolitan area with a limited number of articles each month has to be highly selective about what it prints. Naturally, articles written with our readers in mind will interest us most. Our typical readers live along the lakefront or in other affluent communities, mainly in the suburbs. They have had more than four years of college and hold unusually high-paying jobs, often professional or managerial. Many are parents. They are well read and are interested in the arts and social issues. They go out several times a week to the city's theatres, music halls, and restaurants. They travel widely.

Procedures. Usually we assign or buy articles only after they have been discussed in editorial conferences, so put your queries in writing and send us samples of your best published work. In your query, tell us why you think your idea would interest our particular readers and why you are especially well qualified to write it.

Should we assign the story, you will be contacted by an articles editor, who will negotiate deadline and payment and outline the main features of the article we expect to receive. We will then send you a contract to sign and return.

Payment is on acceptance. What we pay depends on the length of your manuscript, the extent and nature of your research, and the importance we attach to the subject. You will be reimbursed for all reasonable expenses. Although we have paid both more and less, the following ranges will give you an idea of our rates:

Feature articles (including sidebars)	$350-$1,500
Fiction	$500-$1,000
Supplemental sidebars	$150-$250
Short articles (columns)	$275-$600
Book reviews	$100-$125

Standards. These are not hard-and-fast rules, and they don't apply to every article. If you have questions, discuss them with your articles editor.

1. A well-organized story usually answers a single question—often a very simple one. You may not know what it is at first, but after a little research you and your articles editor should be able to formulate one, and the answer ought to be the core of your story.

2. Your research should help you support a point of view. Your story is less likely to be successful if you merely present all sides of an issue and hope that the reader will discern the truth, or if you force a point of view that is not substantiated by your research, or if you tailor your research to validate a preconception.

3. A good magazine story is a good *story*. It doesn't just describe a state of affairs. It tells how and why the situation came about, who was instrumental in making it happen, what it means to the reader, and what the future holds. Often, novelistic devices can be effective: description, narrative, anecdote, dialogue, sensory detail. But if the situation in the story is not intrinsically interesting or does not have consequences that affect our readers, it might not be appropriate for us.

4. A good story usually focuses on individuals. Although institutions take action, it is ultimately individuals who make them act and whose lives are affected. A writer can make almost any story more vivid, and even more truthful, by concentrating on the people involved—their personalities, backgrounds, and motives—on what they stood to gain and lose, and on how they fared.

5. Good stories are rewritten stories. Our readers' time is limited; your manuscript should be a distilled version of your original draft. Remember: We don't pay by the word.

6. Above all, a good magazine story is believable and fair. Any person or institution whose character or actions have been impugned by the author or by anyone quoted in the article has a right to rebut those charges within the article. If that person or institution declines comment, say so in your story. *Chicago* magazine's libel insurance does not cover free-lance writers.

THE
MAGAZINE
FOR GOURMET
CHOCOLATE
LOVERS

WRITER'S GUIDELINES

CHOCOLATIER welcomes inquiries from food writers and cooks.
The query should include a concise story proposal, detailing
the approach and treatment the writer wishes to pursue.
If recipes are part of the story, recipe titles, descriptions of the dish and information regarding its origin
should be included as well as one or two actual recipes
for testing and evaluation. We are interested only in
original material that has not appeared elsewhere. A
resume and samples of previously published work should
also be submitted.

CHOCOLATIER'S audience consists of chocolate lovers.
Not all of our readers are knowledgeable about the world
of chocolate, so topics of discussion can range from
the simple to the sophisticated. What we are looking
for are, simply, good stories about chocolate and
related subjects. Ideas may cover generic and specific
food topics, restaurants, chefs, cooking schools,
techniques, travel, beverages, entertaining and humor.
Though story ideas need not be totally chocolate oriented
(e.g. a cheesecake story would not consist of only
chocolate cheesecakes), generic topics should include
a chocolate variation or two.

Please allow one month for consideration of your
proposal. Address typed inquiries to:

CHOCOLATIER
Articles Editor
45 West 34th Street
Suite 407
New York, NY 10001

CHOICES

For Entrepreneurial Women

2311 Pontius Avenue, Los Angeles, California 90064

CHOICES EDITORIAL STYLE SHEET

TYPES OF ARTICLES:

BUSINESS BEATS--A regular column featuring news briefs, updated business information, and spotlights of women in business who don't warrant full feature coverage. (350-500 words)

DIVERSIONS--A visual column highlighting the "person" part of the businessperson. These include travel, entertainment, new products and new developments that contribute to the physical and mental well-being of a woman. (300-500 words)

FRANCHISE FOCUS--A column highlighting franchise opportunities available. (500-750 words)

STARTING YOUR OWN--An article focusing on the basic, how-to steps of setting up a particular business. (1500-2000 words)

FEATURES--Try to answer the following questions:
1. What was the initial reason for starting a business?
2. What motivated that woman to start a business?
3. How did she do it (get "nuts&boltsy"), specifically who did she call, what did she say, obstacles/problems to overcome, etc.
4. Did she have past business experience/how obtained?
5. What specific problems faced her because she is a woman/how overcame.
6. Did she make any mistakes--what were they/how overcame?
7. Future goals.
8. Advise for a woman starting her own business.
9. Find statistics to back up statements if applicable.
10. If she was a mom with family, did she have to become a "super mom"/were there pressures from the family?
11. If she was already working, what made her decide to start off on her own.
12. Please include practical information so another woman can follow this woman's example.
(1500-2000 words)

PHYSICAL FORMAT:

1. Please use good quality bond <u>white</u> 8 1/2 X 11 paper. No onion skin, colored or lined paper.

2. Articles must be typed and double-spaced.

3. Special care must be used in proper names, dates, figures, etc.

4. Include with your article a complete list of your sources, whether or not we have supplied you with them or you've found them yourself. This will facilitate verifying names, dates, etc. Put your bibliography of sources used on a separate sheet of paper at the end of your article.

5. Count the words you have written and place the number in the upper-right-hand corner of the first page of your article.

6. If you send photos, please include signed model release forms.

CHOICES Magazine assumes no responsibility for unsolicited materials.

Christian HERALD MAGAZINE

For editorial contributors

THE PECULIAR SLANT OF CHRISTIAN HERALD MAGAZINE
by Dean Merrill, Editor

Christian Herald is a general-audience magazine, but that does not mean its editorial formula is generalist. We intend to meet a certain kind of thirst among our readers.

First, a word about those 205,000 readers. Christian Herald is, to put it in a phrase, the magazine of "ordinary Christian adults." Regular folk in the pew. Protestantism's rank and file. Not so much the young and boisterous, not the zealots of the left or the right. Instead, the great, steady middle, from about age 30 and up, whose earlier grabbing for the gusto has now matured. Their lives are less ruled by passions and crusades than by a simple desire "to act justly and to love mercy and to walk humbly with (their) God" (Micah 6:8).

What are they thirsting for? What do they want from a magazine?

We happen to believe the following two things are not at the top of the list:
* "Challenge," exhortation, urgency, pushing, nudging, come-on-let's-do-better. We all need some of this--and we often get a good dose on Sunday morning.
* Inspiration/encouragement/uplift/"blessing." This is somewhat the opposite of "challenge"--and we need regular doses of this, too, in order to feel better about ourselves. We all like to be stroked.

The problem is, a magazine has a hard time doing this as effectively as a singer, a motivational speaker, or even a good Christian friend face to face in your living room. It's not impossible, but the journalism has to be very good.

So what reader needs can we serve in print? Christian Herald's answer is:

The thirst for practical, believable models in the Christian life. The thirst to know whether anybody else just like me is really living the way the preachers say. The thirst to figure out how to be a doer of the Word in the midst of mortgage payments, future shock, and Murphy's law.

A magazine that consistently provides practical, down-to-earth examples of real Christianity in action can be the missing link in many a spiritual life. The Christian world today has a surplus of preaching and a shortage of living, a surplus of telling and a shortage of showing. So our tone or voicing says, "We don't lecture you, order you around. We're you're friends, fellow pilgrims on the way. We're not an authority figure in your life; we're your peers.

"Our taboo words are 'should/need to/ought/we must.' In the best journalistic tradition we intend to show, not tell."

Instead of saying, "You ought to do something about abortion," we tell the story of what one woman and her husband learned through the experience of sheltering an unwed expectant mother for five months.

Instead of saying, "You ought to have family devotions," we show people who are having family devotions and what they do when their kids misbehave.

EXECUTIVE OFFICE: 40 Overlook Drive, Chappaqua, New York 10514 (914) 769-9000

Instead of saying, "We've got to stop pornography," we run an article on "How Jerry Kirk and (Jane Doe) Cleaned Up Cincinnati," where, I'm told, you cannot find an adult bookstore or massage parlor within the city limits. The same is true of Atlanta, thanks to a diligent Christian D.A.

Instead of exhorting couples to be more loving toward each other, we show the honest rekindling of love in one couple's life--not in a sappy sort of way, but believably.

We are not satisfied with "nice articles." We go for the nerve endings--the spots where readers are hurting or are perplexed. We get them to stand up and cheer for the light as it pushes back the darkness--and then want to do likewise.

This does not mean every article must be first-person, like Guideposts. We run topical articles as well, IF they are believable, reality-based, and well illustrated with people stories. Theory is not enough. We also use photo essays, Q&A, and most of the other journalistic formats.

We continue to do people covers, but with bite. Celebrity stories are fine if they are more than "celebrity stories." If a celebrity can demonstrate the solution to a felt need or problem of the readers, fine. If all the story says is "See the famous Christian," that's not good enough. The acid test of a celebrity story is whether the non-fan is intrigued by it. Does the housewife who normally ignores golf find something about this famous Christian golfer that's fascinating?

Every article must pass through the grid of "Will the common Christian care about this?" Our magazine is people-centered rather than issue- or cause-centered. This is a magazine of Christian realism.

Queries and manuscripts are welcome.

Specific needs for standing columns:

For "Kids of the Kingdom"--funny or revealing things that happened to you in the process of raising/teaching/working with Christian kids (75-200 words). $20 upon acceptance.

For "The Two of Us"--memorable, humorous, and/or touching moments in the life of a Christian marriage. Times to cherish--the "glue" that holds a marriage together. The exact opposite of the complaint stories you hear in every beauty salon and barber shop (75-200 words). $20 upon acceptance.

For "One Last Word" (back page)--a moment or experience in your everyday Christian living/ministry that surprisingly took on a deeper meaning. Needs a wistful touch at the end (700-1,000). $100 upon acceptance.

WHAT WE LOOK FOR IN CHRISTIANITY TODAY ARTICLES:

A. Good Ideas.

    1. fresh, creative ideas that plow up new ground.
    2. that fit the purpose and stance of CHRISTIANITY TODAY.
    3. that are useful to the reader; that answer the question: "Good for what?"
    4. that contain new insights, wisdom, judgment, analysis, interpretation.
    5. that are interesting to CHRISTIANITY TODAY readers.

B. Evidence of Hard Work.
    1. not superficial generalities.
    2. strong supporting evidence for the article's major proposition.
    3. careful diagnosis and solutions.
    4. related to the real world.
       a. not limited to academic research.
       b. related to real problems and needs.
    5. correlation with and application of Christian values and principles.

C. A Strong Logical Case.
    1. point-by-point, with transitions.
    2. shows the reader where you are going and why.
    3. makes clear what you are trying to prove.

D. Compelling Opening and Conclusion.
    1. introductory paragraphs that hold attention.
    2. an ending that summarizes and provokes thought.

E. Careful Craftmanship.
    1. not necessarily a literary masterpiece, but . . .
    2. high regard for language and style, words, punctuation, grammar, etc.
    3. colorful, vivid, moving language.
    4. simplicity, clarity, readability.
    5. no technical jargon or professional academic language.
    6. adherence to our word limits, usually 2,700 to 3,000 words. The Ministries and Speaking Out columns use 900-word articles of a practical nature every other issue. Refiner's Fire and book reviews are normally commissioned. Letters of inquiry are requested before these are sent.
    7. fresh, clean, legible manuscript copy, typed double-spaced. (We prefer exclusive original submissions. If you have sent your manuscript to another magazine, please advise.) Word processor printouts, as long as they are clear, are acceptable. We prefer these to be on 8½ X 11 inch sheets.

- -

CHRISTIANITY TODAY expects query letters before manuscripts are sent.

1. Material should not be submitted without first becoming thoroughly familiar with the magazine's content over a period of time.

2. Outline your article proposal. State your subject, theme, proposition and your main points.

3. Outline your research, experience, qualifications.

4. Supply full bibliographical data for all quoted material. Indicate Scripture versions used.

Payment: Essays purchased at $100.00 and up for columns, and $200 and up for articles. Reimbursement upon acceptance.

CompleteWoman

ASSOCIATED PUBLICATIONS, INC.
Continental Bank Building
1165 North Clark Street, Chicago, Illinois 60610 • (312) 266-8680

Thank you for your interest in submitting material to Complete Woman.
We welcome all manuscripts and cartoons/illustrations that address
the concerns of today's woman. Topics may vary over a range, including
positive approaches to home, family, career, health, relationships,
and self-improvement. Subject matter is limited only by your imagination
and understanding of what it means to be a complete woman in today's
society.

Manuscripts should be typed, double-spaced, with wide margins, and
should be between 1000 and 2200 words in length, including any sidebar
or supplementary material. A stamped, self-addressed envelope must
accompany all manuscripts, cartoons, and queries submitted for consideration, or they will not be returned. Because all materials are
received on speculation only, we suggest you query us before sending
your articles.

Complete Woman is published bimonthly. We pay upon publication (during
the month of the cover), and after publication, all rights to your
original materials revert to you.

We look forward to seeing your work.

Sincerely,

Lori L. Lewis

Lori L. Lewis
Editorial Assistant

COMPUTE!'s Gazette for Commodore
AUTHOR GUIDE

COMPUTE!'s GAZETTE for Commodore is looking for interesting, useful articles aimed at beginning to intermediate Commodore users. If you have an article idea or a good original program, we'd like to see it. Don't worry if you are not a professional writer. We are more concerned with the content of an article than its style. Simply try to be clear in your writing and check your program for any bugs.

COMPUTE!'s GAZETTE for Commodore is a consumer-oriented magazine for Commodore users who want to get the most out of their computers in a non-technical way. It is aimed primarily at home users, not all of whom necessarily want to become expert programmers. If your article covers a more advanced or technical topic, you may choose to submit it to our companion publication, COMPUTE!. If you submit an article to one of our magazines and we believe it would be more suitable to the other, we will transfer your submission to the right editors. The basic editorial requirements for publication are the same for both magazines; so are the payment rates.

The following guidelines will permit your good ideas and programs to be more easily edited and published. Most of these suggestions serve to improve the speed and accuracy of publication:

1. The upper left corner of the first page should contain your name, address, telephone number, and the date of submission.

2. The following information should appear in the upper right corner of the first page. If your article is specifically directed to a particular Commodore machine, such as the Commodore 64, please state which one. In addition, please indicate the memory requirements of programs.

3. The underlined title of the article should start about 2/3 of the way down the first page.

4. Following pages should be typed normally, except that in the upper right corner there should be an abbreviation of the title, your last name, and the page number. For example: Memory Map/Smith/2.

5. Short programs (under 20 lines) can easily be included within the text. Longer programs should be separate listings. *It is essential that we have a copy of the program, recorded twice, on a tape or disk.* The tape or disk should be labeled with your name and the title of the article. Tapes are fairly sturdy, but disks need to be enclosed within plastic or cardboard mailers (available at photography, stationery, or computer supply stores).

It is far easier for others to type in your program if you use CHR$(X) values and TAB(X) or SPC(X) instead of cursor manipulations to format your output. For five carriage returns, FOR I=1 TO 5:PRINT:NEXT is far more "portable" to other computers with other BASICs and also easier to type in. And, instead of a dozen right-cursor symbols, why not simply use PRINT SPC(12)? A quick check through your pro-

gram—making these substitutions—would be greatly appreciated by your editors and by your readers.

6. If your article is accepted and you have since made improvements to the program, please submit an entirely new tape or disk and a new copy of the article reflecting the update. We cannot easily make revisions to programs and articles. It is necessary that you send the revised version as if it were a new submission entirely, but be sure to indicate that your submission is a revised version by writing "Revision" on the envelope and the article.

7. All lines within the text of the article should be spaced so that there is about 1/2-inch between them. A one-inch margin should be left at the right, left, top, and bottom of each page. No hyphens should be used at the ends of lines to break words. And please do not justify. Leave the lines ragged.

8. Standard typing paper should be used (no onionskin or other thin paper) and typing should be on one side of the paper only (upper- and lowercase).

9. Sheets should be attached together with a paper clip. Staples should not be used.

10. A good general rule is to spell out the numbers zero through ten in your article and write higher numbers as numerals (1024). The exceptions to this are: Figure 5, Table 3, TAB(4), etc. Within ordinary text, however, the zero through ten should appear as words, not numbers. Also, symbols and abbreviations should not be used within text: use "and" (not &), "reference" (not ref.), "through" (not thru).

11. For greater clarity, use all capitals when referring to keys (RETURN, TAB, ESC, SHIFT), BASIC words (LIST, RND, GOTO), and three languages (BASIC, APL, PILOT). Headlines and subheads should, however, be initial caps only, and emphasized words are not capitalized. If you wish to emphasize, underline the word and it will be italicized during typesetting.

12. COMPUTE!'s GAZETTE for Commodore pays between $50 and $600 for published articles. In general, the rate reflects the length and quality of the article. Payment is made upon acceptance of an article. Following submission (Editorial Department, COMPUTE!'s GAZETTE for Commodore, P.O. Box 5406, Greensboro, NC 27403) it will take from four to six weeks for us to reply. If your work is accepted, you will be notified by a letter which will include a contract for you to sign and return. Rejected manuscripts are returned to authors who enclose a self-addressed, stamped envelope. We do not consider articles which are multiple submissions. If you wish to send an article to another magazine for consideration, please do not submit it to us.

13. Articles can be of any length—from a single-line routine to a multi-issue series. The average article is about four to eight double-spaced, typed pages.

14. If you want to include photographs, they should be 5×7, black-and-white glossies.

Computing
for Business®
7330 Adams St., Paramount, CA 90723

CASE STUDY ARTICLES

In an effort to better serve the needs of our readers, COMPUTING FOR BUSINESS magazine is searching for interesting and informative case study features—articles about how specific businesses implemented microcomputer systems or software packages and reaped benefits in the form of increased productivity and/or more efficient managament (or failed to reap benefits due to product deficiency, poor planning, or other factors).

Are you aware of any businesses, large or small, that have recently implemented microcomputer hardware and/or software? If so, we are interested in articles documenting their experiences from the time they selected the equipment to the point of tangible results from implementation.

To maintain a consistency in these articles, there are several points that should be covered in each story. They are as follows:

* A brief overview of the situation before purchasing the micro or software.

* The reasons for purchasing the merchandise.

* The selection process and the criteria involved.

* The implementation process, including any problems encountered.

* The costs involved, and the benefits in terms of increased productivity and/or improved efficiency of operations.

* Any plans the business may have for future expansion of the system (or software).

Be sure to include any other points you may consider important. These articles should run 2,000-3,000 words.

We encourage each author to take several pictures (35mm black-and-white) of the internal and external working environment. Feel free to be creative. Price range for the articles is $50-80 per published page.

If you are interested, please outline some ideas in writing and send them to us. Every suggestion will be given serious consideration.

Computing for Business®

ARTICLE SUBMISSION PROCEDURE

The editorial department at COMPUTING FOR BUSINESS magazine is always happy to review unsolicited articles to consider for publication. The following guidelines on preparing manuscripts will afford authors the best opportunity possible to receive placement in the magazine.

Our editorial focus is on microcomputer applications for businesses. Unique and unusual methods wherein various businesses can obtain efficient use of their systems are of interest. The fields of law, medicine, retail sales, accounting and recordkeeping, filing, and all manner of useful office functions are emphasized. Case studies of how particular businesses computerized their operations are encouraged. Step-by-step procedures, including planning, product selections, and implementation should be detailed. (See our separate sheet for full details on case study articles.)

Our agenda calls for articles on such topics as business graphics, word processing, computerized communications and networking, and business hardware/software in various capabilities and price categories. (Potential hardware and software reviewers should look over our review guideline policies printed on a separate sheet.)

Useful applications stories involving particular products (i.e., "Sales Forecasting with SuperCalc 2") are also very much of interest. Good quality program listings, accompanied by articles explaining the programs, are sure bets for serious consideration during our screening process. The listings should be no more than 60 characters wide, with no wrap-around lines. Unlined paper and a new ribbon should be used. Sample runs should also be included. In the article, variables should be described. The system utilized in composing the program should be detailed—operating systems, language type and version, and any necessary peripherals.

Manuscripts should be prefaced by a brief synopsis of the article. Copy should be typed or printed out double-spaced with one-inch margins. Minimum text length is 1,500 words, whether or not the article is accompanied by a program listing. Photos should be numbered and have a brief description attached to each. Tables, listings, etc. should be on separate pages and each should have a caption. Authors must submit a statement of background and expertise.

Articles intended for a particular month should be in our office no later than four months prior to the cover date (i.e., May 1 for the September issue). If you prefer to query before preparing the manuscript, the same deadline applies. Please make the query letter detailed enough so that we may evaluate the appropriateness of your proposal to our editorial needs. Telephone queries are discouraged.

The publisher assumes no responsibility for artwork, photos, or manuscripts. No acknowledgement is made unless the submission is accompanied by a large, stamped return envelope. A minimum of six weeks should be allowed for a response. The payment rate ranges from $50-$80 per published page.

All manuscripts and queries should be addressed to: Editorial Department, COMPUTING FOR BUSINESS, 7330 Adams St., Paramount, CA 90723.

CONSUMERS DIGEST

GUIDELINES FOR WRITERS

CONSUMERS DIGEST is written "for people who demand value." This means we try
to help our readers make lifestyle, purchasing, and investing decisions that
benefit their personal lives. To do this, we evaluate products that could be
used in the home or during leisure time: housewares, cars, clothing, food,
electronics, fitness equipment, etc. We identify products by brand name and
evaluate them thoroughly and objectively. We tell our readers which products
are Best Buys, where to buy recommended products (especially discount sources)
and how much they should expect to pay. We put emphasis on the positive, not
the negative.

However, the editorial concept of CONSUMERS DIGEST goes far beyond product
advice. We show our readers how to obtain the best value for the services
they need: doctor, hospital, lawyer, financial adviser, etc. We present the
latest scientific advice on how to eat right, get the right amount and kind
of exercise, and stay healthy. We build "quality of life" into most articles.
We offer advice on how our readers can spend their travel and entertainment
dollars for maximum enjoyment at the lowest possible cost. We like stories
about developing trends, and occasionally we let the readers peek into the
crystal ball at the lives they will lead, the homes they will live in, the
cars they will drive, and the products they will be using in the future. As
a monthly magazine, we can't hope to compete with TV, newspapers, or weekly
magazines; so our pieces must contain provocative "digging" or take an unusual
perspective.

The typical CONSUMERS DIGEST reader is about 42 years old (although the age
range is extremely wide, from the 20s through the retirement years). The
readership is fairly evenly divided between males and females. Most readers
are married and own their homes; their everage household income is about $35,000
--extraordinarily high for any magazine. They have disposable money and they
want to spend it--wisely. They are frequent and well-informed purchasers of
cars, electronics, and indeed, all consumer goods.

CONSUMERS DIGEST is published 10 times a year, including special Buying Guide
issues published biannually. Ideally, articles are scheduled and assigned
four to six months in advance of publication. Articles must be thoroughly
researched, well-documented, and professionally written. You can expect your
work to be subject to intense scrutiny. We make frequent use of charts, graphs,
and lists of "bests." Writers should be well-acquainted with the product or
service they are writing about and be prepared to render objective opinions
concerning value and reliability. To enliven the article, anecdotes and quotes
from experts should be included, along with comments reflecting the experiences
of others with the subject. People relate to other people's experiences.
Product Best Buys generally represent the best value for the money spent and
should be easily obtained nationally.

Article lengths generally range from 1,000 to 3,000 words. First-time contributors should query, including clips of recently published work and a self-
addressed, stamped envelope. A query should be comprehensive enough to give
a realistic idea of how the subject would be handled. Assignments are based
on acceptance of a comprehensive outline. Payment for all rights is approximately 25 cents per assigned work, and generally is made when the article is
deemed acceptable for publication.

Queries should be sent to Frank L. Bowers, Editor, CONSUMERS DIGEST, 5705 N.
Lincoln Ave., Chicago, IL 60659; phone (1-312) 275-3590.

© CONSUMERS DIGEST, INC.

The COOK'S Magazine
THE MAGAZINE OF COOKING IN AMERICA

March 10, 1986

WRITER'S GUIDELINES

COOK'S is looking for lively, informative articles that describe food and restaurant trends in the United States or that give hands-on cooking techniques. Queries are welcome for:

MAJOR FOOD ARTICLES.. $375.00
Describes trends in food and cooking or details fundamental cooking techniques. Includes seven or eight recipes.

SHORTER FOOD ARTICLES.. $200.00
Short text plus four or five recipes.

SCIENCE OF COOKING.. $250.00
Explanation of how a particular aspect of cooking works. Includes one or two recipes if appropriate. Recent topics include knife sharpening and the science of butter.

PEAK PRODUCE... $300.00
Article plus eight to ten recipes focusing on a specific seasonal ingredient or type of ingredient.

IF YOU ARE INTERESTED IN PROPOSING AN ARTICLE TO COOK'S:

1. Direct a brief, to-the-point query letter to the editor. In three or four sentences outline your idea. List several recipe ideas.

2.   Enclose a recent writing sample and two original recipes. The recipes and writing samples <u>do not</u> in any way have to be related to your proposal; they are samples of your style and ability.

We do not use previously published material or recipes that call for prepared ingredients such as canned soups.

Enclose a stamped, self-addressed envelope with your submission. COOK'S IS NOT RESPONSIBLE FOR UNSOLICITED MANUSCRIPTS.

2710 NORTH AVENUE
BRIDGEPORT, CONNECTICUT 06604
203-366-4155

Cosmopolitan

224 WEST 57TH STREET, NEW YORK, N.Y. 10019

COSMOPOLITAN, 224 West 57th Street, N.Y., N.Y. 10019

Helen Gurley Brown, Editor. Issued monthly, $1.75 a copy, $21.00 a year.

Non-Fiction: Roberta Ashley, Executive Editor. Magazine aims at young career women. All non-fiction should tell these readers 1) how they can improve their lives, 2) better enjoy their lives, and 3) live better lives. Within this sphere, articles can be of the widest range, from celebrity profiles to psychological/ sociological pieces of humor. Crisp, incisive, entertaining writing is a must, with a heavy emphasis on reader involvement. Full-length articles should be about 5,000 words, features 1,000 to 3,000 words. Payment for full-lengthers usually varies from $750 to $1500, but this is open to negotiation. Payment for features is proportionately less.

Fiction: Betty Kelly, Fiction and Books Editor. Stories must have solid upbeat plots, and sharp characterization. They should focus on contemporary man-woman relationships. Sophisticated handling and sensitive approach is a must, and female protagonists are preferred since our readers most easily identify with them. Short-shorts range from 1,500 words to 3,000 words; Short-stories from 4,000 to 6,000 words. Payment is $1,000 and up for short stories, from $300 to $600 for short-shorts. Previously published serious novels and mystery and suspense novels are sought for condensing and excerpting; payment here is open to negotiation, with the author's agent or hard cover publisher.

All submissions must be accompanied by a stamped, self-addressed envelope.

COSMOPOLITAN IS A PUBLICATION OF HEARST MAGAZINES, A DIVISION OF THE HEARST CORPORATION

See *Mid-Atlantic Country Magazine.*

Cycle World Magazine
CBS Publications*

1499 Monrovia Avenue
Newport Beach, CA 92663
Telephone (714) 720-5300
TWX (910) 596-1353

TO PROSPECTIVE CYCLE WORLD CONTRIBUTORS

Thanks for your interest and welcome to a tough market.

Tough because while we're always in the market for stories, we only buy material we can't produce ourselves. Most of the magazine consists of tests, evaluations, news and competition coverage, so we don't buy much outside material.

Out standard rate of payment is $150 per published page, that is, if you sell us a four-page article, text and pictures, we pay you $600. (We pay on acceptance.)

We pay $25-$100 for black and white photographs only, double that for color.

Manuscripts must be submitted on standard size paper, typewritten and double spaced, with ample (1-inch minimum) margins for editing. Most freelance photography will be in black and white, and should be submitted as 8 x 10-in. glossy or semi-glossy prints.

A note on color pictures: We run only a few full color pages each month. Mostly we use the pages for the feature articles, tests, etc. We like color. We use it when and where we can. But do not send only full color photographs. We need to be able to use an outside article where it will fit. If we have no black and white art, we can't make it fit as well and we're liable not to use the article.

Our needs include brief stories on significant racing events; technical features; how-to features involving mechanical modification; informative, well-researched travel stores, brightly written, or in a humorous vein; satire, and fiction. We would also like to see photo-features on original custom bikes, classic and antique machines, and nicely crafted competition and street specials.

We expect material of professional quality, submitted in a professional manner. Please include a stamped, self-addressed envelope with all material submitted and make sure that your name, address and telephone number appear on the manuscript and on the back of each photograph submitted. All subject matter pictures in photographs should be identified in captions.

A query letter will help us and you. If we're overstocked on fiction and travel pieces (we usually are) it will save time and effort on both sides if we say no before you do the work. But, when we ask to see a story, that doesn't mean we promise to buy it. We cannot assume any obligation.

Please see the attached PUBLICATION RIGHTS sheet for additional information.

*A Division of CBS Inc.

Photographers:

Photographic work is bought by our publication in three different ways.

1. Special Assignment

   In which we initiate the assignment for our own special use.
   All material produced during that assignment is our exclusive
   property, may not be used by the photographer for any other
   purpose, and usually will not be reassigned at a future date.
   We will retain all such negatives and transparencies in our
   files.

2. Guaranteed Minimum Assignment

   In which we ask a photographer to cover an event or photograph
   a particular subject and guarantee him/her a minimum payment no
   matter how much of this material we use. Example: You send us
   an agreed-upon number of prints from a race, and we pay the
   minimum. If we use more than the minimum value, we will pay you
   space rates. In turn, you must give us "first refusal rights"
   on everything taken during a Guaranteed Minimum Assignment and
   you may not submit to anyone else until we've made our selection.
   Reprint rights may be assigned subject to the conditions stated
   under Publication Rights.

3. Freelance Submissions or Submissions on Speculation

   We buy all rights on that material which we use, require exclusivity,
   and reprint rights may be reassigned subject to the conditions stated
   under Publication Rights.

Releases:

If you use a model in any photograph that is submitted to us, you must
obtain permission in writing for this photograph to be published. Such
releases must be submitted to the publisher on request. (Note: Model
releases are not required for photographs taken in public places, provided
they are not of such intimate nature as to cause embarrassment to the
person or persons in the photograph.) We will not make payment to any model
unless prior arrangement has been made.

Artists:

We purchase all publication rights to artwork. We regard the original art
as the artist's property, however, and will return it on request. The artist
may then sell the original artwork, but only for display, not for publication.
These conditions may be modified in certain circumstances but only when worked
out prior to publication.

General:

If you are in doubt about the rights you are selling or if you have a special
circumstance which necessitates an unusual agreement between you and the
publisher, discuss it with the editor at the time the material is submitted.

CYCLE WORLD MAGAZINE

PUBLICATION RIGHTS

What you are selling to us: Rights.
So that you will understand what rights you are selling when you submit
manuscripts, photographs or artwork to CBS Magazines, we have prepared
the following outline.

Publication Rights

As a condition of sale, the contributor should understand that we buy all
publication rights to articles, photographs and artwork. This means that
you may not submit this material to any other publication without our
permission.

On your request, we will reassign publication rights back to you provided
this does not conflict with our possible future use of this material.
  Exceptions: We will not reassign rights back to the contributor on covers,
  color spreads (either photographic or artwork), road test photos, or
  special assignment photos.

Your guarantees to us:
You must guarantee that material submitted to us is exclusive to us. If it
is being offered to another publication, or if it has already been sold or
published, even in another form, we have the right to know this.

Writers

We buy all rights and will reassign rights only on the conditions stated above.
For writers who want book rights, foreign publication rights, etc., there is
usually no problem. But check with us at the time the material is submitted.

If you send us the work of another person (either photographer, artist or writer)
as a part of your submitted work, it is your responsibility to have obtained
permission to submit this work to us. This applies to a photograph or a drawing
you have obtained to illustrate the article, or a quote from copyrighted material
that has appeared elsewhere. It is also the contributor's responsibility to pay
for such material, when necessary, and we will not make separate payment to such
secondary contributors unless this is worked out with the editor prior to the
material's acceptance by us.

TEXAS' LEADING NEWSPAPER

The Dallas Morning News

```
DALLAS LIFE MAGAZINE WRITER GUIDELINES:

The magazine frequently prints free-lance material,
however very few unsolicited manuscripts are published.
All pieces  must have a strong Dallas angle, and we
generally avoid  straight lifestyle/service pieces even
if they do have a Dallas focus.

Inside stories run 1,000-2,000 words and covers 3,000-3,500.
Inside pieces pay $325 (home stories under 400 words
pay $200), and covers pay $650. Poetry is not accepted
and fiction is printed about once a year.  Queries are
answered if SASE is included. Payment on acceptance.
About 6-week lead time.

Thank you for your interest.




Melissa East
Editor
```

CAT FANCY
DOG FANCY
BIRD TALK
HORSE ILLUSTRATED
magazines

Editorial Offices
P.O. Box 6050
Mission Viejo, California 92690
Telephone (714) 240-6001

WRITER'S GUIDELINES

Thank you for your interest in our publications. We would be pleased
to see your material. Below we have listed some of the publication
requirements of CAT FANCY, DOG FANCY, HORSE ILLUSTRATED, and BIRD TALK
to assist you in preparing submissions.

ARTICLES

CAT FANCY, DOG FANCY, and BIRD TALK are directed at the general pet-
owning population and written for an adult audience. HORSE ILLUSTRATED
is directed at the amateur competition and pleasure horse owner. We
suggest that you read past issues of the magazines to acquaint yourself
with the types of material we use. Past issues may be obtained by sending $3.00 to the above address. We need informative articles, limited to
3,000 words or less, on the care and training of cats, dogs, birds, and
horses (health, nutrition, training, etc.); photo-essays on historical
and current events dealing with cats, dogs, birds, and horses; how-to
articles; human interest stories; and good fiction, with the animal
as the primary focus of interest. We rarely use stories in which
the animals speak as though they were human. We use a breed article in
each issue, but these articles are assigned. Please query if you have
a breed article in mind.

Manuscripts should be typewritten, double-spaced with wide margins. We
prefer that articles be accompanied with appropriate art in the form of
professional-quality color tranparencies or black & white photographs
(NOT SNAP SHOTS) or professional illustrations. Additional guidelines are
available for artists and photographers.

We are always happy to review material on speculation, but with the exception of fiction, the best working procedure is to query before preparing the article. Our usual rate of payment is 3 cents per printed
word, (5 cents if accompanied by good quality photographs). Payment is
made in the latter part of the cover month in which your article appears,
(i.e., if your piece was in the November issue you would be paid in the
latter part of November). We buy first American rights only--all other
rights revert back to the author.

POETRY--CAT FANCY ONLY

We use a limited number of poems in each issue. Competition is fierce!
Payment is $10 and payment is made as it is for articles. We prefer
short poems, but we will use longer works that can be illustrated. Payment for longer, special-use poems is $25.

We cannot assume responsibility for material submitted, but we assure you
that reasonable care will be taken in handling your work. If you would
like a response to your work, PLEASE INCLUDE A SELF-ADDRESSED, STAMPED
ENVELOPE.

Historical Times, Inc.
2245 Kohn Road/Box 8200
Harrisburg, PA 17105
(717) 657-9555

American History Illustrated
British Heritage
Civil War Times
Country Journal
Early American Life
Fly Fisherman
Opus
The New England Skiers' Guide
The Original New England Guide

Museum Editions Limited
Historical Times Travel

MEMO TO AUTHORS:

EARLY AMERICAN LIFE combines elements of history, antiques collecting, home decorating, food, travel, architecture, hobbies, arts and crafts into a final product that is designed to help our readers bring something of the warmth and beauty of early America into their lives. It has a bit of the personality of a home service magazine, a touch of history, lots of how-to, and accurate information on traveling to historic sites and restorations. We try to achieve a balance of these subjects in each issue.

EARLY AMERICAN LIFE tries to be a warm, personal magazine in its approach to readers. While we insist upon sound research and accuracy, we reject articles that are written in the style of a doctor's thesis. Our time period is generally 1700-1900. One exception is when a story begins in that period but must be completed with information after 1900. We prefer a tight, economical style without padding or unnecessary words and phrases. We can use articles from 1,000 to 3,000 words.

Since almost all articles are illustrated, we prefer that you submit pictures, drawings, etc. with your manuscript. Always indicate source for full credit.

If you can give our readers a story that is interesting and entertaining, and at the same time give them something they can use in their own lives, you may have written something that we will buy. (We pay upon acceptance and are not averse to buying for inventory except in categories where we are well stocked.)

Sincerely,

Frances Carnahan
Editor

FC:jc

EASTERN AIRLINES *Review*

Don Dewey, editor

Coverage: Primarily east of the Rockies

Format: Selected reprints from magazines, plus art and entertainment events
             listings across the Eastern Airlines system.

EASTERN REVIEW'S exciting and provocative articles focus on our
       nation's cities, people, fashion, international travel and
       feature articles from notable publications. Full color
       portfolios showcase the newest exhibitions in art and photo-
       graphy. A lively overview of entertainment events in the
       east keeps the reader abreast of current trends. A special
       color portfolio each month is presented in English and in
       Spanish for Eastern's growing South American market. A special
       edition is presented each month for the million-a-year Shuttle
       passengers. This edition focuses on major events and guidelines
       to Washington, Boston and New York.

   For further information, see PSA Magazine.

THE Elks MAGAZINE

WRITER'S GUIDELINES

THE ELKS MAGAZINE goes out 10 times each year to the 1.6 million members of the B.P.O.E. Editorially it is a general-interest magazine. This should not imply, however, the articles are just a rehash of existing material. Because most topics have been covered at one time or another in THE ELKS MAGAZINE, an article to be considered must be fresh, provocative, thought-provoking, well-researched and documented. A thumbnail profile of the "average" reader would be a person over 40, with some college, and an above average income, located in a town of 500,000 or less.

Regular columns deal with medicine, retirement, business, and travel. Leads and back-of-book features are possible on these topics (except travel), but the angle must differ appreciably.

NOT NEEDED: FICTION, TRAVEL, POLITICAL OR RELIGIOUS ARTICLES, FILLERS, AND POETRY.

General Editorial falls into two basic areas.

BACK-OF-BOOK: Articles of information, business, contemporary life problems and situations, or just interesting topics, ranging from medicine, science, and history, to sports. 1500-2000 words.

LEAD: Vary widely in subject matter. Must be tightly written, timely, and authoritative (sources usually requested). 2500-3000 words.

EDITORIAL REQUIREMENTS

Query: A must. Do not send an article without a written query first. DO NOT PHONE.

S.A.S.E.: A must. THE ELKS MAGAZINE cannot accept responsibility for manuscripts sent without a S.A.S.E.

Rights: First North American Serial Rights.

Photos: Purchased as part of a manuscript package ONLY. Will be returned after publication on request.

Rates: Start at $150 for back-of-book features. Lead articles start at about $300, with increases for frequent contributors. Payment is made upon acceptance. S.S. No. must be submitted with your manuscript.

Please direct all editorial queries to:
Herbert H. Gates, Managing Editor
THE ELKS MAGAZINE
425 W. Diversey Pkwy.
Chicago, IL 60614

ENTREPRENEUR MAGAZINE EDITORIAL STYLE SHEET

Writers submitting material to *Entrepreneur* should be aware that any manuscript presented which does not fit the following criteria (and thus requires an extensive rewrite) can reduce the payment from 50 to 75 percent of the normal price.

WHO ARE THE READERS? Primarily readers are in or on the edge of the upper-middle-class socioeconomic level. Most (69 percent) are businessmen, executives, lawyers and accountants. Awareness of modern business techniques is high. However, the language used should be plain, since 31 percent of the readers have only a high-school education or minimal amounts of college training. This sector of the readership is composed of young, salesman types looking for a way to make a quick buck.

We are trying to produce three different results from our stories: awareness of the newest, most profitable ways to make money as an independent businessman; instruction and education that are unique to the featured business; enthusiasm for the particular business.

Enthusiasm and confidence are as important to the success of a business as having sufficient capital and education—sometimes even compensating for lack of education.

In the opening paragraphs of each article the writer should try to "sell" the reader on starting this business, but with facts and figures rather than unsupported opinions.

Word conservation is very important. After completing your first draft, go back, cut and condense. Flowery phrases are inappropriate. The readers are hard-headed businessmen, reading for profit, not pleasure.

After the introduction, which is actually an overview of the market and possibilities for the featured business, the instructions for starting the business must be described in a logical order. Pretend you are starting the business yourself and list every step from conception through grand opening. *These steps must be in a logical sequence. Don't jump around.*

The following is a list of information that should be reported on:

1. Profit - how much to expect.
2. Exact costs - everything it takes to set up, open and operate.
3. Equipment - what to buy.
4. Economy - ways to save money on equipment, fixtures, etc.
5. Rent - how much to pay.
6. Location - how to choose the best
7. Licenses and permits - what to expect and how to get them if unusual.
8. Merchandise - what to buy, how to buy, where to buy.
9. If retail - how to lay out your store and display your wares.
10. Decorating ideas - quick, cheap and impressive.
11. Signs - how much, how big, where, and what to say.
12. Employees - whom to hire, where, and what to pay.
13. Advertising - how, where, when, and how much.
14. Promotion - best gimmicks, completely detailed.
15. Knowledge - where to find it, buy it, or rent it.
16. Financing - how to finance your opening costs, how to finance your sales to customers.
17. Customers - how to bring them in and keep them.
18. Pricing - What price to set in selling your products or services.

HOW TO ACQUIRE INFORMATION FOR FEATURES: Usually business owners are secretive if they feel they have a hot, highly profitable business. However, ego satisfaction is often stronger than the desire to keep the details of a business secret. Strong, clever interview techniques are usually necessary.

The most difficult data to extract from a business owner are gross sales and net profit. Often the most successful in the field of endeavor will be the easiest from which to obtain this information—one-upmanship!

There are tricks to figuring gross sales when the owner won't divulge these data. For example, we did a feature on the balloon concessionaire at Disneyland. The owner would not give us a clue as to his gross sales. Our reporter then asked a seemingly innocuous question, "Who supplies your helium?" The helium supplier also thought the question was academic, "How many tanks of helium does so and so buy?"

The business owner told our reporter the percentages of sales in various-size balloons. A balloon supplier provided the quantity of helium used for each size. From there it was simple mathematics. (By the way, high-profit businesses often are not obvious. That balloon concessionaire netted close to $100,000 annually before taxes.)

If you encounter resistance, offer to keep the source confidential. Sometimes this procedure will be unnecessary if there is an association serving the field. It will usually have typical operating percentages available.

Don't bother going to your local library for information on small businesses—there's nothing of any current value there.

In closing, remember that we buy specifics, not generalities, and all facts and figures must be backed up with sources for verification. Anyone who can present acceptable material can look forward to regular assignments.

The Editor

TYPES OF ARTICLES:

Featurettes (1,800 to 2,000 words, 12 to 18 cents per word): Discussing a unique business. Use quotes.

Celebrity Entrepreneur (2,000 to 2,500 words, 15 to 20 cents per word): A profile of a celebrity who has also started a business. Past issues have featured Joan Collins, Gene Barry, and Ernest Borgnine. Query first.

Young Millionaire of the Month (1,800 to 2,000 words, 15 to 20 cents per word): A "Horatio Alger"-type story. Someone under age 40 whose ideas paid off.

PHYSICAL FORMAT: The following rules are to be followed to facilitate editing of submitted material and to speed up the word count for payment.

1. Please use good quality bond *white* 8½ × 11 paper. No onion skin, colored or lined paper.
2. Articles must be typed. A clear, preferably new ribbon should be used. Special care must be used in proper names, dates, figures, etc.
3. *Everything is to be double-spaced.* This is essential.
4. Include with your article *a complete list of your SOURCES*, whether or not we have supplied you with them or you've found them yourself. This will facilitate verifying names, dates, etc. Put your bibliography of sources used on a separate sheet of paper at the end of your article.
5. Count the words you have written and place the number in the upper-right-hand corner of the first page of your article.
6. Enclose your *signed* writer's release when you mail your article. We buy *all* rights.

SEND ALL SUBMISSIONS TO: EDITOR, ENTREPRENEUR MAGAZINE, 2311 PONTIUS AVE., LOS ANGELES, CA 90064

Esquire

GUIDELINES FOR UNSOLICITED MANUSCRIPTS

1. Esquire accepts unsolicited manuscripts, although we cannot take responsibility for the return of any unsolicited materials.

2. For fiction pieces: It is best to send the finished manuscript. We will consider short stories only; please do not send full-length novels.

3. For non-fiction: We prefer receiving a query letter together with some published feature writing samples, rather than receiving a finished manuscript. However, writers who have not been published as yet should send the finished article.

4. Suggested length for non-fiction manuscripts is 1,500 to 4,000 words.

5. Fees vary. We pay upon acceptance of an article.

6. We try to answer all query letters and to return manuscripts that have not been accepted within four weeks.

7. In all correspondence with us, please include a self-addressed, stamped envelope. Manuscripts to be returned if not accepted must include an envelope with sufficient postage.

2 PARK AVENUE, NEW YORK, NEW YORK 10016

WRITER'S GUIDELINES

**UNSOLICITED POETRY IS NO LONGER BEING ACCEPTED. PLEASE QUERY FIRST BEFORE SUBMITTING NON-FICTION MANUSCRIPTS. **

All manuscripts by writers not on assignment or new to our magazine must be submitted on speculation. Manuscripts are then read and evaluated by the editors (allow us six to eight weeks) and accepted or rejected at the end of that time. Please don't let this discourage you. Many of the articles you've seen in ESSENCE have been submitted in this manner.

All manuscripts must be typed and double-spaced. Most articles fall between 1500 and 3000 words. We urge you to submit a photostatic copy of your original manuscript. We cannot be responsible for originals. Type your name, address and telephone number on the first page of the manuscript and include a stamped self-addressed envelope when posting it. Payment for articles is made on acceptance for publication.

We look forward to hearing from you.

SENDING A QUERY LETTER

If you want to write for ESSENCE, you should query us. On one (1) typewritten page explain: 1) The topic 2) Points to be discussed 3) Length of manuscript 4) Why you think our readers would be interested.

If we want to see the manuscript, we'll send you a note asking you to submit it.

THE EXECUTIVE FEMALE

The Executive Female is a bi-monthly magazine published by the National Association for Female Executives. Its goal is to provide up-to-date information on career advancement and financial planning for the independent, upwardly mobile businesswoman and female entrepreneur.

QUERY LETTERS OUTLINING ARTICLE IDEAS PREFERRED.

If manuscripts are submitted, they must be typed double-space on 8½ x 11" white paper, including quoted material and references. Two copies should be submitted to speed up the review process. Please do not send originals.

Title of article, author's name and affiliation, and full address (including zip code) to which correspondence should be sent should be included on a separate sheet.

Articles on any aspect of career advancement and financial planning for women are welcomed. During the coming year, features and departments will deal with the broad topics outlined below.

FEATURES: Preferred length of features is 6 to 12 manuscript pages (typewritten). Longer manuscripts will be considered only if the quality and timeliness warrant.

TOPICS:

Investment	Career Goal Setting and Advancement
Coping with Inflation	(changing careers, new careers,
Money-Saving Ideas	career counseling, changes in
Financial Planning	the work force and in work style
Business Communication	affecting women)

COLUMNS: Preferred length of columns is 6 to 8 manuscript pages (typewritten). Regular columns include:

$$$ AND YOU -- Specific financial issues, i.e. social security, tax planning.
HORIZONS -- Career planning, personal and professional goal-setting.
PROFILES -- Interviews with successful women in a wide range of fields.
ENTREPRENEUR'S CORNER -- Successful female business owners with unique perspectives.

Payment depends on length and nature of article.

SEND QUERY LETTERS (or manuscripts) to: Editor
The Executive Female
1041 Third Avenue, 2nd floor
New York, NY 10021

Thank you for your interest. We look forward to hearing from you.

EDITORIAL REQUIREMENTS

EXPECTING MAGAZINE
685 Third Avenue
New York City, New York 10017

EXPECTING is for every pregnant woman with emphasis on the first-time mother-to-be.

Feature articles--1200 to 1800 words. Subjects cover every aspect of pregnancy, birth and the postpartum period: emotional and physical changes of pregnancy; prenatal development; budgeting; nursery and layette planning; working while pregnant; consideration of older children; diet; minor discomforts; husband-wife relations; childbirth preparation. In short, any subject that would be of interest to a woman at this period of her life when so many changes are occurring in both her body and outlook.

We prefer medical doctors, registered nurses and nurse-midwives to do strictly medical articles, but are glad to see anything personal-experience oriented if written knowledgeably. We are always open to suggestions from writers who can work with doctors to produce by-line features. We do not use fiction, but occasionally use poetry.

Payment for general articles is $100 to $300, slightly higher rates for specialists, on acceptance.

A reader-contributed column, "Happenings," features brief anecdotes on unusual or amusing occurrences during pregnancy. Payment, $10 is on publication. Manuscripts cannot be returned.

THE MONEY MANAGEMENT MAGAZINE

305 East 46th Street
New York, NY 10017
(212) 319-6868

WRITER'S GUIDELINES

FACT is a money management and personal finance magazine. Our readers are individuals who are fairly sophisticated about investing. We attempt to provide them with specific details on new investment products, ideas and opportunities.

FACT articles are concise and packed with useful information. Most pieces that we publish are accompanied by sidebars or tables. We use full-color photos to illustrate articles. Sources for these photos usually are suggested by the author. When a company that sells investments (or provides information about them) is mentioned in FACT, we try to include an address and phone number.

We regularly cover stocks, bonds, mutual funds, precious metals, banking, real estate, taxes, collectibles, insurance and investing by computer. Suggesting a good piece (1500 to 1800 words) for one of these departments is the best way to attract our attention. Send a query. DO NOT SEND A MANUSCRIPT.

Fact Finding, Investment Report Card, Investor News Wire, Money Facts, Wall Street Facts, Washington Facts and our various Monitors are all done in-house.

We are not a business magazine. If we do feature a particular industry in a cover section, it will be from the investor's viewpoint. Industry cover stories are usually assigned to experts in the field.

We do not use personal experience articles ("How I Made Money In The Market") or general pieces ("All About Mutual Funds"). If you want to write for FACT, suggest a specific topic, and show us in a query that you know how to handle it. Include clips of your published works.

THE EDITORS

488 Madison Avenue, New York, N.Y. 10022

Thank you for your recent letter.

Potential FAMILY CIRCLE contributors should pay careful attention to the following points:

1. Take a close look at FAMILY CIRCLE for some knowledge of format and an understanding of the subjects we have tackled in the past, remembering that it is a special kind of magazine with many millions of readers.

2. In some instances, it is advisable that a letter of inquiry or outline be submitted concerning your article suggestion. If interested, we will request to review your manuscript on speculation.

3. Manuscripts should be typed, double-spaced, on business letter or legal-size paper. Handwritten submissions will be returned unread.

4. Maximum length for short stories and articles is 2,500 words; for poetry, approximately 20 lines.

5. FAMILY CIRCLE does not consider multiple submissions.

6. Submissions and queries must be accompanied by self-addressed, stamped envelopes of sufficient size or--if mailed from abroad--by International Reply Coupons, available at post offices throughout the world.

7. FAMILY CIRCLE takes good care of manuscripts; however, owing to the fact that mail is sometimes mislaid by the U.S. Post Office, we cannot assume complete responsibility for them. Be sure to have a carbon copy of every manuscript you submit.

Again, thanks for your interest.

THE EDITORS

FAMILY COMPUTING

A PUBLICATION OF ■■ SCHOLASTIC INC.

Dear Writer:

Thank you for your interest in FAMILY COMPUTING.

We are always looking for new writers with original ideas and, of course, well-written, well-researched articles.

The following are guidelines for submission of story ideas to our publication. Generally, we prefer written queries rather than telephone calls or unsolicited manuscripts.

When formulating story suggestions for FAMILY COMPUTING, keep in mind our specific audience -- the family that has already purchased its first computer, or plans to purchase one soon. We are most interested in stories about how families much like our readers are putting their computers to good use.

When submitting a proposal, please keep your query limited to one page. Include a possible lead, potential source, the type of machine being used (when applicable) and a brief statement describing the story's application to our readers. Be sure to enclose your resume and writing samples, as well as your current address and phone number(s), with the time you can be reached.

The best way to acquaint yourself with our style is to examine several previous issues of FAMILY COMPUTING. Also, please note that story lengths usually run from 1,000 to 3,000 words, depending on the subject matter.

We will try to reply within a few weeks by mail or phone. However, in case of a delay, keep in mind that we have numerous queries to examine.

Thanks for your cooperation. We look forward to working with you in the future.

Sincerely,

June Rogoznica
June Rogoznica
Managing Editor

730 BROADWAY, NEW YORK, NY 10003. (212) 505-3000

AMERICA'S NO. 1
SPORTSMAN'S MAGAZINE

1515 BROADWAY • NEW YORK, NEW YORK 10036 • TEL. (212) 719-6000

FIELD & STREAM is issued monthly at $ 1.75 per copy or $ 13.94 for a year's subscription. We accept very little fiction and no verse.

FIELD & STREAM is a broad-based outdoor service Magazine. Our editorial content ranges from very basic "How It's Done" filler stories that tell in pictures (or drawings) and words how an outdoor technique is accomplished or device is made, to feature articles of penetrating depth about national conservation, game management, and resource management issues, and recreational hunting, fishing, travel, nature, and outdoor equipment. We also publish nostalgia and descriptive writing -- "mood pieces" on hunting and fishing -- and we publish humor.

The key word for most of our articles is service. The "Me and Joe" story rarely works, with the exception of well-written adventure articles. With the exception of Canada and Mexico, most of our foreign material is staff written.

Preferably, both where-to-go and how-to articles should be well illustrated with color photographs, but we do buy manuscripts without photographs.

FIELD & STREAM encourages authors to submit queries -- article outlines with photographs -- rather than complete stories. Article length for features is 2,000 to 2,500 words; "How It's Done"* fillers run 500 to 900 words. Payment depends on the experience of the author and the quality of his work, and ranges from $ 500 to four figures per feature article, on acceptance, and $ 250 for fillers. "Did You Know?" is a front-of-the-book filler department which provides information on game, fish, and the natural world that is useful to hunters and fishermen. "Did You Know?" runs in three sizes -- 300 words, 550 words, and 700 words. Payment is $ 350 on acceptance.

It is a common practice to buy pictures and stories as packages. When pictures are purchased separately, however, the rates are $ 75 and up for black-and-white. Rates for color are $ 450 depending on size used on single page; $ 800 for partial spread; $ 900 for full spread; and $ 1,000 and up for cover.

FIELD & STREAM also publishes special Regional Sections so readers can enjoy feature articles on hunting and fishing in their own areas of the country. The Sections are geographically broken down into Northeast, Midwest, Far West, West, and South, and appear 12 months a year.

CBS MAGAZINES/a division of CBS Inc.

page 2

Cartoons should be submitted as finished black-and-white sketches about 8x10 in size. Payment is $100.00 per cartoon.

FIELD & STREAM reports within 60 days. We buy First World Rights for color and black-and-white photographs, for manuscripts, and for cartoons. We return those rights to you after publication.

HOW TO KEEP YOUR QUERIES FROM BEING "QUEERIES"

There are three basic reasons for sending queries to an editor: 1) to avoid wasting time on a useless project; 2) to determine if an editor is interested in your idea; and 3) to learn how the editor wants an idea to be handled, ie: as a photo story or a full-length piece.

There are some things a query won't do. The long-cherished idea that a cleverly written query will automatically produce a firm assignment to write an article is, for the most part, fodder for writers' magazines and "how-to-write" books. A query will rarely elicit a commitment to buy the finished article or bring advance payment. Instead the editor will ask to see the article on "speculation."

GENERAL QUERY INFORMATION

Type on white paper, not transparent bond. Double space and keep it neat. Handwritten material is not acceptable.

Organize the ideas in your query exactly as you would outline before writing the actual story. Be sure to emphasize what makes the particular angle of your article different. An angle is just a hook to hang the story on. It should give the article a fresh approach and provide it with unity. An angle is the difference between writing on the idea of "Bass Fishing is Fun" as compared to "Drive Your Bass Buggy."

Brief sketches of some of the anecdotes you might use in the completed article help an editor to judge the kind of material you have, as well as your ability to write it. Some authors like to present the opening paragraph or two of the explanatory material (roughly 5-6 paragraphs) before outlining the remainder of the article. But however it is done, slanting and organization are important in a query. And so is brevity!

page 3

Photographs should be included with a query whenever possible. Color slides, preferably 35mm, and contact proofs of black-and-white negatives on 8x10-inch sheets are perfectly acceptable. Good photography will help to sell a story faster, but this often requires that some groundwork be done on the proposed article before the query is sent in. However, submitting good photographs will permit an editor to develop the idea as a photo story if he chooses, thus saving you the time it takes to write a full-length article.

If a query is just a page or two with a covering letter, it can be mailed in a regular envelope. If photographs are included, package them in plastic sheets surrounded by cardboard, and send them flat in a manila envelope. Address the package to the editor of the magazine, unless you have already discussed it with someone else there.

All editors have dislikes. One is duplicated queries that are sent out to several magazines at the same time. If your idea is good and you want it to land in the best possible spot, start with the top magazine and work down. Writers who send duplicate queries obviously are looking for the best offer, and no editor wants to get into a bidding war. There is also the complex problem that arises when more than one editor approves the same query. The only thing you can do then is change your name and start all over again.

When an editor answers your query positively, he may suggest ways the story can be developed and written, pictures that are needed, when he would like to see your complete manuscript, etc. He will almost always say that he would like to see your complete manuscript "on speculation," which is the nearest thing to a firm buy indication that you'll get. At least you know you're on the right track.

page 4

PHOTOGRAPHY FOR FIELD & STREAM

In recent years the tools of photography have improved greatly, and so has competition in the sale of good photographs. Since many of FIELD & STREAM's articles are illustrated with color photographs, it is important that writers and photographers know what our picture needs are. The photographs we use are often submitted with an article, but FIELD & STREAM does buy many photographs separately. We usually buy First World Rights when purchasing photographs and return the photographs and the rights to you. When submitting photographs, be sure to send them by registered mail.

REQUIREMENTS FOR BOTH BLACK-AND-WHITE AND COLOR PHOTOGRAPHS

HOW MANY? Writers who regularly sell to us usually submit an average of 50 color photographs with each article. We seldom illustrate an article with mixed color and b&w, but if you have really good b&w prints, send them along with your color. If you have good color photographs, but fewer than 20, don't throw in some obviously bad or unsuitable photographs just to bring the number up. We don't judge article illustrations by the numbers.

CAPTION MATERIAL. We do not ask authors or photographers to write captions for their photographs. What we do need, however, is information about what each photograph shows. This includes the names of persons, the area, the nature of the activity, and most important, the point the picture makes. Write your name and address on a separate sheet of paper for b&w prints, and glue it to the back of the photograph. SLIDES SHOULD ALWAYS CARRY YOUR NAME. Don't attach caption information to color photographs. Number your pictures, and then, on a sheet of manuscript paper, write the information opposite the corresponding numbers.

COMPOSITION. A few elementary "rules" can help you sell photographs. In general scenes, it is better not to have the horizon cutting directly across the center of the picture. Action, people walking, animals, fish, etc., should MOVE INTO THE PICTURE, not out of it. The main object in a picture should be off-center toward one of the corners, not in the middle. Try "framing" occasionally. A tree limb extending across an otherwise vacant sky adds a stop for the eye and depth to the scene. All these "rules" can't be followed in any one picture, but they help. And don't be surprised if we buy pictures that ignore these "rules" completely. Above all, do not take pictures of people staring into the camera.

page 5

CONTRAST. Black-and-white and color photographs are opposite on this. Black-and-white photographs need contrast to give them depth, but not to the point where the black areas are solid black and the whites are bleached clean. Prints should have visible detail in the large dark and light areas. Color, on the other hand, is best when flatly lit. Outdoors, that means shooting with the sun behind you, or behind and slightly to one side. Overexposure is a major fault in color slides. If proper exposure of light areas means that faces or other important details of the photographs will be too dark to reproduce properly, move your position or wait for better light conditions.

ACTION. Without it, pictures are often uninteresting, so when taking pictures for illustrations, try to include a person doing something, or an animal moving. Of course, there are times when action can't be achieved, but a whole set of pictures showing dead fish or game, beautiful scenes, or still lifes can't be used.

EXPOSURES AND FILL-IN FLASH. In black-and-white photography, errors in judgment of light can be corrected somewhat in printing, but this is not the case with color film. We prefer color photographs that are exposed perfectly, but if you have some that are exceptional but somewhat under-exposed or dark, we can sometimes bring them out in engraving. So send them along, even though they aren't just right. It is important to use fill-in flash, both in black-and-white and color photography. Probably the most important use of this technique is in lighting faces that would otherwise be obscured by shadow. This goes for both sunny and overcast days.

VARIETY. We often receive a selection of photographs that isn't a selection at all--just a number of pictures of the same scene or object. A good selection must have variety--no two pictures alike except for a good reason. Here are a few tips:

> Change subject matter and background often; photograph close-ups, overall scenes, companions, shots of scenic beauty, anything unusual. Variety in pictures is difficult to achieve, so carry a camera all the time and use it. Remember that the cost of film is nothing compared to the price of the trip, so take lots of pictures.

BLACK & WHITE PRINTS. We like 8x10 b&w prints which are big enough to study easily. We don't like photographs larger than that because they are too big for our files. We do not require negatives with enlargements, but sometimes ask for them later so we can have photographs reprinted.

page 6

PACKAGING. This is most important! Photographs should be packaged so
they will not be damaged in the mail. A mailing envelope one-half-inch
larger on all sides than the prints is good. Use pieces of cardboard
bigger than the pictures for stiffeners. Enclose a SELF-ADDRESSED,
STAMPED ENVELOPE (SASE).

COLOR PHOTOGRAPHS ONLY

SIZE. FIELD & STREAM considers slides from 35mm up. The magazine has
no preference in size, but the great majority of our color illustrations
are made from either 35mm or 2¼-inch film. The slide mounts supplied by
processors are fine for submission. We prefer color slides, not prints.
Please make sure your name shows on the mounts of the slides to avoid
confusion.

PACKAGING. Don't package each of your slides in individual envelopes.
It's a bother when judging them. The best idea for slides is 8½ x 11
see-through plastic sheets with pockets for slides. Pack these sheets
between cardboard stiffeners and mail in manila envelopes.

COLOR QUALITY. The quality of color is important. Often a whole set of
slides will be rejected because they have a peculiar shade of color
overall, or too much blue or red or green. This is not always the fault
of the photographer, except when it stems from his trying to cut costs
in film and processing. But if your slides have a predominant cast of
one color, we probably won't be able to use them.

COLOR HIGHLIGHTS. Color pictures are of little use when they are drab.
An otherwise colorless or dull scene can be livened up a great deal by
the addition of a spot of bright color. People in brightly colored
(within reason) clothing can often help greatly. Watch out especially
for hat or cap shadow obscuring a face. You can solve this problem by
using fill flash or by getting the hat off the subject. You would cry if
you knew how many cover candidates and inside photographs have failed over
the years for this one reason.

In addition to article illustration, we are always looking for cover photographs, in color, which may be vertical or horizontal. Whenever possible,
do not center the subject. Sometimes you must grab whatever you can get,
but try to remember: a cover picture must have room at the left for cover
lines.

51 Atlantic Avenue, Floral Park, N. Y. 11001
Telephone 516 352-9700

ARTICLE REQUIREMENTS

Color features run to 2,500 words, with 2,000 preferred. Subject matter can be where-to on a hot fishing site, how-to on tackle and techniques, tips on taking individual species, or a story on one lake, or an entire region, either fresh-water or salt. Photography requirements: 35mm or larger color transparencies--originals, not duplicates. Please use vinyl or plastic slide sheets. Also like some b&w glossies to supplement color. Payment for complete text/photo package is $300. Cover, $300 extra. All transparencies should be identified as to photographer and subject, and all must be accompanied by a detailed caption sheet.

Black-and-white or unillustrated featurettes are occasionally considered. These can be on anything remotely connected with fishing. Length to 1,000 words. Payment $75-$150, depending on length and photos.

In general, queries are preferred, though we're very receptive to unsolicited submissions accompanied by smashing photography. Always include sufficient postage or funds for safest return of materials--certified or registered is recommended for valuable photos. Manuscripts must be typed, double-spaced, and all submissions are on speculation. We buy First North American Serial Rights. Lively writing appreciated; avoid anecdotes. Save how-to-get-there facts (costs, distances, recommended outfitters, transportation, etc.) for sidebar at the end except as they blend smoothly with main text. Such data should be as current as possible. Finally, don't be offended by a form reject--when possible, editors will add a personal postscript. Volume of submissions makes individual replies often impossible.

Ford Times

Ford Times, Room 765, The American Road
P.O. Box 1899, Dearborn, MI 48121-1899

Writer's Guidelines

Although it is published by an auto company, the magazine prints no more automotive-related articles than do most general-interest publications targeted for a family audience. The primary editorial goal is to be lively, informative, contemporary, and—above all—interesting.

Subject Matter: Almost anything that relates to current life (no nostalgia, please) in North America that is upbeat and in good taste. We are particularly interested in articles that appeal to readers in the 18-35 age group. Major categories:

- Topical (trends, lifestyles);
- Places of interest (narrow-view pieces rather than conventional broad-scope destination stories, e.g., the guest houses of New Orleans' French Quarter rather than New Orleans in general);
- Profiles of interesting people, well known or otherwise;
- First-person accounts of unusual vacation trips or real-life travel "adventures";
- Unusual sporting events or outdoor activities;
- Food and cooking (Note: Restaurant stories are usually prepared by the staff, as is the "Favorite Restaurant Recipes" feature);
- Humor (ranging from vacation/travel-dining anecdotes for "Road Show" to full-length articles or essays).

To a far lesser degree, we also publish stories with an international flavor. Such stories should fit the categories cited for North American pieces. International subjects comprise less than 10 percent of our editorial content, but we are interested in the broadened scope they give the magazine and are always on the lookout for those that fit our editorial format.

Length: We have three categories: Full-length manuscripts range from 1,200-1,500 words. Medium-length from 800-1,200 words. Short from 500-800 words. "Road Show" anecdotes and "Glove Compartment" items range up to 150 words.

Rates: $500-$750 for full-length manuscripts; $350 for medium-length; $200 for short. (One-third kill fees are paid on assigned stories which are rejected.) Published "Road Show" and "Glove Compartment" items get $50. Payment in all categories is made on acceptance.

Terms: We buy first-time publication rights.

Submissions: Queries are required for all but anecdotes and humor pieces. Volume prevents us from reviewing unsolicited manuscripts. Always include a self-addressed, stamped return envelope with your query.

Photographs: We need bright, lively photos that not only support the text but contribute to strong graphic display. Transparencies (Kodachrome is the first choice) are preferred, but high-quality 8 x 10 color prints may be acceptable. If color isn't available, black-and-white prints may be submitted. Complete caption information should be provided for each photo. (Note: Publication releases are required from anyone who is readily identifiable in a photograph.) If photos aren't available, snapshots, postcards, brochures, etc., may be submitted for artwork reference.

Photo Fees: These are based on our one-time use—$150 for a picture printed less than full page in the magazine, $350 full page or larger. A payment of $500 is made for a cover picture. Payment for photos is made upon publication.

The Editors

Ford Times is published by Ford Motor Company, The American Road, Dearborn, Michigan 48121-1899

FRETS MAGAZINE
Writers' Guidelines

WHERE TO START

The best preparation any writer can do before submitting a query or a manuscript to *Frets* is to sit down with several issues of the magazine and analyze them. Carefully. Most of the manuscripts we reject shouldn't have been submitted to us in the first place: The writers simply didn't take the time to ask themselves whether what they had to offer was in line with what we regularly print.

We are a special-interest publication. *Frets* bills itself as "The Magazine For Acoustic String Musicians." Literally 99% of our readers are musicians who play banjo, violin, mandolin, guitar (the majority interest), or some other acoustic string instrument. They read the magazine chiefly because they want to learn to play better, they want to learn about the techniques and equipment of artists they admire, and they want to learn more about the instruments themselves. Please note how often the word "learn" crops up here. Although we strive to be entertaining, *Frets* is fundamentally an educational magazine.

WHAT WE LOOK FOR IN AN ARTICLE

Content is the most important criterion for us in evaluating a query or a manuscript. We want to know if the material will have something useful to teach our readers, and if so, whether it will be sufficiently important to them to justify making room for it in an issue of *Frets*. If the article is about an artist, is the artist's reputation big enough to excite the readers' interest? Or is there something else there that gives the story an edge in the tight competition for space in our pages?

Professionalism is something else we look at closely. For us, that breaks down into two areas: expertise and craftsmanship. Is the writer knowledgeable about the subject? Is he or she sufficiently conversant with the music, or the techniques, or the historical background involved so that the key points are brought out and communicated accurately to the reader? Are there any gaps in the information, indicating that the writer has missed something through ignorance or carelessness? Second, is the writing clear, expressive, and well-organized—or would the piece need a lot of editing to bring it up to our standards? (It's surprising how often we actually get *query* letters that are marred by misspellings and typographical errors.)

Given the nature of our coverage, there are times when we'll buy a less-than-well-written manuscript because its writer is an expert on a particular subject. But we won't buy a superbly written article that is lacking in substance. We are always looking for good writers, however, and when we find them we keep their names on file.

HOW WE DO BUSINESS WITH WRITERS

Like most magazines, we would rather get a query letter than get a manuscript sent on speculation. (Unless time is really of the essence, we prefer a letter to a phone call.) It doesn't take long to read a query, so we're more apt to read it carefully. And if we decide we like something the writer wants to do, but we'd prefer a slightly different slant, it's easier on the writer to simply write to our requirements than it is to do wholesale revisions on a finished manuscript—or to throw the manuscript out altogether and start from scratch. We also like to see samples of the writer's published work.

Regarding manuscripts:

[Frets requests]
that they be typed, in black ink, on 8¼″ x 11″ bond paper (no lightweight paper, please). Text should be double-spaced, with left and right margins of about 1¼″. We will accept dot-matrix word processor printouts so long as they are clean and legible, and their quality comes close to typed manuscripts.

We try to respond to submissions within two to four weeks, at most. Sometimes our workload is such that a response takes longer, and in those cases we aren't offended if a writer calls to check on the status of the submitted item.

Frets pays on acceptance for editorial material. In other words, once we've determined that we want to use a manuscript, we'll buy it. The writer doesn't have to wait until publication to get paid.

On photographs, however, check requests don't go to GPI's accounting department until after an issue is sent to the printer. That's because on a given story, we might pull a good picture two days before deadline to substitute a *great* picture just turned in by a freelance photographer; or we might find that a story is running long, and pull a photo or two so that vital text matter won't have to be cut.

The upshot is that until the magazine goes off to press, we don't know precisely which photos will be running in it. After an issue is finished, our Art Director initiates the payment proceedings for photos and other graphic elements.

In some cases, we'll pay a flat fee for a story and accompanying pictures. Typically that is how we make arrangements for material in our *Frets* Visits and *Frets* Repair Shop departments, where pictures of equipment or technical procedures are an integral part of a story. Without the illustrations, there wouldn't be an article. But as a rule, manuscript acquisition is the job of the editors, and photo acquisition is the job of the art department.

We generally pay between $100 and $250 for feature articles, depending on length and content. Short pieces in *Frets* may run between 900 and 1,200 words in length; a cover story may be as long as 3,500 words. We pay more for cover stories, nearly all of which are written on an assignment basis. Contributors who have written satisfactorily for us before are paid fees that are slightly higher on the scale. Payment for photos ranges between $35-$50 for inside black-and-white to $150-$250 for cover color. Photo terms are spelled out in greater detail in the GPI Photo Guidelines, which are available on request.

When we assign a deadline for a piece, we expect it to be observed. Frequently, advance promotional material (such as that in *Frets'* "Coming Next Month" box) commits us to running certain stories. Our printing deadlines are firm, and late materials create expensive delays. Editorially we are always working at least three months ahead of our publication dates—and even longer for special issues.

Writers are requested to sign and return a standard GPI Writers Agreement form when submitting a manuscript. The form specifies which rights are transferred to GPI when we buy a story, and which rights the writer retains. A sample is available on request.

SOME POINTERS ON WRITING FOR *FRETS*

There are certain kinds of information we like to include in our articles, and certain ways we like it to be presented. We're appreciative whenever a writer takes time to become familiar with our stylistic idiosyncrasies. That simplifies our work in copy editing.

Following are some specific guidelines that will be helpful in preparing copy for *Frets*:

• Because all GPI publications are geared toward serious musicians, rather than just toward music fans, a story lead should immediately and solidly establish a reason for musician/readers to get into the article. Will it teach them something new about the instruments they play? Will it improve their grasp of music principles? Will it satisfy their curiosity about a favorite artist? That kind of information needs to be up front.

• People should always be clearly identified within the context of their music. *Frets* has a diversified readership, and not all readers will be able to recognize "Scott Joplin" as a ragtime composer, "Haydn" as classical composer Joseph Haydn, or "Tony Trischka" as a progressive banjoist. "He worked with the Osborne Brothers" might seem to be a sufficiently clear statement, in and of itself—but some readers might not know the Osborne Brothers from the Osmond Brothers, nor the Osmond Brothers from the Allman Brothers. It's

FRETS MAGAZINE
Writers' Guidelines

essential to be specific about who and what people are.

- In an artist profile, the writer must convey what it is that makes the player unique, and whom the artist has influenced or been influenced by.
- When a manufacturer, instrument builder, repair shop, or other business is named in an article, the company address should be listed at the first reference. (Readers may want to write for more information.)
- When a record album is mentioned, we like to see the label and album number included—along with the label's address, if it isn't one of the "majors" like CBS or A&M. These details also should be cited in any discography. (Articles about artists or groups should include discographies as a matter of course.)
- Spellings of the names of people, companies, places, instrument types, and so forth should all be carefully checked.
- In *Frets* parlance, banjos, guitars, mandolins, and related instruments have *fret*-boards; violin family instruments have (fretless) *finger*boards. Adjustable instrument necks are equipped with *truss* rods, not *tension* rods. Flat-top guitars have glued-on *pickguards*; arch-top guitars and mandolins have elevated *finger-rests*.
- A pet peeve: "Etc." belongs in notes and memos, not in the text of magazine articles.
- References to instrument tunings—non-standard tunings in particular—should include the pitches involved and the sequence they follow. Example: "He plays guitar in 'dropped-*D*' tuning [*D A D G B E*, sixth string through first string]."

INTERVIEWS AND INTERVIEWING

Interviews in *Frets* may follow either a narrative format, in which the interviewee's responses are woven into the fabric of an article; or a Q/A format, in which the interviewer's questions and the interviewee's answers appear together. In each case, the interview article opens with introductory narrative material.

As a rule, the Q/A format should only be used when the dialogue offers a particularly lively exchange between the interviewer and the subject. Routine background details—such as the subject's date and place of birth, early influences, and so on—should be relegated to the introduction, unless there is something especially colorful or revealing in the subject's response to a background question.

The flow of an interview should be smooth from beginning to end, with related topics grouped together and presented in a coherent order. This may require careful editing on the writer's part. Word-for-word transcriptions of an interview tape rarely are satisfactory from the standpoint of logical progression: Interviewees often jump from topic to topic, or take off on unex-

pected tangents when responding to a line of questioning. And statements that make sense within the context of the face-to-face interview, when body language is part of the message, may come across as gibberish when printed word for word.

Interviews should be free from inside jokes, exchanges of a strictly personal nature, or anything else that might tend to make readers feel as though they were outsiders. The interviewer should function as an extension of the reader's curiosity, rather than as an obtrusive intermediary. In our opinion, the best interviewers keep a very low profile. (A rare exception: artist-to-artist interviews, where readers will be interested in the ideas and personalities of both people involved.)

It's important to remember that every interview has an objective and a focus. At the start, it helps to let the subject know just what areas are going to be covered. Background material is a safe opener, and reviewing such basic information can give the subject time to settle into the interview.

Although few people today freeze at the sight of a tape recorder, as a courtesy it's wise to ask permission before recording an interview. (Paper and pencil should be on hand, just in case permission is refused.) Once set up and running, the recorder is best left alone—so that it fades into the woodwork as much as possible.

We've found that the best material usually comes out when the interviewee is allowed to talk at leisure. Some counterproductive techniques: rushing to fill the pauses in the conversation, or changing topics before the interviewee has finished a thought. Open-ended questions, rather than questions that can fizzle out in simple "Yes" or "No" answers, are most effective.

It's important to press for specifics when the interviewee is talking about a musical concept. So far as is practical, chords, scales, and playing techniques should be diagrammed—or at least explained in detail. Those are the things our readers are buying the magazine to get.

A good sign-off for the session: "Is there anything else you'd like to add; or is there anything you've always wished somebody had asked you about your work?" Sometimes the second part of that question works well at the start of the session, to loosen up a self-conscious or uncommunicative interviewee.

The closing formalities should also include getting the interviewee's phone number, so that fuzzy details can later be checked and follow-up questions asked. It's wise to exchange numbers, so that the interviewee is free to call back with any important afterthoughts.

Occasionally an interviewee asks to see a copy of the transcript. Once it gets to *Frets*, it's our material. We discourage interviewees' pre-publication reviews of transcripts and manuscripts, because every so often somebody wants to get involved in the

actual authorship of a piece being written about them. That leads to press agentry, not journalism. As a courtesy, we sometimes allow interviewees to check stories for verification of facts; but we don't guarantee that opportunity.

QUESTIONS WE LIKE TO ASK

The following is a list of questions that represent the areas we're most concerned with in any interview with a musician. We aren't suggesting that the list be followed slavishly. These are, after all, writer's *guidelines*. A good writer can sense what to ask, how to ask it, when to keep digging on a promising vein of information, and when to move on to new ground. (And a careful researcher will have learned ahead of time the answers to many of these questions, anyway.)

We've presented the questions in checklist form in the belief that they will be helpful to any writer who is preparing to interview someone for *Frets*. We aren't trying to do the writers' thinking for them. Rather, our wish is to free the first-time contributor from worrying about just which details *have* to be covered, so that he or she can work creatively in conducting an interview.

☐ Did you come from a musical family? What parts of your upbringing prepared you for what you do now?

☐ When did you begin to play? What was your first instrument? In what sequence did you learn other instruments (if any), and why?

☐ How did you learn—from teachers, other players, books, records, or just on your own?

☐ Do you read music? Tablature? Have you ever studied music theory?

☐ What were your early performing experiences like? What was your first paying job as a musician?

☐ Who were your influences? (Specific artists, groups, records, and so on.)

☐ How did your playing style evolve? Do feel that your technique is continually developing, or are there periods when it stays at a plateau? Does that bother you, and if so, why? Is there anything you do to regain momentum?

☐ What other artists have you worked with? How did you get together with them?

☐ What do you see as having been the milestones of your career so far, in terms of groups you've been with, performances you've given, albums you've released, and so on? (Date as accurately as possible.) How do you feel about the various musical roles you've played—in terms of which were most educational, or most satisfying?

☐ What sort of advice would you give to young players who wanted to pattern themselves after you? What essential first steps would they need to take? What would they need to watch out for?

☐ What are your feelings about studio

FRETS MAGAZINE
Writers' Guidelines

work? Are there any special recording processes or setups that you favor? Is it easy to work with producers? What kind of latitude do you have?

☐ What are your favorite kinds of venues for performing? Why?

☐ How do you handle the pacing and sequencing of songs within a set? What are the most important considerations in putting together a live program? A record?

☐ Is every part of your show planned, or do you like to work spontaneously?

☐ How do you gauge how well you are going over with an audience? Do you change your delivery or change material if things *aren't* working, and if so, how?

☐ What do you feel is the best kind of response you can get from a crowd?

☐ What steps do you take to make sure your sound will be optimum in a performance? Do you carry your own sound system? Do you have a road crew, and if so, how large is it?

☐ Do you like traveling, being on the road—or does it seem more like a neccessary and unavoidable part of the job?

☐ What kind of practice schedule do you follow now, if any? Is practicing something you approach systematically?

☐ In practicing, how much time and effort do you devote to exercise and study in various areas (such as sight reading, reviewing old material, learning new tunes).

☐ Do you use a metronome? Do you ever practice mentally—without instrument in hand?

☐ What do you think are the most effective areas of your playing technique? Why? How has your technique changed or improved over the years? What techniques have you learned from other players?

☐ Do you anchor your playing (picking) hand anywhere on the instrument's body? If so, where?

☐ What do you do to bring out different tone colors on your instrument?

☐ Do you use any non-standard tunings? If so, what material have you recorded with them.

☐ Do you play styles other than the one for which you are noted?

☐ How do you approach a solo? Do you build from scales? Modes? Chords? Inversions? Do you have certain favorite positions on the instrument for soloing?

☐ How do you structure a solo—in terms of dynamics, changes in register, key modulations, and so on? How much of it is a conscious process?

☐ How do you go about writing your music? What elements come first, and what elements are filled in later?

☐ What is your main instrument (type, brand, model) today? Why?

☐ How do you like your instrument(s) set up—stock, or customized in some way?

Is there a particular repairperson who does all your work for you?

☐ Is your choice of a studio instrument different from your choice for live performing? If so, why? On what records do your favorite instruments appear?

☐ What microphones do you prefer in the studio?

☐ How prepared are you prior to going in the studio? How much of your recorded music do you improvise?

☐ Do you use any electronic effects in your work? If so, which ones (e.g., stereo chorus, flanger, delay line), what are their makes and model numbers, and why do you use them? How do you set them up and control them?

☐ What do you see as the main problems in amplifying acoustic music? Do you carry your own amplification equipment, and if so, could you please describe it?

☐ How do you prefer to work through a house PA system? Do you discuss your needs with the sound engineer, and if so, are there specific things you request? How do different PA systems affect your concert sound?

☐ If you play in a band, how do the members interact? If there is more than one soloists, how are soloing duties worked out?

☐ How did your latest tour or recording project come about? What interests you most about it? When will it be finished?

☐ If you play both acoustic and electric instruments, do you experience difficulties in switching between them? Do skills transfer from your acoustic instruments to your electric instruments?

☐ Is the music you play at home, for your own enjoyment, different from what you play professionally? Would you say there is a gap between your personal tastes and what is marketable to your audiences?

☐ Do you know of any other articles about you that are currently being written or considered? If so, by whom—and when are they expected to appear?

—*The Editors*

20085 Stevens Creek, Cupertino, CA 95014

FRIENDS

**THE
CHEVY OWNERS'
MAGAZINE**

30400 VAN DYKE
WARREN, MICHIGAN 48093
(313) 575-9400
800 232-6266

STORY REQUIREMENTS AND GUIDELINES

FRIENDS is a controlled-circulation magazine which goes to approximately 1,000,000 readers monthly. The editorial scope is national and subject matter is general, but all stories must have a Chevrolet tie-in.

Appropriate subjects for FRIENDS stories would include profiles of Chevrolet-owner celebrities, travel stories on destinations reachable by automobile (United States only), unusual uses of Chevrolet products, stories on Chevrolet motorsports, unusual Chevrolet collectors and features on sporting events of television productions sponsored by Chevrolet. If it's an exciting subject that relates to the world of Chevrolet, we'd probably like to see it.

All stories concerning new Chevrolet products are either staff-assigned or staff-written.

Story length ranges from 600 to 1,200 words, and FRIENDS rates start at $300. When applicable, good color-transparency photography should accompany the text. Signed releases are required for anyone mentioned or quoted in the story or depicted in the photography.

Stories should be typewritten and double-spaced. Do not send your only copy, as we cannot be responsible for unsolicited submissions. Simultaneous submissions should be identified as such. Letter-quality computer printouts are acceptable.

First-time contributors are urged to query first with clips of previously published material. All material should be accompanied by a self-addressed envelope with sufficient postage for its return.

Bear in mind that most FRIENDS rejections are because of one of these four reasons:
    1) Topic not sufficiently narrowed.
    2) Topic too dry.
    3) Topic not of interest to national-scope audience.
    4) Topic does not tie-in to Chevrolet.
    5) Topic too closely duplicates story in stock.

FRIENDS pays on acceptance, after receiving all necessary releases and the author's invoice in triplicate, including the author's federal identification (Social Security) number.

FRIENDS

THE
CHEVY OWNERS'
MAGAZINE

30400 VAN DYKE
WARREN, MICHIGAN 48093
(313) 575-9400
800 232-6266

PHOTOGRAPHIC REQUIREMENTS FOR FRIENDS MAGAZINE

1. Preferred format for most stories is 35MM (except food, product or other "set-up" shots, for which a larger format will give better results).

2. Always provide ample coverage -- overshoot and bracket to insure technical and editorial perfection.

3. Aside from "straight" photographic coverage, always look for the unusual approach. Use filters, a variety of lenses or any other technical means to achieve suitable special effects.

4. Avoid the use of flash when possible.

5. When the situation permits, shoot in early morning or late afternoon -- avoid the harsh light of midday.

6. For color submit only transparencies; for black & white submit a few appropriate 8" X 10" prints along with contact sheets and negatives.

MONTCALM PUBLISHING CORPORATION
800 SECOND AVE. NEW YORK, N.Y. 10017 212-986-9600

EDITORIAL GUIDELINES

Your name should appear on all pages of the manuscript.

Pseudonyms: may be used.

Fiction length: 1000 to 3000 words.

Lead articles: 2000 to 3500 words.

Humor: 1000 to 1500 words.

Profiles and interviews: 3000 to 3500 words, includes introduction.

How-to and self-help articles: 1500 to 3000 words.

It is best to send queries for all non-fiction manuscripts, though non-fiction manuscripts will be considered.

Payment depends on length as well as type of article. Humor generally averages $500; fiction between $350 and $750; articles between $350 and $1500. Payment is made one-half within four weeks of acceptance, the other half on publication.

It usually takes from six to ten weeks to come to a final decision on manuscripts.

Suggestion: Study a copy of GALLERY ... it is your best guide-line.

Unsolicited manuscripts MUST be accompanied by a stamped, self-addressed envelope, or they will not be returned.

MONTCALM PUBLISHING CORP.

Editorial Department

GENTLEMEN'S QUARTERLY, Conde Nast, 350 Madison Avenue, New York, NY 10017.
Editor-in-Chief: Arthur Cooper. Managing Editor: Eliot Kaplan. Circ: 607,000.
Emphasizes fashion, general interest, and service features for men ages 25-45
with a large discretionary income. Monthly magazine. Pays 25% kill fee.
Byline given. Pays on acceptance. Submit seasonal/holiday material 4-6 months
in advance. Does not accept simultaneous submissions. SASE. Reports in
one month. Nonfiction subjects cover politics, personality profiles, lifestyles,
trends, grooming, nutrition, health, fitness, sports, travel, money, investment and
business matters. Buys 4-6 mss/issue. Query with clips of previously published
work or ms. Length: 1500-4000 words. Pays $750-3000.

Columns/Departments: Eliot Kaplan, managing editor. Body & Soul (fitness,
nutrition and grooming); Money (investments); Going in Style (travel);
Health; Music; Tech (consumer electronics); Dining In (food); Wine & Spirits;
Humor; Fiction; Games (sports); Books; The Male Animal (essays by men on
life); All About Adam (non-fiction by women about men). Buys 5-8 per issue.
Query with clips of previously published work or ms. Length: 1000-2500 words.
Pays $750-2000.

Tips: "The best way to break in is through the columns, especially Male Animal,
All About Adam, Games, Health or Humor."

GLAMOUR.

Thank you for your note. These facts about GLAMOUR should help you.

Most of our readers are women between the ages of eighteen and thirty-five, and articles that are slanted to our older readers must work for the younger ones as well. We do not publish short stories or poems, and we steer away from stories that depend on very current events because the material will be out of date by the time a piece can be written and published.

Of course, we're always happy to see completed articles, but it's really more sensible to send us a proposal or outline first. We may have a similar article assigned or in print, or we may be able to help you bring your proposal into better focus.

We publish articles of three lengths. "Viewpoint", our opinion page, is approximately 1000 words, for which we pay $450. As the name implies, "Viewpoint" works best when the writer has a strong point to make about a topic. For short articles of 1500-2000 words, we pay $1000 and up; for longer manuscripts of 2000 or more words, we pay $1200 and up. Manuscripts should be typed and double-spaced, and a self-addressed stamped envelope should be enclosed.

Thank you again for your interest in GLAMOUR.

Sincerely,

Janet Chan

Janet Chan
Articles Editor

Golf Digest accepts fillers, poems, cartoons, photographs, artwork and manuscripts on a speculative basis. Our procedure is to route them through the editorial staff and, based on the consensus, a submittal is accepted for publication or return to the author. This takes from six to eight weeks. Payment is made upon acceptance and is based on length and content.

You should address your submittal to the attention of the "Submittal Editor" (artwork goes to the Art Director) and be sure to enclose a self-addressed, stamped envelope, as we cannot otherwise guarantee the return of unsolicited material.

Golf Digest is a monthly, with approximately 25 per cent of its feature content written by free-lancers. Readership is 95 percent male, median age is 52. Circulation about 1,150,000, with estimated readership 2.6 million. Rates for free lance articles run from $100 for the shorter "Digest" items to about $300 for one-page articles up to $2,000 for specially-assigned major features. We pay expenses on assignments. Kill fee: 25 per cent. We buy all rights. Number of submissions received weekly: 25 to 30. Reply time to queries: immediate. Our lead time is two months, and issues are planned five to six months in advance.

All of our instructional material is done in house, by editors in collaboration with tour pros or our instructional staff of teachers.

Cartoons are welcome; one is generally used each month.

We will frequently request articles on a spec basis, particularly if done by a writer previously untried at Golf Digest.

Galleys are not shown, but the writer is advised of any major editing changes.

In sum, golf is a difficult sport to write, and traditionally does not support many free-lancers. But we are always on the lookout for fresh, new material, and we reply immediately to queries.

 380 MADISON AVENUE, NEW YORK, N.Y. 10017, TELEPHONE: (212) 687-3000

GUIDELINES FOR WRITERS, PHOTOGRAPHERS AND ARTISTS

GOLF Magazine is written and edited for golfers who are serious about the game and all its elements. The emphasis is on golf for males, age 15-80, mostly college-educated.

The primary areas of coverage are golf instruction and the professional tours (mens' and ladies'). Most instruction pieces are written by staff editors or the magazine's contributing playing and teaching pros. Articles on tour professionals are occasionally open to outside contributors. About 20% of the material is freelance written.

Other areas of coverage include golf history and travel (places to play around the world), both of which are sometimes open to outside writers, and equipment, fashion, and golf notes, which are handled by the staff.

GOLF is not interested in poetry, personal opinions (except in the "Letters" column), or fiction. We do look for humorous features, but only as they apply to the game.

Writers hoping to contribute must be well-versed in the game of golf, its language, and its idiosyncrasies. Instructional pieces must be written by recognized experts. Profiles of tour players, which are an outsider's best hope for contributing, must reflect a strong knowledge of golf, so are best handled by those intimate with the game.

Articles usually run 1,000 to 2,500 words; payment is $350 to $1000. Queries are required with all submissions, but we prefer a query first before any material is sent. Address queries to the Features Editor or Instruction Editor.

Unsolicited material cannot be acknowledged unless accompanied by a self-addressed stamped envelope. Proper postage is required. We cannot be responsible for the loss of unsolicited materials. Response to submission is within 4 weeks.

Artwork: Prefer transparencies or 8X10-inch photograph of original work to be considered. Photographs: 8X10-inch black-and-white glossy prints only; screened prints are not acceptable. Color--transparencies only, 35mm slides preferred. Payment is up to $500 per color photo; black-and-white, up to $35. Address art material to Art Director.

PUBLISHED BY TIMES MIRROR MAGAZINES, INC.

AND THE PRINTING INDUSTRY ®

875 Third Avenue New York. NY 10022
212-605-9574

EDITORIAL DATA

Contributed Material

GRAPHIC ARTS MONTHLY considers for publication articles
that relate specifically to printing and allied trades
such as ink and paper manufacturing, prepress equipment,
press accessories, plant equipment, art and layout
materials, composition, postpress (binding, addressing,
mailing, transportation), trade services and
miscellaneous.

Articles should be of modest length (about 2,000 words),
must be beneficial to printers and printing management
personnel, written objectively, and related to problem
solving in the industry. All noteworthy material will be
considered if it is directed to cost savings, quality
enhancement, maximized safety, or increased productivity.

Contributors are encouraged to submit appropriate
illustrations - color or black-and-white photographs, line
drawings, etc. - along with their copy.

The Editors

Technical Publishing
DB a company of
The Dun & Bradstreet Corporation

AMERICA'S FAMILY PUBLICATION

Guidelines for Free-Lancers

Free-lance writers and photographers have long played a major role in providing quality material for publication in Grit. Those who have been most successful have educated themselves to know Grit and appreciate the audience to which it addresses itself.

What Is Grit?

Grit is a tabloid-size national weekly. It offers helpful, inspiring, uplifting articles and features which are both informative and entertaining.

Grit is people-oriented. Even when presenting articles about places and things, Grit tries to do so through the experiences of people. Rather than tell you how to do something, Grit is more likely to show you how someone else has done it.

Grit is published for a general readership in small-town and rural America. It aims to provide articles and illustrations of interest to every member of the family—from the child who has just learned to read, to great-grandparents and all ages between.

Grit is easily accessible. Boys and girls throughout America sell it door to door. More and more newsstands, supermarkets, and other places where periodicals are sold are now handling Grit. And Grit is available by mail subscription.

What Material Does Grit Look for From Free-Lancers?

Grit wants well-written *stories about individuals and groups who are making an important contribution to their neighbors, community, and/or the American way of life*. Grit is also interested in *patriotic stories having an immediate tie-in with a date*. Avoid sermonizing, but report interestingly and accurately so that readers will be inspired.

Stories about men, women, teen-agers, and children have always been a major part of Grit's editorial diet. You might well become a contributor of some of them.

Grit wants *stories about religion,* of how churches raise money or develop successful programs that are unusual and set them apart from other congregations: *stories about the spirit of a community.* stressing local traditions that bind people together: *stories about families.* featuring experiences of families who live in small towns or run small-town businesses. In addition. Grit has a *Grit Family of the Week* feature that focuses on families who have shared an exciting adventure, overcome adversity or have shown unusual creativity.

Grit also wants *stories about how people cope in providing the necessities of life* — food. clothing and shelter: *stories about people and their jobs.* featuring persons who have surmounted hardships in order to work or are in unusual occupations, and *stories about recreation,* emphasizing travel, sports and hobbies.

Grit constantly seeks *articles about small towns* recovering from adversity. small towns moving forward in innovative ways which other communities might profitably imitate. and unusual small-town celebrations, major anniversaries, and so on. Each should have significance beyond that of an annual town carnival and the like. If you can, *present the material around an individual who is deeply involved in the event. movement —whatever — or present it through his or her eyes.* That will make a sale more likely.

Grit believes *private enterprise* is the backbone of the American economic system and wants stories that show it is as a desirable and vital aspect of American life. The *stories should be about specific individuals doing admirable things successfully.* They should show the value of honesty, thrift. hard work, generosity, and other positive attributes as keys to better living.

Find a theme, whatever the subject, so that you will have a story to submit. Write of someone's unusual contribution to family, community, school, church etc. as concisely and interestingly as you can; don't send us a biographical profile or a dull compilation of information.

Don't overlook the story of a child involved in a noteworthy activity, situation. or adventure, nor the great-grandfather or great-grandmother either. Show people being good, kind. helpful; instructive, entertaining, inspiring; laughing, crying, solemn, wise. *Show the positive side of life* so that others can rejoice or weep with the subjects of your tale.

Grit needs brief anecdotal and other items that are unusually interesting. They should be amusing, heartwarming, or inspiring mini-features—tiny slices of life—and run from 30 words up.

Humorous verse and brief quips are needed for the "Talelights" column, with two four-line rhymes used in each issue. Keep the verse in meter and be sure the rhyme is true; near-rhymes are out. *Traditional-style light and serious verse* of four to 16 lines is sought for the "Poetry Just for You" column. Same rules apply.

Specific Do's and Don'ts
For Writers and Photographers

Successful writers for Grit must be competent and disciplined. *Manuscripts should be 300-500 words* and, with editing, be publishable as submitted. With few exceptions, stories should be accompanied by good-quality black-and-white photos or color transparencies, and each illustration should be accompanied by cutlines identifying people and objects and telling accurately what is happening.

Keep copy strong in human interest. Write concisely in simple, direct language (active not passive voice).

Always include the complete name and mailing address of the persons about whom you write.

Double-space all manuscripts and type the writer's name and address, including ZIP Code, on the first page.

Black-and-white illustrated articles should, if keyed to a date, reach Grit at least six weeks before the date, preferably earlier. Avoid submitting snapshots. We will work with good 5x7-inch glossies but prefer 8x10s.

In submitting transparencies, remember that Grit publishes on newsprint and therefore requires sharp, bright, contrasting colors for best reproduction. Strive for a variety of colors; avoid monotones (greens, reds, browns, etc.) and strongly complementary colors such as orange and red unless contrasting color also is present.

Avoid all shadows across faces and strong shadows generally. Depending on the situation, that may require use of fill-in flash even in daytime.

If faces have an unnatural tint — blue, green, purple, strong yellow, etc.—don't bother submitting the transparency.

With 35mm film, Kodachrome 64 generally does a good job. However, don't hesitate to submit slides taken with other brands of film. Also, if you have good-quality larger-size color transparencies, we're especially interested in considering them.

Cover art must be simple in composition and usable in vertical format. Chances of selling a cover will be improved if the transparency is accompanied by a strong story and additional color and/or B&W art.

Generally, *illustrations*, whether color or black and white, *should include action or implied action*. In other words, they should be of persons or animals doing something interesting in an eye-appealing setting.

Single photographs that stand alone must be accompanied by 50-100 words of meaningful caption information. The information should be of such nature that it will add to the significance of the illustration and vice versa.

Always enclose a self-addressed, stamped envelope when submitting copy, photos, queries, or other material requiring a reply. Otherwise, as a matter of policy, material not purchased will be placed temporarily on hold and then disposed of.

If you hope to sell regularly to Grit, you would be wise to subscribe and review Grit's approach and contents from time to time.

By following these guidelines carefully, you should produce the kind of material Grit needs.

Where to Send Your Queries
Or Manuscripts and Illustrations

Address all queries and material submitted on speculation for Grit's editorial consideration to: M. Joanne Decker, Assignment Editor, Grit, 208 West Third Street, Williamsport, Pa. 17701.

Grit's Standard Rates
For Words and Pictures

First rights: for copy, 12 cents a word; for accompanying B&W photos, $25 each; for B&W photos and captions that stand alone, $35; for verse, $6 for four lines or fewer plus 50 cents a line for each additional line.

Color for front cover, $100.

Second or reprint rights: For copy, 6 cents a word; for accompanying B&W photos, $10 each; for B&W photos and captions that stand alone, $15.

All payments are made upon acceptance of material, which is usually evaluated by the Board of Editors within 2 or 3 weeks.

GUESTINFORMANT

EDITOR
Maryanne Larson

PUBLICATION PROFILE

Guest Informant is a hardcover city guidebook, published annually and placed in the rooms of select hotels in 31 cities and resorts nationwide. Each four-color edition is an editorial and pictorial compendium of information about the city and its environs. Guest Informant is designed to acquaint business people and tourists with the city's shops and restaurants.
    In each edition, articles, sidebars and listings highlight the arts, sightseeing attractions, neighborhoods, sports and leisure-time activities. Shopping and dining profiles are listed alphabetically in separate sections of the book.

READER PROFILE

Guest Informant is edited for business travelers and sophisticated visitors who are interested in the city's cultural, sightseeing and recreational offerings, and who patronize the city's finer shops and restaurants.

WRITERS' GUIDELINES

60-80% free-lance written ON ASSIGNMENT ONLY.

Article lengths: 500 to 1,400 words.

Deadlines: Usually 4 weeks.

Pay within 30 days; writers' fees from 30¢ per word.

NO unsolicited manuscripts, poetry, fiction or controversial material.

Send business-size s.a.s.e. for list of markets. Include writing samples that are informative, lively and readable. Query ONLY if familiar with publication. Send $5.00 for sample copy.

Topics: (city specific) city overview, performing and visual arts, neighborhoods, sightseeing, sports, business, real estate; (multi-market) wine, travel tips, business trends, other special interest.

AMERICA'S FOREMOST HOTEL ROOM MAGAZINE | 21220 Erwin St., Woodland Hills, CA 91367 | (818) 716-7484

747 Third Avenue
New York, N.Y. 10017
(212) 754-2200

GUIDEPOSTS MAGAZINE

Guideposts magazine is a monthly, inspirational, interfaith, non-profit publication written by people from all walks of life. Its articles present tested methods for developing courage, strength and positive attitudes through faith in God. As of January, 1985 the magazine Audit Bureau of Circulation verified 4.2 million paid circulation and it is ranked by the Magazine Publishers Association as 14th in circulation among all magazines in the U.S.

In March of 1985, the magazine celebrated its fortieth year of publication. Editors-in-Chief and Publishers are Ruth Stafford Peale and Norman Vincent Peale. Deputy Publisher, J. Wendell Forbes. Editor, Van Varner. Editorial offices: 747 Third Avenue, New York, New York 10017. Buisiness offices: Carmel, New York 10512.

Guideposts

747 THIRD AVENUE • NEW YORK, N.Y. 10017 • TELEPHONE 212-754-2200

EFFECTIVE AS APRIL, 1985

EDITORIAL NEEDS

A typical Guideposts story is a first-person narrative written in simple, dramatic, anecdotal style with a spiritual point that the reader can "take away" and apply to his or her own life. It may be your own or someone else's first-person story.

Observe the following as you write your Guideposts story:

1. Don't try to tell an entire life story in a few pages. Focus on <u>one</u> specific happening in a person's life. The emphasis should be on <u>one</u> individual. If it's the story of a disaster, then stick to the viewpoint of one rescuer or rescued individual. If the story is about an organization, tell it through the eyes of a worker or one who has been helped. Bring in as few people as possible to keep the reader's interest with the dominant character.

2. Decide what your spiritual point or emphasis will be. Don't forget: <u>We want our readers to take away a message or insight that they can use in their own lives</u>. Everything in the article should be tied in with this specific theme.

3. Don't leave unanswered questions. Give all the facts so that the reader will know what happened. Let reader feel as if he were there, seeing the characters hearing them talk. Depict the situation, conflicts, the struggle and then tell how person was changed or problem solved.

<u>NOTE</u>: We do not use the essay or sermon-type material nor do we present stories about deceased people. We do not evaluate book-length manuscripts.

We do use third-person presentations in our QUIET PEOPLE feature -- a one-page telling of the good an individual does for others. Contact us in advance about QUIET PEOPLE submissions. We also use very short fillers with an anecdote and spiritual point.

Newspaper or magazine clippings often form the basis of articles in Guideposts. We are not able to pay for this type of material and will not return clippings unless the sender specifically asks us to do so. We are grateful for story suggestions but, again, cannot pay for such leads.

<u>PAYMENTS</u>:
a. Short features up to approximately 250 words (including FRAGILE MOMENTS, poems--though we use very little verse.) -- $10-$25

b. Short manuscripts of approximately 250-750 words (QUIET PEOPLE, one or two-page stories.) -- $50-$200.

c. Full-length manuscripts -- 750 to 1500 words -- from $200 to $400. Occasionally we make higher payments.

MANUSCRIPTS SHOULD BE TYPED, DOUBLE-SPACED, AND ACCOMPANIED BY A STAMPED, SELF-ADDRESSED ENVELOPE.

Remember the best rule of all: STUDY THE MAGAZINE!

■ HARPER'S MAGAZINE   TWO PARK AVENUE   NEW YORK, NEW YORK 10016   (212) 481-5220 ■

HARPER'S

Harper's almost never publishes
unsolicited articles. We are happy
to consider unsolicited non-fiction
manuscripts and queries, but they
must be accompanied by a stamped,
self-addressed envelope. We do not
consider unsolicited fiction and
poetry, because we publish so little
and our small staff cannot give such
works the review they deserve.

                    The Editors

1700 BROADWAY, NEW YORK, NEW YORK 10019 • (212) 903-5000

WRITER'S GUIDELINES

Harper's Bazaar is for women, late 20's and above, middle income
and above, sophisticated and aware, with at least two years of
college. Most combine families, professions, travel, often more
than one home. They are active and concerned over what's happening in the arts, their communities, the world. We publish articles
on food, wine and spirits, travel, education, financial matters,
successful women, careers, health and sexuality. Please read
several issues of our publication before submitting, as we have
a very specific writing style. We accept no unsolicited ms.
Query first. Enclose SASE. Payment is determined by the type
and length of the article.

Health
MAGAZINE

GUIDELINES FOR WRITERS

HEALTH magazine's feature articles generally focus on fresh, innovative approaches to diet, fitness, exercise and nutrition, and advances in preventive medicine and health care.

Here are some basic guidelines for writing a HEALTH story:

CONTENT: We look for upbeat, informative pieces on new ways to exercise and keep fit or unusual solutions to common problems of mental and physical well-being, home and institutional health care, child-rearing and family relations. We prefer features with an angle to roundups.

Prospective contributors should avoid proposing exposé-style pieces on controversial subjects that are likely to be found on the evening news (for example, reports on how patients are neglected by mental health workers). Also to be avoided are stories centering around warnings about negative trends and developments (such as discussions on the increases in teenage pregnancy or certain communicable diseases) and any other topics that are likely to frighten or depress readers. Articles on health problems that affect only a small percentage of the populace or treatments and forms of therapy not available to the average person are also out.

STYLE: Warm, lively and down to earth. We prefer that articles 'show' the reader through scene and dramatic example, rather than 'tell' him or her in didactic, essay-like prose. Explain all complicated medical terms; remember that most of our readers are lay people, not scientists or doctors.

LENGTH: 1,500 - 3,000 words.

RATES: $350 - $1,100 depending on length and amount of research involved.

As you work on ideas, please remember:

° It's always better to query us before sending your manuscript. A one-paragraph query is sufficient.
° If you do send a manuscript, please enclose a stamped, self-addressed envelope.
° We take 4-8 weeks to reply, and the large number of manuscripts we receive precludes our answering each writer personally.

HEALTH magazine was formerly titled FAMILY HEALTH.

Three Park Avenue New York, New York 10016 (212) 340 9200

BREAKTHROUGHS GUIDELINES

HEALTH's monthly Breakthroughs column is a readable compendium of brand-new developments in the health field.

SOURCES: Items based on word-of-mouth information are the most likely to be new and the least likely to turn up in other magazines. If you have your own network of contacts in the research field-- or can develop such a network--your chances of producing acceptable Breakthroughs are much greater. Medical journals are suitable sources if the facts are checked out further with the doctor or organization mentioned in the article.

CONTENT: Breakthroughs are grouped by subject: Eats (food), Looks (beauty), Brainwaves (psychology), Power (fitness), Kids, Frontiers (cardiology, dentistry and similar heavy medical areas). They encompass cures or treatments, advances in equipment, innovative trends in patient care, useful discoveries. Avoid animal studies; experiments must be on a reasonable sample of humans. Also avoid negative-sounding advances--for example, a finding that interferon has proven to be less effective against cancer than was originally thought.

STYLE: Lively, optimistic: Breakthroughs should be fun to write and read. Explain all complicated terms; our readers are lay people, not scientists or doctors. About 75% of our readers are women; median age is in the 30's.

RATE AND LENGTH: $150 for 200 to 400 words.

LAST WORD: Please don't forget to:

° Include several original quotes in your item. <u>This implies an interview with the surgeon, scientist, inventor or MD in question.</u>

° If your interview subject is an MD or a PhD, please indicate so.

° Ask your interview subject about the future of the medicine/treatment. Is it available in the United States? If so, where? If not, when is it expected to be?

° Ask your interview subject if we may list his/her name and address at the end of the item as a source of further information.

° Ask your interview subject if he/she has relevant photographs or diagrams. No head shots! We are looking for art that helps in the understanding of the material.

° Enclose a bill with your finished piece, bearing your name and address, name of the item and fee, signature, <u>Social Security number</u> and the date. We will also pay phone expenses if you submit a clearly marked phone bill (this can be sent in later). All other expenses must first be cleared with the Breakthroughs editor.

° Send a list of your sources and their phone numbers with the finished article, and also your background material if the proposal originated with you.

BREAKTHROUGHS EDITOR

CRAFTS

We want fresh, novel, tested ideas, with clear directions. We require a well-made sample to be submitted with each craft idea. Project must require only salvage materials or inexpensive, easy-to-obtain materials. The wider the age range, the better; especially desirable if easy enough for primary grades or preschoolers. We are particularly interested in ideas for projects that result in the creation of interesting toys and games and attractive, useful gift items.

VERSE

We seldom buy verse.

FINGER PLAYS/ACTION PLAYS

Should have lots of action. Must be easy for very young child to grasp and for parents to dramatize, step-by-step, with hands, fingers, and body movements. Should not be too wordy. $25.

GENERAL INFORMATION

We don't pay persons under 15 for contributions.

No inquiries needed. We buy all rights, including copyright, and do not consider material previously published.

All material is paid for on acceptance.

Be sure to enclose with manuscript a self-addressed, stamped envelope for its possible return.

EDITORIAL REQUIREMENTS AND PAYMENT SCHEDULES

Editorial Offices, 803 Church Street, Honesdale, Pa. 18431

HIGHLIGHTS FOR CHILDREN is published monthly (except bimonthly July-August) for children from 2 to 12. Circulation is over 1,500,000. Sold by subscription only.

FICTION

We carry stories up to 900 words appealing to both girls and boys. Stories should begin with action rather than description. Create a story which children 8 to 12 will want to read, capturing interest in the first few sentences. If children 3 to 7 will also enjoy hearing this same story, it is especially valuable to us. We print no stories just to be read aloud and we seldom choose rhyming stories.

Our greatest current need is for stories for beginning readers, (600 words or under) having strong plot and great suspense, short sentences, and much action.

We like stories in which listeners or readers can imagine themselves the leading character and wish to emulate the traits of this person—stories which don't emphasize money values, but imperishables. Any moral teaching must be indirect and subtle. We particularly need stories with female leads, humorous stories, stories with urban settings, and stories of adventure. We welcome stories that accurately portray other cultures and religious observances, and stories that leave a good emotional and moral residue.

Suggestions of war, crime, and violence are taboo. HIGHLIGHTS aims to exalt the preciousness of every person regardless of sex, family background, social status, religion, race, or nationality. We aim to foster wholesome human relations.

We accept a story on its merit whether written by a novice or by an experienced writer. We pay 6 cents and up per word and prefer to see the manuscript rather than a query.

FACTUAL FEATURES

We are always looking for gifted writers, especially engineers, scientists, historians, artists, musicians, etc., who, having a rich background in their respective fields, can interpret to children useful, interesting, verifiable facts. References or sources of information must be included with submission. Photos or art reference material are helpful when we evaluate such submissions.

Also, we want authors who write from firsthand experience and can interpret well the ways of life, especially of children, in other countries; who show appreciation of cultural differences; and who don't leave the impression that our ways always are the best. In short, writers who can help foster world brotherhood.

Biographies stressing the early lives of individuals who have made significant contributions through their own efforts are particularly welcome.

Science and other factual articles within 900 words, $60 and up.

PARTIES

We want original party plans for children, giving clever ideas and themes clearly described in 300 to 800 words, including drawings or samples of items to be illustrated. $30-$50.

HISTORIC PRESERVATION

GUIDELINES FOR FREELANCERS

Thank you for your interest in contributing to <u>Historic Preservation</u>. The magazine is published by the National Trust for Historic Preservation, a national, nonprofit private organization dedicated to the preservation of America's significant architectural and cultural resources. HP is published every other month and is distributed as a benefit of membership to the Trust's more than 140,000 members. The magazine is also sold on selected newsstands across the country.

Most of the articles and photographs in the magazine are submitted by freelancers, and consequently queries are quite welcome. Our story ideas come from a variety of sources--freelancers, the magazine staff and preservationists around the country. We encourage freelancers to share their enthusiasms with us: If you find something fascinating, there's a good chance our readers will be interested, too. Articles cover a very wide range of subjects--from rural preservation issues to design and social problems in inner cities; from oral history and maritime preservation to carousels and cemeteries. We are always looking for lively upbeat stories and interesting personalities, but we are also actively looking for ways to alert our readers to problems in the preservation field.

We regularly cover recent residential restorations, so we have a particular interest in stories about outstanding old houses and the families that have rescued and revived them. To help us evaluate these queries, please include photos of the house--snapshots will do--showing exterior and interior views. If we are interested in pursuing the house you propose, we'll send professional photographers, unless existing color photographs of high quality are available. Finally, we'd like to see more humor, interesting restorations, personal essays and how-to suggestions, including not only restoration but also gardening, cooking, antiquing, etc.

WRITERS

If you are a writer and you have an idea for an article, please query us first by sending a short--not more than a page--summary of what you want to write about. Send two or three writing samples if you have them. Telephone queries make us unhappy. Include a stamped, self-addressed envelope and your phone number. You will normally hear within two weeks. We generally use articles written by professional freelance writers, but queries from preservationists and others with interest or knowledge in a particular field are also welcome.

National Trust for Historic Preservation, 1785 Massachusetts Avenue, N.W., Washington, D.C. 20036   202/673-4084

AUTHOR'S GUIDE

Much of the writing and photography that appears in **Home Mechanix** is done by freelance contributors. This guide provides basic information about our editorial needs and requirements, along with our rates of payment, which are made on acceptance. An understanding of HM's editorial content is a prerequisite for selling us an article, so take the time to carefully examine several recent issues.

The subject you propose should be genuinely interesting and have application to the majority of our readers. We stress creativity, originality and good design, and will publish only technically accurate information. Our emphasis is always on quality.

The **Home Mechanix** cover line—"Helps you manage your house and auto better"—indicates our general focus. More specifically, we aim to provide information that our readers can act on, or use, to solve problems and improve their lives.

For the most part, we are **NOT** interested in the following type of stories:
—The Gee-Whiz type of articles—action or adventure that traditionally appeared in magazines such as **Home Mechanix** in previous years.
—Stories that focus primarily on individuals rather than on product, project or technique. The idea always is that the technique or project can be easily duplicated by readers.
—We are not interested in purely historical or very technical subjects. **Home Mechanix** wants stories that are exciting because they are good ideas for home, shop, yard and auto. In a story where you want to emphasize that there is a new or unusual development, or product, be specific about what makes that development new or better.

HOME IMPROVEMENT AND WORKSHOP—Our how-to articles cover a broad spectrum of reader interest, ranging from building and home improvement projects to woodworking. Generally, we're interested in any project that you have done to improve your home. How-to stories should focus on one specific project, with step-by-step instructions for building. Remember to include such information as the time and cost of a project and the materials used. All how-to stories must be well illustrated with photos and drawings.

AUTOMOTIVE—Our automotive coverage encompasses how-to (car repair, care and maintenance), driving reports and vehicle comparisons, as well as evaluations on the latest automotive tools, supplies and other aftermarket products. We cover vehicles—including trucks, vans, etc.—that tend to have appeal to the family or homeowner. While most automotive articles are staff-written, certain assignments are given to qualified freelancers.

CONSUMER PRODUCTS AND SERVICES—Although our general editorial content focuses on house and car, this third department of our magazine is the most varied. It encompasses such subjects as gardening, satellite TV, energy, home entertainment systems, boating, buying guides, bicycles, design and hobbies, to name just a few. If the subject affects your home or car, it is probably of interest to us. We are not interested in space or adventure stories, or subjects dealing with military hardware.

PHOTOGRAPHS—A good lead photograph—the picture that should bring the reader into the story—is extremely important. It should clearly convey the theme of the story and what follows. An article on building a desk, for instance, might show someone actually using the finished desk. Other photos should demonstrate the materials and steps used in building the desk. Take plenty of photos while you build a project. It is better to have too many photos rather than too few.

If your story is on how to build something, show the finished product in a natural setting with as little background clutter as possible. For action, always try to have one or two people in the lead shot—not just posing, but involved with the project. Try to make your subject stand out by using the proper background—light for a dark subject, dark background for a light-colored subject. Step-by-step black-and-white photos should be supplied for each sequence of the project—construction, assembly, finishing. The preferred format is 8 x 10 glossy prints. Show the author (or builder) using tools and materials in the workshop environment. Again, your best guide is to study how-to stories published in HM.

You can use 2¼ x 2¼" or 35mm. Regardless of what kind of camera you use, take close-up pictures of the technique or idea and make certain they are sharp and with good contrast. To evaluate your submission, contact prints are acceptable. If we buy your piece, we may ask for the negatives, which will be returned if requested.

Every photo should be keyed with a letter corresponding to its caption, which is keyed with the same letter. Use ink or grease pencil in the margin at the bottom. If a sequence of photos is submitted, be certain to key the photos in order.

A caption should be supplied for every photo; each must focus on the action taking place in the picture. Type the captions on a separate sheet of paper—at 40 characters per line—and key each one to correspond with the keyed photo.

Regarding art scrap: It is not necessary to do an inked, finished drawing suitable for publication. However, we do require pencil drawings that are accurate and adequate for our technical artists to work from. Various parts of the project should be keyed (labeled) and two materials lists are required:

1. The shopping list, which the builder uses when he goes to buy the materials and,

2. The cutting list—that is, the actual sizes of the parts as they appear on the technical art.

TEXT—Submit your text on 8½ x 11 white bond paper and type it double-spaced to 34 characters per line, 20 lines per page. The cover page should contain the author's full name and address and the title of the story. Succeeding pages should bear the author's last name and story title at the top left, with page numbers at the top right. We're not interested in a word or line count; use the number of words that are required to tell the story clearly and fully.

RATES OF PAYMENT

RATES OF PAYMENT—Payment is based upon several factors: intrinsic merit, the number of published pages the story will occupy and the staff time required to ready the story for publication. Generally, payment for a two-page article is $600; for a one-pager, it's $300. A ready-to-publish article with professional-quality photos, on the other hand, will command around $500 per published page.

Occasionally, on assignments, we offer a flat fee if we are undecided how many pages an article will run.

If we simply buy your idea or lead to a story (e.g., you send us the name of someone who has just completed a unique kitchen remodeling), expect a finder's fee payment in the $100 range, in addition to expenses. We buy all rights and pay upon acceptance.

SUBMISSIONS

SUBMISSIONS—Submit material to the appropriate department editor:

General features ......**Executive Editor Harry Wicks**
Home improvement & workshop .....**Michael Morris**
Automotive ....**Don Chaikin**
Consumer products ....**Arline Inge**

Short articles may be submitted without a query. However, as a rule, it is recommended that you submit a query for longer articles. All submissions are made on a speculative basis only.

All submissions must be accompanied by a stamped, self-addressed envelope if you want rejected material returned. We emphasize again reading several current issues of HM so you can see how we present an article. We'll be happy to consider anything you think fits the bill.—*The Editors*

HELPS YOU MANAGE YOUR HOUSE AND AUTO BETTER

1515 Broadway
New York, NY 10036
212/719-6631

AUTHORS' GUIDELINES FOR HORIZON MAGAZINE

I. Horizon Is Interested In Articles On

    A. Theater
    B. Art and artists
    C. Movies
    D. Photography and photographers
    E. Architecture
    F. Sculpture and sculptors
    G. Literature about the writers and/or their works
    H. Film and film makers
    I. Crafts and craftsmen
    J. Performers and their roles
    K. Dance, dancers and choreographers
    L. Theater and actors
    M. Music, musicians, conductors and composers
    N. Television

II. General Rules

    A. Style

        1. Manuscripts must be double spaced
        2. Horizon uses a style based on the Chicago Manual of Style
        3. Please send two copies with a stamped, self-addressed return envelope
        4. Please enclose a biography of fifty to seventy-five words
        5. Include illustrations (both black and white and color) with as much identifying and credit information as possible or give information where illustrations can be found

    B. Manuscripts.

        1. Each manuscript, which should be based on original work, should be between 1,500-2,500 words
        2. Horizon also welcomes outlines suggesting topics
        3. All manuscripts are subject to editing in Horizon's style
        4. The editorial staff may direct that certain portions of manuscripts be rewritten or cut
        5. Rejected manuscripts will be returned (if postage is included) in eight to twelve weeks
        6. The price paid for each manuscript is subject to negotiation and and will be paid upon publication
        7. All articles will be scheduled for publication at the convenience of Horizon magazine

Please direct all questions regarding policy in writing to:

Jennifer W. Graham
Senior Editor
Horizon Magazine
P. O. Drawer 30
Tuscaloosa, Alabama   35402

WRITER'S GUIDE

HOROSCOPE Publications
Dell Publishing Co., Inc.
1 Dag Hammarskjold Plaza
(245 E. 47th Street)
New York, NY 10017

Julia A. Wagner, Editor-in-Chief (212)605-3439

Ronnie J. Grishman, Associate Editor (212)605-3441

Diane Pilatsky, Assistant Editor (212)605-3442

Ed Kajkowski, Assistant Editor (212)605-3440

* * *

WRITER'S GUIDE

Dell's HOROSCOPE Publications

This guide has been prepared for your benefit. It is suggested that you read it carefully before you begin to prepare your manuscript. If you have a question that is not answered herein, do not hesitate to call or write us about it.

* * *

PAPER--Use "mimeo bond" or an equivalent. This texture of paper absorbs typewriter ribbon ink. Avoid the use of corrasable bond, for the typewriter ribbon ink tends to smear or rub off on this quality paper. Onionskin can be used for the carbon copy but should never be used for the original copy. The size of the paper should be 8½x11--not 8½x13 or 8½x14. The paper on which this guide is printed is a sample of the type of paper you should use for the original copy.

TYPING--Leave at least 1" margins around each page; i.e., top and bottom, left and right. Double-space the entire manuscript, including any quoted material used. ("Double-space" has been underlined for a specific reason. Some makes of typewriters have a space adjustment for 1½ spaces. This spacing does not allow our copyeditors and proofreaders the space necessary between lines for making changes and marking corrections.) Please do not prepare your manuscript with your typewriter set for 1½ spaces between lines. Indent five spacesfor paragraph breaks. Single-spaced or handwritten manuscripts are unacceptable.

NUMBER OF COPIES--The original (ribbon copy) manuscript must be accompanied by one carbon or one xerox copy. If charts are used

WRITER'S GUIDE, Dell's HOROSCOPE Publications   2

with an article, they, too, must be submitted in duplicate. Do
not staple the original copy; use a clip instead. You may staple
the duplicate.

RUNNING HEADS--The title of your article must appear from page 2
on in the upper left-hand corner.

TYPEWRITER RIBBON--Use a medium- or dark-inked ribbon. Faint
type is hard to read. If your ribbon is dried out or worn, please
replace it with a new ribbon.

NAME AND ADDRESS--In the upper left-hand corner of the first page
of your manuscript, give your name and address in full. Your
Social Security Number should appear under the address.

DUAL AUTHORSHIP--If your manuscript is a collaborative effort,
indicate the author (put an asterisk by the name) who is to receive the payment in the event that the manuscript is accepted.
Split payments are not made.

WORD COUNT--In the upper right-hand corner of the first page of
your manuscript, give the exact or approximate word count. If
this information is not given, we will approximate the word
count if your manuscript is accepted.

LENGTH--A manuscript should be between 1,500-2,000 words long--
and no longer.

PAGINATION--Number the pages consecutively throughout the manuscript in the upper right-hand corner.

DATES--Spell out the names of the months. Express a date in
this manner: September 12, 1924, not the 12th of September, 1924.

HOROSCOPE HOUSES--Spell out the house number; for example, first,
second, third, etc. Do not use 1st, 2nd, 3rd, etc.

ASPECTS--When you mention aspects between planets, put the plan-

et making the aspect to the other planet first. For example,
Venus trine Uranus, not Uranus trine Venus. In a series of aspects, list them in sequence from the nearest to the farthest
from the Sun. For example, the Sun trine Venus, Mercury square
Jupiter, Mars conjunction Jupiter, Saturn sextile Neptune, etc.,
instead of the other way around.

ASTROLOGICAL SIGNS--We prefer that you use the following dates
for the signs of the zodiac:

ARIES	March 21-April 20
TAURUS	April 21-May 21
GEMINI	May 22-June 21
CANCER	June 22-July 23
LEO	July 24-August 23
VIRGO	August 24-September 23
LIBRA	September 24-October 23
SCORPIO	October 24-November 22
SAGITTARIUS	November 23-December 21
CAPRICORN	December 22-January 20
AQUARIUS	January 21-February 19
PISCES	February 20-March 20

SPELLING--Use Webster's Seventh New Collegiate Dictionary (1976
edition). Where two spellings are given for a word, use the
preferred one; i.e., the first one listed in the dictionary.
Do not use shortened spellings for words, such as "thru" for
through, "altho" for although, etc.

DIVISION OF WORDS--If you are uncertain about where a word should
be divided at the end of a line, look it up in the dictionary.

HELPFUL GUIDES--Two books that will be helpful to you in prepar-

WRITER'S GUIDE, Dell's HOROSCOPE Publications   4

ing your manuscript are: Writer's Guide and Index to English,
published by Scott, Foresman & Co. Words into Type, 3rd edition, published by Prentice-Hall.

TOPICS--HOROSCOPE Publications are strictly astrological in content. We do not accept articles on numerology, phrenology, gra-
phology, palmistry, spiritualism, or witchcraft. If you are in
doubt about your topic, please do not hesitate to check with us
before you prepare your manuscript for submission to us.

TIMELY TOPICS--We work five months ahead of an issue date. If
your article deals with a timely subject and must be published
in a specific issue, it must reach us six months ahead of that
issue date so that we will have sufficient time for reviewing
it for possible publication. Please keep in mind the issue in
which an article will appear so that you do not include fore-
casts based on dates before that issue date. For example, if
your article is for the March issue, don't include in it fore-
casts that precede that particular month. Project yourself into
the issue for which you are writing.

RESEARCH, ARTICLES BASED ON--If your article deals with research
involving a large number of charts, present the chart data in a
table (see EXHIBIT A). We cannot reproduce all of the charts
with the article because of space limitations, but you must submit the charts with all of the necessary data on each so that we
can double-check for accuracy.

CHARTS, SOURCES FOR--Charts based on verified data appear in:
Lois M. Rodden's The American Book of Charts, published by Astro
Computing Services, distributed by Para Research, Rockport, MA
01966; Michel and Francoise Gauquelin's The Gauquelin Book of

American Charts, published by Astro Computing Services, distributed by Para Research, Inc., Whistlestop Mall, Rockport, MA 01966; Lois M. Rodden's Profiles of Women, published by the American Federation of Astrologers, Inc., POB 22040, Tempe, AZ 85282. Do not use Marc Penfield's An Astrological Who's Who, for the charts presented therein cannot be verified.

TWO-PART ARTICLES--It is rare that we accept a two-part article. Query us first before you submit one to us.

SERIES--If you are planning to prepare a series of articles, check it out with us ahead of time, for we do not generally accept series unless it is of an unusual nature.

REGULAR FEATURES IN HOROSCOPE--At the present time, the regular features are: STOCK-MARKET OUTLOOK, PLANETS AND YOU, ASTROLOGY AT WORK, METROSCOPE, WHO IS SHE? (HE?), CHILDREN, BOOK REVIEWS, WHAT'S IN A NAME?, HOROSCOPES AND DAILIES, LOOKING AHEAD, THE MAJOR TRANSITS AND YOUR SUN-SIGN, YOUR INDIVIDUAL PLANET FORECAST, YEAR AHEAD, HOUR GUIDE, LOVE--MONEY--HEALTH, SELF-GUIDANCE CHART, LUCKY ZODIACAL NUMBERS, SAFETY FIRST, and ASTRO-WORD PUZZLE. Become familiar with these features so that you do not submit material that duplicates them.

SUN-SIGN ARTICLES--If you are writing a Sun-Sign article, address the sign. Use the second person--the one spoken to--you. This way, the material becomes personalized and you will avoid the awkward he/she, his/her construction.

QUOTATIONS--If you quote material that goes over 50 words, you must get the permission of the copyright holder to do so. The copyright holder may want to know how you are going to use the material and may want to review your manuscript. He may give you permission to use the material gratis--or he may ask that you pay a fee for it. This fee must be absorbed by you. Clearance for use of quoted material must accompany your manuscript.

SOURCES--When you are doing your rsearch, check your sources carefully, especially if you run across conflicting statements. Primary sources are, of course, preferred to secondary ones. List your sources at the end of your article.

AUDIENCE--We have a mixed readership. The age group ranges from the teens to the octogenarians. They are on the beginners, intermediate, or advanced level. Don't slant your material to the female market unless it is intended for this group alone.

FILLERS--Each one should be no shorter than 25 words and no longer than 150 words. At least 10 fillers should be submitted at one time. Less than that number will be rejected. Do not number the fillers. The first line of each filler should be indented three spaces. Place three asterisks between fillers. See EXHIBIT B.

ADJECTIVES FOR SIGNS--Arian/Aries, Taurean/Taurus, Geminian/Gemini, Cancerian/Cancer, Leo/Leo, Virgoan/Virgo, Libran/Libra, Scorpio/Scorpio, Sagittarian/Sagittarius, Capricornian/Capricorn, Aquarian/Aquarius, Piscean/Pisces.

SIMULTANEOUS SUBMISSIONS--These are unacceptable for the simple reason that an article could also be purchased by the editor of a competitive magazine. Only material guaranteed exclusive to HOROSCOPE Publications will be considered by our staff.

RIGHTS--We buy all rights to each manuscript we accept for publication. If yours is restricted, do not submit it to us, for we are internationally published and cannot buy limited rights.

WRITER'S GUIDE, Dell's HOROSCOPE Publications   7

REPRINTS--We do not reprint articles that have been published in other astrological publications.

TERMS--You convey all rights in a manuscript to the drawer, including the exclusive unlimited right to reproduce the manuscript in all languages throughout the world in any and all of Dell's publications, and the right to secure copyright therein, and all versions thereof throughout the world. You warrant that you are the sole owner of the manuscript and that the manuscript does not contain any matter contrary to law. Remember that plagiarism is a legal offense, and you alone must answer such a charge if it is leveled against any material included in a manuscript we have accepted for publication.

REVIEW OF MANUSCRIPTS--If your manuscript deals with a topic which is not of a timely nature, please allow us nine weeks to review it for acceptance or rejection. Manuscripts of a timely nature will be reviewed within a month.

CLEAN COPY/DIRTY COPY--EXHIBIT C is a sample of clean copy, while EXHIBIT D is a sample of dirty copy. If we feel that your manuscript is going to fall in the latter category, we will reject it for the simple reason that we do not have the staff to retype material and dirty copy costs more to set.

PAYMENT--It is our policy to pay for manuscripts upon acceptance. Our current payment ranges from $150.00 to $200.00. Consideration is made for complexity of material in an article. Payment is handled by computer.

BACKGROUND IN ASTROLOGY--If you have not submitted material to us before, we would appreciate receiving a resume from you.

SUBMISSION OF MANUSCRIPT--Send your manuscript (original and

WRITER'S GUIDE, Dell's HOROSCOPE Publications   8

duplicate) to: Julia A. Wagner, Editor-in-Chief, HOROSCOPE
Publications, 1 Dag Hammarskjold Plaza (245 E. 47th Street),
New York, NY 10017. Mail flat in a 9x12 manila envelope. In-
close a self-addressed envelope with sufficient postage for its
return in the event it is rejected. (Do not glue the postage
on the return envelope, but clip it thereon.)

the fumes of alcohol. There does not seem to be any stellar reason why she should show symptoms of cirrhosis. This lady suffered from delirium tremens, but the D.T.'s are actually reactive symptoms consequent upon withdrawal. Thus, in the case of a chronic alcoholic, deprivation of alcohol can have the effect of bringing on the D.T.'s. It is, therefore, not a condition which would be symbolized in a horoscope.

Case No. 4: female born Sunday (Sun), October 18, 1908. Her condition was uncomplicated by the presence of other maladies. Her addiction to alcohol would be traceable to the Moon square Mercury, as that is a configuration which would affect the nervous system and so render her liable to succumb to defeatism. The presence of Mars opposition Saturn suggests that her natural will to dominate was defeated by an unhappy marriage.

Case No. 5: male born Wednesday (Mercury), September 11, 1912. His addiction to alcohol is directly traceable to his Mercury square Saturn. Beyond chronic alcoholism, there were no other complications. But it should be noted that this gentleman has Jupiter opposition Saturn in his horoscope, which shows that obstruction to the liver could quite easily occur.

Case No. 6: male born Monday (Moon), September 25, 1871. Addiction in his case appeared to spring from Jupiter square Neptune (which is the mark of the real inebriate), as the influence of this configuration results in a form of constitution capable of readily succumbing to alcohol.

Case No. 7: female born Saturday (Saturn), March 11, 1911. She was unfortunate inasmuch as apart from chronic alcoholism, she was also suffering from syphilis (which means spirochaeti were probably circulating in her blood along with the alcohol). This is a supposition which is supported by the concrete testimony of the basic configuration of her horoscope: a Mars-Uranus conjunction opposite her Moon square Saturn. She was undoubtedly compensating for her hard lot in life by imbibing alcohol in quantity.

Hor. No.	Day	Asc.	Sun	Moon	Mercury	Venus	Mars	Jupiter	Saturn	Uranus	Neptune
1.	Sat.	♒ 8°	♉ 10°	♏ 1°	♈ 13°	♉ 9°	♊ 21°	♉ 8½°	♎ 7¼°	♏ 8¼°	♊ 9¼°
2.	Wed.	♊ 8	♈ 21½	♎ 9	♉ 11	♉ 24	♒ 22	♏ 12	♉ 7½	♑ 29	♋ 18¼
3.	Sun.	♊ 24	♈ 22¾	♋ 2	♈ 7	♓ 7¼	♈ 19½	♒ 13	♑ 27¼	♐ 21¼	♊ 29
4.	Sun.	♓ 22	♎ 25	♌ 12	♏ 13½	♍ 11½	♎ 5½	♍ 7	♈ 5½	♑ 13¼	♋ 17
5.	Wed.	♐ 15	♍ 18½	♍ 25	♍ 1	♎ 6¾	♎ 5¾	♐ 8	♊ 4	♑ 29¾	♋ 25½
6.	Mon.	♑ 19	♎ 2	♒ 25	♍ 18½	♎ 3½	♏ 28¾	♋ 25¾	♑ 3½	♌ 0½	♈ 23¼
7.	Sat.	♑ 0	♓ 19½	♌ 10	♓ 11	♈ 14½	♑ 28½	♏ 14½	♉ 3¾	♑ 28¼	♋ 19
8.	Thu.	♋ 28	♌ 20	♉ 13	♌ 3½	♎ 3	♍ 29¼	♒ 17	♊ 29	♒ 9¼	♋ 28¼
9.	Sun.	♌ 29	♐ 16¾	♎ 1	♏ 29¼	♐ 2	♎ 15¼	♋ 8½	♓ 9	♑ 7½	♋ 12
10.	Fri.	♓ 2	♏ 4½	♎ 5	♏ 11	♎ 10	♍ 24½	♎ 7	♎ 2½	♓ 5¼	♌ 15¼
11.	Mon.	♈ 8	♎ 26	♍ 24	♏ 11'	♍ 16	♍ 6½	♌ 15	♍ 8¼	♒ 28	♌ 11½
12.	Wed.	♑ 0	♑ 28	♑ 24	♐ 12½	♏ 28¼	♓ 25¾	♈ 15¼	♎ 12	♏ 9½	♊ 9½
13.	Wed.	♈ 1	♉ 23¾	♈ 15½	♉ 25	♉ 27¾	♍ 1½	♑ 12¾	♑ 16	♐ 15¾	♊ 27¾
14.	Wed.	♍ 28	♋ 19½	♓ 0	♊ 29	♌ 27	♐ 11¼	♎ 10¾	♎ 2	♓ 13½	♌ 14¾
15.	Mon.	♈ 1	♏ 19	♑ 17	♏ 17	♐ 5½	♎ 16	♏ 27¼	♎ 26¼	♓ 13¾	♌ 20½
16.	Sun.	♑ 24	♎ 28	♋ 27	♏ 22½	♎ 18	♈ 27¼	♋ 6½	♎ 28	♏ 14½	♊ 15½
17.	Mon.	♎ 1	♉ 6	♌ 18	♈ 10½	♈ 18	♎ 29	♌ 9	♏ 5	♓ 5½	♌ 8¾
18.	Sat.	♊ 17	♐ 18	♈ 3	♑ 3	♐ 21	♏ 23	♏ 6	♉ 0¼	♑ 23¾	♋ 21
19.	Wed.	♍ 21	♋ 1½	♍ 9	♊ 19¼	♋ 16½	♓ 17	♍ 8½	♈ 21¾	♑ 19¾	♋ 16¼
20.	Mon.	♊ 1	♋ 6	♏ 6	♊ 19¼	♋ 22½	♓ 19½	♍ 9	♈ 22	♑ 19½	♋ 16½
21.	Sun.	♏ 27	♈ 1	♑ 22	♓ 12	♈ 28	♎ 10	♓ 7¼	♒ 6¾	♐ 25½	♋ 1

EXHIBIT A

One man whose Sun, Mercury, and Neptune are precisely conjunct in Virgo is an absolutely terrible conversationlist. His problem is not a lack of articulation skills. Quite the contrary! It seems once he starts talking, he just won't shut up. Mercury combust the Sun and afflicted by Neptune does not make him nebulous or confusing in speech, but it does make him totally unself-conscious about the poor effect he creates; and he is totally unaware of how rudely he monopolizes conversations. He is not truly insensitive towards others; rather, he is oblivious of them.

* * *

It's business first, pleasure later with a Taurean. Never influence him to retract his decision, for he will simply fidget restlessly, fearful that he is wasting time.

* * *

Those who have natal Sun conjunction Jupiter can really get on other people's nerves. Very little seems to ruffle them, for they are perennially cheerful and optimistic. Even when their outlook obviously irritates more serious folks, they remain blithely unconcerned and unoffended.

* * *

When natal Mars is afflicted, women may become regretfully sloppy in matters of self-defense and protection. Since Mars rules young males, at this time men are potentially combative, volatile, and violent. Although this affliction may play out in a number of ways, astrologers do know that a common denominator in the horoscopes of battered women is adverse aspects involving Mars and/or Uranus. Women, therefore, should exercise caution and suspicion when natal Mars is

EXHIBIT B

CLEAN COPY

may be one to try to organize and thu ill the void of blind fate with reason.   Such interests have long been associated with Sagittarians, Pisceans, and, of course, their ruling planet, Jupiter.

Garth Allen, whose small but powerful book Taking the Kid Gloves off Astrology" (Clancy Publications, Tucson, AZ, 1957) has remained a foundation of modern psychological interpretation of planets, described under Jupiter a process by which an infant "creates" its mother. The baby feels hunger and eventually is fed, so it comes to believe (insofar as infants can believe anything) that its need has "created" the need's fulfillment. Incapable of thought complex enough to recognize forces outside of itself, it assumes that the hunger brought into being the thing that fulfilled it. This psychological process, described originally by psychiatrist Ferenczi, seems a little less off-the-wall when one considers in the modern world a phenomenon like people who truly believe that God, after creating the Universe, particularly empowered them and their friends to run it.

This is nothing new, however, as in more ancient times the ruler was considered by most to be the appointed regent of heaven; and doctrines like the Divine Right of Kings, or the social systems described in books like the "I Ching" show amply that moral authority and God are frequently seen as the same force, a force that often displays a marked sense of "Manifest Destiny" when confronted with differing beliefs.

In a more highly socialized world like that of the present, authority and morals are usually more inwardly than outwardly enforced; and Jupiter symbolizes this inner conscience or ethical set of standards that militates, for example, that at least 99 percent of humanity considers it a crime to kill another human.

EXHIBIT C

DIRTY COPY

9/10 text [15A]

~~F~~or forty-five years, this ~~very~~ beautiful ~~lady~~ *woman* has been ~~tueing~~ *enthralling* audiences ~~from ingenue to doyene, giving them the time of their lives.~~ *with her subtly sensuous style* Today she ~~receives~~ *generates* as much ~~adulation as she did~~ *excitement* ~~as~~ *when she worked as* a ~~talented~~ chorus line dancer ~~in 1932~~ in a ~~New York~~ nightclub. *At the time,* ~~With transiting Saturn trine her mars she~~ *Transiting* was willing to discipline ~~herself, especially as with~~ transiting Uranus in Aries in close sextile to her ~~natal~~ Mercury ~~that~~ *in Gemini* introduced her to an exciting new world and gave her powerful singing voice *its first* ~~a real tryout.~~ *Sun in Aquarius trine her Mars in Gemini assured her of the steady determination* ~~When she refers to your audiences enthusiastic reception she~~ *to start her climb to the top, while* ~~asks herself "how does the old broad do it?"~~

When she was ~~As a~~ three year old ~~child~~ her parents separated and she was farmed out ~~among~~ *to* various relatives in different parts of the country. Transiting Neptune *in Leo* was moving slowly to ~~the~~ square of her Scorpio *Moon in* ~~moon~~ (an aspect she has at birth), ~~that~~ show~~ed~~*ing* ~~small~~ preparation for the many subtle and *unstable* ~~insecure~~ environments to which she had to adapt. [In her fearfulness, she never permitted herself to love ~~anybody~~ *anyone* because she knew that soon she would be shifted to *yet* another ~~set of circumstances~~ *even later* in a family that was alien to her. ~~The fixed square of~~ *A square from the Moon to a Saturn=Neptune* ~~Saturn conjunct Neptune square the moon~~ caused her *to seek escape* ~~to protect herself~~ from unfamiliar surroundings ~~and she~~ *by* creat~~ed~~*ing* an *imaginary* ~~artificial~~ environment ~~to keep her from being too trusting. In addition~~ *she* felt emotionally trapped without the loving support of her mother (the Moon). These were ~~a set of~~ very inhibiting ~~aspects~~ *circumstances* for a *young* child ~~so young~~. Fortunately, her ~~moon trines her sun helped~~ *Sun=Moon* *gifted her with an inner stability which* her to accept responsibility and ~~gradually gave her~~ *blossomed into self-* confidence. As she ~~grew more~~ mature this trine showed her how to mobilize her varied talents and established good timing as she moved along in her creative world.

HORSE AND HORSEMAN

Box HH, 34249 Camino Capistrano, Capistrano Beach, Calif. 92624

EDITORIAL REQUIREMENTS

Manuscripts should be typed, double-spaced, on one side of the paper. Typical full-length articles run from about six to twelve pages of manuscript. It is not necessary to count the words, as we do not pay by the word.

We recommend that you retain a copy of your manuscript for your files. This is against the possibility of loss in the mail or due to some other cause. Each typed page should have the author's name and address in the upper left-hand corner, to ensure payment should the title page become separated from the manuscript. Please include your social security number on the title page, along with a phone number and the time at which you can be reached there.

As to the mechanics of preparing your manuscript, we recommend that you review a few copies of HORSE and HORSEMAN with a view toward absorbing the general writing style customarily employed.

We never purchase articles sight-unseen from those with whose work we are unfamiliar and recommend a query letter first. We then will indicate whether we are or are not interested in seeing the article as outlined and described. Accordingly, all manuscripts should be accompanied by return postage. We will not accept liability for unsolicited manuscripts, photographs or artwork.

As to what we want: As our main audience is comprised of pleasure horseowners, we present material of interest to them for the most part. We do, however, cover the rest of the equine world, from rodeo to play-days, on a somewhat lesser scale. Training tips, do-it-yourself pieces, grooming and feeding, stable management, tack maintenance, sports, personalities and general features of horse-related nature are sought. We do not publish puzzles, poems or sketches, unless the latter supports a story. We put more emphasis on informing than on merely entertaining.

The likelihood that we will purchase and use a given article is strongly affected by the amount and quality of the artwork accompanying it. Good black and white photos, with accurate caption information, are a decided asset to your manuscript, so far as we are concerned. Should you desire the return of any photos, indicate those to be returned upon submission of the manuscript. If you care to supply negatives with your manuscript — black and white, full-frame 35mm or larger — we will make prints for our use and return your negatives. If you furnish negatives, be sure they are suitably protected and identified with your name and address on the envelope or wrapper.

We use color photos with most of the editorial content of the magazine and frequently illustrate a story totally in color (4 to 6 views). Therefore, good, original color transparencies (preferably Kodachrome 25 or Kodachrome 64) in support of the manuscript are welcomed. However, these should be supplemented with black and white photos or other artwork. We have a good darkroom and, if absolutely necessary, can make black and white prints from color negatives (such as Kodacolor) or from positive color transparencies (such as Kodachrome slides). However, this entails a great deal of extra work.

Submission of color transparencies for possible cover use is encouraged. We prefer 35mm format and, in this format, only Kodachrome transparencies will be considered. Detailed caption information must accompany each transparency submitted. Transparencies not selected will be returned promptly when accompanying postage is included. Payment rates depend on the content and quality of the individual transparencies. Originals only are acceptable -- no dupes!

We pay upon acceptance and the amount is determined by the length and quality of the manuscript and illustrations as well as, to some extent, the amount of work we have to do on it to make it suitable for our purposes. If it's weak on artwork and we have to shoot additional photos, this will reduce the amount we will pay for that story. In short, the less we have to do to a story, the more it is worth to us. As a general guide, payments run from about $75 to $200, rarely higher than that. Cover photos are $75 to $100.

CAT FANCY
DOG FANCY
BIRD TALK
HORSE ILLUSTRATED
magazines

Editorial Offices
P.O. Box 6050
Mission Viejo, California 92690
Telepone (714) 240-6001

WRITER'S GUILELINES

Thank you for your interest in our publcations. We would be pleased to see your material. Below we have listed some of the publication requirements of CAT FANCY, DOG FANCY, BIRD TALK and HORSE ILLUSTRATED *to assist you in preparing submissions.*

ARTICLES

CAT FANCY, DOG FANCY and BIRD TALK are directed at the general pet owning population and written for an adult audience. HORSE ILLUSTRATED *is directed at the amateur competition and pleasure horse owner. We suggest that you read past issues of the magazines to aquaint yourself with the types of material we use. Past issues may be obtained by sending $3.00 to the above address. We need informative articles, limited to 3,000 words or less, on the care and training of cats, dogs, birds and horses (health, nutrition, training, etc..); photo essays on historical and current events dealing with cats, dogs, birds and horses; how-to articles; human interest stories; and good fiction, with the animal as the primary focus of interest. We rarely use stories in which the animal speaks as though they were human. We use a breed article in each issue, but these articles are assigned. Please query if you have a breed article in mind.*

Manuscripts should be typewritten, double spaced with wide margins. We prefer that articles be accompanied with appropriate art in the form of professional- quality color transparancies or black and white photographs (NOT SNAP SHOTS) or professional illustrations. Additional guidelines are available for artists and photographers.

We are always happy to review material on speculation, but with the exception of fiction, the best working procedure is to query before preparing an article. Our usual rate of payment is 3 to 5 cents per printed word, (5 cents if accompanied by good quality photographes). Payment is made in the latter part of the cover month in which your article appears, (i.e., if your piece was in the November issue you would be paid in the latter part of November). We buy first American rights only-- all other rights revert back to the author.

POETRY--CAT FANCY ONLY

We use a limited number of poems in each issue. Competition is fierce!! Payment is $10.00 and payment is made as it is for articles. We prefer short poems, but we will use longer works that can be illustrated. Payment for longer, special-use poems is $25.

We cannot assume responsibility for material submitted, but we assure you that reasonable care will be taken in handling your work. YOU MUST INCLUDE A SELF-ADDRESSED, STAMPED ENVELOPE WITH EACH SUBMISSION.

HORTICULTURE
EDITORIAL GUIDELINES

It is our intention to make Horticulture, The Magazine of American Gardening, an authoritative and informative source of gardening information, as well as a stimulating and visually attractive publication. To succeed in this objective, you must be thorough in your coverage of a subject and careful in checking sources. Equally important, your approach to stories must be intelligent--raising and answering the questions a sophisticated gardener or reader would ask.

The following outline is intended to serve as a checklist of important elements that should be part of a properly developed plant profile. It is not intended to suggest any order, priority, or relative importance. And it is only a suggestion of some of the elements that could be contained in a garden article that is not specifically a plant profile. We do not insist that every point be included in every article, but each one's relevance should always be considered. Whenever possible, relate your own experience with growing the plant.

Plant Profiles:

The objective is to give a fully developed profile of a plant, its place in nature and in a garden. The presentation should be such that a generally interested reader will find it entertaining reading and a specifically interested reader will be able to glean the information needed to make a decision about whether to grow the plant. In most cases, the writer should present the information in a readable form--not as a recipe.

Taxonomy:

What is the family, genus, species, and cultivar?
To what well-known garden plant is it closely related (and in what way?)
If a hybrid, what are its parents? Who made the cross and when?

Culture:

What is the plant's range of requirements in terms of:

temperature	transplanting
light/exposure	water needs
soil type	humidity
soil pH	pollination
fertilizer	propagation (both technique
wind tolerance	and timing)
pollution tolerance	pruning needs
dormancy	container culture
flowering and fruiting	special requirements

In general, this information should indicate what is needed for the plant to perform well--not merely to survive.

Description of plant should indicate:

height	annual, perennial, or woody
width	deciduous or evergreen

bloom time	scarcity or endangered status
flower color	foliage size, shape, and color
flower size	native habitat and adaptation
fragrance	approximate life expectancy
time to ripen fruit	poisonous or allergenic qualities
storage of fruit	insect susceptibilities
rate of growth	disease susceptibilities

Availability:

Where can one buy or at least observe the plant (its fruit, seed, etc.)?
Roughly, what should it cost?
What is the best size plant to buy and why?
When is the best time to plant?

Use:

What is the primary function of this plant: ornamental, edible, wildlife repellant, wildlife attractant, etc.?
What else can it be used for?
Does its use vary with the climate?
What are the traditional uses versus new possibilities?
With what plants or structures does it work well?

Sources:

List references for controversial facts or figures that might be challanged.
List nurseries, garden centers, or mail-order companies that offer the plant.

When submitting a manuscript:

Your manuscript should be neatly typed and double-spaced; include your name at the top of each page. While all manuscripts and photos are handled with care, safe return of unsolicited material is not guaranteed. All materials MUST be accompanied by an SASE.

You will receive an acknowledgement from us shortly after your piece arrives.

Thank you, and good luck.

Editorial Department
Horticulture, The Magazine of American Gardening
755 Boylston St., Boston, Mass. 02116
617-247-4100

HOUSE BEAUTIFUL

1700 Broadway, New York, NY 10019

(212) 903 5000

Thank you for your inquiry about HOUSE BEAUTIFUL's guidelines for free-lance writers.

1. We are primarily interested in service articles dealing strictly with the home. We use no fiction or poetry.

2. Be sure to study the style and contents of a few recent issues before submitting any articles.

3. We have monthly columns on beauty, travel, pets and gardening-- only in very rare instances do we use free-lance material on these subjects.

4. We prefer receiving queries rather than finished manuscripts-- this will save you time. If we are interested in an idea, we will ask you to send in the article on speculation.

5. Most of our articles are between 1,200 and 1,500 words.

6. Send seasonal ideas five to six months before the season, i.e. Christmas.

7. Please label with your complete name and address every page, caption, photo, etc., that you send us. We receive many articles and queries, and it is very easy for unlabeled material to become separated.

8. Type your articles double-spaced on white paper, leaving at least a two-inch margin on the top and one inch on the remaining margins.

9. Any submissions sent without a stamped, self-addressed envelope will not be returned to writers.

10. Address all articles, queries and related correspondence to Carol Cooper Garey, Senior Editor/Copy, HOUSE BEAUTIFUL, 1700 Broadway, New York, NY 10019.

Thank you again for your interest in HOUSE BEAUTIFUL.

HOUSE BEAUTIFUL IS A PUBLICATION OF HEARST MAGAZINES, A DIVISION OF THE HEARST CORPORATION

LARRY FLYNT PUBLICATIONS

HUSTLER FICTION/ARTICLE SPECIFICATIONS

All submissions should be written in a simple, straightforward style which is easily readable and not academic. PLEASE: All manuscripts must include a return envelope, STAMPED AND SELF-ADDRESSED. All others will be destroyed. Allow six weeks for response.

Prices quoted are base rates and are negotiable depending on the writer's previous publishing credits and the subject matter to be covered.

FICTION:

4,500 words, $1,000.00 (+)

At present we are buying stories with emphasis on erotic themes. These may be adventure, action, mystery or horror stories, but the tone and theme must involve sex and eroticism. The main sex scene should be a minimum of one-and-a-half pages in length. However, the erotic nature of the story must not be subordinate to the characterizations and plot; the sex must grow logically from the people and the plot, not be contrived or forced.

Stories should start fast and continue to move forward, with a minimum of flashbacks, preferably none at all. The dialogue should sound authentic and carry the story forward as well as reveal the story's characters.

We do not buy poetry, science-fiction, satire, or humorous fiction. Please refrain from stories with drug themes, sex with minors, incest, homosexual themes or blasphemy.

ARTICLES:

4,500 words, $1,200.00 (+)

a. Hard-hitting, documented exposes.
b. Highly readable, well-researched material on all social, religious, political and sexual topics.

NOTE: All information, statistics and quotations used in articles must be verifiable. (Every article is thoroughly checked by our Research Department.) Please refrain from using the first-person singular. Query first.

- over -

PROFILE:

4,500 words, $1,200.00 (+)

Up-close and personal looks at well-known or trend-setting invidviduals. Absolutely no promotional copy.   Please refrain from using the first person singular. Query first.

INTERVIEW:

5,000 words, $1,200.00 (+)

Candid interviews with well-known or trend-setting individuals. Interviews must be penetrating and probing, pushing the subject to reveal as much as possible of himself/herself. Absolutely no promotional copy. Query first.

KINKY KORNER:

1,500 words, $100.00 (+)

First-person account of an unusual sexual adventure. Style should be verbal, not literary, using little dialogue and no "fancy writing". Tone should be realistic, titillating and celebrate human sexuality. Kinky behavior should not be merely superficial but must stem from inner needs. It must be highly offbeat to qualify, yet must be believable. Please refrain from using sex with minors or incest. Sexual encounters should be described in exact detail as to action and position of participants at all times. Study of printed Kinky Korners is a must.

IN BUSINESS

WRITERS' GUIDELINES

IN BUSINESS magazine, published bimonthly, is a how-to management and lifestyle magazine for persons who currently run their own small business -- or who would like to start one. The editorial pages contain detailed case histories of small enterprises in a wide range of fields, as well as columns on financing, marketing, taxes, and legal issues. Emphasis is given to innovative and independent businesses.

For all profiles, we request figures on start up costs; annual sales; projected sales; how the business is financed; management techniques; marketing strategies; success and failure prevention tips; handling growth; dealing with competition; going from regional to national distribution. How-to management pieces must include theory and case histories, e.g., 10 easy marketing ideas with real life examples; accounting principles used by the following five types of companies. We also accept historical pieces as they relate to surviving in a recessionary economy, marketing strategies used, profiles of entrepreneurs. We generally do not accept articles on "hot" franchise business opportunities, get rich quick schemes, "how my neighbor makes lots of money arranging flowers".

Full length articles average about 2,000 words. Writers should query with a detailed description/outline of proposed article and include one or two clips of published work. Please state availability of black and white photos; contact sheets should be submitted with the article. We prefer captions, model releases, and identification of subjects. First North American rights are purchased. Article payments range from $100 to $200; photos range from $15 to $25 per print used. Payment is on publication. Kill fees are uncommon and minimal.

Departments cover small business computing, book reviews, money management, investing tips, and write ups on "New and Growing" businesses. These range in length from 250 to 700 words; payment ranges from $25 to $75. Seasonal material should be submitted at least three months in advance of publication date, e.g., August 15th for November-December. A self-addressed stamped envelope is requested for return of submissions. We report on queries within six weeks, manuscripts within four weeks. A sample copy is $2.95. The best tip we have is to read several issues of IN BUSINESS to understand the editorial focus -- and then send detailed query.

Nora Goldstein for the
Editors of IN BUSINESS

8/84

THE JG PRESS INC

BOX 323, EMMAUS, PA 18049 (215) 967-4135

GUIDELINES FOR CONTRIBUTORS

Inc.

THE MAGAZINE FOR GROWING COMPANIES
38 COMMERCIAL WHARF
BOSTON, MASSACHUSETTS 02110
(617) 227-4700
TELEX 710-321-0523

INC. welcomes queries from writers. If you are interested in writing a story for INC., you should first read several issues of the magazine to become thoroughly familiar with the kinds of stories we have published in the past. INC.'s goal is to provide its readers, the managers of small companies with sales in the $500,000 to $100 million range, with practical advice and insights into the management of their businesses.

Payment for an INC. story varies, depending in part on the length of the manuscript, the amount of research involved, and the degree of editing required. Feature rates range from $600 to $2,500. Department rates start at $150 for very short items. For the longer departments, rates range from $400 to $1,000. Features are rarely longer than 2,500 words. Short department items should not be more than 300 words; the longer departments run about 1,000 to 1,500 words.

INC. normally buys all rights, but usually agrees to subsequent sale or publication of purchased material provided INC. receives appropriate credit. If contributors wish to sell only first serial rights, the fee will be reduced by about $200.

INC. will reimburse contributors for reasonable, itemized expenses.

Kill fees are paid when an assigned story proves unsuitable for publication. The fees range from under 10% for first time contributors to 30% for stories assigned to regular contributors. Expenses are usually paid to writers whose stories are killed. Payment of a kill fee constitutes purchase of the research and story treatment, unless otherwise agreed to by the editors.

Writers assigned stories receive copies of an agreement detailing the fee, the kill fee, the deadline, and the rights to the story. Payment is initiated upon acceptance of a completed manuscript.

Submit all queries in writing to the Submissions Editor, INC. Magazine, 38 Commercial Wharf, Boston, MA 02110. Do not telephone. Queries will be reviewed within 1 - 2 months, and the writer will be notified by mail.

8/85

BEYOND THE BOTTOM LINE

Brief Notes About What INC. Looks for in a Story

Like any national magazine, INC. receives hundreds
of news releases and queries each month about our interest
in stories focusing on companies and people. Very few of
these lead to stories in the magazine. In part, this
is a result of space limitations. Equally important,
though, is a lack of understanding about the kind of
stories INC. looks for.

In simplest terms, INC. is interested not only in
the "what" of a business story but in the "how." Traditional
business journalism begins and ends with the financial
success or failure achieved by a company and its leaders,
liberally spiced with predictions about the future of
the market segment the company may serve. While a good
INC. story will of course contain those elements, we
also want to know, as specifically as possible, about
the experience which produced the results.

The reason is simple: INC. exists to help owners
and managers of small companies do a better job of running
their own business. Experience is the best teacher, and
we want our readers to be able to learn from a piece how
they might take similar advantage or avoid similar
disaster.

Taking the above into account, it's obvious that a
successful outside query to INC. will be one that goes
beyond the profit and loss statement or the scientific
brilliance of a company or a concept. Help us understand
what is unique about the way in which the principals
have approached an opportunity or a problem and you'll be
far more likely to pique our interest.

inCider

MICROCOMPUTING • INCIDER • 80 MICRO • HOT COCO • RUN • JR • 73 MAGAZINE

80 Pine Street/Peterborough, NH 03458/1 (800) 441-4403

Dear Author:

    As requested, a copy of inCider's Writer's Guidelines is enclosed. We are revamping our original guidelines, which had become outdated over the last few years. The material we are sending you today is an interim version.

    We have also enclosed a confidential author "spec sheet". Please take a few minutes to fill out and return it when you submit your first manuscript.

    Thanks for your interest in inCider. We look forward to hearing from you soon. Don't hesitate to call us with any questions you may have.

Best Regards,

Susan Gubernat
Managing Editor

The Editors at inCider

/ld

CW COMMUNICATIONS/PETERBOROUGH

An Ever-So-Brief Guide to Writing for inCider

Okay, you have got a great idea for an Apple computing article for inCider. Now what? For a no-fail, quick-start way to develop your subject, do a little brainstorming on your word processor. Your objective is to extract everything you know about your subject. Pay no heed to order or sequence. Don't burden yourself with complete sentences. Just get everything down in black and white.

Now that you have generated your material, reassemble it in outline form. You will quickly spot natural lines of division between topics and subtopics, and recognize as well items that are tangential and even off-track for this particular piece. Chances are you will want to make some topical block moves later on, but at least you've got a blueprint.

Wading into It: The Lead

Don't drain your juices trying for a Dickensian lead. It is better to say something quick and direct than to waste your time on foot-shuffling introductions that some hard-nosed copy editor is just going to chop anyway. Say up front what you are talking about and briefly address those reader needs your article will satisfy. Sell the article.

Now the stage is set for the rest of the story. It's at this point that your outline earns its keep. Use it like a road map to chart a logical course through the subject. Since you have already determined the gist of your article, you'll find the writing comes more easily at this stage.

When have you said enough about a particular aspect of your topic? A good rule of thumb is to leave nothing to the reader's imagination. Swamp him with details. Immerse her in knowledge. Fortify him with thought. (But don't baffle her with BS.) If you've said too much, a good editor will quickly trim the fat with no harm done. Say too little and we've got problems.

While you're writing, here are a few tips to keep in mind:

1). Style is elusive; content is finite. We stress the latter and so should you.
2). Be precise, but not clinical. Visualize yourself explaining the subject to a close friend.
3). Keep your sentences short.
4). Ditto for paragraphs.
5). Everyday vocabulary will assure a comfortable fit for the reader.
6). Remember the road to literary ruin is strewn with pompous $5 words.

7). Be specific; give examples.
8). Have fun. You´d be surprised at the increased readership an upbeat tempo generates.

Finally, when your article is done, close it quickly, using
the same logic advised for writing a lead.

About Illustrations

Diagrams can be useful in conveying your message. So don´t
be afraid to sketch one out if you think it will illuminate
the article. These should be done on separate sheets of
paper, not couched in the text. Unless you´re extremely artistic, we´ll have your sketch re-drawn by a professional illustrator, so don´t get hung up about how the sketch looks.
Do take pains to clearly label the elements of the illustration and give it an appropriate title.

If it´s possible and/or relevant to include a computer print-
out (e.g., a screen dump of a business graph) by all means
include it. Make it as sharp and professional as you can.
The same holds true for photographs.

About Manuscripts

Your article must be typewritten, either on a printer or a
standard typewriter. Dot-matrix type is acceptable, though
letter-quality is preferred. In either case, make sure that
you have a decent ribbon in your machine so that we´ll be
working from reasonably dark copy.

Number the pages. Go easy on capitalization. And double-
space your copy. Everything you can do to make the manuscript neater, more explicit, and self-explanatory increases
your chances of selling it.

If a program listing accompanies the article, we´ll need a
printout of it and a copy of the program on disk. If your
article has no program listing, it´s still an excellent idea
to send us the manuscript on disk in addition to hard copy.
We´ve recently interfaced our editorial Apples to our typesetting equipment, and if we have your text already in electronic form it can save us a lot of keyboarding.

One immutable condition: Please don´t send us a manuscript
that you have sent, or will shortly send, to another
magazine. Double submissions can only lead to hassles and
there´s a very good chance that NOBODY will end up buying
your piece.

How much do we pay? That depends on your topic, your skill
as a writer, our needs at the time of submission, among other

things. But our author payments generally run anywhere from
$100 for a minor article up to $500 for a nicely done
feature.   On rare occasions we buy longer manuscripts and
break them up into monthly segments, but we prefer stand-
alone works.

Our policy is to buy all rights to a manuscript. Also,
please bear in mind that payment does not guarantee publication. Unforeseen circumstances could force us to suspend
publication of an article indefinitely, though this is rare.

Finally, once we begin production of your story you will have
the opportunity to correct any errors that may have been
introduced during the editing process. This is accomplished
through author´s proofs (or galleys) which we ask you to
check over and send back by return mail.

That, in a nutshell, is it. Since 1982, we´ve had the
pleasure of working with hundreds of fine authors, many
of whom never knew they had a flair for writing until they
gave it that all-important first try. So whether it´s your
first or your fiftieth article, get it down on paper and send
it along to inCider. Apple America waits.

inCider

INCIDER • 80 MICRO • HOT COCO • RUN • 73 MAGAZINE

80 Pine Street/Peterborough, NH 03458/1 (800) 441-4403

Author Information Sheet
CONFIDENTIAL

Name _____

Street Address _____

City/State/Zip _____

Occupation _____

Phone: Home _____ Office _____

Social Security Number _____

A. SYSTEM CONFIGURATION

_____ Apple II	_____ Apple III	_____ Printer
_____ Apple II +	_____ Apple III +	_____ 80-Column Card
_____ Apple IIe	_____ Macintosh	_____ Serial Card
_____ Apple IIc	_____ Modem	_____ CP/M

Other _____

What word processor do you use? _____

B. AREAS OF EXPERTISE (Please check all that apply)

_____ Utilities	_____ Games	_____ Hardware construction
_____ Spreadsheets	_____ Business Appl.	_____ Home Applications
_____ Education	_____ Graphics	_____ Music/Speech Synthesis
_____ Robotics	_____ Word Processing	_____ Telecommunications
_____ DBMS	_____ Networking	_____ Information Services
_____ AI	_____ Bulletin Boards	

Other _____

C. LANGUAGE FLUENCY

_____ 6502 Assembly	_____ Applesoft BASIC	_____ Pascal
_____ Forth	_____ Logo	_____ Lisp

Other _____

D. If you are interested in reviewing new products for inCider, please check the following categories.

_____ Hardware Reviews	_____ Printers	_____ Modems
_____ Software Reviews		_____ Educational

Other _____

Note: If you are a new author with inCider, clippings of your previous work would be appreciated. Please return this to inCider, 80 Pine St., Peterborough, NH 03458 within 30 days.

CW COMMUNICATIONS/PETERBOROUGH

Writer guidelines

The following is an abridged version of the writer guidelines that we give to all potential contributors. (Of course, our review board members are welcome to propose non-review articles to us, although editors other than the Senior Editor/Reviews are likely to review such proposals.)

Independent writers who are interested in submitting free-lance material to us should be familiar with using a personal computer and with the personal computer industry and must be able to work fast. We recommend that you read several issues to familiarize yourself with our style and news angle before proposing any stories. Please understand that we are a newsmagazine trying to cover a very broad field of interest; we appreciate very highly writers who do not waste our time by proposing story ideas that belong in a monthly feature magazine or a product-specific magazine.

InfoWorld covers anything and everything that is significant and interesting to people who need to know what's happening as the personal computer "revolution" progresses. We do not cover events or trends of minor interest or of very specialized interest. We maintain a large staff of professional journalists, who write most of our news and news-feature stories. As a result, we do not buy much free-lance material, except for reviews. Writing reviews requires a separate arrangement with the Senior Editor/Reviews. Of the total of about 250 to 400 free-lance manuscripts we purchase each year, nearly 80 percent are reviews.

We buy articles from independent writers in the following situations:

We buy news features from writers who have special access to sources that we cannot obtain. Special access may mean a story that originates overseas (where we do not presently have any full-time staff or correspondents) or it may mean access to a recently announced, but undelivered, product that promises to be very important.

We buy articles and features for several special issues, reports, and publications. In the magazine, we schedule a number of annual special issues every year, including our "Products of the Year Awards" in January, our "Back to School" issue in September, our *"InfoWorld* 100" in the spring, and other annuals that may offer special opportunities for free-lance submissions. We also publish quarterly Special Reports as inserts in the magazine. They focus on topics of interest to a specialized portion of our audience, are more tutorial than news-oriented, and are written entirely by independent writers. We also publish several special publications. Our biannual *"InfoWorld* In Review" retrospective is a compilation and re-editing of the highlights of *InfoWorld* every six months.

Most of the articles we buy are reviews of hardware and software products and on-line services. Product reviews are commissioned according to strict guidelines. Independent writers who want to review products for *InfoWorld* must qualify for membership on our review board, essentially by being well-versed in one or two significant product areas and by demonstrating their analytical and writing abilities. Potential reviewers should apply to the Senior Editor/Reviews for membership on the Review Board.

We publish four weekly columns, two of which are written by independent writers, and have one regular contributor on retainer. At this time, we are not interested in reviewing new column ideas.

If you would like to propose an article, start by sending us a very brief query (one or two paragraphs). Do not call us on the telephone until you have established a relationship with one of our editors and have figured out what we are really looking for.

We will try to respond within three or four weeks, faster if your query deals with a very timely subject. Please recognize, however, that we are set up to be primarily a staff-written magazine and are not as well-organized to respond to independent writers as is a free-lance-written feature magazine.

We will respond either with a form letter that tells you that we do not want the article that you proposed and why we don't want it or we will call and assign the article to you. In the latter case, we will usually revise the idea you proposed. Please pay particular attention to those revisions, since your willingness to work to our specifications will affect the success you have in dealing with us in the future.

We will give you a deadline with your assignment. Because *InfoWorld* is a newsweekly, we have strict production deadlines, which writers must meet. If you do not meet your deadline or if you ask for extensions too frequently, we are not likely to ask you to write more than one article. Once we have accepted an article, we cannot guarantee an exact publication date. Articles usually appear within two to four weeks of acceptance.

Once we have given you an assignment, do not hesitate to call the assigning editor. We prefer to hear about problems or changes in direction as soon as possible, and we always stand ready to help writers complete their assignments when we can.

Payments and copyrights: Our established fees for articles can vary from $25 to $300 per article, depending on length and difficulty. We will pay you for an article when we deem it acceptable, and usually process the payment within two weeks of acceptance. We give a byline for all contributed articles, and we offer a standard kill fee of 30 percent for any article we deem unacceptable for publication. If we do not publish an accepted article, we will pay the full fee.

While it is not a common policy among magazines in general, *InfoWorld* buys all copyrights worldwide and for all methods of publication including print, broadcast, and electronic forms, including all reprint rights. We maintain this policy because we are a division of a company that publishes similar magazines and newspapers all over the world and our parent company wants to achieve some of the efficiences that come from the capability of these publications to share articles and news stories. It would be a nightmare to keep track of different copyrights to different articles in more than 50 publications in 26 countries. It is, therefore, incumbent upon you to decide in advance whether we are paying you enough money to acquire all of the rights in the article(s) you might write for us.

(Not to let you get away without a plug, however, we also feel that *InfoWorld*'s low payment rates are compensated for somewhat because the magazine is read nearly universally by all of the chief and executive editors who are responsible for buying articles for the most important magazines and newspapers.)

Photographs: We encourage reviewers who have the appropriate skill and equipment to take photographs to illustrate the written review. We prefer these to stock photos acquired from the manufacturer or public relations agencies. If you take photographs for reviews, you will be reimbursed for film and other materials used. You will also receive a photo credit.

These arrangements are different from those we offer to independent, professional photographers who shoot on assignment for news stories and features. If you have questions regarding those requirements and rates, please contact the Executive Editor.

September 1984

A GUIDE FOR WILDLIFE BIOLOGISTS AND OTHER SCIENTISTS WRITING

FOR INTERNATIONAL WILDLIFE MAGAZINE

Write to:

Jonathan Fisher
Managing Editor
International Wildlife Magazine
National Wildlife Federation
8925 Leesburg Pike
Vienna, Virginia 22180

The magazine: International Wildlife is a "popular" magazine published for the National Wildlife Federation, largest conservation organization in the U.S.   Its circulation is 400,000. International
Wildlife, which covers wildlife and related subjects outside the U.S.,
is a sister magazine to National Wildlife. Each magazine comes out six
times per year.

Subjects covered: Species status reports, personal adventure, personality profiles, environmental and wildlife issues, indigenous people,
natural history, humor, scientific trends, new research, how-to or
virtually any subject that touches on wildlife or the environment.

Length: Most stories run 1,500 to 3,000 words (8-15 double-spaced
typewritten pages). Some stories as short as 500 words are also published.

Photographs: It is not necessary to submit photographs with an
article; however, superlative color transparencies can make a story
package much more appealing, particularly since International Wildlife
is in large part a colorful picture magazine. Professional-quality
35mm transparencies are preferred. (Use Kodachrome film with Kodak
processing.) They should cover a variety of subjects: scene-setting
pictures in the location of the story; shots of the author at work;

-2-

close-up, middle-distance and panoramic wildlife shots; behavior pictures; pictures which illustrate special points covered in the story. These should appeal to a lay audience and should be technically sharp and well exposed. Key each picture to a caption sheet which identifies people, wildlife and situations in the picture. (Photo guidelines are available on request.)

Payment: Payment for major features begins at $800 and ranges upward, depending on how many magazine pages are used for the story. The magazine usually buys all rights to text and one-time rights to photographs, plus promotion and reprint rights. Photos and text submitted together will be purchased as a package. Text payment is made on acceptance of the article.

How to approach the magazine with an article: Write a one- or two-page proposal letter to Jonathan Fisher, Managing Editor, (International Wildlife Magazine, National Wildlife Federation, 8925 Leesburg Pike, Vienna, Virginia 22180) outlining what you would cover and how you would organize this material. This should be a tightly written specific "selling" letter designed to make the story compelling to the editors. You should also include sample pictures if you have them and a brief note about your background.

If the proposal has promise, the editors, after first outlining payment for an acceptable article and setting other ground rules, will invite you to submit a finished manuscript on speculation. (That is, they reserve the right to reject the story with no payment should they find the finished article unacceptable.) If you have sold to the magazine previously, the "on speculation" stipulation may be waived.

Because of new copyright laws in the U.S., you will be sent a copyright form to be signed and returned (it outlines rights purchased and other conditions).

Referee: Please provide the names of two authorities who know the subject you are writing about. We will ask them to review your edited manuscript.

The audience: International Wildlife readers include conservationists, biologists, wildlife managers and other wildlife professionals, but the vast majority are not wildlife oriented. In fact, International Wildlife caters specifically to the unconverted -- those people who may have only a passing interest in wildlife. Consequently, our writers should avoid a common pitfall: talking only to people like themselves. International Wildlife is in competition with TV and hundreds of other periodicals for the limited attention, attention spans and time of busy people. So our functions include attracting readers with engaging subjects, pictures and layouts, then holding them with interesting and entertaining, as well as instructional, text.

Why we want scientists to write for us: Much of our publication is written by professional journalists, trained in popular writing and adept at translating the jargon or complicated language and concepts of specialists into lay language. But the first-hand observations, richness of experience and grasp of their subject that scientists can

-3-

bring to our readers is important to us, too. We need the diversity of
both kinds of writing. We also feel that the scientific community has
an obligation to make its work understandable to the general public,
particularly at a time when wild places and wildlife are disappearing
so rapidly from the earth.

Problems of writing for the public: A scientific paper and a popular
magazine article are two distinctly different animals. Many scientists have great difficulty shifting gears from one to the other.
Among the most common mistakes: 1) Using scientific, academic vocabulary; 2) Assuming that the audience knows more than it does (even
relatively simple terms such as "home range" and "dominance hierarchy"
can be foreign to a reader); 3) Dull writing; 4) Poor article structure
or organization; every article should have a structural backbone, and
nothing should deviate from that; 5) Inability to zero in on a piece of
a broad subject and to focus on the most interesting aspect; 6) Failure
to simplify (minor sub-topics and their ramifications are usually of
little interest to popular readers); 7) Failure to put an article into
a general perspective or to orient the reader; 8) Reluctance to inject
personality into an article or to relate personal anecdotes (readers
don't like stiff scientists; they like real people who can let their
hair down); 9) Failure to pinpoint inherently interesting or significant subjects for popular consumption.

Recipes for writing: There are no recipes, no pat answers, no formulas
for writing for a popular audience. Our articles may take the form of
a diary or journal, a series of short impressions, questions and answers or, more commonly, a conventional first-person account. Execution is everything.

On the other hand, most researchers share both common field experiences and common problems in writing about those experiences. They know
the animal or subject they are studying intimately. They have had
personal contact with it in the field, often in exotic places. They
can take a reader along vicariously on a field expedition. They have
the reservoir of experiences for making their subject lively and provocative. They have the potential to grab people who would probably
prefer to be watching the Miami Dolphins over a beer; but they often
have little experience writing for a non-professional audience.

For all that, there is one structure that has worked particularly well
for some researchers who have written for us in the past. It is
offered here as a guide for a particular kind of article (to be used
where appropriate -- or ignored altogether):

Story Structure for Wildlife Researchers

I.   Opener -- colorful personal anecdote involving researcher obser-
      ving the animal (example: author follows lactating cheetah to
      her cubs -- a first for a wildlife researcher).

II.   Orientation paragraph -- author tells what he is doing and what problem he is hoping to solve (example: he's in the field at the Serengeti because cheetah numbers are dropping and if he learns about their ecology, he may devise a strategy for saving them).

III. Chronological narrative starting from the beginning of the field work:

A. Researcher decides how to solve problem (example: he decides to radio track the female referred to in the opening anecdote).

B. Frequent observations of the animal, offered in anecdotal form, reveal its natural history to researcher, and to the reader who is now vicariously along for the ride.

1. As portrait of the animal unfolds, researcher is faced with personal crises (example: he gets bitten by a tsetse fly, black mamba and big black-maned lion on successive days but miraculously manages to overcome these to move on ahead to his goal).

2. He faces professional crises (example: the cheetah he has tracked most successfully dies, but he finds 18 others and devises a new technique for recognizing individuals).

IV.   Recommendation -- his work over, the researcher says what must be done to save the species.

V.   Closer -- a final anecdote to say farewell to the beast that now has a prospect for a secure future (example: on day before he leaves the Serengeti, a cheetah rips his tent to tatters, a symbol that the animal is forever wild).

Representative articles written by scientists or wildlife professionals:

1. "I Witnessed a Massacre" by Karl G. Van Orsdol (Ph.D. candidate at Cambridge), January-February 1980. While the author is studying lions in Uganda, a Tanzanian "army of liberation" moves in and slaughters some of the world's most magnificent wildlife. A poignant tale of personal courage and sorrow.

2. "The Selling of the Zebra" by Norman Myers (wildlife ecologist and consultant), January-February 1978. The shocking story, by a Nairobi-based biologist, of how Grevy's and other zebras have been pushed toward extinction by poachers who sell the skins to be used for rugs, wall hangings and even telephone-book covers.

3. "Kill Him or Leave Him Alone?" by John G. Sidle (former Peace Corps biologist in Zaire), March-April 1978. Dramatic experiences with hippos in the field are a launching pad to a discussion of a controversial wildlife issue -- a species' ability to control its own numbers and the related question of whether wildlife managers should crop some individuals to save the rest.

4. "Monkeys in the Bank" by Russell A. Mittermeier (Harvard Museum of Comparative Zoology and N.Y. Zoological Society), March-April 1978. A look at efforts of world-renowned conservationist Adelmar F. Coimbra-Filho of Brazil to save the lion tamarin. A story of a remarkable man as well as one of the world's rarest monkeys.

5. "The Rocky Road to Survival" by John Perry (vice chairman, IUCN Survival Service Commission), May-June 1976. A look at some of the strategies being set up around the world to save populations of disappearing animals. One bit of news: zoo breeding may not be all it's cracked up to be.

6. "The Lioness is a Lousy Mother" by George B. Schaller (N.Y. Zoological Society), November-December 1978. Despite moments of maternal devotion, reports the National Book Award winner, the lioness is also likely to be a selfish and neglectful parent. First-person anecdotes help bring the thesis to life.

7. "I Probe the Jungle's Last Frontier" by Donald R. Perry (Ph.D. candidate in biology), November-December 1980. A daring biologist spins a treetop web of ropes -- a dizzying new technique to study life in Costa Rica's rain forest canopy. Even Spiderman would be envious of such adventure.

8. "Our Seven Years With Hyenas" by Mark and Delia Owens (Ph.D. candidates at the University of California, Davis), November-December 1982. Endangered brown hyenas are not solitary animals, as once thought; they even adopt orphan young. A riveting, literate and warmly personal account of hardship, disappointment and discovery during a 7-year period in the Kalahari Desert.

9. "The World's Rarest Birds" by Warren B. King (Ph.D. in ornithology; compiler of the Red Data Book on Birds), September-October 1981. What are the rarest birds in the world? How did they get that way? Using colorful, tightly written case histories and summaries, the author draws some valuable generalizations and tells what people are doing to help.

10. "Hermits of the Jungle" by Peter S. Rodman (primatologist at University of California, Davis), May-June 1977. Why, when all other apes and monkeys stick together, are orangutans loners? Relying heavily on personal experiences with orangs in the jungles of East Kalimantan, the author tackles this intriguing natural history question.

11. "A Most Preposterous Beast" by Andrew Laurie (Fellow of Selwyn College, Cambridge), July-August 1977. What will become of the Indian rhino, one of the world's most unlikely creatures? The author spent three years in Chitawan Park, Nepal, much of it on elephant back, finding out. He combines a status report with first-hand observations of natural history and an account of his own narrow escape from death.

-6-

12. "Baby Crocs in a Valley of Death" by Dhruva Basu (naturalist trained at Madras Snake Park and Crocodile Bank), January-February 1980. Saving an endangered Indian crocodile called the gharial requires braving a no-man's land aswarm with marauding bandits.

13. "Silverback Calls the Shots" by Kelly and Sandy Harcourt (wildlife biologists associated with Cambridge University), January-February 1980. Instead of telling everything they learned while living with gorillas in Rwanda, the authors focus on one topic: how the full-grown male holds his band together.

14. "His 'Crop' is Crocodiles" by Jerome Montague (Ph.D. candidate at Michigan State), March-April 1981. In a remarkable money-earning scheme, remote bush people in Papua, New Guinea are "farming" crocs. That's good for the people. It's also good for wild crocs. The author -- who worked on the project for two years -- relates some of the difficult "public relations" problems involved with convincing a nomadic people to participate in this novel conservation program.

15. "Butterflies: Now You See Them..." by Robert Michael Pyle (consultant to IUCN), January-February 1981. From Britain to Brazil, butterflies are in trouble. Collectors often get the blame, but habitat loss is the real villain. A series of case studies helps bring the subject to life.

16. "'Talking' with Monkeys and Great Apes" by Robert M. Seyfarth (Department of Anthropology, UCLA), March-April 1982. Great apes in captivity are "conversing" with our species using the sign language of the deaf. In the wild, scientists -- including the author -- are studying vocal signals in monkeys. What does it all tell us about intelligence? And what does the whole subject have to say about some ill feeling within the scientific community?

17. "Art of the Alias" by Edward S. Ross (curator emeritus of entomology, California Academy of Sciences), March-April 1983. In the insect world, camouflage, mimicry and other "adaptive illusions" help individuals escape predators. The story illustrates how -- through the talented "camera eye" of a man who has spent a lifetime studying and photographing the subject.

18. "Catch a Lizard, Use a Lizard" by Walter Auffenberg (curator of herpetology, Florida State Museum), November-December 1982. In parts of Southeast Asia, people are eating water monitors into oblivion. Using fascinating information gathered from years in the field, the author tells how these animals are being used -- and what it all means for their conservation.

SEPTEMBER 1984

INTERNATIONAL WILDLIFE MAGAZINE -- A GUIDE FOR WRITERS

The magazine: International Wildlife is a "popular" consumer magazine published for the National Wildlife Federation, largest conservation organization in the U.S. Its circulation is 400,000. International Wildlife, which covers wildlife and a wide range of related subjects outside the U.S., is a sister magazine to National Wildlife. Each magazine comes out six times a year.

Kinds of articles published: Wildlife profiles, species status reports, personal adventure, personality profiles, environmental and wildlife issues, scientific trends, humor, poetic essays, how-to's, man's relationship to the land, place stories, gee whiz, wildlife art, historical pieces.

Length: Most stories run 1,500 to 3,000 words.

Payment: Payment begins at $500 for short features and ranges substantially upwards for longer stories. The magazine buys all rights to text and one-time rights to photographs, plus reprint and promotion rights for the National Wildlife Federation. Pictures and text submitted together will be purchased as a package. Payment is on acceptance.

Photographs: It is not necessary to submit photos with an article; however, superlative color transparencies can make a story package much more appealing, particularly since International Wildlife is in large part a colorful picture magazine. Professional-quality 35mm Kodachrome transparencies are preferred. They should cover a variety of subjects: scene-setting pictures in the location of the story; shots of the author or subject at work; close-up, middle-distance and panoramic wildlife shots; behavior pictures; pictures which illustrate special points covered in the story. These should appeal to a lay audience and should be technically sharp and well-exposed. Key each picture to a caption sheet which identifies people, wildlife, location and situations in the picture.

How to approach the magazine with an article: Write a one- or two-page proposal letter to Jonathan Fisher, Managing Editor, International Wildlife, 1412 16th St., NW, Washington, D.C. 20036. Outline what you would cover and how you would organize the material. This should be a tightly written specific "selling" letter designed to make the story compelling to the editors. You should also include sample pictures, if you have them, a brief note about your background, and samples of your magazine writing.

Assignments: All assignments will be made or confirmed in writing. The assignment letter will outline payment, length, delivery date and other suggestions or ground rules. That will be accompanied by a transfer of rights form to be signed and returned.

The audience: International Wildlife readers include conservationists, biologists, wildlife managers and other wildlife professionals, but the majority are not wildlife oriented. In fact, International

Wildlife caters to the unconverted -- those people who may have only a passing interest in wildlife. Consequently, our writers should avoid a common pitfall: talking only to an "in group." International Wildlife is in competition with TV and hundreds of other periodicals for the limited attention, attention spans and time of busy people. So our functions include attracting readers with engaging subjects, pictures and layouts, then holding them with interesting and entertaining, as well as instructional text.

Story Ideas: Too much environmental writing is self-serving and dull. Yet even the dullest subject can be made interesting. The challenge is to come up with new approaches, new slants, new angles. We appreciate creative thinking and novel ways to cover conventional subjects. Even more, we appreciate proposals on unconventional or unusual subjects.

Editing: Some stories require very little editing; many are edited heavily. A copy of the edited story goes to the writer for comment prior to publication. Edited stories are also sent to scientific authorities for comment and for a check of all factual material.

Writing we like: We've published everything from poetic nature essays to field journals, and we are reluctant to say that one kind of writing serves our purposes more than another. But we do appreciate the following:

1. Lean copy.   We want every word to count. Cut out extraneous material; avoid convoluted sentences.

2. Tight structure. Every piece must have a structural backbone. Just as every paragraph should have a topic sentence, every story should have a topic paragraph, a "billboard" that points the way for the reader, telling him exactly what the story is about and where it is going to take him. This orientation paragraph should generally appear high up in the story, preferably immediately after the lead.

3. Hard reporting. We want the whole story, with specific hard facts reported from primary sources. Use the phone. Don't be satisfied with general quotations; get colorful quotes that say something. Get the latest statistics and numbers. Cover all sides, but don't get so close to the story that you can no longer distinguish what is important.

4. Engaging leads. Write them to entice the readers into the piece.

5. Understandable language. Avoid the lingo of biologists or wildlife managers. Remember, our readers, no matter how well educated, are just folks.

-3-

6. Anecdotes.   They help bring most copy to life. Use them.

7. Punchy endings. Don't leave us with flat closers, such as story summaries or innocuous platitudes about environmental lessons. The ender, as with the lead, should be a high point of the story.

<u>Stories we've run</u>: We urge all contributors to study past issues of the magazine before submitting proposals. The following articles have appeared in recent issues. They are listed here to indicate the variety and types of pieces that we need:

"Kangaroo Shooter at Work" by J. F. Shaw (May-June 1979). The story zeroes in on the work of a professional kangaroo killer in Australia as a way of getting into the broader issues of what Australia should do about managing its big marsupials.

"Never Trust Nanook" by Fred Bruemmer (July-August 1979). A standard species profile comes to life thanks to numerous on-scene observations by the author, who has spent much of his life in the Canadian Arctic, some of it working with polar-bear scientists.

"Gift of the Incas" by Noel Vietmeyer (September-October 1984). When the Conquistadors invaded Peru, they took the potato back with them to Europe, leaving several dozen important crops that are only now being rediscovered.

"Trial by Ice" by Lee Williams (May-June 1979). In 1911 a trio of scientists braved 150 miles of Antarctic ice fields, in mid-winter, all to procure a curious treasure: three penquin eggs. This historical piece recreates their adventure.

"Artful Catchers, Deadly Prey" by Zahida Whitaker (March-April 1979). India's Irula tribesmen live off a land of cobras and honey, but their special relationship with nature and the land is changing fast.

"The Tiger in Billy Singh" by Emily and Per Ola d'Aulaire (March-April 1983). An eccentric Indian -- the subject of this personality profile -- is as independent and controversial as the big cat he's trying to protect.

"Detective Auffenberg Gets His Beast" by Walter Auffenberg (March-April 1979). The author takes us on a vicarious, first-person journey in search of a huge lizard that had never been seen alive. In fact, even a dead Gray's Monitor had not been found in 130 years. Our man gets his beast -- alive.

"The Bizarre, Violent, Funny World of the Wild Pig" by Edward Ricciuti (March-April 1979). A collection of short, sometimes way out, but always interesting items about pigs.

"To Catch an Eggnapper" by Ivor Smullen (November-December 1978). In Britain, egg-collecting is still a big hobby, but the Royal Society

-4-

for the Protection of Birds is waging a war on the eggnappers. This amusing article details some of the Society's battles.

"Something's Out There" by Richard Critchfield (January-February 1979). In Nepal, stories of the abominable snowman may not be all myth. The author, who has long collected Yeti stories in Nepal, takes a look.

"Firewood, the Poor Man's Burden" by Erik Elkholm (May-June 1978). For more than a third of humanity, the real energy crisis is not scarcity of petroleum but of firewood. The author takes us from the Ecuadorian Andes to the edges of the Sahara Desert to examine the problem.

"Now that the Last Hunt is Over" by Eric Robins (March-April 1979). Kenya's swashbuckling safari guides are passing quietly into history and legend. This piece takes a look at vanishing Africana.

"Wild in London" by Chad Neighbor (March-April 1984). An urban ecologist named David Goode is searching for dumps, cemeteries and old railroad beds in London, and this profile looks at him as a way to discuss broader issues of urban wildlife.

"Cowboys & Capybaras" by Fiona Sunquist (March-April 1984). In Venezuela, these 100-pound rodents are rounded up and clubbed to death -- for food. Result: Since they have a use, their prospects for survival have increased.

"Saving the Trees, Saving Ourselves" by David Alexander (January-February 1984). Chipko, a grass roots political movement in India, is saving forests from destruction as village women stand up to bulldozers.

"Jungle Rx" by Virginia Morell (May-June 1984). Scientists adept at both botany and anthropology are scrambling to learn from witch doctors before these healers disappear along with their jungle pharmacopoeia.

"Adrift on Greenland's Ice" by Bryan Alexander (May-June 1984). A photographer's trip to document an Eskimo walrus hunt becomes a struggle for survival in the north as the hunting party is marooned on floating ice.

"No Place to Hide" by Sam Iker (September-October 1983). Nuclear war is the ultimate environmental disaster and scientists piecing together what it might mean now see a world of darkness and cold. This story was the first to report this subject in any popular media.

INTERNATIONAL WILDLIFE MAGAZINE
1412 16th St., NW
Washington, D.C.
20036

ISLANDS

AN INTERNATIONAL MAGAZINE

EDITORIAL GUIDELINES

Thank you for your interest in submitting articles or photography to ISLANDS. The most important thing a prospective contributor should do is read the magazine. If you don't have access to a back issue, we'll mail you one for $4.85. Subscriptions cost $18 for a year.

ISLANDS is an international, bimonthly publication written and edited for island enthusiasts. Each issue of the magazine contains a major centerpiece of five to six thousand words, three or four feature articles of roughly 2,500 words, and two or three topical articles for our departments, each of which generally runs approximately 1,500 words. The proportion of text to photography averages 40:60.

We invite articles from many different perspectives: historical, exploratory, cultural, etc. We ask our authors to avoid the typical travel magazine style and concentrate on stimulating and informative pieces that tell the reader something he or she might not know about a particular island. We prefer articles with a sharp focus. We do not accept fiction or poetry.

Any author who wishes to be commissioned should send a detailed proposal for an article, an estimate of costs (if applicable) and samples of previously published work. Material submitted on speculation is welcome. Just be sure to include a self-addressed envelope and adequate postage to ensure prompt return of your material. Allow at least six weeks for a response--it takes time to consider each proposal or manuscript.

Fine color photography is a special attraction of ISLANDS, and we look for superb composition, image quality and editorial applicability. Please label slides with name and address, submit in protective sleeves and include abbreviated captions and return postage.

ISLANDS pays $.25 and up per published word for features and $75 to $300 per photograph, depending on usage. Commissioned photographic assignments are negotiated. For writers, payment of a 50 percent acceptance fee is made within 15 days of acceptance of the manuscript, with the balance paid within 30 days of publication. If ISLANDS rejects a commissioned article, it will pay a 25% kill fee. For photographers, payment is made within 30 days of publication. Contributors receive three copies of the magazine.

ISLANDS PUBLISHING COMPANY, 3886 STATE STREET, SANTA BARBARA, CA 93105 (805) 682-7177

KIWANIS

A MAGAZINE FOR COMMUNITY LEADERS

A WRITER'S GUIDE TO KIWANIS MAGAZINE

KIWANIS magazine is a fifty-two-page monthly publication, except for combined June-July and November-December issues. It is distributed to the 290,000 members of Kiwanis International in North America, as well as to clubs in more than seventy other overseas nations. Although KIWANIS is the official publication of this men's service organization and is responsible for reporting organizational news, each issue also includes from five to seven feature articles geared to the interests of Kiwanians and their families.

Kiwanis club members are business and professional men who are actively involved in community service. To help you identify the audience to which you are writing, here are some statistics on KIWANIS magazine readers:

- Median age -- 55

- Median household income -- $44,900

- Manager/administrator -- 49%
  Business owner -- 18%
  Professional -- 14%

- Median size of company/business -- 32 employees

- Graduated high school -- 97%
  Attended/graduated college -- 84%

- Married -- 88%

- Own a home -- 94%
  Market value of home -- $98,000

Kiwanians are interested in a variety of subjects, and, hence, free-lance written manuscripts submitted to KIWANIS may deal with almost any topic of interest to an intelligent male audience. Editorial need is primarily for articles on current business, social, humanitarian, youth, self-improvement, and community-related topics. Other subjects of continuing appeal include international issues, health and fitness, family relations, leisure-time use and recreation, travel, sports, consumer trends, education, and transportation.

The magazine has a special need for articles on business and professional topics that will directly assist readers in their own businesses and careers.

Some of KIWANIS magazine's recent titles have included: "Quality Circles: Reshaping Business," "Unmasking Terrorism," "The Plight of the Homeless," "Dentistry's New Dynamics," "The Double Threat of Diabetes," "Looking Out for Latchkey Kids," "Urban Forests Take Root," and "How to Manage Time."

Articles published in KIWANIS are of two general types: serious and light nonfiction. (No fiction, poetry, filler items, jokes, or first-person accounts are used.) Manuscripts should be between 2,000 and 3,000 words in length (eight to twelve pages, typed double-spaced). Payment is on acceptance, ranging from $400 to $1,000 depending on current editorial need, depth of treatment, appeal to the magazine's readership, and other factors. Queries are preferred to manuscript submissions.

-2-

Proposed articles are tested against two major criteria: They should (1) be about an overall subject rather than an individual person, place, organization, or event, and (2) have applicability in the lives and concerns of KIWANIS magazine's readership.

In addition, an article, when feasible, should be international in scope, providing information from various world regions. Writers should be aware that KIWANIS is not an exclusively US magazine--it has readers in Canada, Europe, Central and South America, Australia, Africa, and Asia as well. Terms such as "our nation" and "our president" must be avoided. Articles on global topics, particularly if they have a strong bearing on current US developments, could be ideally suited for KIWANIS.

In all manuscripts, a writer's treatment of a subject must be objective and in depth, and each major point should be substantiated by illustrative examples and quotes from persons involved in the subject or qualified to speak on it. The question "why?" should be as important as "what?" and perceptive analysis and balanced treatment are valued highly. Serious articles should not contain intrusions of the writer's views. Writing style should not be pedantic but rather smooth, personable, and to the point, with anecdotes, description, and human detail where appropriate.

Treatment of light subjects must be as authoritative as serious topics, but humorous examples and comparisons and a lighter writing style are valued where needed.

An article's lead must be <u>strong</u>, drawing the reader's attention and setting the tone of the piece. It should be followed by a clear statement of the article's central point: The reader should quickly know what he is going to read about and why.

Manuscripts also should contain pertinent background and historic information, as well as a balanced presentation of issues. Firsthand interviews as well as research of published sources are essential. All information should be the most current available on the subject. And the article's conclusion should summarize the consequences of what has been said.

Writers should keep in mind a crucial point: If you do not find what you are writing to be interesting, neither will the reader. Strive to present new concepts and valuable information with a creative writing style.

Photos are not essential, but they are desirable when they are of high quality and add substantially to the impact of the text. Black-and-white photos should be 8-by-10-inch glossy prints; color transparencies are used but less often. All photos should be captioned and are purchased as part of the manuscript package.

Chuck Jonak
Executive Editor
KIWANIS Magazine
3636 Woodview Trace
Indianapolis, Indiana 46268
(317) 875-8755

Three Park Avenue   New York City 10016   Telephone 212 340 9200

Thank you for your letter of inquiry with regard to editorial guidelines for Ladies' Home Journal.

In order not to restrict the originality and creative content of our material, the Journal has no set guidelines. However, if you want to write for LHJ, the best advice we can give you is to do a little research on your own. Read the Journal from cover to cover. In this manner you will become familiar with its editorial content and at the same time be able to tailor your work to meet its needs.

A few helpful hints:

- Read back issues.

- It is requested that you submit queries rather than full-length manuscripts. Keep your query to a minumum, one to two pages at most, citing the lead, how you will document, research and develop your story. Please be specific.

- If you have been published before, include a few samples of your writing style, list of credits and a resume.

- Fiction must be submitted through an agent, but otherwise an agent is optional. Unproven writers may be asked to write on speculation (in which case there is no fee if an article is unacceptable). Payment, length, and deadlines will be discussed on assignment and the writer is paid on acceptance.

- Average story length is 3,000 words.

- Submissions for "A Woman Today" should be approximately 1,500 words and should be written in the first person, and typed double-space. These must be true-life stories. Enclose a stamped, self-addressed envelope and mail to Box WT, Ladies' Home Journal. Response may take as long as three months.

- Remember, that we have at least a three-month lead time, and seasonal material is uaually assigned four or five months in advance.

- Always enclose a stamped, self-addressed envelope. We are not responsible for unsolicited material.

In closing, the Journal welcomes your story ideas and gives careful individual attention to each and every one.

Thank you for your interest.

                              Sincerely,

                              THE EDITORS

Downey
Communications,
Inc.

1732 Wisconsin Ave., N.W.
Washington, D.C.
20007

Telephone
(202)
944-4000

The Military Lifestyle Magazine

EDITORIAL GUIDELINES

(revised 10/83)

LADYCOM is a privately-owned magazine published ten times a year (June/July
and November/December issues are combined) for wives of American servicemen.
Appearing in two editions -- United States and Overseas -- LADYCOM includes
in-depth articles of interest to members of the military domestic community.
About 80 percent of the articles in LADYCOM are written by freelancers. The
balance is staff-produced.

The editor is interested in purchasing well-researched articles on parenting;
travel to military locales; analyses of benefits, military lifestyle situations,
and family finances; health and beauty care; and consumer awareness. It's
essential that these subjects have a military angle. Straight general interest
articles will be discouraged.

LADYCOM publishes short stories (fiction) about personal aspects of military
life about four times per year. Payment for fiction runs from $100 to $200.

Many of LADYCOM's contributors are military wives or service members. Many
have an intimate knowledge of military life and are able to write from the
special point of view we seek for LADYCOM. However, a number of freelancers
without military backgrounds have done fine work for LADYCOM, and the editor
is always interested in thoughtful queries from freelancers willing to go the
extra distance to tailor their material to our audience. Payment ranges from
$50 for light, humorous essays to $500 for in-depth, complex articles about
military life.

Freelancers interested in contributing to LADYCOM should submit a clear,
specific outline on a topic that would be of interest to military wives aged
20-40. Subject, sources, expected length of article, types of interviews,
and angle should be clearly explained in written queries. First-time writers
submit articles on speculation; after an article has been accepted, the editor
will negotiate a fee with a writer before another article is assigned. Payment
is rendered at the time of publication, although payment will be made earlier if
the article has to be held for more than six months.

Article length is set by the editor at the time the assignment is made. The
average length of articles in LADYCOM is about 1,500 words.

LADYCOM's lead time is about six months.

Address queries to: Hope M. Daniels, Editor, LADYCOM, 1732
Wisconsin Avenue, NW, Washington, DC 20007. No phone queries.

Downey
Communications,
Inc.

1732 Wisconsin Ave., N.W.
Washington, D.C.
20007

Telephone
(202)
944-4000

ladycom

The Military Lifestyle Magazine

GUIDELINES FOR MANUSCRIPT PREPARATION

Style.   Ladycom follows the Associated Press Stylebook and Libel Manual. Please follow it carefully, especially with regard to use of numerals, hyphenation, capitalization and trademark terms.

Attribution. Ladycom editorial policy prefers that individuals be fully identified by first and last name, title (if a professional where title is relevant), and city and state where they reside. It is particularly important that military members be correctly identified with regard to rank and duty title. It should be clear at all times to whom ideas and direct quotes are being attributed, and the person to whom they are attributed should be fully identified.

Exceptions to this are occasional extensions of anonymity to persons divulging important but somewhat controversial and sensitive ideas, and who do not wish to be publicly associated with the thought. Ladycom offers this anonymity to persons on a very selective basis. Any writer undertaking an article where such requests are likely should discuss their resolution with the editor prior to conducting interviews.

Where anonymity has been used, the attribution should attempt to give an idea of the individual's role or status in relation to the idea expressed, for example:

"a squadron commander's wife"

"an Air Force retiree with extensive experience in human resource management"

"a former wives' club president who resigned under pressure from a club at a base in the South"

Age, Appearance, Rank. Ladycom makes as few references to age, race, appearance and rank or rate as possible, except when such references are essential to the telling of a story. However, when rank is omitted, the writer is expected to give a complete description of the servicemember's job responsibilities, including duty title.

MANUSCRIPT GUIDELINES
Page 2

Spelling. Writers who contribute to Ladycom are expected
to double-check the spelling of proper names, geographical
names and military acronyms. Ask the person you are interviewing
to spell first and last names, no matter how common or easy the
name sounds. There really are a lot of ways to spell John Smith!
With contributions coming to us from all over the world, it's
impossible, in many cases, for us to check these spellings ourselves.

Length. If Ladycom has specified a word length, please
make the manuscript come as close to that length as possible.
A manuscript submitted to us that is excessively long will be
returned to the author for cutting.

Editing. Editing of manuscripts consists of fine-tuning
and, when necessary, condensing and reorganizing. Rewriting
by our staff is rarely necessary and is done only when time
constraints prevent returning the article to the author
for revision or when the writer is clearly unable to re-attack
the article.

Relations with sources and facilitators. Public Affairs
offices at military installations will help you arrange
interviews with active-duty personnel. In very few cases
can active-duty persons speak with a writer without clearance
from Public Affairs. This is just a formality, however, and
Ladycom asks writers to touch base with Public Affairs as a
matter of courtesy.

We also permit writers to review quotes obtained in
interviews with the person interviewed. This makes people
more comfortable and eliminates errors in fact and context.
However, it is against Ladycom policy for contributors to
submit entire articles for review by anyone outside the
magazine, including sources, public affairs personnel and
others. Occasionally, however, such a requirement will be
asked of the writer before the interview will be granted.
Should this happen, please contact Hope M. Daniels at Ladycom
and she will handle this. It's been our experience, however,
that permitting an interviewee to review his or her quotes
will suffice.

It's not necessary to contact Public Affairs if you are
interviewing family members unless they are connected with
an installation function about which you are writing.

When in doubt about whether to contact Public Affairs,
contact them. It fosters good relations.

Purchase of Rights. Ladycom buys first North American
serial rights for its articles. Contributors are free to
resell their articles after publication, but not before.

Ladycom often receives requests from various groups,
asking for permission to copy and distribute an article.

MANUSCRIPT GUIDELINES
Page 3

We give permission routinely if the reprint will be used for educational or nonprofit purposes. However, if the request is for use which could mean a resale for the writer, we attempt to get a fee for the writer and notify the writer of the other publication's interest in his or her article. Usually, we are able to help with the resale.

Expenses. Documented expenses for telephone calls, car mileage and some other expenses are reimbursable. Before running up any expenses, however, writers should have a firm assignment and a discussion with the editor as to precisely which expenses are allowable on that article. Persons writing on spec should not expect to be reimbursed for expenses connected with the article unless the article is purchased, at which time they should submit records of their expenses.

Copies. Each contributor to Ladycom will receive two copies of the issue in which their article appears. Additional copies may be purchased for the cost of postage. Send $1 per copy when you order extras.

23 West 26th Street, New York, N.Y. 10010 • (212) 689-3933

Thank you for your query.

We are always interested in reviewing an author's manuscript with the understanding that the manuscript is submitted on speculation and, if accepted, is paid for upon publication.

Our rates are: $75.00 for short articles; $125.00 for longer articles; and $10.00 for each photo used.

Longer articles submitted for consideration should run from 2000-2500 words, preferably written in a warm, informal but well-informed style. Appropriate subjects include "how-to" crafts and hobbies; knitted and crocheted projects; sewing; saving and/or making money at home; child care; health; antiques; nostalgia and losing weight. We are especially looking for inspirational accounts of people overcoming hardships, and individuals or non-profit organizations that are doing charitable or volunteer work of importance to their communities. We publish fiction but seldom publish poetry. When applicable, clear black and white glossy photographs should accompany material submitted.

One-page articles typically run between 600-1000 words, and often deal with nostalgic topics, such as a favorite old baking dish, a farewell to a former home. We also accept some shorter pieces on food topics, e.g., a collection of zucchini recipes for summer's end.

The best way to arrive at an idea of our style and content is to ob- tain the last three issues and read them cover to cover.

We regret that we cannot supply sample copies unless you send us $1.75 plus $1.00 for postage and handling.

Unsolicited manuscripts and photographs will be returned only when accompanied by a self-addressed, stamped envelope.

Thank you for you interest in LADY'S CIRCLE!

                                        THE EDITORS

444 North Larchmont Boulevard • Box 74908 • Los Angeles, California 90004 • Telephone (213) 469-3901

Let's LIVE® MAGAZINE

GUIDELINES FOR CONTRIBUTORS

ARTICLE LENGTH: 1,000 words (minimum) to 2,500 words (maximum). We will accept 750-word "My Story" or thoughtful "The Last Word" features if exceptionally well crafted.

SUBJECT MATTER: Let's LIVE pays from $50 (My Story) to $250 for articles by qualified professionals (M.D.s, Ph.D.s, or equivalent) in preventive medicine, nutrition, or other sciences devoted to good health (of both mind and body), physical conditioning and proper diet. We will consider similar articles by non-professionals if thoroughly researched and accurately documented, or if developed around Q & A interviews with recognized and/or highly accredited doctors or authorities in the field.

Whenever possible, articles should be accompanied by photos. These may be of the person interviewed or of the individual or subject written about, or of all three. We prefer color slides or negatives, but will accept sharp, well-composed B&W and/or color prints, (preferably 4X5 to 8X10) along with explanatory captions. Payment: B&W....$17.50 each, or $35 total for three or more; Color....$35 each, or $85 total for three or more. We pay only for pictures published. Pictures are returned upon request.

We prefer a query letter and brief outline of the story idea prior to consideration of any article, but will accept a finished manuscript for consideration without obligation if accompanied by a stamped, self-addressed envelope. If acceptable for publication in Let's LIVE, articles will either be commissioned in writing (contingent on the publisher's approval of the manuscript) or author will be notified of the manuscript's acceptance at a quoted rate of payment. (Payment for articles and photos are made on publication; rates vary and are not based on cents-per-word, but on quality, length and subject matter) Generally, replies to queries are made in 4 to 6 weeks; articles not accepted for publication are returned in 2 to 3 weeks.

POLICY NOTE: It is the policy of Let's LIVE that NO brand names be mentioned in any article.

DEADLINE: 10 weeks prior to cover date (generally, magazines are on sale 10 days to 2 weeks in advance thereof) For example: The July issue goes on sale around June 18; copy should be received no later than April 20.

MECHANICAL REQUIREMENTS: Double-spaced text; set off subheads four spaces; leave 1 3/4" lefthand margin, 1 1/2" bottom margin; allow at least two inches above and below title; number pages in upper right-hand corner. Be sure to type name, address and telephone number in single-spaced block at upper left-hand corner. Please avoid using erasable paper - it smudges.

THE LION welcomes freelance contributions in two categories: 1. General interest articles which reflect the humanitarian, community betterment and self-improvement philosophy of Lions International. 2. Articles and photo features about impressive and unusual Lions Club community service projects.

Because ours is an international magazine, read by over half a million Lions Club members, submitted material should not be of purely local or national interest, but must have general appeal to warrant international readership.

All material is given careful and hopeful study, and reports are made (except in unusual circumstances) within one week. Advance queries on feature articles save your time and ours. Article length not over 2,000 words, subject to editing and payable on acceptance. Photos, 5 x 7 glossies or larger. No fillers, gags, quizzes or poems. Material must be accompanied by self-addressed, postage-paid return envelopes. Address all submissions to

Senior Editor

THE LION MAGAZINE

300 22nd Street   **Oak Brook, Illinois 60570**

THE
MAGAZINE
OF
SOUTHERN CALIFORNIA

LosAngeles

Thank you for your interest in Los Angeles Magazine. The
primary editorial role of the magazine is that of a sophisticated, authoritative guide to getting the most out of life
in the Los Angeles area. Our editorial content deals with
subjects of special local importance in Southern California,
with an emphasis on people, places, events, trends, local
problems and issues, pleasures and lifestyles. The magazine
also comments on provocative new ideas shaping or affecting
the readers' environment; and explores the wide spectrum of
options and opportunities available in the vast, diverse and
sometimes bewildering Southern California area.

The articles we publish reach an audience of 162,000
that is made up of college-educated, upper-middle-class men
and women between the ages of 25 and 55. Our average reader
age is approximately 40, with an average income of $50,000 to
$60,000.

Articles are assigned only on the basis of written proposals.
Either query letters or completed manuscripts may be submitted,
and both should be accompanied by a self-addressed-stamped
envelope. Departments are approximately 1500 words long and
payment, on acceptance, will be $300; rates for longer feature
stories vary according to subject matter and length. There is
a 30% kill fee for accepted articles that do not get published.
All story suggestions should be mailed to Lew Harris, Executive
Editor. Allow up to three weeks for a reply. If possible,
writers should include recent clips and/or biographical information. Los Angeles Magazine purchases First North American
Rights.

It is only fair to say that Los Angeles Magazine accepts only
a small percentage of the suggestions it receives. However,
you can be sure that anything you submit will receive close
attention.

1888 CENTURY PARK EAST · SUITE 920 · LOS ANGELES, CALIFORNIA 90067

TELEPHONE AREA 213 · ADVERTISING 557-7553 · BUSINESS 557-7592 · CIRCULATION 557-7551 · EDITORIAL 557-7569 · EXECUTIVE 557-7592 · PRODUCTION 557-7594

MADEMOISELLE 350 madison avenue new york ny 10017 212-880-8800

WRITING FOR MADEMOISELLE

We look for quality fiction and non-fiction. Subject matter must
be of interest to women 18 to 25 years old. No topic is taboo--we
welcome articles and stories on controversial subjects, so long as
the handling is tasteful. Personal reminiscences and humorous
pieces are also welcome.

Fiction should be approximately 2,000 to 2,500 words long; articles
run from 1,000 to 2,500 words.

A prospective writer should start by submitting either an outline or
a proposal for an article. Authors with whose work we are unfamiliar
should send tearsheets of previous writings (preferably published).
Occasionally we consider articles that have been submitted on speculation, but the great majority of the material we publish is written
on assignment.

We no longer publish poetry in MADEMOISELLE.

Address all articles/non-fiction to: Articles Editor (at the above address).
Address all fiction to: Fiction Editor (at the above address).
Please include a self-addressed, stamped envelope with the submission.

We appreciate your interest in MADEMOISELLE and hope we've been helpful.

the condé nast publications inc

Writer's Guidelines for Submitting Manuscripts to *Mature Living*

Mature Living, a leisure reading magazine, is designed for senior adults 60 and older and works 12-15 months ahead. We're looking for unique, creative manuscripts that are characterized by human interest and Christian warmth. Write with simplicity and clarity. Give evidence of research.

Mature Living prefers to purchase all rights (with some exceptions). Due to copyright laws, the Baptist Sunday School Board requires a signed contract for the purchase of all manuscripts except those for which pay is less than $25 and/or items which will be used only once.

Mature Living claims the editorial privilege of editing, abridging, and condensing as needed. Purchase of a manuscript is an intent, but not necessarily a promise, to publish. The editors further retain the right to illustrate manuscripts as they deem appropriate.

Here are some of the types of manuscripts we're interested in:

General
These articles may deal with a variety of subjects related to senior adult life, such as: contemporary interests and issues, problems and adjustments of aging, how-to hobbies and crafts, and other topics of special concern or interest. Preferred length is either 450 or 925 words. In a few instances, 1550 words is acceptable for exceptional copy.

Nostalgia
Each issue includes an "I Remember When . . ." feature. It should recall a past experience/event that most readers can identify with. It should have uniqueness and highlight some value or truth. It may include humor. If possible, include old photographs (see note on photos) for an illustration or as a basis for an artist's sketch. Preferred length is 925 words.

Travel
Travel articles should have general appeal that includes interesting information and descriptive experiences. Readers must be able to mentally picture the sequence and occasion being narrated. Quality black-and-white pictures or sharp color slides (no Polaroids) that illustrate the article should be included with descriptive cutlines. Preferred length is 750 words and 6 to 8 photos.

Fiction
High quality fiction, relating to senior adults, should strive for creativity, strong story line, underscore a truth, and provide enjoyable leisure reading. Place the word *fiction* at the top of the title page. Preferred length either 925 or 1550 words.

Profiles
Profiles should be 25 lines (42 typewritten characters per line) and recognize a senior adult for some accomplishment or highly interesting or unusual experience. A profile *must* include a quality, action black-and-white picture suitable for reproduction showing the person actively engaged in his activity (no Polaroids). Payment for a profile is $10 at the time of *acceptance,* and $15 for an original picture at the time of *publication.*

Cracker Barrel
Each issue includes a page of brief, humorous, original items. Payment is $5 for each item.

Grandparents' Brag Board
These accounts of something said or done by **your** grandchild or great-grandchild (preferably humorous, or showing unusual insight) must be brief, accurate, and original. Payment is $5 each.

Poetry
Mature Living accepts a limited amount of quality poetry that has a direct relationship and interest to seniors. Payment is $5 to $20.

Information About Submitting a Manuscript
- **Enclose a self-addressed, stamped envelope if you want your manuscript returned; otherwise; it will be discarded.**
- Don't send previously published manuscripts or simultaneous submissions.
- Keep a duplicate copy for your files. Allow 8 weeks for a reply from the editors.
- Don't ask what issue an accepted manuscript will appear in. This isn't determined until the late stages of publication.
- Don't query about a manuscript you're working on; send the manuscript. Limit each mailing to two manuscripts.
- Writers will receive, without cost, 3 advance copies of an issue in which their manuscripts are published. Extra copies should be ordered from Materials Services Department, 127 Ninth Avenue, North, Nashville, TN 37234.
- *Mature Living* cannot accept responsibility for photos and slides that may be lost in one of the processes of publication. If pictures are old and rare, sender may have them reproduced locally, and send copies. If the manuscript and pictures are accepted, Art Services Department will reimburse cost of reproducing pictures if an invoice is enclosed.

Specification
- Set your typewriter margins on 20 and 62 (42 characters a line) and type within that line. Double space on regular (not erasable) white bond paper.
- **Put your name (as you want it to appear in print), address, and Social Security number on the first page and your name on every page.**
- Correct all spelling, document unique material, and rewrite to conform with preferred lengths.

Payment
The rate of payment set by the Baptist Sunday School Board is 4¢ per word for all rights, (15 percent less for first rights) for the part of any manuscript accepted for publication. Checks are issued once each month. It may be 60 days after acceptance of a manuscript before payment is received. Use of original pictures, negatives, and slides is paid for by Art Services Department *at the time of publication.* Payment will vary with size, type, and use. Pictures will be retained in editorial files until the issue in which they appear has been released.

The Editors, *Mature Living*
127 Ninth Avenue, North, MSN 140
Nashville, TN 37234

McCall's

WRITER'S GUIDELINES

Thank you for your inquiry. All manuscripts are submitted on speculation at the author's risk. We cannot accept responsibility for unsolicited manuscripts. They should be typewritten, double-spaced and accompanied by a stamped, self-addressed envelope of sufficient size to contain the manuscript. Manuscripts are usually read and processed in 6-8 weeks. Study recent back issues carefully before submitting. Articles dealing with food, fashion, beauty, home decorating & appliances are staff-produced. McCall's purchases material in the following categories:

FICTION
Requirements for short stories include well-developed characters and valid, well-motivated plots. Love stories, family relationships and humor geared toward young adults are preferred. We generally publish stories with con-temporary American settings. Stories that are grim, depressing, fragmentary, concerned with themes of abnormality or violence are not solicited. The average length is approximately 3,000 words; however, we are also looking for short-shorts up to 2,000 words. All manuscripts should be addressed to Helen DelMonte, Fiction Editor.

ARTICLES
McCall's is in the market for human interest narratives, personal essays and humor pieces--1,000 to 3,000 words in length. With the exception of humor pieces, editors should be queried for interest. We are also interested in seasonal stories--new ways of looking at holidays. Keep in mind that Christmas comes in July at McCall's; send ideas well in advance. Specifically, the sections listed below frequently use material from free-lancers:

> THE MOTHER'S PAGE (edited by Maryann Brinley) These are short items that may be humorous, helpful, inspiring, reassuring--an excellent outlet for mothers to relate their experiences. Pays $100 and up.
> VITAL SIGNS (edited by Judith Stone) This monthly section consists of short items on health and medical news. "'Vital Signs' pieces are, in some ways, like kids: they're short and demanding," says editor Judith Stone. Pay varies.
> BACK TALK ——————————————————— On the last page of every issue we publish a 1000-word essay in which the writer makes a firm statement of opinion, often taking an unexpected or unpopular point of view. Whether humorous or serious in tone, the piece must reflect the writer's strong feelings on the subject. Pays $1,000.
> VIP-ZIP ——————————————————— This high-demography regional section provides an excellent opportunity to break into the magazine. Largely service-oriented, it covers travel, decorating and home entertainment. The editors are also interested in short essays (humorous or serious) and in profiles for the Singular Woman feature. The woman spotlighted here has accomplished something not expected of her and is someone our readers can admire. Pay varies.

230 Park Avenue, New York, N.Y. 10169

MD MAGAZINE

Thirty East Sixtieth Street, New York, N.Y. 10022
telephone 212/355-5432

A.J. VOGL
Editor

Writer's Guidelines

MD is a cultural magazine. Our purpose is to enrich the personal and professional lives of its readers -- 160,000 physicians in private practice. To accomplish this end, MD publishes articles and departments that range over a broad spectrum of subjects -- among them, medicine, science, the fine arts, literature, history, biography, music, sports, travel, entertainment, and social issues.

The typical MD reader is a male physician about 45 years old, intelligent without necessarily being intellectual, with higher-than-average income and a taste for the finer things of life. Often our reader's specialized education has forced him to bypass "culture" during college and medical school. Although our typical reader is male, some 12% of our readers are female physicians, and many doctors' wives are keen readers of MD, too. So keep women in mind when writing for MD.

Our target reader is by no means a sitting duck. He may receive as many as 50 medical magazines every month. We must compete with every one of them to get the doctor to pick up MD and read it.

For this reason, you must use every journalistic device in your arsenal to interest him in your article -- an arresting angle, a snappy lead, boxes and sidebars, etc. Most important of all, your article should have a sharp focus. We don't like articles that are conceptually frail or try to cover too much ground.

Every article proposal should be submitted to us with a title. It may be a working title, but for an article proposal it should work for you. If it doesn't sell us, you'll never have the chance to sell the reader. Some examples of MD titles may give you an idea of what we're looking for. The subjects of the articles have nothing in common, but we believe that their titles do -- the ability to stop a busy reader and get him to look at a blurb or photo -- and then to start reading.

If Renoir Had Worn Glasses (about whether and how visual problems can explain a painter's work)

A World Without America (about one of the world's oldest surviving globes)

The 6 Most Underrated Artists in the U.S.

The Last of the Gentleman Crooks

What Singers Other Singers Admire Most

Urban Scrawl (about graffiti)

A Vacation Like No Other on this Earth (about ballooning in France).

Whenever possible, interview primary sources and quote them by name. Writing from secondary sources usually shows in the finished product. The reader should feel you're comfortable with the subject. The tone of your article should be authoritative but not academic. When dealing with a subject that doesn't have a natural cultural context (e.g. sports) be sure to establish one. Most of our articles are written in the third person. We don't rule out the first-person approach, but it should be used only for the best of reasons -- that it enables you to tell your story better.

Above all, ask yourself: Why should MD publish your article now? You believe it's a good story. How do we convince the reader of that? Ask yourself: Is yours the most interesting and manageable angle? Does it tell the reader what he wants to know? Does it provide him with a reason to read the article?

The Essentials

All article ideas should be queried first. Do not send unsolicited manuscripts. SASE required.

We do not customarily assign travel articles. If you choose to write a travel piece for us on spec, it is also best to query first -- to make sure we haven't recently published one on your subject, or haven't a similar article in inventory.

Sample copies are available for $1. You can get a good idea of MD and its approach to culture from a close reading of the magazine.

Length: Department installments run 1,200 to 1,500 words, feature articles from 2,500 to 3,000 words.

Rates: Our rates range from $250 to $700. Payment for a specific feature or department installment varies according to length, subject matter, and how much work is required.

Payment is upon acceptance. In practice, allow 30 days for payment. We do not usually pay expenses beyond the usual phone calls, carfare, etc. required to research an article. You must submit receipts to be reimbursed. If you have any questions about whether an expense is justified or reimbursable, query the editor before making the expenditures.

Rights: We buy first North American rights. We reserve the right to reprint the article in other MD publications. In this event, you will receive one-half the fee you received for the MD article. Also, if the article is reprinted elsewhere, we will pay you half of any monies we receive from the article's republication. Our kill fee is one-third the negotiated fee.

Manuscripts should be typed and double spaced. With your article submit your social security number and a brief biographical sketch that we can draw upon for an author's blurb.

GUIDE TO AUTHORS

Medical Times is a monthly clinical journal that goes to over 100,000 primary care physicians in office practice throughout the country—that is, family physicians, general practitioners, internists, and osteopathic physicians. Articles should be geared to this audience. The editors are interested in review-type articles that have practical, everyday clinical application, not in research activity and findings which are not yet applicable in the office or at the bedside. Articles should be original and unpublished. All articles are subject to a standard peer review process. Authors will be notified of any major recommended revisions, but routine editorial changes will be made to conform to *Medical Times* style. Galleys will be sent to the author prior to publication.

Manuscripts and all accompanying material should be sent to Susan Carr Jenkins, Executive Editor, *Medical Times,* 80 Shore Road, Port Washington, New York 11050.

Specifications

1. Length should be about eight to ten typewritten pages on 8½ × 11 inch paper, double spaced, 1½ inch margins, in triplicate. Subheads should be inserted at reasonable intervals.

2. Please prepare a section of Key Points to precede the article which highlights the 3 or 4 most significant points presented in the paper. This should be limited to about 100 words

3. All abbreviations should be explained. In most cases, abbreviations should not be used, but spelled out.

4. Drugs—Both generic and trade names should be given. When there are three or more trade names for a particular drug, the generic name alone will suffice.

5. The title page should include the title, all authors' names and their primary affiliations, city, and state, plus an address for future correspondence and a phone number where the authors can be reached during normal business hours.

6. Photos and slides should be labeled "top" and numbered to correlate with legends which should be typed on a separate page. Tables also should appear on separate sheets, numbered and titled. We *must* have written permission if you wish to reproduce material (e.g., tables, charts, figures) from another journal. A credit line should be submitted for any photographs or artwork.

7. References should be limited to ten if possible and numbered consecutively as they appear in the text. The form used by *Index Medicus* should be used.

8. A black and white photo and a *curriculum vitae* for each author should accompany the manuscript.

The Detroit News

615 Lafayette Blvd./Detroit/Michigan 48231

Dear Letter Writer:

Here are a few guidelines for stories for MICHIGAN magazine:

-- All stories (with the possible exception of fiction) must
   have some sort of Michigan angle or connection (even if it's
   a somewhat tenuous one). Subject matter may vary, but we're
   looking for things with broad appeal for the cover, in
   particular.

-- Cover stories tend to run 2,500 to 3,000 words; secondary
   stories, 2,000 to 2,500. That's flexible, of course.
   Cover stories pay $500 to $650; secondary stories, $250 to
   $450.

-- We'll consider any art submitted with a story. We prefer
   color slides or 4-by-5 transparencies. We pay $150 per
   color page, $350 for covers. If a story doesn't come with
   art, we'll arrange for it ourselves.

-- We're interested in fiction -- preferably by Michigan authors
   or set in the Midwest or Michigan itself.

That's about it. If you have more specific questions, you're
welcome to call (222-2620).

Sincerely,

Cynthia Boal-Janssens
Editor, MICHIGAN magazine

/pb

THE ATRIUM, SUITE 205
277 SOUTH WASHINGTON STREET
ALEXANDRIA, VIRGINIA 22314 (703) 548-6177

GUIDELINES FOR PHOTOGRAPHERS, ILLUSTRATORS, AND WRITERS:

* Queries are recommended at first, rather than sending a completed manuscript or photo/art file. Also, please be patient: We have a small staff, and a large number of interested freelance writers, illustrators and photographers.

* All material should be typewritten, double-spaced on 8x11 white paper. Please include your name, address, phone number(s) and Social Security number.

* It is understood that all material is submitted on a "speculation only" basis. The magazine accepts no responsibility for unsolicited photographs, illustrations, or stories -- all of which must be accompanied by stamped, self-addressed envelopes if their return is expected.

* If accepted, payment is on actual publication. The following rates are based on the assumption we are purchasing only first rights or one-time use rights:
        Photos, Illustrations: $50 for each full photograph or illustration (whether in black and white or in color); $40 for less than full-page; $35 for 1/6-page or smaller. Covers: up to $300 if assigned; less if "found" in submitted material. Expenses for assigned photography are paid on a case-by-case basis.
        Stories: $3.50 per column inch for printed material, minimum.

* A word about what we're looking to buy: Quite simply, the best words and art about the Mid-Atlantic region. The range of subjects is wide: From outdoor sports to history, from arts and crafts to real estate, from human interest stories to light photo essays, from food to interior design. The material must be focused on some part (or all) of the Mid-Atlantic region -- Delaware, District of Columbia, Maryland, New Jersey, North Carolina, Pennsylvania, Virginia, West Virginia. The material MUST have a local or regional angle. Articles and art that include Mid-Atlantic people are preferred. Thanks for your interest in Mid-Atlantic Country.

Jim Scott
Editor
July 1986

MID-ATLANTIC LIVING AT ITS BEST

170 Fifth Avenue • New York, NY 10010 • Telephone (212) 989-8700 • Telex 424018 ROWECOM

Writer's Guidelines

Miniature Collector is published bimonthly for collectors and makers of dollhouses, dollhouse furnishings and dolls and other miniatures. We focus on, but are not limited to, pieces in the scale of one inch equals one foot. We publish profession-ally written articles that are illustrated with color or black-and-white photographs of high quality. Queries submitted with sample photographs (color transparencies or black-and-white glossy prints) will be given top consideration. Querying by tele-phone is not acceptable. Most first articles are written on speculation. Length ranges from 500 to 1,500 words, with most articles published being under 1,000 words.

Articles: profile, and examine the work of, artisans involved in the making of minia-tures; visit outstanding public and private collections; profile well-known collectors and celebrities who collect miniatures. We are especially interested in articles for our Projects & Plans section that detail do-it-yourself projects that can be accom-plished easily in the average workshop. Diagrams, illustrations and/or photographs should accompany instructions for such projects. Miniature Collector is a consumer magazine, and so we do not publish articles on retail shops or large businesses.

Our readers are knowledgeable in the field and so articles should not dwell on the difficulty of making little things, or the "cute" qualities inherent in the small. We are looking for detailed, and lively articles aimed at a specialized audience.

MC guidelines/page 2

Manuscripts and queries should be typed, double-spaced, on one side of the paper only and should be accompanied by a stamped, self-addressed envelope. We will respond within six to eight weeks and regret that we cannot offer individual comments on any submissions.

Rates for accepted material vary, but rarely exceed $200. Payment is made upon publication.

Writers are strongly advised to study an issue of <u>Miniature Collector</u> before submitting any material. Sample copies are available by request (one per writer) for $1.00.

# # # # #

A CBS MAGAZINE
One Park Avenue, New York, New York 10016

WRITERS' GUIDELINES

1. We are a consumer bridal publication. All articles must be of direct interest to the engaged or newly married couple.

2. Send query letter with a brief outline of areas to be covered or complete manuscript to: Mary Ann Cavlin, Managing Editor. Enclose a stamped self-addressed envelope for response or return of material.

3. If you are a published author, send two clips with your query.

4. Queries usually are answered within three weeks of receipt.

5. Article lengths range from short features, 500 to 800 words, to main features, 1500 to 2000 words.

6. Prefer typed, double-spaced manuscript or computer letter-quality print-out. Dot-matrix and multiple submissions not acceptable.

7. Assignments may be made on speculation or with a 20 percent kill fee provision depending on circumstances.

8. Purchase first periodical publishing rights. Payment on acceptance.

Editorial (212) 503-3888
Advertising (212) 503-3800

General Editorial, Photography and Art Requirements and Rates

For MODERN MATURITY

215 Long Beach Boulevard
Long Beach, CA   90801

We are in the market for material of interest to older readers
in these categories:

o   Human Interest (celebrities in education, science, art, etc.,
       as well as unknowns)
o   Practical information on living (health, personal, finances,
       housing, food, etc.)
o   Inspiration
o   Americana
o   Nostalgia
o   Fiction
o   Information and commentary on science and technology and their
       effects on life and living conditions, present and future
o   How-to and crafts
o   Short verse, humor, puzzles and tips

These pieces run from one to four pages of the magazine in length,
including pictures. Wordage: 500 to 2,500

— — — — — — — — — — — —

PICTURE REQUIREMENTS
       Black and white, 8 x 10
       Color - any size

— — — — — — — — — — — —

RATES OF PAYMENT
       Articles: $2,000 - 1,000 words Major
                           $1,000 -   500   "   Shorts
                           $ 750 -   350   "   Departments & Columns
                           $ 400 -   150   "   Short Shorts

       Puzzles: $ 150
       Cartoons: $ 100
       Verse: $ 35
       Tips and humor: $ 15
       Photography: $ 750 - Color - Front Cover Page
                           $ 600 - Color - Inside Cover Page

Color	Full Page	3/4 Page	1/2 Page	1/4 Page or less
	$ 500	$ 400	$ 250	$ 150
B/W	$ 300	$ 250	$ 150	$ 75

       Photographer Assignment: $300 a day - $150 for 1/2 day
                                 $100 a day for travel
       Illustration: $ 150 - $1,500

Money Maker

5705 N. Lincoln Ave. Chicago, IL 60659   312-275-3590

GUIDELINES FOR WRITERS

"Useful investment advice for unsophisticated investors" is the overriding editorial concept of MONEY MAKER.

This means that many of our readers are neophytes when it comes to investments and finance, and we aim to provide jargon-free investment analysis and advice regarding stocks, bonds, stock options, real estate, commodities, commodity options, IRAs, mutual funds, tax shelters, precious and strategic metals, coins, gems, collectibles and antiques, financial futures, penny stocks, REITs, new issues, foreign currencies, Treasury issues, bank CDs, and on and on - anything that is relevant to investing, especially as regards new or small investors.

However, the editorial concept of MONEY MAKER goes beyond specific investment advice. We also provide educational articles about the basics of investing, such as dealing effectively with a stockbroker, the mechanics of various investment markets, basic guidelines for sophisticated m-rket strategies, and the rudiments of market analysis. Our articles range from step-by-step instructions for investing in all areas, to highly sophisticated analyses of stock industry groups. In addition, we present interesting concepts to our readers, ranging from franchise opportunities to the consequences of tax reform to new markets and market strategies to profiles of successful investors. Most importantly, we go a step beyond all other financial publications when we strive to give our readers very practical advice - specific recommendations which they can put to use in their own investment portfolios.

If we feel a particular investment area has strong potential, we recommend specific investment vehicles, such as common stocks, which will help our readers profit from our analysis. If we feel an investment area is overvalued or weak, we warn our readers to avoid it. Our goal is to encourage our readers to invest wisely, and we attempt to provide the guidance that will allow a newcomer to proceed safely and profitably.

The typical MONEY MAKER reader is about 49 years old (although the age range is extremely wide, from early 20s through post-retirement). The male/female ratio is about 60/40; most readers are married and own their homes. Average household income is between $42,000 and $58,000; a majority of readers are college-educated. Although many have larger sums available for investment, we operate on the assumption that our readers have investible capital of $5000-$10,000.

MONEY MAKER is published six times a year on a bi-monthly schedule beginning with the December/January issue, plus an annual Investment Guide issue published as a market primer in January. Articles are scheduled and assigned according to topical interest, commonly three to six months prior to publication. Deadlines to writers are the first Friday of the month two months in advance of the publication date. Articles must be thoroughly researched, well-documented, and professionally written and completed under contract. Charts, tables, graphs and sidebars are frequently used and are expected from writers. Authors must be well-acquainted with the investment areas they discuss and should be prepared to render subjective and objective opinions about profit potential and risk.

Articles range in length from 1000 to 4000 words. First-time contributors submit manuscripts on speculation. Assigned articles are based on a comprehensive outline. Payment starts at $.20 per assigned word, paid on acceptance. Kill fees of 50% are paid for assigned articles that are not accepted.

A MINISTRY OF THE MOODY BIBLE INSTITUTE

GUIDELINES FOR WRITERS

OUR PURPOSE:

MOODY MONTHLY exists to encourage and equip Christians—men and women who have received God the Son, the Lord Jesus Christ, as their own Savior—to live biblically. That process involves focusing on God's Word for doctrine, reproof as needed, correction, and instruction in righteousness.

OUR READERS:

MOODY MONTHLY readership encompasses an estimated one million individuals each month (circulation 225,000) focused in the United States and Canada, but including missionaries and others worldwide. Seventy percent of our readers have some college education or its equivalent. Twenty-three percent are in the 25-34 age bracket; 28 percent are 35-49; 30 percent are 50-64; 16 percent are 65 or older; 76 percent are married.

OUR CONTENTS:

MOODY MONTHLY is a conservative evangelical monthly. It is neither a study magazine nor a journal. Rather, it's a popular, Bible-centered, family magazine reflecting diverse interest.

Seventy percent of the articles printed are assigned to qualified writers. The best opportunities for free-lance writers are the following departments:

First Person—This is our gospel tract, the only article written for non-Christians. A personal testimony written by the author (we will accept "as told to's"). The objective is to tell a person's testimony in such a way that the reader will understand the gospel and want to receive Christ as Savior. Length up to 1,000 words.

Essential Points:
1. Conflict.
   What kept this person from Christ?
2. Conversion. Must include:
   a. Christ's death for his/her sin.
   b. Repentance from sin.
   c. Faith in Christ alone for salvation.
   Include appropriate Scripture.
3. Change.
   How is this person a new creation in Christ? This must relate to the conflict that introduced the article. Show how Christ has resolved the conflict or is resolving the conflict.

Avoid testimonies of professional entertainers and athletes, public figures, and new Christians (received Christ less than two years ago).

News Feature—An expanded factual account of a current news event giving obvious evidence of thorough research. Journalistic in style; length up to 1,200 words.

Parenting—Provides practical guidance for parents solidly based on biblical principles. Target a specific need parents can relate to. In corporate scriptural truths and insights from recognized authorities on parenting. Draw from your own experience for illustrations. Length up to 1,500 words.

People—Shows a person's faith that works, faith in action. Write about one aspect of a person's life—employment, family, special interest, school, etc.—showing how he or she lives Christ in that environment and ministers to others. The person's actions must clearly result from personal faith in Christ. Avoid telling the reader everything about this person's background and testimony. Include significant background information that relates to the person's current walk with Christ. Use anecdotes. Quote the individual and those who know him or her. Above all, *show* the reader this person's faith that works. Don't *tell* the reader. Length up to 1,000 words. Avoid Christian workers, entertainers, athletes, public figures.

Non-departmental articles cover a broad range of topics. They must present a specific viewpoint. Length up to 2,000 words.

2101 WEST HOWARD STREET, CHICAGO, ILLINOIS 60645 | 312 274-2535

OUR PROCEDURE:

MOODY MONTHLY does not accept unsolicited manuscripts. Writers must first write a query letter and secure permission to forward their manuscripts. We frown on queries by telephone.

Query letters should reflect an understanding of MOODY MONTHLY's aim, slant, and viewpoint that can only be gained by studying a number of recent issues. In your letter, include:

> A working title to help editors grasp your idea quickly.
> A statement suggesting why your idea is significant.
> A brief outline, including summaries of anecdotes and biblical support.
> Suggested length.
> Availability of pictures.
> How soon you can get the manuscript to us.
> Your qualifications to write on the particular subject.
> Your writing experience.

Always include a self-addressed stamped envelope for our response. We cannot guarantee a response without an SASE.

POETRY AND FICTION:

A query is not required for poetry, but do not send more than three poems at one time. We do not use poems of prayer. We seldom use rhyming poetry. We prefer poems with two levels of meaning. The poem should offer fresh insights into biblical truth or Christian living.

Poems submitted without an SASE will not be returned.

We require a query for fiction. Manuscripts submitted without first securing permission from the managing editor will not be returned.

MANUSCRIPT FORMAT:

MOODY MONTHLY uses an optical character reader to scan articles into our computer system for editing. Follow these guidelines to ensure that your copy is readable to the scanner:

— Use 8½ by 11 paper.
— Use paper ranging in weight from 16 to 30 pounds.
— Type copy double-spaced with a carbon ribbon, or print copy using a Selectric or Daisy Wheel printer.
— The optical character reader "reads" the following type styles:
  Courier 10   Courier 12   Letter Gothic   Pica
  Elite   Prestige Elite   Prestige Pica
  If possible, use an electric typewriter with one of the above type styles.
— If you use correction fluid or correction tape, submit a good quality photocopy of the original.
— Allow at least ½ inch margins from the top, bottom, and sides of the page.
— Do not write on your manuscript.

Type the total number of words in the upper right corner. Return the writer information sheet sent in response to your query. Always include an SASE for the return of your manuscript should it not meet our needs.

PAYMENT:

On acceptance, we pay 10 cents a word for sharp, well-edited copy; less for articles that require heavy editing by the editors. We will pay more for brilliant copy—well-researched, significant, articulate. Payment for poetry ranges from $25 to $50.

MOODY MONTHLY buys first rights, meaning we purchase one-time-use rights. All rights return to the author once the article has been published. We seldom purchase reprint rights.

POLICY:

We examine all manuscripts on speculation. A positive response to a query does not guarantee purchase.

You grant MOODY MONTHLY the right to edit or abridge the manuscript for layout purposes and affirm that the article has not already appeared in print and that it has not been simultaneously submitted to other publications. You affirm that you are the sole and true author of the article.

ADDRESS:

Managing Editor
MOODY MONTHLY
2101 W. Howard St.
Chicago, IL 60645

THE MOTHER EARTH NEWS

Information for ~~Pen~~ Potential Contributors

UPDATED MARCH 1984

THE MOTHER EARTH NEWS® is a bimonthly magazine primarily slanted to the growing number of individuals who are interested in building a more rational and self-directed way of life for themselves. The publication places heavy emphasis on alternative lifestyles, ecology, working with nature, and doing more with less. Readership ages range from the very early teens to over 90, with a peak among dynamic, think-for-themselves young adults.

WE USE ARTICLES ON

- gardening
- small businesses
- unusual self-employment income enterprises
- ultra low-cost ($150 to $3,000) shelters
- attractive, energy-efficient dwellings
- alternative energy systems
- raising livestock
- workshop projects
- old-time and traditional crafts
- wholistic health
- wild foods
- down-home adventure and travel
- firsthand reports from "them that's doin'"
- recycling, environment, conservation
- food preparation and preservation
- home decorating
- small-town and urban self-sufficiency

WE DON'T USE

- fiction
- articles that complain about a problem without offering a solution
- articles about untested ideas

GET THE IDEA? We're interested in real life and real living. Not the cheap, prefab, prepackaged, plastic existence that most other magazines cover. And we NEVER preach. We NEVER tell anyone WHAT to do. We NEVER tell anyone to actually DO anything. We just say, "Hey, look. There are other ways of living than the old deadening 9-to-5 routine. Here they are. Do with them as you will."

WE USE ARTICLES that range from 200 to 3,000 words in length. Keep all submissions tight, informative, solid, factual, and—maybe—just a little light and easy to digest. NO PADDING ALLOWED! And *please*: no wife jokes and no hokey "my husband is all thumbs" humor. They belong to a vanishing age. MOTHER deals in integrity, honesty, dignity, concern for fellow passengers on Spaceship Earth, and here's-how-to-do-it facts.

GETTING IN TOUCH is easy. You may send your finished feature article manuscript—complete with photographs —directly to our Submissions Editor, or you may query that editor first *by letter*. (Telephone queries *cannot* be answered satisfactorily.) Your manuscript must stand on its own merits, however, whether you've sent it in "over the transom" or whether you've first written to ask us if we'd like to see your piece.

Your thorough knowledge of our publication can be a big timesaver. If you see that we've just run an article that covers the same territory you'd like to suggest, you'll know that we wouldn't be ready to treat that subject again immediately. Check our indexes, too, so you'll know what we've done on the topic in past issues.

After you've queried on a particular item and we've told you we'd like to take a look, please don't wait months or even years to send the manuscript for which you whetted our appetites with your glowing query letter. If we don't hear from you within eight weeks or so, we're pretty apt to figure that you aren't going to send the manuscript . . . and we'll turn our enthusiasm elsewhere.

ASSIGNMENTS and affirmative answers to queries are not one and the same thing. If we respond to your letter of inquiry by saying we'll consider your piece, the article will still be subject to careful scrutiny and must meet our needs and standards in order to be accepted. Assigned articles are generally those that we ourselves have initiated.

PHOTOS ARE IMPORTANT HERE. Good pictures may tip the balance when your article is being weighed for acceptance or rejection. Many of the ideas presented in our pages can be "shown" more clearly than "told," and one good illustration is often worth several paragraphs of complicated explanation.

Certain articles—for instance those on crafts, wild foods, gardening, and decorating—all but *demand* color photos. We like 35mm slides, but will look at other transparencies and (reluctantly) at color prints with negatives included.

For black-and-white pictures, we prefer 8 X 10 glossies, and we like to have you submit both the prints and the negatives.

Please send your photographs *with* the article they illustrate. Your slides are most easily handled when inserted in protective plastic transparency-holder pages. These have twelve 2-1/4-inch or twenty 35mm-size pockets on one page. If you have only a few transparencies to submit, you can cut the page in strips or in half.

We'd suggest that you keep duplicate copies of any photos that you send to us. If your manuscript is purchased, we will keep the photos until the article is published.

We also buy a few—but very few—pictures (with captions included) to supplement our stock photo files. Payment for these begins at $25.

WE PAY (upon acceptance) a flat rate for a complete manuscript/photo package. Our basic rule of thumb is $100 for the amount we'd use on one page of the magazine. That means we start at $20 for the real shorties and at $100 for the average general article. We go up to $600 for some feature pieces.

We buy all rights. However, after publication of our edited version, the rights to your original material may be reassigned to you. Then you may resell the unedited version as many times as you like.

COLUMNS AND DEPARTMENTS

● *PROFILES* uses pieces from 250 to 500 words detailing the accomplishments of interesting people (known and unknown) involved in any field regularly covered by the magazine. A sharp, glossy, black-and-white action photo of the person should be included. Address material for this department to Profiles Editor. Payment for accepted material is $50 for the report/photo package.

● *BARTERS & BOOTSTRAPS: Barters* features unusual, beneficial exchanges of skills, labor, and other commodities. Each short report (of an actual barter transaction) that's good enough to print brings the writer a one-year subscription in exchange.

Bootstraps describes successful home or small businesses that were inspired by articles in the magazine itself. Tell us the why, when, and where of your business, and how much "seed money" it took to start the venture. If yours is one that's chosen for publication, your payment will be a two-year subscription to THE MOTHER EARTH NEWS®. Address your reports for these subjects to Barters & Bootstraps Editor.

● *FIELDBOOK* presents poems appropriate to MOTHER. Please take the time to look over what we've published in this section. If you can't honestly say you can equal or better that body of work, don't send us anything. Furthermore, all unsolicited submissions should be sent *without* self-addressed, stamped envelopes and should be addressed specifically to Fieldbook. We won't return or comment on unused poems: Only those accepted for publication will be acknowledged.

● *MOM'S MARKETPLACE* tells about products of interest to MOTHER's readers. If you have information on an item you think our readers should know about, send it to New Products Editor.

● *ACCESS* provides names and addresses that will help in the search for information on self-sufficiency and living the good life. Suggestions for this page— which typically include books, reports, pamphlets, records, or almost any *other* form of available information—are invited, and you should address them to Access Editor.

HERE'S HOW TO SUBMIT YOUR WORK

● All manuscripts should be double-spaced, typed with a black ribbon on white 8-1/2 X 11 paper.

● Your name, address, phone number, and social security number should be noted on the upper left corner of the first page of each manuscript.

● Put your name on each item you send us . . . including *all* of the photos, etc. accompanying your article.

● Manuscripts that are mailed flat are not opened by machine and are therefore less apt to be damaged in transit.

● Please enclose a bibliography of the written material you've used for reference in preparing your article.

● Seasonal material should be submitted at least six months in advance.

● Include your telephone number on all correspondence about your manuscript.

WE'LL REPLY almost immediately to query letters. Completed manuscripts often take longer to evaluate because they're read by several staff members before a final decision is made. If we keep your work several weeks, you'll know that we're giving it serious consideration.

ADDRESS all queries and manuscripts—except specific column/department material already noted—to Submissions Editor. Enclose return postage. The mailing address for ALL editorial departments is:

The Mother Earth News®
105 Stoney Mountain Road
Hendersonville, NC 28791

Please retain this information for your files.

KB501

1663 MISSION STREET • SAN FRANCISCO, CA 94103
(415) 558-8881 • CABLE: MOTHER, SAN FRANCISCO, CA

INFORMATION FOR WRITERS

Queries: Before asking a writer to go ahead with a proposed story, we like to see an outline or query letter at least a page or two long. Besides sketching out what you intend to cover, the query should spell out clearly just how you plan to make the story lively and readable. Is the story news? Will you be writing about your own experiences? Basing your story on a profile or a person? Using extended dramatic scenes? How will you give the article narrative suspense? The lack of sensitivity to what's needed to make a reader read a story is the most common reason we turn down article ideas. No matter how worthy your topic, a query must answer the question: What here is going to make a reader not interested in this subject sit up and read?

Here are several other factors to keep in mind:

* Will the story be dated by the time it appears in print? We have a three-month lead time; in March, for example, we're already producing the June issue.

* Is the story too local? It should be broad enough in scope to hold the interest of a national audience.

* Have we carried a similar article within the last three years? If so, the story you're proposing would have to be written from a truly original perspective.

* Has the subject you want to write about already been covered by other publications? We try to offer our readers significant stories or analyses that haven't gotten attention elsewhere.

If we're not familiar with your work, please send two or three photocopies of previously published articles along with your query. Please query us in writing, not by phone.

Frontlines: In the magazine's Frontlines section of shorter items we often use amazing statistics, quotations from public figures, news items underreported by the conventional press, etc. Address all material to Frontlines Editor. We pay $50 to $250, depending on length and the amount of research required, for commissioned Frontlines stories.

<u>Rates</u>: We generally pay $1000 for standard features, and $500 to $600 for columns of 1000 to 2000 words. Kill fees are one-quarter of the purchase price of an assigned article. Writers' expenses are paid by prior agreement. Payment is made on acceptance. (The above rates do not apply to forthcoming books.) Two or three articles from each issue are included in a regular syndication package sent to dailies and alternative weeklies across the country. Authors receive half of the revenue generated by sales to these papers. Occasionally an outside syndication network (i.e., the New York Times Syndicate, King Features, etc.) will pick up a <u>Mother Jones</u> piece. Again, revenues from such sales or from any other sales are shared with the writer on a 50-50 basis. Authors have made $300 and more through our syndication efforts.

<u>What kinds of material we're looking for</u>: No formulas apply here; the best guide is to read recent issues of the magazine.* We frequently publish fictional short stories, and occasionally run excerpts from soon-to-be-published fiction and non-fiction books. We specialize in our own brand of investigative reporting, which focuses on corporate and government cover-ups. We carry certain kinds of human interest stories--see, for example, "Revenge of a DES Son" (MJ, Feb./March '83), about a corporate lawyer who sued his ex-client when he found their drug had given <u>him</u> cancer, and "The Glow Boys" (MJ, Nov. '82), about the workers who clean up radiation in atomic plants. We are interested in profiles ("The Great Indian Power Grab," MJ, Jan. '82, a profile of Peter MacDonald) and interviews ("Tom Brokaw Is Mad As Heck," MJ, April '83), as well as political essays ("The Politics of Porn," MJ, April '80), overseas reportage ("Inside the Slaughterhouse," MJ, June '83), economic analysis ("The Unlevel Playing Field," MJ, Aug. '82) personal voice essays (our series on life and love in the eighties, "The Way We Are," which started in April '83), trend-spotting ("They Are The Japanese," MJ, Aug. '82), proposals for social reform ("The Illusion of Safety," Parts I & II, MJ, June '82 and MJ, July '82), and coverage of the arts (especially music). Our regular columns on books, health and economics are generally written by contributing editors, but we're always looking for good profiles of people making a positive impact for our Strategies column. Please note that we do not carry poetry or list upcoming events.

<u>Manuscripts</u>: All unsolicited manuscripts must include a stamped return envelope or they will not be returned.

* If these are not available to you, back copies can be purchased for $3 apiece (including postage and handling); subscriptions are $12 a year. Address orders to Reader Service Department, <u>Mother Jones</u>, 1663 Mission St., 2nd floor, San Francisco, CA 94103.

MOTORHOME

Guideline for Writers and Photographers

MOTORHOME is the only monthly magazine devoted exclusively to self-propelled RVs: mini, micro-mini and Class A motorhomes and customized buses. MOTORHOME readers range in age from young couples with and without children to mature people of retirement age, and their interests range from how-to RV projects to travel destinations. The primary prerequisite for all material submitted to MH is that it be RV oriented, written with an RV focus, for this specialized audience. Studying recent issues will help clarify our approach.

All manuscripts must be submitted for our exclusive publication. (They have not appeared elsewhere, nor are they being submitted for publication to another publisher simultaneously.) Manuscripts should be typed, double-spaced and include the author's name, address and telephone number as well as the total number of words. MOTORHOME will return material including photographs and other artwork if it is not appropriate for our use, providing a self-addressed, stamped

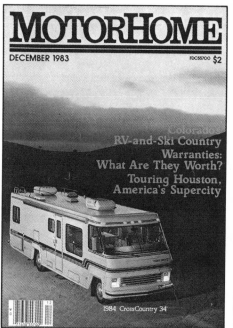

envelope is enclosed.

Whenever possible, give names, addresses and telephone numbers of contacts or agency personnel who can verify operating dates and other details on campgrounds and attractions described in the manuscript. Every effort will be made by MH staff to confirm such facts prior to publication. It is also a good idea to enclose brochures describing events mentioned in the manuscript, along with maps.

MOTORHOME reserves the right to edit all manuscripts for style or length but will discuss any major changes with the author, whenever possible. Manuscript acknowledgments are sent upon receipt; acceptance or rejection notification usually follows within 30 to 45 days. Written queries are advisable; telephone queries are not always convenient. Seasonal articles must be received at least four months ahead of publication date in order to be considered. Payment is upon publication and ranges from $75 for small articles (such as *Guest Commentary* essays) to $350 for major features (such as travel stories).

Photo Requirements

Quality and suitability of photographs often determine acceptance or rejection of manuscripts. Travel features should be accompanied by a minimum of 10 color transparencies—all originals. At least one or two must include motorhomes. Authors are encouraged to offer a large selection of scenic and RV photos, because manuscripts that are not adequately illustrated regrettably must be returned, even if the manuscript is of good quality. How-to and personality articles usually are printed with black-and-white prints, which should be 8 x 10-inch glossies, although smaller sizes will be considered if they are of sufficient quality. If prints are of marginal quality, please send negatives so they can be reprinted by our professional photo lab.

All photos and slides should be numbered with an accompanying caption sheet identifying each one. If possible, it is wise to write the photographer's name on each one also, to ensure return of the photos or slides. Photos or slides provided by someone other than the manuscript author should be clearly identified for photo credit.

Although photographic essays are not published in MH magazine, we will consider scenic RV photos for possible use with future articles or on the cover. Any photos clearly featuring people should be accompanied by statements of permission for their appearance.

MOTORHOME purchases first North American rights and will return all transparencies and photos after publication, along with those that were not used, whenever possible. Please include a self-addressed, stamped envelope for this purpose. We can not accept responsibility for unsolicited material.

Travel Features

MOTORHOME publishes several major travel features each month, many of which are written by free-lancers. These generally are between 1,000 and 2,000 words in length, although exceptions are considered. (Short travel articles averaging approximately 1,000 words are used in the *Short-Stop* column, which includes one or two color or black-and-white photos.) Travel destinations are virtually unlimited—as long as they are accessible by motorhome—and range from Canada to Mexico and around the world, in addition to the United States. Each travel story needs a map detailing routes, campgrounds and specific sights mentioned in the copy. (Maps are redrawn by staff artists, so it is not necessary to obtain permission for publication.) Descriptions of little-known attractions and activities are good elements for an article, as are personal observations on the character of a specific area and its inhabitants. The adventure aspect of RV travel can be a very strong element.

A wide variety of quality color slides is essential for a travel feature in this magazine, and again, at least one or two *must* include a motorhome in the appropriate setting.

Human Interest Features

Articles about people are regularly included in MOTORHOME. They may focus on ordinary people with very unusual hobbies, or very unusual people who are RV owners. A strong RV connection is a must. Photo usage normally is black and white, but color will be considered if accompanied by black-and-white photos also.

Do-It-Yourself Articles

Motorhome enthusiasts are interested in learning how to do it themselves, even though many may not be mechanically inclined. Typical how-to projects include making tool boxes or magazine racks, but sometimes these projects involve major modifications of a coach. In all cases, there must be ample illustrations, either black-and-white photos or sketches, to fully show the reader how to accomplish the project at hand. Staff artists will make professional illustrations from rough sketches, so contributors need not be artists themselves.

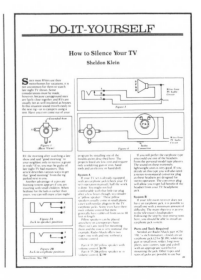

Technical Articles

Although vehicle tests are staff written or assigned to contributing editors, we welcome additional technical articles on almost any subject related to RVs—from brakes to solar heating. They should be comprehensive, accurate and clearly written. Black-and-white 8 x 10 photos are suggested, although illustrations may be used as well. Rough sketches will be sufficient for staff artists to render camera-ready artwork. Article length depends upon the subject matter, but generally should be between 1,000 and 2,000 words.

Shifting Gears

Thoughtful handling of the shift lever can improve fuel consumption, uphill speed and driving pleasure

Don Alexander

Miscellany

Hobbies such as fishing, hunting, rockhounding, archery, hiking and spelunking are good subjects for articles if written from the RVer's point of view. These should be accompanied by appropriate photos showing people participating in the activity; be sure to get their permission if they are clearly identifiable. These may be illustrated by black-and-white prints or color transparencies, or both.

Humor articles are appropriate if written from the RVer's point of view. Readers enjoy stories about RVers who are laughing at themselves, rather than at someone else. Typical stories describe the novice's mistakes, seen from the vantage point of a wiser, more experienced motorhomer—but there is a lot of potential in every aspect of RVing if given the right slant.

Guest Commentary is a regular column which presents a reader's unsolicited essay on a subject he or she feels strongly about, such as pets in campgrounds, overnight campground restrictions or inconsiderate fellow campers. No photos are required, since this is essentially a long letter. A nominal payment is offered for published *Guest Commentary* contributions, which usually run no more than 1,000 words in length.

Address all queries and manuscript to: Editor, MOTORHOME, TL Enterprises Inc., 29901 Agoura Road, Agoura, California 91301; (213) 991-4980.

A Tall Tale For Lofty RVers

otherwise known as a guide to survival in a motorhome that is shorter than you are

Gail Hallas

Dear Writer:

Thank you for your interest in contributing to Ms. We do read unsolicited manuscripts: poetry, fiction, and non-fiction articles or profiles. Manuscripts are considered for body-of-the book articles (3,000 word limit; 12 typed pages) or for front-of-the-book features (1,500 word limit; six typed pages), and are purchased at competitive magazine prices.

Please mail completed, typed manuscripts to Manuscript Reader, Ms. Magazine, 119 West 40th Street, New York, NY 10018, indicating on the envelope what type of piece you are submitting. No manuscript will be read unless accompanied by a self-addressed, stamped envelope. Expect to wait at least six weeks for a reply.

Please bear in mind that we accept fewer that one in 2,000 unsolicited manuscripts, and will not read manuscripts being simultaneously submitted to other publications.

The editorial content of Ms. reflects women's rising awareness of their changing roles, the reasons for the change, and the consequences to women, to lifestyles, and to society.

Sincerely,

THE EDITORS

119 West 40th Street,
New York, New York 10018
212 · 719 · 9800

National Geographic **Traveler**

GUIDELINES FOR WRITERS

National Geographic <u>Traveler</u> is a quarterly publication of the National Geographic Society. <u>Traveler's</u> purpose, like that of its parent organization, is to increase and diffuse geographic knowledge, and it does so by making travel experiences more interesting, meaningful, and enjoyable for its subscribers.

FORMAT
<u>Traveler</u> is newsweekly size (about 8½" x 11"), with roughly 160 editorial pages. There are several regular departments and as many as 10 feature articles in each issue, each presented with photography and text in a 2:1 ratio.

SCOPE
<u>Traveler</u> highlights mostly U.S. and Canadian subjects, but about 10% of its articles cover other foreign destinations--most often Europe, Mexico, and the Caribbean, occasionally the Pacific. In all cases we are interested in places accessible to most travelers--not just the most intrepid or the very wealthy.

<u>Traveler</u> articles are usually narrow in scope; for example, we do not cover whole states or regions. Subjects of particular interest to us are national parks, historic places, cities and parts of cities, sport and resort-oriented travel, regional crafts and cooking, and places of archaeological interest. Articles may narrate a particular kind of trip-- by boat, raft, or car, for example--or evoke a place through a mood piece.

STORY PROPOSALS
Article ideas may be generated by <u>Traveler</u> editors and assigned to free-lance writers, or we may accept proposals by writers or photographers. All proposals are given careful consideration, but because of the need for seasonal and evenly distributed regional coverage as well as for a mix of kinds of travel, otherwise excellent proposals simply may not work for us or may be long postponed. Because of our lead time--9 to 12 months-- writers should not expect to get a confirmed assignment on a few weeks' notice.

Story proposals should be 1-2 pages long and should highlight why the destination is of interest to <u>Traveler</u>. The prospective writer should include relevant published clippings, a resume, or some indication of areas of expertise, and a note explaining how he or she is a suitable person to write the article. We are not interested in previously completed manuscripts or stories written in connection with some commercial arrangement or "familiarization" trip.

Prospective contributors doing preliminary research for a story must avoid giving the impression that they are representing the National Geographic Society or <u>Traveler</u>. They may use the name of the magazine only if they have a definite assignment. When <u>Traveler</u> gives an assignment to a writer or photographer, the terms are clearly stated in a written contract.

-2-

LENGTH AND FEE
        Most Traveler articles range from 1500 to 5000 words, depending
on the subject. Fees vary from $1500 to about $5000 depending on length,
importance, and writer's experience.

STYLE
        In general, Traveler articles avoid a guidebook approach. Although
we do not wish to impose rigid restrictions on a writer's individual style,
we have found our most successful contributions share certain characteristics,
notably a strong sense of the author's personality and experiences and a
high literary quality. The places are brought to life through the writer's
eyes, and his or her experiences are used to deepen those of the reader.

        Service information is generally given separately at the end
of the article in a section that includes "how to get there," lists
(but no recommendations) of places to stay and to eat, places of interest
nearby, opening and closing times of attractions, and where to obtain more
information. This section is prepared by researchers on the Traveler staff,
although the writer is expected to send along as much service information
as possible with his or her manuscript.

National Geographic Traveler
National Geographic Society
Washington, D.C. 20036

Revised 6/83

GUIDELINES

For Contributors to National Geographic WORLD

WORLD IS:

- A monthly picture magazine for young readers, age 8 and older

- Available only from the National Geographic Society

- A full-color publication with an 8 1/2 x 10 3/4 inch page format and a picture-to-text ratio of three to one

WORLD EDITORS REVIEW:

- Top-quality pictures on a variety of subjects of interest to children: science, nature, sports, adventure, industry, unusual experiences, how-to-do-it projects (Children featured in picture stories should be older than 7 and younger than 16.)

- Imaginative, eye-catching action photographs with a strong visual story line and, where appropriate, humor

- Sharp, professional quality transparencies (35 mm and 2 1/4, 4 x 5 or larger)

- Transparencies that are suitable for our regular features: Kids Did It!, Far-out Facts, and What in the World...?

- Proposals for picture stories (Please send applicable samples of your photographic work.)

- Original game ideas

WORLD EDITORS WILL NOT REVIEW:

- Black-and-white prints, color prints, duplicate transparencies, or motion-picture frames

- Poetry, fiction, or manuscripts (All stories are written by staff members, and contract writers.)

- Unsolicited drawings or paintings (All art is done by assignment.)

- Adaptations of standard games (Examples: find-a-word games or crossword puzzles.)

WORLD BUYS:

- Transparencies: $200 per published page, payment prorated for smaller uses, minimum payment $75, front covers and poster front $400

- Games or puzzles: $25 for original games or puzzles (We reserve the right to edit and adapt to our use.)

- Children's contributions: $10 for art, photographs, or games

HOW TO SUBMIT:

- Query in writing before investing time and money in shooting a story. Address letters to National Geographic WORLD, Submissions Editor, 1145 17th Street N.W., Washington, D.C. 20036.

- When submitting transparencies, include a brief summary of the proposed story plus specific caption information for each picture. It is our policy to identify in the magazine all individuals featured in pictures. We need full name, place of residence, telephone number, and--for a child--age. For animals, we need species name and the date and location of the photograph. (Be as specific as possible. If the photograph was made in a zoo, include the name.)

- Write your name, as you wish it to appear in the picture credits, on every transparency mount or label.

- Include your Social Security number with your cover letter. If we decide to use your material, we will need this to make payment.

WHAT TO EXPECT:

- Your material will be reviewed by staff members. Part of the editorial process in connection with pictures for children sometimes entails display of sample layouts to a limited number of children to determine interest level.

- You will be notified of our decision concerning your transparencies as soon as possible. We will make every attempt to return your pictures quickly, but we cannot agree to pay holding fees or penalties if they are not returned by a given date.

- The standard practice in the industry requires that we make certain editing and layout uses of your photographs in order to publish them. Payment is made after the final layout is approved, usually three months before publication.

- All contributors receive three complimentary copies of the issue in which their work appears. Additional copies may be purchased at reduced rates. Address requests for extra copies to Mr. Paul Tylor, Member Relations Manager, National Geographic Society, 1145 17th Street N.W., Washington, D.C. 20036. Please advise us in advance of the publication date if you plan to purchase 50 copies or more. Special rates can be arranged for bulk orders.

NATIONAL GEOGRAPHIC WORLD STORY PROPOSAL

Photographer: _____
Address: _____
_____
_____
Phone: (____) _____

In order to consider your story proposal, we must have a clear description of the focus and visual possibilities. A narrow focus is essential because we generally have very limited space—from one to six pages for a photo story. It usually helps to have at least half a dozen photo possibilities described in some detail. The focus should not exceed a paragraph, and picture ideas should be limited to one sentence each. It is important to be very specific about what action is available for pictures. Please include the ages of any children involved in the story.

Focus paragraph:

Photo possibilities:

1. _____
2. _____
3. _____
4. _____
5. _____
6. _____

Ages of children involved in the activity: _____

Name and address of organization and coach or leader of activity:

_____
_____
_____

Telephone: _____

NATIONAL REVIEW

We publish freelance articles, book reviews and short satirical prose fillers. Articles should be factual reports on some aspect of the current scene with as little editorializing as possible while keeping in mind that National Review is a journal of opinion which serves a conservative audience. We prefer articles of 3,000 words or less but do occasionally publish freelance pieces that run up to 5,000 words.

Queries about articles should be addressed to: Articles Editor, NR., 150 E. 35th St. NYC 10016; queries about book reviews and other cultural matters to Books, Arts & Manners Editor Chilton Williamson Jr., 1025 Beech Street, Kemmerer, Wyo. 83101. All submissions should be double-spaced, and accompanied by SASE.

AN INTRODUCTION TO NATIONAL WILDLIFE

FOR WRITERS AND PHOTOGRAPHERS

PUBLISHERS: NATIONAL WILDLIFE magazine is published six times a year by the National Wildlife Federation, a non-profit, non-government organization with 50 state affiliates. The largest conservation group in the U.S., the Federation has long been a leader in educating the public about environmental problems.

NATIONAL WILDLIFE magazine is a membership publication. A NATIONAL WILDLIFE membership is $12.00 per year. A World Membership is $19.00 per year and includes six issues of INTERNATIONAL WILDLIFE, as well as six issues of NATIONAL WILDLIFE.

EDITORIAL OFFICES: The creative and editorial functions of NATIONAL WILDLIFE magazine are the responsibility of the National Wildlife Federation, 1412 16th Street, NW, Washington, D.C. 20036, Editor, John L. Strohm; Managing Editor, Mark Wexler; Photo Editor, John Nuhn. Send all editorial correspondence to this address.

CONTENT: Readers will find beauty, adventure, human interest, an occasional shock, some humor and a little crusading. We try to be provocative, sometimes challenging, always interesting and relevant.

OPPORTUNITIES FOR WRITERS

Although we have staff writers and roving editors, we depend heavily upon outside contributions. Therefore, we are eager for your ideas and suggestions.

AUDIENCE: Our 800,000 subscribers are concerned about the environment, and they appreciate the drama and beauty of all wildlife, both plant and animal. Some of them are environmental activists. Some are hunters and fishermen. Some are armchair travelers who enjoy reading about fascinating places and wildlife.

STYLE: We want vital, active writing that holds the reader once our dramatic photography and artwork have attracted him. Our style is heavily anecdotal, and we often encourage a personalized, subjective approach.

LENGTH AND DEADLINES: Short articles are approximately 1000 to 2000 words, longer ones are 2500 to 3000 words. Our planning calls for submission of a detailed text proposal six months before publication.

QUERIES: In several paragraphs, give us a clear feeling for the story's content, structure, topical peg and illustration needs. We will reply within a few weeks.

PAYMENT: Competitive with other quality magazines. Payment upon acceptance.

TYPES OF ARTICLES NEEDED: We are looking for story ideas and articles covering a wide variety of subjects; for example:

-2-

A. <u>WILDLIFE</u>: In-depth stories about wildlife in all parts of the United States. Birds, mammals, reptiles, fish, flowers, trees.

   1. In-depth profiles of a single species: Example: "Can the Grizzly survive the 20th century?" Or the mountain lion, the osprey, the buffalo, etc.? Interesting historical lore about the species should be included, as well as habitat, "life style," anecdotes, etc.

   2. Constant battle between diminishing habitat and encroachment of man. The confrontation between the needs of an industrial society and the need to preserve our environment.

   3. Adventure narratives involving wildlife. These can include hunting, but hunting should not be the main focus of the narrative.

B. <u>NATURE ESSAYS</u>: Occasionally we buy essays that move the heart as well as the mind. Their focus can be almost anything -- mountains, rivers, lakes, forest, the seashore, etc. -- and the writing must be excellent.

C. <u>MAN: THE STORY OF MAN AND HOW HE LIVES</u>:

   1. A week with a Seminole medicine man -- last of a vanishing breed.

   2. A day in the life of an Oregon forester.

   3. The last of the old decoy makers.

D. <u>MAN AND HIS ENVIRONMENT</u>:

   1. Ecology of an area: The story of the Appalachians -- man, wildlife, plant life, problems.

   2. <u>POLLUTION</u>:

      a. Air
      b. Water
      c. Noise
      d. Land

E. <u>WHAT YOU CAN DO</u>: Many of our readers are activists...like to get things done...we try to show them how...how a city was cleaned up...a park area saved...a legislature educated in the need for sound environmental legislation, etc.

F. <u>TRAVEL</u>: We use an occasional, unusual travel story with adventure overtones...making the experience an extension of the National Wildlife Federation's interest in hiking, camping and outdoor recreation. Not the usual how-to travel story, but one that takes the reader to off-beat parts of our country for a quality experience with nature.

-3-

REMEMBER: We also publish INTERNATIONAL WILDLIFE, and are always interested in top stories from around the world.

NOTE TO PHOTOGRAPHERS: If you also shoot pictures -- so much the better -- let's see them. We are always interested in photograph and text "packages."

OPPORTUNITIES FOR PHOTOGRAPHERS

NATIONAL WILDLIFE magazine depends heavily on contributions from photographers, both professionals and outstanding amateurs.

COLOR: We want your sharpest color transparencies, 35mm and larger. Our preference in film is Kodachrome. We need the originals, which will, of course, be returned.

BLACK AND WHITE: We also need outstanding B/W photographs.

SUBJECTS:

A. MAMMALS, BIRDS, FISH, REPTILES, INSECTS:

1. Action pictures of the chase, the flight, the kill.

2. Close-ups: both conventional and from unusual angles.

3. Sequence shots: The hatching of an alligator...A moth emerging...How the timber wolf stalks its prey, etc.

4. The family story: Example: All the American Wildcats.

5. The picture narrative: Tell a story with your photographs and long captions.

6. On the particularly dramatic picture -- give us a paragraph on how you made the photo, camera, exposure, film, conditions, etc.

7. The photographer's story. How you stalked the moose... how you photographed the California condor, etc.

B. FLOWERS AND PLANT LIFE

1. Single close-up of blossoms, rare and not so rare.

2. Series: Flowers of the Rockies...Trees of the Olympic Peninsula...Life in the Louisiana Swampland...The Flowering Shrubs of the old South...Plant Life in the Smokies ...Rockhounding in the Badlands.

-4-

C. SCENICS

1. Single, dramatic scenics which might be used for a cover
    or a full spread.

2. Series, alternating long shots with close-ups: Examples:
    The Story of Mt. Whitney...Lake Superior Wonderland.

3. The TEN most photographed sights in the Northwest...or
    Southwest.

D. ECOLOGICAL SERIES

1. Life along the Colorado -- man, birds, animals, plant
    life. Or Life in the Sonora Desert...or Life on the
    Great Plains.

E. MAN...AND HOW HE LIVES

1. A day in the life of: "A Porpoise Handler in Marineland"
                          "A Game Warden in Virginia"

2. How man is despoiling his environment: Photographs of
    Air Pollution...Water Pollution examples...Land Pollution
    examples...Over-population Problems...Soil Erosion...Food
    Problems.

We are always looking for that distinctive single photo...the
springly, dramatic, colorful, human interest photo that remains
in the reader's mind and heart for months to come. We call
them Favorite Photos, and use them frequently.

RATES: We pay competitive rates for top photos. Purchase
of rights follows customary publishing practices. (We buy
single photos or groups.)

SUBMISSIONS: The only way we can tell whether we can use
your photos is to see them. Please mail them to: Photo Editor,
NATIONAL WILDLIFE, 1412 16th St., NW, Washington, D.C. 20036

REMEMBER: We also publish INTERNATIONAL WILDLIFE and are
always looking for top photos from around the world. Queries
on both magazines, for photos, should be directed to the
Photo Editor (address as above).

Nation's Business

PUBLISHED BY THE CHAMBER OF COMMERCE OF THE UNITED STATES

1615 H STREET, N. W.
WASHINGTON, D. C. 20062

In response to your letter of
NATION'S BUSINESS occasionally takes unsolicited
freelance manuscripts. It is advisable to write
first with a summary of the idea and enclose a phone
number to facilitate communication. It is also
advisable to have a pretty good idea of what type
of magazine this is--an idea that will be obtained
by reading a number of issues.

Manuscripts should be typed, double-spaced
74 units to the line, with ample margins. Each page
should be numbered at the top and have an identifying
slug. The first page should also have, at the top,
the author's name, address and phone number.

Articles should be written in lively, easy-
to-understand style and contain illustrative anecdotes
and quotations wherever possible.

Standard article length: 1,500 words. Payment
is subject to agreement.

Freelance ideas may be submitted to the Editor,
NATION'S BUSINESS. Our present editor is Robert T. Gray.

Cordially,

Nation's Business

Henry Altman Managing Editor	Chamber of Commerce of the United States	1615 H Street, N.W. Washington, D.C. 20062 202/▮▮▮▮▮ 463 5650

We have received the material you submitted under the date of
and we thank you for giving us an opportunity to consider it.

Please be advised that:

_____We plan on using all or part of this material in our magazine, and
a staff member will contact you at the appropriate time.

_____We are considering use of this material, and will notify you of our
decision.

_____Our staff writers and contributing editors meet our needs in the area
covered by your material.

_____Our editorial content consists primarily of Washington-based activities
affecting business, management techniques helpful in the day-to-day operation of a
business and profiles on successful business people. I regret that your material does
not fit any of these categories.

_____Our standard article runs 6 to 8, double-spaced, typewritten pages, and
your material does not lend itself to the editing necessary to bring it within those
limits.

_____Your submission does not meet our editorial needs at this time.

Because of the heavy volume of letters, press releases, manuscripts and
other material submitted to our editorial offices, we are unable to consult in person
or by telephone on our evaluation of each submission. We request your cooperation in
this regard.

Sincerely,

NATURAL HISTORY

MAGAZINE OF THE AMERICAN MUSEUM OF NATURAL HISTORY • CENTRAL PARK WEST AT 79TH STREET, NEW YORK, N.Y. 10024 • 873-1300 • CABLE: MUSEOLOGY

GUIDELINES FOR SUBMITTING MANUSCRIPTS TO NATURAL HISTORY MAGAZINE

1. Natural History magazine is published by The American Museum of Natural History, Central Park West at 79th Street, N.Y., N.Y. 10024.

2. Manuscripts or article proposals should be sent to The Editors, Natural History magazine, at the above address.

3. Natural History includes articles on the biological sciences, ecology, anthropology, archeology, earth science, and astronomy. Six to eight major articles are published in each issue.

4. Most of the articles in Natural History are written by professional scientists and scholars. High standards of writing and research are expected. The magazine does not lobby for causes.

5. Natural History is read by scientists, teachers, students, and an intelligent lay audience. Technical jargon should be avoided.

6. Manuscript preparation:

   The length of accepted manuscripts is usually between 2,000 and 3,500 words.

   A self-addressed, stamped envelope should be included with unsolicited manuscripts.

   Footnotes should not be used.

   Manuscript should be typed, double spaced, with at least one-inch margins.

7. Manuscript disposition:

   Receipt of manuscript will be acknowledged.

   Accepted manuscripts may receive extensive editing.

   Edit orial decisions are usually made within two to six weeks.

   Unaccepted manuscripts are returned.

   When an article will appear depends on editorial need.

   Criticism or suggestions for unused articles will not be provided.

8. If an article is accepted for publication, an author's photograph and biographical information, especially on field experience relating to the article, are required.

9. A fee, generally in the range of $600 to $750 for full-length articles, is paid upon publication.

10. Copyright is held by The American Museum of Natural History.

Thank you for your offer to contribute to New Age.

New Age is a national monthly magazine of new ideas and traditional values for readers who take an active interest in personal growth, health, and contemporary social issues. Editorial interests include humanistic lifestyles, environmental concerns, politics, self-improvement, relationships, progressive businesses, practical spirituality, and arts and culture.

Our readers are successful, innovative people who have incorporated '60s values into their '80s lifestyles. We are looking for quality writing and thorough reporting that will keep this audience informed and entertained.

We publish features (2000-4000 words), columns (750-1500 words), short news items (500 words), and first-person narratives (750-1500 words). To get an idea of our content, style, and format, please look over a recent issue (available at newsstands and bookstores, or send $2.50 for a sample copy).

It is best to send a query letter before preparing a lengthy article, although we will consider unsolicited material. When sending queries, please include clips of recent work. All manuscripts, photographs, and artwork must be accompanied by a stamped, self-addressed envelope. Please do not send originals, as the magazine cannot be held responsible for loss or damage of unsolicited material. We will try to respond as quickly as possible to all submissions--usually within four to six weeks.

Our payment rates for published material are comparable to those of other national magazines. Fees and payment schedules are determined on an individual basis by assignment or upon acceptance.

New Woman

215 Lexington Avenue, New York, New York 10016   Telephone: 685-4790

GUIDELINES FOR WRITERS

Most articles in NEW WOMAN are reprints. We do commission some
original pieces. And <u>occasionally</u> we accept an appropriate article
from a query.

The best guidelines for suitable NEW WOMAN material are found
within the contents of the magazine. Please query first. If the
topic seems right for us, we will ask to see the manuscript on
speculation.

Thank you for your interest in NEW WOMAN.

Rosemarie Lennon
Reader Service Editor

NEW YORK MAGAZINE • 755 SECOND AVENUE, NEW YORK, NEW YORK 10017 • (212) 880-0700

WRITER'S GUIDELINES

New York publishes nonfiction relating to New York City. Preferred topics include profiles of New Yorkers, health/ medicine, behavior/lifestyle, investigative reporting, and service articles (articles giving consumers guidance on matters ranging from where to shop to how to determine which bank will give you the best service). No fiction or poetry is accepted.

The magazine has a staff of columnists who cover the arts, politics, business, fashion, the media, and advertising. However, features on these subjects are accepted.

Word length: 1,800 to 5,000 words.

Rate of pay: varies.

Procedure: Submit a query describing the article you wish to write. Include as much detail as possible. Samples of previously published work should be included.

Complete manuscripts will also be considered, but must be accompanied by self-addressed envelope.

We cannot assume responsibility for unsolicited material.

Reply: three weeks.

Thank you for your interest.

The Editor

nibble® Author's Guide

GENERAL AUTHOR INFORMATION

Thank you for your interest in writing for *Nibble*! The aim of *Nibble* is to help readers learn how to use their Apple computers more effectively...and to have fun doing it. Although we publish product reviews, tutorials, and general interest articles, our major emphasis is on programs and programming methods. We are interested in games, utilities, home and personal information management, finance, music, and most other applications that attract our readers to the Apple II series and Macintosh. Programs published in *Nibble* have a potential readership in excess of 150,000 people in the U.S. and over 50 other countries!

If you have a favorite program that you think would be of general interest, we would like to see it. This guide explains the submission process and our general requirements for submissions. Please read it carefully, and follow the suggestions which are pertinent to your particular submission. This will not only make both our jobs easier, but it will also increase the chances that your submission will be accepted for publication.

Your Submission Package

Obviously, the actual materials in your submission will depend on whether you are submitting a program and article or just an article. However, the following items should be a part of all submissions:

1. A cover letter that describes the article and/or program. Be sure to include your name, address and telephone number on this letter, as well as on the first sheet of your article.

2. A manuscript typed in upper- and lower-case and double-spaced on clean, white paper and a disk copy of the manuscript text if a word processor was used to produce it.

3. If your submission is a program, you should include both a printed listing and a disk copy of your program. All of the files on the disk should be described in your cover letter. A short demonstration program that "showcases" your submission is often very helpful.

4. When appropriate, illustrations, photographs, diagrams, screen dumps, charts, tables, or program runs should be included to clarify your article/program. These should each be on a separate piece of paper attached to the documentation. (Where applicable, they should also be on disk.) Such artwork need not be professionally done, but should be of sufficient quality that our artists will be able to accurately render the final work.

Be certain to label all of the separate parts of your submission with your name and address, including any disks you submit. You need not include return postage with your submission.

Submissions should be sent to:

Nibble Magazine
MicroSPARC, Inc.
45 Winthrop St.
Concord, MA 01742
Attn: Programs Editor

What Happens Next?

When we receive your submission, we will immediately mail a postcard acknowledging its receipt. It then enters an evaluation cycle during which programs are run and tested and manuscripts are carefully read. This usually takes 4-6 weeks. When we have finished our evaluation, you will receive notification from us. If your work is accepted for publication, we will make you a royalty offer at this time. Occasionally we will ask an author to revise a submission either to bring it more in line with *Nibble*'s standards, or to fix a minor program bug. In this case, the royalty offer is contingent on the successful modification of the work. If we are unable to accept your material, it will be returned to you with a letter of explanation.

Royalties

Our author remuneration is typically in the $40 to $250 range, though payments for major features range between $400 and $500. The actual amount is dependent upon a combination of factors, the most important of which are the clarity of the article/program and the appeal that we feel your work will have to *Nibble* readers. Full payment is normally made approximately two weeks after we receive your acceptance of our offer for your article/program.

When we purchase your article/program, we are buying exclusive publishing and marketing rights. In each issue of *Nibble*, we normally offer two diskettes containing the major programs in that issue for a 90-day period at a relatively low "introductory" price. Since this is a service to our readers and the price is close to our cost, we cannot offer additional remuneration for disk sales made during that period.

However, if your program is selected for the *Nibble* disk, when the 90-day period has expired, we normally re-price the disk and continue to advertise it. At that time, we begin paying a 20% royalty on the pro-rata share of the price that your program earns. For example, if a disk contains three programs of equal magnitude (from different authors) and sells for $30, your pro-rata share is 20% X $10.00 (less any discounts for volume dealer sales). We accumulate sales figures and pay the royalty at the end of each calendar quarter in the year. Royalties are paid through the third year following publication of your article.

Further, if your article is selected for our annual anthology, the *Nibble Express*, we normally duplicate the original author remuneration. You can see that this can mount up quite rapidly.

Contributing Editors

After having accepted your first article(s), we may invite you to become a Contributing Editor to *Nibble*. If we extend this invitation, we will ask for your commitment to submit at least three significant articles/programs per year in exchange for:

1. Carrying your name on our masthead.
2. Assuring very fast turnaround on publication decisions.
3. A complimentary subscription to *Nibble*.

Becoming a Contributing Editor is by invitation only.

ARTICLE AND PROGRAMMING GUIDELINES

Articles

The article that describes a program submission should include the following main sections in the order outlined:

1. What your program is and what it does.
2. How to use your program.
3. How to type in the necessary program files and save them to disk.
4. How it works and how the programming methods might be used elsewhere.
5. How to customize or modify the program for individual needs.

A Few Words on Writing Style

Like you, most *Nibble* readers are Apple programmers and users. When they start to read your article, they want to know right away what the program does. Use the first few paragraphs of your article to say generally what the program does and how it will help the reader. Give the reader an overview of the program, a sort of thumbnail sketch. Feel free to be creative and draw the reader in. Is there something about your program that makes it stand out from others like it? Take the time to elaborate a little. Similarly, you might want to use your concluding paragraphs to make a few general remarks about the program or just some parting words of advice.

Remember, you're not just a programmer now, you're a *Nibble* author. It's up to you to communicate your ideas in a clear, understandable style. Try to maintain an engaging tone throughout the article; after all, you're the reader's guide through the complexities of Apple programming.

One of the best methods of conveying the proper use of a program is to include a sample session. If this technique is employed, the narration should use the second person pronoun, you, rather than the first person, I or we.

If your program adapts routines that have been published elsewhere, it is important to give credit to the source of the routines. If your program uses another author's routines, we will ask you to obtain written permission from that author to use them.

Programming Guidelines

All programs, regardless of length, should be submitted on disk. Unless modifications to the disk operating system are necessary for the submission, the standard version should be used. Protected disks are unacceptable. Apple II series programs should be written in Applesoft, 6502 assembly language, or Pascal. Macintosh programs should be written in Microsoft BASIC, Apple MacBASIC, 6800 assembly language, or Apple MacPascal.

The following suggestions are general programming guidelines; not all will be applicable to your specific program. However, these guidelines are used in the evaluation process, so following them will not only increase the chances of having your submission accepted, but it will also reduce the amount of modification we may request in an otherwise acceptable program. You may find it useful to use this list as a final checklist before mailing your submission.

User Interface
- All input should be error trapped and range checked to prevent avoidable user errors. Areas of particular concern are errors that may cause:
  - a. a system crash
  - b. the loss of data (particularly through disk errors)
  - c. the screen display to become "scrambled"

- To avoid the accidental loss of information, confirmation should be required when opting to quit a program.

- A program should provide a graceful way to exit that restores the computer to a normal state.

- Long pauses during which the computer is active but appears "frozen" should be accompanied by a reassuring "Please Wait" type of message.

- The use of control keys should be consistent throughout the program. <RETURN> should be used to accept a choice, and <ESC> should be used to quit or exit a routine.

- If possible, programs that use cursor control should use the standard diamond of the I, J, K and M keys. When possible, the arrow keys on the //e and //c should also be implemented.

- The display of flashing text can be very annoying and should be used judiciously.

- Because many readers do not have paddles or joysticks, games that use these peripherals should also include a keyboard option.

- Instructions presented on the screen should be readable. This may often be accomplished by leaving a space between printed lines. In most cases, text should be displayed in upper-case only so that the program will be compatible with older Apple II's. If possible, text displays should be useable in both 40- and 80-column modes.

- Using the SPEED statement or "timing loops" to slow the display of text, particularly in instructions, can be frustrating and should be avoided. A better alternative is to print a full page of text at a time, and prompt the user to press any key to continue the execution of the program.

- To be useful to the largest number of readers, characters that are only accessible from the //e and //c keyboards should be avoided.

- It is much easier for readers to type in lines that contain repeated characters if a REMark designates the number of repetitions. For example:

100 PRINT "   ": REM 21 SPACES

Disk I/O
- Programs that can make use of more than one disk drive should allow users to specify and/or change the configuration to conform to their system.

- When prompting for the disk drive and/or slot, the prompt for the slot should precede the prompt for the drive number.

- During the input of a file name, the name should be displayed on its own line so that it will fit on the screen, regardless of its length.

- Programs that require the user to access the disk by file name should include a CATALOG option.

- The program should initialize all necessary data files during its first run so that it will function correctly regardless of the prior existence of these files.

- A test file that demonstrates the program's ability to deal with its size limitations should be included on the test disk.

Programming Conventions
- Variable names that contain the letter O and the digit 0 should be avoided.

- There should be no "hidden" control characters in a program (i.e., within quotation marks or REM statements). When control characters are necessary for the function of the program, the CHR$ form should be used either directly or in a variable assignment. (For example, both of the following are acceptable: **PRINT CHR$(4)"CLOSE"** and **D$ = CHR$(4): PRINT D$"CLOSE"**

- A program should not assume that a binary file which is necessary for its operation is loaded, but should explicitly load the file at the beginning of its execution.

- Control characters should not be appended to file names, since this may cause confusion when readers attempt to delete unwanted data files.

- Programs that use the Hi-Res graphics display (page 1) and that are long enough to require loading above this display should let the first line of the program change the pointers and then restart the program as follows:

```
10 IF PEEK(104) <> 64 THEN POKE 103,1: POKE
   104,64: POKE 16384,0: PRINT CHR$(4)"RUN EXAMPLE"
20 REM ACTUAL START OF PROGRAM NAMED "EXAMPLE"
```

- Since readers often like to shorten or speed up a program by removing REMarks, GOTO's and GOSUB's should not branch directly to REMark statements.

- All Applesoft program lines should be less than 239 characters long so that they may be entered without using the line editors or the question mark (?) abbreviation for PRINT.

PRODOS COMPATIBILITY

To reach the largest number of readers, programs should be as compatible as possible with both DOS 3.3 and ProDOS. When possible, programs that include disk access, either to load binary files or to read data files, should be written to conform with ProDOS. To ensure the greatest possible compatibility with both DOS 3.3 and ProDOS, program submissions should adhere to the following guidelines. In the event that exceptions are necessary for the program to function properly, the article should include information on the location of the incompatible code.

File Names

All file names should follow the ProDOS standard. ProDOS file names may be up to 15 characters long, and must start with a capital letter. The rest of the characters may be any combination of letters, digits, and periods. Spaces are not allowed, and any lower-case letters will be converted to upper-case automatically.

INIT

The INIT command no longer exists under ProDOS and should no longer be used.

MON and NOMON

Neither MON nor NOMON are supported by ProDOS and should no longer be used.

MAXFILES

MAXFILES is not supported by ProDOS. Although its use is discouraged, submissions written under DOS 3.3 may need to use MAXFILES. The documentation should clearly state this and give the location of the MAXFILES statement.

VERIFY

The function of VERIFY under ProDOS is simply to verify the existence of a file on the disk. It no longer checks the integrity of the data, and should not be used to do so. It is no longer possible to DELETE a file that has just been OPENed. Because of this, files should be verified under the control of an error trap before they are opened. The rather common practice of writing a text file with the OPEN-DELETE-OPEN-WRITE sequence will not work under ProDOS and should no longer be used. You may use instead OPEN-CLOSE-DELETE-OPEN-WRITE.

CAT and CATALOG

Under ProDOS, the CAT command results in a 40-column catalog, and the CATALOG command displays an 80-column catalog. When

it is necessary to include one of these in your program, the documentation should include a reference to the line containing the statement.

PR# and IN#

These commands must be preceded by a <CTRL>D. For example, to direct output to a printer connected to slot one, the statement: PRINT CHR$(4)"PR#1" would be used.

HIMEM

The HIMEM statement must use a value that lies on an even page boundary. That is, the hexadecimal equivalent of the value specified must end in two zeros.

CHR$(4)

<CTRL>D must precede all ProDOS commands that are issued from within a program, just like DOS 3.3. However, the concatenation of CHR$(13) and CHR$(4) which is commonly used to clear the input buffer before issuing a <CTRL>D does not work under ProDOS and should no longer be used.

Directory Trees

Although ProDOS allows the use of directory trees, all of the files pertinent to a program submission should be contained in the top level directory. To maintain program compatibility with DOS 3.3, data files used by a program should not access lower level directories.

ERROR HANDLING

All error messages should be displayed until the user presses a key. Also, whenever possible, an error should cause the program to try again after attempting to correct the error. This is particularly important for disk errors.

It is important to maintain the integrity of the screen display when trapping errors. Information should not scroll off the screen as a result of displaying an error message.

HARDWARE

A parts list, including approximate costs, should be included with hardware construction projects. Any special tools or parts that may not be familiar to the reader should be explained in the article.

SPECIAL EDITORIAL REQUIREMENTS

To avoid paste-up errors and to simplify the task of typing in published listings, programs should be numbered consecutively by tens starting with line 10.

For assembly language programs, the source code should be submitted as well as the object code (on disk) along with the name of the assembler that was used. Also, a remark in the first few lines of source code should indicate the name of the assembler used.

For readers who do not have printers and for those who have their printer interface card in a different slot, the documentation should note the lines in which output is directed toward a specific slot or in which special printer codes are specified.

FOR FURTHER INFORMATION

An excellent source of information on program design in general and the idiosyncrasies of the different models of the Apple II is the booklet *Design Guidelines*. To obtain a free copy, write to: Apple Computer, Inc., Developer Relations, MS 23-AF, 20525 Mariani Avenue, Cupertino, CA 95014.

Northwest Magazine

1320 S.W. Broadway
Portland, OR 97201
503-221-8228

Guidelines for writers and photographers

Northwest Magazine is distributed as part of The Sunday Oregonian, the Pacific Northwest's largest newspaper. Circulation is more than 400,000 with subscribers concentrated in Oregon and southwest Washington and widespread distribution reaching into Idaho, northern California and the balance of Washington. The Sunday Oregonian therefore provides maximum regional exposure for free-lance writers and photographers.

Northwest Magazine is, in turn, The Sunday Oregonian's major free-lance market. An entirely new editing staff has been directing the magazine since the summer of 1982, and a major program of expansion and improvement has been under way since then. Projections are that the need for free-lance material will increase.

The magazine's audience

Northwest Magazine, like any other free-lance market, is most accessible to writers and photographers who understand its format and produce material suitable for its intended audience. The best guide to format is the magazine itself. Read it regularly if you live within its circulation area; send for sample copies if you do not.

The magazine is designed for the well-educated, 25-to-49-year-old reader. The target audience is affluent and spends a relatively high proportion of its income and time on leisure activities, including reading, dining out, music, the arts, drama, destination travel and outdoor activities such as hiking and skiing.

If you intend to produce for the magazine, you should assume a fairly sophisticated audience. Your readers will be heavy media consumers, and they will be familiar with quality contemporary styles in both writing and graphic design. Your work will have to measure up.

Your audience also will expect substance, not the innocuous fluff that passes for "lifestyle journalism" in some publications. The magazine's editors intend to offer serious treatments of important regional issues. Humor and lifestyle stories will be part of the editorial mix, but even those should include perceptive analysis of culture and social structure. A good Northwest Magazine feature enhances the meaning of the reader's life by drawing parallels, detecting patterns and investigating the complexities of modern life.

The magazine's title is the best clue to its intended level of interest. Its niche is as a chronicle of the Pacific Northwest, and every article should relate to the region in some tangible way. Articles that fail to reach beyond downtown Portland are no more appropriate than articles focused on Peru.

Suitable topics

No topic is out of bounds if it conforms to the general assumptions that guide the magazine's editorial policy. The possibilities are endless and the editors always are delighted to discover appropriate material that opens new subjects.

In general, however, acceptable story ideas will fall into the following categories:

REGIONAL ISSUE STORIES — 3,000-5,000-word in-depth articles that go beyond daily press reports in analyzing the impact of major Pacific Northwest news developments. Writers of such stories should adhere to the most rigorous reporting standards and should have extensive experience in dealing with sensitive material.

PERSONALITY PROFILES — 1,000-3,000-word, slice-of-life stories that provide an inside look at the region's movers and shakers. The magazine usually profiles younger men and women who are in some way influencing the region as it develops. Outstanding writers, artists, politicians, performers, attorneys, physicians, educators, sports figures, architects and the like all are fair game. Ordinarily, your subject should be high in name recognition. But talented unknowns also are valid profile subjects.

Sometimes, a personality profile can provide an effective vehicle for analyzing a significant regional issue.

LIFESTYLE TRENDS — 1,000-2,500-word articles that examine some aspect of developing Northwest culture. The treatment usually will be light and sophisticated, and the subject matter can range from developments in *haute cuisine* to the most mundane aspects of popular culture. The key question is, "What's different about the way Northwesterners are living their lives this year?"

TRAVEL — 1,000-2,000-word guides to travel destinations within the Pacific Northwest. Out-of-the-way inns, resorts, lodges and hotels are of particular interest. Traditional Northwest destinations are acceptable topics only if the writer can present suggestions for new ways to enjoy old haunts. Make travel directions fairly explicit and include useful information on rates, reservation procedures, equipment and clothing needs and so on.

OUTDOOR RECREATION — 1,000-2,000-word guides to outdoor activities appealing to younger readers from primarily urban backgrounds. Traditional hunting and fishing topics are covered elsewhere in The Oregonian. But hiking, skiing, rafting and innovative suggestions for enjoying a short outdoor experience all are acceptable magazine topics.

SCIENCE AND BUSINESS NEWS — 1,000-3,000-word articles that profile major developments at Northwest research centers and business firms. Whenever possible, tie such developments to their practical impact on the region. Other institutional profiles, such as articles on schools, studios, theaters and so on, also are good candidates.

THE ARTS — The magazine draws heavily on The Oregonian's staff critics for arts coverage in the Portland metropolitan area. But the editors appreciate free-lance submissions on developments in music, dance, the visual arts, theater and handicrafts in other parts of the region. Arts stories should take the form of a short profile of the artist or of a developing body of artistic work, rather than a conventional critical review.

FASHION AND DESIGN — Photo essays with 500-800-word explanations of innovative approaches to regional clothing, interior design, residential architecture, landscaping and product design. Extensive caption information on important design features should be provided with the photographs.

PERSONAL ESSAYS — 800-1,000-word essays that reveal personal insights about some aspect of the Northwest experience. Personal essays can be extremely creative in their literary approach, but they should follow traditional essay standards for tight focus and unity.

LITERARY ARTS — Poems and short articles on Pacific Northwest writers are appropriate submissions to the magazine's regular "Literary Arts" section. Queries and submissions should be directed to the book editor, The Oregonian, with a note explaining that the submission is for the Literary Arts section.

TOPICS WITH LITTLE CHANCE OF SUCCESS — As a general rule, the magazine does not publish history without some contemporary angle, stories about the free-lancer's vacation travels, boilerplate light features without some Pacific Northwest angle, specific "how-to" articles and stories that promote a particular product or service.

Photographic requirements

Northwest Magazine buys free-lance photo essays and photographic story illustrations on a regular basis. The editors also will consider individual feature photographs with a distinctive Pacific Northwest flavor.

Photographers should submit either color slides (preferably Kodachrome) or black-and-white contact prints with negatives. Completed black-and-white prints are acceptable from established photographers with extensive professional experience.

The editors encourage accomplished photographers to submit resumes and portfolios so that they may be considered when work is available in their local areas.

NORTHWEST MAGAZINE GUIDELINES
PAGE 3

Submission format and procedures

The magazine's editors prefer written queries for all free-lance submissions. A query usually saves time for everybody concerned. The editors can evaluate the idea before wading through a full-length manuscript. The writer or photographer avoids time wasted on inappropriate ideas and benefits from editorial direction in completing the story. Generally, written queries will receive a reply within two weeks of their arrival at the magazine.

The editors will evaluate completed manuscripts submitted on speculation. But spec manuscripts submitted without a query have a far lower acceptance rate than those submitted after a query and a response from the editors.

When you do submit a manuscript, follow the Associated Press Stylebook on all questions of style and usage. Free-lancers who intend to submit to the magazine regularly should have their own copy of the stylebook, although submissions will not be rejected just because they follow some other style guide. The main point is that writers should follow one style consistently and that manuscripts should be relatively free of typos, misspellings and errors in grammar or usage.

Manuscripts should follow conventional free-lance magazine submission guidelines. Consult Writers' Market or some similar guide if you are unfamiliar with standard procedures. In general, manuscripts should be typed double-space on non-erasable paper. Include your name, address and telephone number on the opening page as well as your name and a slug line on each following page. Close with an end mark and include "(more)" at the bottom of each page before the close.

Address manuscripts and related correspondence to:

The Editor; Northwest Magazine
The Oregonian
1320 S.W. Broadway
Portland, OR 97201

All correspondence should include a self-addressed envelope. Attach postage to the envelope with a paper clip. If your stamps aren't used, they will be returned to you.

Writers should consider illustration possibilities when preparing and submitting manuscripts. The editors will consider drawings or other illustration material submitted with manuscripts. If the writer does not submit photographs, a list of photo possibilities — including names, addresses and telephone numbers — is appreciated.

Prose style

Good writing is, most of all, fresh and creative. It therefore defies definition. Successful Northwest Magazine free-lancers nonetheless share some basic stylistic traits.

First of all, manuscripts submitted to the magazine should be *involving* . Picture your reader pulling the magazine from the newspaper and setting it aside for a good read in front of a cozy fire. Then produce the kind of prose that makes that kind of reading one of life's most rewarding experiences.

Involving writing draws readers into different times or places. It fills the imagination with the sight, sound, smell, taste and touch of a world apart from the daily grind. It entertains, no matter how serious its subject. It informs, but it does so as the byproduct of a pleasurable experience.

Look to the best of contemporary writers for the literary techniques designed to accomplish that purpose. Today's outstanding non-fiction writers borrow heavily from fiction writers for everything but their content. They tell stories through scenic construction. They fill their writing with the kind of concrete color and sensory detail that allow readers to participate in the narrative. They use creative figures of speech to stimulate readers with fresh imagery and they use words in provocative new ways. Anecdotes, vignettes and dialogue help them inject dramatic tension into their writing and they use a variety of unity devices to hold a compelling focus.

Naturally, some of Northwest Magazine's shorter, more-informational content will deviate from the full-fledged literary treatment found in the best-written cover stories. But it still will avoid the barriers to reader involvement that cripple some manuscripts. Even a short hiking article should avoid passive voice and dry, abstract detail. It should maintain focus on a clearly defined topic and should rely on clear, direct syntax. Its transitions will carry readers smoothly from one point to the next while its carefully constructed paragraphs explore single, identifiable ideas presented in logical order. It will not, in other words, wander all over a confusing landscape of unrelated ideas, dull quotations and preachy rhetoric.

The ultimate outcome of good style is compelling clarity. Any manuscript that achieves that noble end will have a good chance of selling to Northwest Magazine.

Of course, free-lancers who sell to the magazine also sell to one of the West's largest and most influential newspapers. For a newspaper, the fundamental standard is accuracy. So scrupulous attention to facts also should characterize every submission to the magazine. Sloppy reporting will disqualify even the most brilliant literary effort. Fabrication of facts, anecdotes or quotations will sever the magazine's relationship with any free-lancer permanently.

Pay procedures and rates

Northwest Magazine pays on acceptance and checks usually are mailed mid-month the following month. The free-lancer's expenses are included in calculation of the overall rate and should not be billed separately.

The magazine's editors buy first-publication rights for Oregon and Washington. Simultaneous submission to other publications outside the two states is acceptable. The editors usually avoid publication of material that already has appeared anywhere within the Pacific Northwest.

Rates range up to $500 or more for a major cover story involving extensive reporting and research. Inside stories ranging in length from 1,500 to 4,000 words will earn between $150 and $350, depending on quality, length and the amount of research required. Shorter personal essays and similar material usually bring $75-$125. If the editors decide to accept a submission, they will send the free-lancer an acceptance letter that serves as a contract. The letter contains the proposed fee for use of the story or photographs, as well as detailed information on rights and restrictions. If the free-lancer agrees with the terms proposed, he or she should promptly sign the letter and return it to the magazine. Receipt of the letter in the magazine's office sets the standard payroll procedure in motion. ■

OMNI

OMNI PUBLICATIONS INTERNATIONAL LTD., 1965 BROADWAY, NEW YORK, NY 10023-5965. 212-496-6100

FEATURE ARTICLES: Guide to Authors

Feature articles for OMNI cover all branches of science with an emphasis on the future: what will this discovery or technique mean to us next year, in five years, or even by the year 2000? Articles are addressed to a lay audience, about the technical level of Time, Smithsonian or Astronomy.

Articles are assigned only on the basis of written proposals. To save yourself the aggravation of writing on speculation about a topic already assigned, please send a query letter outlining your ideas and a sample of your work. If accepted, you will be sent a contract with specific terms.

Format: The average article totals between 2,500 and 3,500 words, although occasional very short or very long features are also assigned. If one of the sources on which you based your article is difficult to find, to facilitate copy-editing of names and numbers, please include a copy of the source material used.

Always double space your copy and type on one side of the paper. Make sure to keep one or two carbon copies of your manuscript to guard against possible loss in the mail.

Use metric system throughout!

Illustrations: Photographs, drawings or other illustrations should be originals. Either black-and-white or color is acceptable. Photographs should be glossy prints from the ORIGINAL negatives or ORIGINAL transparencies themselves--not duplicate slides, copy prints, or clippings from other publications. All illustrations will be returned.

Bibliography: Please include a list of half a dozen general books and articles on the subject as additional reading.

OMNI

FEATURE ARTICLES: Guide to Authors -2-

Payment: Payment for the manuscript, on acceptance, will range between $800 and $1,250 for the average article; very short or very long features may pay less or more. Expenses (such as mileage or long-distance telephone calls) will also be covered, up to about $50; greater expenses must be discussed first. You must submit an itemized bill for expenses. If a commissioned article is not usable, you will be paid a kill fee of 25% the agreed-upon fee. Payment for illustrations is additional and depends on the number and size of illustrations used, up to a maximum of $250 for a full page. To facilitate payment, please indicate your social security number.

Credit: Articles are by-lined, so please indicate how you want your name to appear.

Also include a short (one page) biographical note about yourself, describing your background and interests, and a glossy black-and-white photgraph--preferably a rather informal, relaxed picture--for use on our authors' page.

Author's Checklist

o Manuscript is double spaced

o All quantities are in the metric system

o A copy of any scarce backup material is enclosed

o List of additional readings is enclosed

o Social security number is given

o Illustrations are included

o Biographical note is included

o Photograph of yourself is included

o Self-addressed stamped envelope is included

OMNI

COLUMNS: Guidelines for Authors

OMNI is a magazine rich in columns. All but one (Games)
are written by freelance writers. The pay is good. The
hours are short. And there is no heavy lifting. To those
interested in doing an OMNI column, we offer the following
information:

Queries. No phone queries please. We work only from written
proposals. If you call in with an idea, we will ask you to
write a proposal on the topic. Save yourself a phone call.
The writer can benefit from this. If an idea is sent to the
SPACE editor, for example, and she'he doesn't find it suitable
for that section, it may be passed along to the STARS editor
who might be ablt to use it.

Length. Most of the editors prefer that the entire column be
able to be contained on one magazine page. That means the copy
should be no longer than 850 words. We can and have run longer
columns, but only after it was specifically cleared with the
editor involved. The reason is simple: When readers see that
little "continued on page ___" at what they think is the end
of the column, their interests starts to fade.

Research. Treat the column as a kind of mini-feature, with a
brief, one paragraph lead and with information collected from
talking to the main source -- scientists, the experts, the
government officials -- whoever is doing the most relevant and
important work. Secondary sources are fine, but interviews
are a must. Good quotes and anecdotes give a column life and
immediacy. They make a story distinctively OMNI's

NOTE: We require the names and phone numbers of primary sources
so we can pass them along to our fact-checking department. The
numbers also come in handy for our phote researchers who are
always searching for the right picture to illustrate the story.

OMNI

COLUMNS: Guidelines for Authors - 2

Payment: We pay on acceptance. Pay ranges from $750 to $850 depending not upon the length of the piece, but on the amount of work required to do the column, the quality of work done, and our familiarity with the writer.

We also reimburse writers for reasonable expenses -- things like long distance phone calls or car mileage -- up to about $50. If the writer anticipates higher costs, the details of reimbursement must be worked out with the column editor beforehand.

For commissioned articles that are not usable we pay a kill fee, 25% of the agreed upon fee.

REMEMBER: Always include a list of sources and their phone numbers with the completed article.

OMNI

WRITER'S GUIDELINES FOR CONTINUUM & ANTIMATTER

Length: Items should be no longer than 300 words, or 75 lines typed to a 27 character width. Our average is about 50 lines. We hate long, long pieces. Don't even bother trying to talk us into one.

Payment: $150.00. Payment does not depend on length. If we can not use an article that we have assigned, we pay a kill fee of $37.50.

Pictures: A photo is needed for virtually every story printed. We do not require that writers provide photos with each story, though that is helpful when possible. We do ask that you keep picture possibilities in mind, however. For instance, if you're writing a story about some sort of new device, find out from the source if the photo is available. You don't have to get the photo, but at least tip us off so our picture editor knows where to look.

Research: We require original research -- like at least a phone interview with the scientists or experts involved. It's okay to get leads from journals, press releases, etc., but please dig up some new facts. Do something to make the story ours.

Point of View (Antimatter): OMNI does not accept the paranormal, the occult, and other "fringe" areas without question. Therefore, where appropriate, please include the opinion of a skeptic who can, at least, try and explain suspect claims. In instances where sources or their claims seem particularly spurious or absurd, a light, humorous approach is often more effective -- and more fun -- than angry depunking.

IMPORTANT: At the end of each item, include the names and phone numbers of all sources you contact for the benefit of our fact checkers. A piece can not be accepted without a source list.

Pamela Weintraub
Antimatter Editor

Dick Teresi
Continuum Editor

FOR THE MAN OF THE WORLD

oui

300 West 43rd Street
New York, N.Y. 10036
212-397-5200

OUI MAGAZINE FICTION/ARTICLE SPECIFICATIONS

All submissions should be typed, double-spaced and as free from typos and editorial marks as possible. ALL MANUSCRIPTS MUST INCLUDE A SELF-ADDRESSED, STAMPED ENVELOPE. All others will be immediately rejected and trashed. Please allow six-to-seven weeks for response.

AUDIENCE: Male-oriented, 18-35 years of age, college educated. OUI readers are looking for something out of the ordinary that will stimulate them mentally as well as physically.

FICTION: The more off-beat the better. Descriptive sexual passages and strong erotic overtones are welcomed but not required. Science fiction, mystery, horror, adventure and comedy are within our realm. OUI does not want such stories as How I Opened Up My Marriage or An Early Morning Affair; plodding, analytical pieces that bog down on page one. Stories on prostitutes, bordellos or massage parlors have been done, done, done and overdone. Create new situations. Investigate new areas. Take chances. Recently published pieces include: The Predator, a hard-hitting crime/ sex story in which a mysterious killer holds a city captive; and Who-Stuck-John, a humorous piece about a man who told the 'inside' story of his good buddy, Lee Harvey Oswald. Length: 2,000-3,000 words.

NON-FICTION: Hard-hitting, well-documented exposes; in-depth pieces on new sexual trends; political intrigue. Recent articles have included: Spykill - The Weapons of Homemade Terror; In Search of Paris Pink (a first-hand report on sex in underground Paris); Sentenced to Death (an inside report on the death penalty); and Oral Sex - Everything You Wanted To Know But Didn't Know Whom To Ask. Length: 2,000-3,000 words. QUERY FIRST.

INTERVIEWS: Q&As with top or up-and-coming female actresses or comtemporary female musicians. Interviews with top male stars on occasion. Recent Q&As have included: Sting, Mick Jagger, Nastassia Kinski, Barbara Carerra and Tanya Roberts. Q&A Length: 1,500-2,000 words. QUERY FIRST.

SERVICE/HOW-TO ARTICLES: Pieces that will be of genuine concern and help to OUI's readers will be given serious consideration. How to make money; how to survive specific situations; how to protect yourself from fraud; etc. are good examples. The pieces must be of national interest and have something new to say. Potential service-oriented pieces could include: the best imported cars for under $15,000; the best gifts for the man/woman with everything; sexual aids for travel in outer space; etc. Again, they must be of national interest and have a new, untapped angle. Length: 1,200-2,000 words. QUERY FIRST.

PAYMENT: Varies for all of the areas discussed. OUI pays on publication.

-- 30 --

Outdoor Life ♣♣♣   380 MADISON AVENUE, NEW YORK, N.Y. 10017, TELEPHONE: (212) 687-3000

WHAT DOES OUTDOOR LIFE BUY?

OUTDOOR LIFE serves the active outdoor sportsman and his family. The magazine emphasizes fishing, hunting, camping, boating, conservation, and closely related subjects.

If you are interested in writing for OUTDOOR LIFE, you should study the magazine. What we publish is your best guide to the kinds of material we seek. Whatever the subject, you must present it in a way that is interesting and honest.

We pay on acceptance. We use no fiction, and we use no poetry.

The best advice is to write a query letter first. Most of the material we buy originates this way.

Do you have something to offer the reader that will help him or her? Just exactly how do you think it will help? How would you present it? If you have photos, send them with your query.

You are better off to be early--even considerably early--with a query than to be even a little late. We think at least a year ahead. Right now we are concerned about what will be in OUTDOOR LIFE a year from now. Writers and photographers should be thinking the same way.

Though we have millions of readers, we never forget that we reach them one at a time. A reader who picks up a copy of OUTDOOR LIFE is asking, "What's in it for me?"

You are writing for an intelligent reader who is eager to learn more about the outdoors. Your job is to make it clear and interesting.

Preparing Manuscripts and Photos

Manuscripts must be typed: double-spaced or triple-spaced. Use a medium-quality non-erasable 8½ x 11½" paper (editing on erasable paper is murder). Number the pages, and type your name and the story title at the top of every page. Leave wide margins. Do not staple or bind manuscript pages. Paper clips are fine.

Black-and-white photos should be professional-quality 8 x 10" glossy prints (we may ask for negatives). Color photos should be the original positive transparencies and of 35mm size or larger. Best way to mount transparencies is in notebook-size plastic holders that hold 20 of the 35mm transparencies. Your name and address should be on the back of each black-and-white print and on the cardboard mount of each transparency. Every print and transparency should be clearly marked with a number.

On a single sheet of paper, write comprehensive captions and key them to the photo numbers. Each caption should tell who (from left to right) and what is shown in photo, describe the action, and tell where and when photo was taken. A reader may also be interested to know how it was taken.

We take every possible precaution in handling unsolicited material. However, we are not responsible for its damage or loss, and any that lacks a properly stamped, self-addressed envelope will not be returned.

PUBLISHED BY TIMES MIRROR MAGAZINES, INC.

380 MADISON AVENUE, NEW YORK, N.Y. 10017, TELEPHONE: (212) 687-3000

HOW TO WRITE A REGIONAL ARTICLE FOR OUTDOOR LIFE

The OUTDOOR LIFE regional article focuses on lakes, rivers, specific geographic locations, counties, shorelines and sometimes whole states or multi-state regions that are of special interest to hunters and fishermen. The article tells what aspect of the area, such as its being rediscovered, restocked or underutilized, will convince our readers to hunt or fish there. In other words, answer the question "What makes this certain area worth my time?"

Be specific when discussing a location. Include regulations, license fees, bag limits, accommodations and facilities pertinent to the area. The majority of your text should consist of "where to" information; the remainder can be utilized for technique or "how to," plus an anecdote, humor, or some other attempt to make the material interesting as well as useful. After reading the article, the reader should know all about the area or know where to obtain further information. Study of a recent issue is the best guideline.

Photographs are of utmost importance--they will often be the deciding factor in acceptance of the package. Submit only black and white prints. Color transparencies are okay, although we use only black and white in regional pages. Photos should be clear, crisp and have good contrast so they reproduce well. Include a caption sheet, and label each photo with your name and address.

Always query first with an article idea. Tell us exactly what you want to write about and why it's worth covering; i.e., an outline of the story. Include your supporting photography with the query package.

If your query is approved, the article is assigned <u>on speculation</u>. Pages and word lengths for regionals are as follows:

        One-pager.....900-1,100 words......$300-$350
        Two-pager...1,400-1,700 words......$450-$550

Rates vary according to quality of article and photos.

Include a stamped, self-addressed envelope with your query, and address it ot the editor of the particular region you're writing about--East, Midwest, South or West.

2--

East Editor
Michael C. Toth
OUTDOOR LIFE MAGAZINE
380 Madison Avenue
New York, N.Y. 10017

Midwest Editor
Gerald Bethge
(same address)

South Editor
George H. Haas
(same address)

West Editor
Stephanie Boyle
(same address)

Submit your idea eight months to one year before the issue
that you feel will be best suited to include your article.
Allow four weeks for a response.

1165 NORTH CLARK STREET • CHICAGO IL 60610 • 312-951-0990

EDITORIAL GUIDELINES
FOR PROSPECTIVE CONTRIBUTORS

OUTSIDE is a national magazine published 12 times a year for active, educated, upscale adults who love the outdoors and are concerned for its preservation. We publish well-written, original articles on all aspects of the outdoors. In particular, we look for solid, seasonal service pieces; profiles of outdoor personalities, regions, wildlife; adventure-oriented sports pieces with a national appeal; in-depth stories on outdoor lifestyles, sciences, activities, and important environmental issues.

Although most of our features are written by experienced writers, we are always interested in fresh ideas and new writers. We will give special attention to news of expeditions, adventures, and novel outdoor experiences, as well as prospects for photo stories. But each article or query we seriously consider, whatever the subject, should present a clear, provocative, and original thesis, not merely a topic or unformed idea. We also expect prospective contributors to be familiar with the magazine.

In addition to the five to seven full-length (2,000 to 4,000 words) articles we publish in each issue, we also carry the following regular freelance-written columns:

Dispatches: News and events relevant to the outdoors; in subject matter a microcosm of the magazine itself. Items are usually 200 to 700 words.

Review: An examination of a particular class of outdoor equipment, with evaluations of new innovations. From 1,000 to 1,500 words. Also, reviews and comments on the new, the classic, and the unusual in both equipment and resources. Items are usually 200 to 500 words.

Field Notes: An account of a particular event or occurrence, especially a sporting event. The specific subject need not be well known, but it should be interesting. From 1,200 to 1,500 words.

Law of the Land: An in-depth look at a current legal or political issue that affects the outdoors. 1,500 to 2,000 words.

Destinations: Activity-oriented travel ideas with a national scope; usually covers four or five locales within a given topic. 1,500 words.

Rates

Articles	$500–$1,500
Dispatches	$100–$200
Hardware/Software	$ 75–$125
Equipage	$400–$500
Field Notes	$500–$750
Law of the Land	$400–$500
Destinations	$400–$500

Payment is on publication; kill fee for assigned pieces is one-quarter of the negotiated article fee.

Photographs & Illustrations

Separate sets of guidelines are available for potential photographic contributors and/or illustrators; if you would like to submit photography or illustrations, please request photo or illustration guidelines from the photo or art departments.

Writing for OUTSIDE

The best source of information is the magazine itself; we suggest you look at several issues to become familiar with our style, subjects, and standards. Please send queries, *not manuscripts,* and include clips of published work. Our response time is usually four to six weeks. If your idea sounds intriguing, it will be discussed at an editorial meeting, where the editors will decide whether to assign the story. If you have little professional writing experience, you may be asked to submit the piece on speculation, without a guaranteed kill fee.

Address editorial correspondence to Articles Editor, OUTSIDE, 1165 N. Clark St., Chicago, IL 60610.

Thank you for considering OUTSIDE.

John Rasmus
Editor

OZARK AIRLINES *Ozark*

Laura Dean Bennett, editor
Coverage: Midwest

Format: Midwestern focus with some national; feature articles (personalities,
            fashion, sports, arts, business, food). Accent on the good life in
            the Midwest with each issue having a central theme.

Ozark magazine, published for Ozark Airlines, features the good life in the American
   Midwest with each issue having a central theme. (For instance, January's theme
   is Business.) One of Ozark's many national destinations outside the Midwest is
   featured each issue. Ozark's main focus being business, lifestyles, personality
   profiles, sports, food, travel, arts and fashion, it caters to a primary audience
   of traveling executives. Ozark also features unique columns, such as "Hometown"
   and "The Right Stuff" in an effort to bring the best of the Midwest to Ozark
   travelers. Each month, Ozark provides "The Ozark Traveler," a column of events
   and services of interest to business and leisure travelers.

For further information, see PSA Magazine.

<u>PACE MAGAZINE</u>

<u>EDITORIAL GUIDELINES</u>

<u>Departments</u>

Communication, Management Direction, Perspective, Forum and To Your Health highlight PACE magazine's regular departments. These speak directly to the business passenger with essential information for conducting business life. New departments include Southeastern Commercial Properties, highlights of commercial property information in the Southeast, and Computer Age, an analysis of business applications.

Other departments include Gallery, the presentation of original works of prominent artists depicting their particular modes of expression, and Cooking, by Dominique D'Ermo of Washington, DC, which takes the gourmet cook into the exotic adventure of cooking the unusual in wild game and delicacies.

These departments are furnished by a group of writers on contract to PACE. Free-lance submissions are not accepted.

<u>Features</u>

Acceptable free-lance features are those that focus on present and future trends in business. PACE magazine is acclaimed for its articles on principles and techniques of business management. This stated editorial mixture is one of progressiveness and readability, thus suiting Piedmont the "up and coming airline."

Below are some of the free-lance titles that have appeared recently in PACE.

Harness Your Selling Power With A Sales Script Book
This aid offers powerful assistance in helping you sell more efficiently.

Stop, Listen -- And Profit
Most executives and business managers spend about 80 percent of their time either listening to someone or being listened to.

Take Pounds Of Pressure Off - Reduce Corporate Stress
Stress management should be an important consideration in developing a healthy company.

MBC: Management By Contract
If we see the logic for needing a contract with everyone else, why not ourselves, too?

(over)

Searching For The Right Search Firm
Executive Search can no longer be considered
a small-time business.

Information Networks - Filling The Gaps
A manager's success may depend on how
well he is able to gather, handle and use
information.

Bulk Mail Gets Personal Service
The new generation of couriers bases its
trade on volume rather than value.

Cafeteria Programs - A New Trend in Employee Benefits
Flexible benefit programs can enable employees
and employers to realize substantial savings.

Diversification - Often Needed, Always Touchy
Beware if your particular strategy for thriving
in troubled times includes added diversity of the
wrong kind for the wrong reasons.

SPECIFIC GUIDELINES:

· The manuscript should be typed and double-spaced.

· The writing style should be lively and entertaining.

· Photographs or illustrations should be included if appropriate.

· We do not publish fiction, first-person narratives or reprints.

· A list of sources including addresses and phone numbers should be
included, if possible.

·
Free-lance material is accepted on speculation. Query letters
are also accepted. No telephone queries or simultaneous submissions.

· We buy First North American Serial Rights. Payment for the article
will be made upon its acceptance.

· You may not resell material until 30 days from the date of its
publication in PACE.

· A self-addressed stamped envelope should be included with submissions
and queries.

Circulation: 1.3 million (monthly) along Piedmont's cross-country
flight route. Our primary readers are upscale business travelers.

If you would like a recent copy of PACE magazine, send $3.00 and a
9 x 12 self-addressed stamped envelope.

Submit material to: Leslie P. Daisy
                             Managing Editor
                             PACE Magazine
                             338 N. Elm Street
                             Greensboro, NC 27401

PAN AM *Clipper*

Richard Kagan, editor
Coverage: Worldwide

Format: General interest stories on travel, the arts, science and technology,
            business, sports, food and beverages, fashion, adventure, humor.
            Designed and edited to appeal to the sophisticated business and
            pleasure traveler on Pan Am's domestic and international routes.
            Articles are urbane in tone, designed for an affluent audience.

PAN AM CLIPPER selects products, places, arts, personalities which measure
     up to an international definition of World Class. Provocative
     articles on art, latest technological developments, business trends,
     fashion, sports, foods and travel provide the reader with inside
     information and color-filled pages of incentive. "Clipper Panorama"
     features special events as well as the latest gadgets, scientific
     discoveries, theatre, culinary happenings and untold art treasures.

For further information, see PSA Magazine.

CONTRIBUTOR'S GUIDE

Thank you for your interest in PARADE. Here are some suggested guidelines for prospective writers but please recognize that the diversity of stories we publish is as great as the 48 million readers we reach every Sunday.

Editorial features must be exclusive and oriented to news, issues or personalities.

Choose a topic that would appeal to as much of PARADE's vast readership as possible. A story about the poor treatment of inmates at a Reno jail might have limited appeal. But the subject of strip searches of women suspects in jails across the entire nation could reach a much broader audience.

Keep your article short and simple. PARADE has room to publish only the most tightly focused story. An article that cannot be gripping and complete at 1500 words is not worth submitting. Also, any story should be aimed at an audience unfamiliar with your subject. If you choose to write about new treatments for mental illness, for example, you should carefully define your terms for everyone.

Write on something you care about deeply. If a topic does not make you happy or sad, angry or elated, chances are that PARADE readers won't care that much either.

PARADE is interested in nationally known figures in all fields. Other areas of interest include: health, consumer and environmental issues, education, community activities (with national applications), the family, sports, science and science-related articles.

Articles should be current, factual, authoritative and 1300 to 1500 words in length. Spot news events are not accepted, as PARADE has a six-week lead time.

PARADE does not solicit or accept freelance work for Personality Parade, Intelligence Report or Laugh Parade. PARADE does not publish fiction, poetry, games, puzzles, quizzes, lists of quotes or "tidbits," or personal columns.

PARADE purchases First North American Rights and will accept completed manuscripts on speculation. Assignments are made on the basis of query letters of one page. PARADE pays a minimum of $1000.

Photographs should have visual impact and be well composed with action-stopping qualities. All photographs must be accompanied by text and accurate caption material. Transparencies of any size are accepted, as are black and white 8 x 10 enlargements or contact sheets. Stock photos: $75 each. Cover: $750, pro-rated for combinations. Assignments: At ASMP rates. Query Photo Editor before submitting material.

PARADE is not responsible for any unsolicited material, manuscripts, transparencies, negatives or photographs. A stamped self-addressed envelope must accompany all submissions. PARADE does not pay service charges. All photographic material will be returned after publication.

Again, thank you for your interest. It is only fair to say that PARADE accepts only a small percentage of the articles it receives. However, you can be sure that anything you submit will receive close attention.

CONTACT: Articles Editor
PARADE Magazine
750 Third Avenue
New York, N.Y. 10017

ARTICLE REQUIREMENTS

WE ARE INTERESTED IN:

> *Articles which offer professional and/or personal insights into family and marriage relationships.*
>
> *Articles that help women to cope with our rapidly changing world.*
>
> *Well-documented articles on the problems and successes of preschool, schoolage, and adolescent children—— and their parents.*
>
> *Good, practical guides to the routines of baby care.*
>
> *Reports of new trends and significant research findings in education and in mental and physical health.*
>
> *Articles encouraging informed citizen action on matters of social concern.*

We prefer a warm, colloquial style of writing, one which avoids the extremes of either slanginess or technical jargon. Anecdotes and examples should be used to illustrate points which can then be summed up by straight exposition.

Articles vary in length from 1,500 to 3,000 words. Payment is on acceptance.

We recommend that writers query us about an article idea before submitting a completed manuscript. Manuscripts should be typed, double-spaced, and must be accompanied by a stamped self-addressed envelope.

Please allow three to four weeks for a reply.

The Editors

PARENTS MAGAZINE

PARENTS MAGAZINE ENTERPRISES 685 THIRD AVENUE, NEW YORK, N.Y. 10017 (212) 878-8700

THE PARIS REVIEW

SUBMISSION OF MANUSCRIPTS

Fiction manuscripts should be submitted to George Plimpton; poetry to Jonathan Galassi c/o The Paris Review, 541 East 72nd Street, New York, NY 10021. We regret that we are not responsible for manuscripts not accompanied by stamped, self-addressed envelopes. Material must be in English and previously unpublished. Translations are acceptable and should be accompanied by a copy of the original text. We suggest to all who submit that they read through several issues of The Paris Review to acquaint themselves with the material that we publish. Copies of The Paris Review are available in many public libraries. Sample copies may be ordered from the Flushing office (45-39 171 Place, Flushing, NY 11358) for $6.00 per copy (includes postage and handling), or $16 for a one year subscription (four issues).

THE AGA KHAN PRIZE FOR FICTION

The Aga Khan Prize for fiction is awarded annually by the editors of The Paris Review for the best previously unpublished short story (1,000—10,000 words) submitted. Work should be submitted between May 1st and June 1st. Winning selection will be announced in the fall issue. The winning manuscript, awarded one thousand dollars, will be published in the following issue of The Paris Review. No applications are necessary; regular submission guidelines apply.

THE BERNARD F. CONNERS PRIZE FOR POETRY

The Bernard F. Conners Prize for Poetry is awarded annually by the editors of The Paris Review for the finest unpublished poem over 300 lines submitted. Work should be submitted between April 1st and May 1st. Winning selection will be announced in the fall issue. The winning manuscript, awarded one thousand dollars, will be published in the following issue of The Paris Review. Please address to The Poetry Editor/BF Conners Prize. No applications necessary; regular submission guidelines apply.

THE JOHN TRAIN HUMOR PRIZE

The John Train Humor Prize is awarded annually for the best previously unpublished work of humorous fiction, nonfiction, or poetry. Manuscripts should be received by March 31st. Judges are Brendan Gill, Lewis Lapham, George Plimpton, John Train. The winning manuscript, awarded $1500, will be published in The Paris Review. Please address to The John Train Humor Prize. Regular submission guidelines apply.

HUNTING

8490 SUNSET BOULEVARD · LOS ANGELES, CALIFORNIA 90069 · (213) 657-5100

GUIDELINES FOR PROSPECTIVE CONTRIBUTORS

Subject matter and storyline must be tailored to the interests of the North American hunter. The best form and guide for this is the magazine itself. We reserve the right to edit any accepted manuscript.

Manuscripts must be typed, double-spaced on plain white paper, with author's name, story title and page number appearing on each page. Length should range between 2,000 and 2,500 words.

Hunting articles should be of a semi-technical nature. We are looking for the How-To article rather than the romance of a hunt. We want our readers to be informed completely about their intended quarry. While not a requirement, hunting anecdotes are preferred, to demonstrate the practical use of methods discussed. Articles of a more general nature, such as building a duck blind, must be keyed to hunting. For example, instead of "Simple and Effective Blind Construction," approach the subject from the standpoint that "Better Blinds Result in More Ducks." Short, one-page filler material is sometimes of interest.

All manuscripts must include photographs sufficient to cover all phases of the subject. Specifically, photos of technical "how-to" interest, live action and trophy shots as well as live game are needed. The photographs must enhance the story and lead the reader into the storyline. Manuscripts submitted without photos will most certainly be rejected. Ideally, black and white photos should be printed on 8"x10" single-weight, glossy paper. Prints must be sharp, with the subject well-defined and properly lighted, printed at a contrast suitable for reproduction. Prints that are fuzzy, very light or dark are not usable. Sharp transparencies are required for color. The best package will have 10 to 12 black and white glossies and a selection of excellent slides (preferably Kodachrome), never less than a total of 15.

Rate of pay depends on physical quality of material submitted (neat, organized, requiring little or no rewrite or clean-up), timeliness of subject matter and reputation of author. Short filler material will earn $100.00; feature material will average between $300.00 and $400.00 including all black and white photos. Color photos will be handled independently; since the quality, subject matter and size vary greatly, each color contribution will be evaluated and the price determined through consultation between author and editor.

Publishers of: HOT ROD • MOTOR TREND • CAR CRAFT
MOTORCYCLIST • DIRT RIDER • 4-WHEEL & OFF-ROAD • PICKUPS & MINI-TRUCKS
CIRCLE TRACK • GUNS & AMMO • PETERSEN'S HUNTING • 'TEEN • PHOTOGRAPHIC
SKIN DIVER • SEA and a variety of SPECIALTY PUBLICATIONS
Offices in: Los Angeles, New York, Chicago, Detroit, Cleveland, Atlanta, Dallas

8490 SUNSET BOULEVARD · LOS ANGELES, CALIFORNIA 90069 · (213) 657-5100

PHOTOGRAPHER'S GUIDELINES

Generally HUNTING Magazine is more interested in hunting photography than in wildlife shots but we do like to have both in our files. In particular, we would like to see more action hunting scenes, with both the game and the hunter in the photo; and action wildlife shots such as birds in flight and running game.

We usually purchase all rights to the photos at the time of publication. We pay $35.00 for each glossy black and white print used in our magazine. If possible, all 35mm transparencies should be Kodachrome rather than Ektachrome since Ektachrome presents a reproduction problem. However, if you have top-quality Ektachrome, we may be able to use it. Rates for color transparencies are:

    Cover: $350.00

    Inside Color: $75.00 - $100.00 per photo,
                    $150.00 maximum for two or
                    more photos on one page.

If you wish to submit 20 to 60 35mm color slides and/or 8"x10" black and white prints, we will consider them for possible use. It is our policy to keep a few of these photos on file which we feel we may be able to use in the near future. Please indicate whether you wish to sell all rights or one-time use only. Also include your social security number and phone number.

Thank you for your interest in Petersen's HUNTING Magazine. We look forward to seeing some of your work.

C. A. Yeseta
Art Director

Publishers of: HOT ROD • MOTOR TREND • CAR CRAFT
MOTORCYCLIST • DIRT RIDER • 4-WHEEL & OFF-ROAD • PICKUPS & MINI-TRUCKS
CIRCLE TRACK • GUNS & AMMO • PETERSEN'S HUNTING • 'TEEN • PHOTOGRAPHIC
SKIN DIVER • SEA and a variety of SPECIALTY PUBLICATIONS
Offices in: Los Angeles, New York, Chicago, Detroit, Cleveland, Atlanta, Dallas

PETERSEN'S
Photographic
MAGAZINE
Writer's and Photographer's Guide

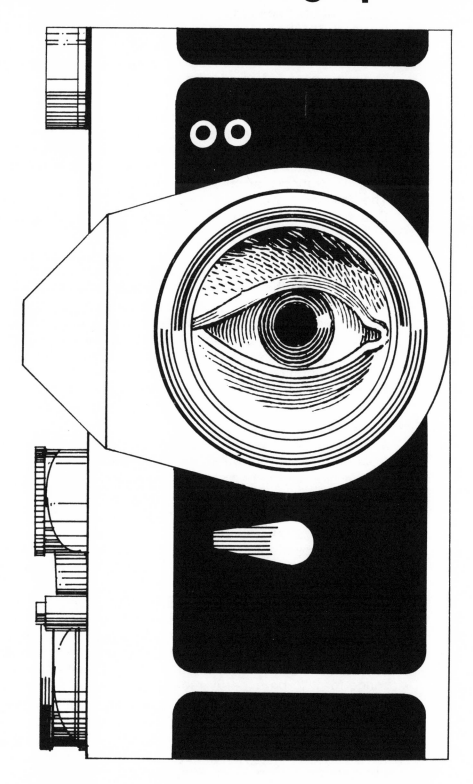

EDITORIAL CONCEPT	PhotoGraphic Magazine is edited for the amateur and advanced beginner in all phases of still- and motion-picture photography. Emphasis is on "how-to" articles, clearly written and well-illustrated, in color and black-and-white. No fiction, cartoons or poetry. Contributions are on speculation, subject to final editorial approval. No assignments.
GENERAL COPY REQUIREMENTS	Typed, double-spaced, single side only. Preferably a maximum of 60 characters to a line. Manuscripts must be submitted in final draft form; captions on a separate sheet. Material may be condensed or portions of the manuscript edited to meet PM requirements.
GENERAL ILLUSTRATION REQUIREMENTS	Because PhotoGraphic Magazine is devoted to photography, all photographic illustrations must be technically accurate, sharp and in focus, well-lighted and printed with a full range of tones. Probably more manuscripts are rejected for poor illustration than any other reason.

The following are general rules-of-thumb for contributors. Doubtless, visual requirements will vary from story to story. However, use the following as a general guide:

1. Photos should be 8×10 glossies or matte prints with a one-inch-wide white margin. The margin is used to mark instructions to the printer. Irreplaceable, one-of-a-kind prints are unacceptable.

2. If a technique or process is the theme of the article, photographs must be submitted that show EACH AND EVERY STEP. We can edit out pictures if we don't have the space to accommodate them. However, we cannot add pictures if we don't have them on hand.

3. Include at least one photograph of materials required, shown all together.

4. Show finished product in one photograph. If details vary from one angle to another, show various angles.

5. Use close-up shot to show any small details or process.

6. If the "how-to" result is an image or effect, try to show in the procedure shots (requirement No. 2) the same example that you're using for the finished result.

7. All step-by-step product shots should be made with a clean, uncluttered background. Seamless paper is recommended for this purpose.

8. If mechanical drawings, plans, cutaways, charts, etc. would be helpful in showing what is to be achieved, please include them. If you don't have the ability to do your own, then submit a rough sketch, properly identified with dimensions and all other information. The Art Director will arrange for it to be expertly redrawn.

9. If the object is small enough to send to us, please do! It will be returned later.

10. All illustration captions must be on a separate sheet of paper, identified by numbers that match corresponding numbers on the prints or illustrations.

FEATURE REQUIREMENTS

COLOR ARTICLES: Color transparencies will not be accepted on the basis of content alone. All color presentations serve an absolute editorial concept. That is, they illustrate a technique, process or how-to article. Cover photographs also illustrate an editorial presentation, and covers are considered editorial material.

PORTFOLIOS: Each month, PhotoGraphic Magazine presents the work of a photographer of high professional accomplishment. Portfolio presentations are in black-and-white. A minimum of 15 prints should accompany each submission, and all details relating to the prints must also accompany the portfolio. If the portfolio is selected, the photographer will be contacted for additional information.

GALLERY: A special three-page section reserved for presenting single photos by readers. There is no limit to the number of prints that may be submitted, transparencies are limited to five per submission. All photos must be identified with name and address. Full technical information and stamped, return mailer must accompany each submission. Textured-finish machine prints are NOT acceptable.

BLACK-AND-WHITE ARTICLES: These can be on virtually any subject that relates to photography. Movies, stills, filters, films, etc. All black-and-white articles must be complete, well-illustrated, and along the lines of how-to, techniques, processes, or general photographic interest.

SUBMISSION REQUIREMENTS

All materials submitted to PhotoGraphic Magazine must be well-wrapped, preferably with heavy cardboard to prevent damage to the enclosed material. All submissions must also be accompanied by a stamped, self-addressed return mailer only. No loose stamps, no money.

PAY RATES

Editorial copy:	$60 per published page/color and black-and-white
Portfolios:	$35 per photograph used
Gallery:	$25 per photograph used
Covers:	As covers are considered part of an editorial presentation, special arrangements will be made with the author/photographer.

ACCEPTANCE

Manuscripts submitted to PhotoGraphic Magazine are considered "accepted" upon publication. All material held on a "tentatively scheduled" basis is subject to change or rejection right up to the time of printing. It is understood that material submitted to PhotoGraphic Magazine is original, free and clear of all copyrights, and in no way infringes upon previously published works. Upon publication, the material is copyrighted by PhotoGraphic Magazine, and permission to reprint any of the material must be obtained, in writing, from the publisher.

SCHEDULING

Generally, the editorial staff of PhotoGraphic Magazine plans issues 5-7 months in advance.

Karen Sue Geller, *Editor*

1500 Walnut Street
Philadelphia, PA 19102
(215) 545-3500

GUIDELINES FOR FREELANCE WRITERS

Articles can run from 1000 to 7000 words. They must be <u>non-fiction</u> with a definite Philadelphia slant and appeal to a sophisticated audience. Stories should flesh out subjects in human terms, illustrating points with specific examples and quotes, and clarifying complex subjects. It is essential that you study our magazine before trying to write for us. We'll send you a sample copy for $3.00.

<u>Query</u> by letter. If you've never written for us before, include magazine clips or the first few pages of the story itself. <u>Unsolicited manuscripts</u> are considered, although we don't read photocopied or simultaneous submissions.

<u>Manuscripts</u> should be typed, double-spaced, on 8½" x 11" white bond with substantial margins. Make corrections in pencil. Send us the original, and keep a copy. Please enclose a SASE with all manuscripts. Address queries and manuscripts to Bill Tonelli, Articles Editor. We report within a month. Seasonal material should be submitted at least three months in advance.

<u>Editing</u> is done to make articles as readable and unimpeachable as possible, although major changes are subject to the writer's agreement.

<u>By-lines</u> are used to give credit to the writer and also to inform our readers. For this reason, we permit pseudonyms or anonymous articles only in exceptional cases.

<u>Payment</u> ranges from $100 upward, depending on the importance of the subject, the effort involved in treating it properly and the amount of editing required. Payment is made on final acceptance. If an assigned article is judged unacceptable, we will pay a kill fee of 20% of the assigned fee. We do not pay a kill fee for unacceptable articles submitted on speculation. We reserve the right to rescind an assignment if the article isn't submitted by the assigned deadline. We make no commitment to run an article in any particular month.

A Subsidiary of Metrocorp

Tips on writing for THE PITTSBURGH Press Sunday Magazine

READERS READ magazines differently than they read newspapers. They subconsciously commit a longer block of time to a magazine story than they do to a newspaper story, which they expect to give them information fast.

The following tips are offered to help smooth the transition into magazine style:

1. Read good magazine writing — Esquire, New York Magazine, New Yorker non-fiction, New York Times Sunday Magazine, Inquirer Magazine of the Philadelphia Inquirer. Some of these are available for perusal at the magazine desk. Note the difference in style between those stories and and regular newspaper stories.

2. Read previous issues of THE PITTSBURGH Press Sunday Magazine to gauge the range of story ideas and how they were handled.

3. Develop a flow to the story. One thought must lead to another, building a story line with smooth transitions. As opposed to newswriting, where you give the reader information in the most efficient way possible, your intention in writing a magazine piece is to tell a story.

4. Stories need narrative. Do not hesitate to develop scenes, characters and situations in your own words.

5. Images often are what the reader best remembers. If the 250-pound spy enters a room like a tiptoeing elephant, say so. Just make sure the images are precise and accurate.

6. Show, don't tell. Instead of telling your readers the room was cold and drafty, give them the details that show the cold — a character puffing clouds of vapor, a flickering candle, the butler wearing mittens. Effective use of detail lets the reader see. Useless, cluttering details should be left out.

7. Keep related thoughts in the same paragraph. In a newspaper story, paragraphs are kept short to speed the reader along. There is no need to artificially break the flow of a magazine story. Paragraphs should signal a reader that a new thought is being introduced.

8. Avoid newspaperese. In the economy of newspaper writing, a man who dedicated his life to police work, who made a career during weekends and midnight shifts and who faced countless dangers for inadequate pay becomes a "28-year police veteran." For the magazine, there is no need to boil the elements of a personality into such efficient language.

9. But don't overwrite. If the subject is not compelling enough to carry it without exaggeration and flowery embellishment, the value of the story immediately comes into question.

10. Don't be afraid to use present tense.

11. Give the story a narrow focus. Rather than a story on the Pittsburgh Symphony, tell us about a cellist's frustrating search for a new cello.

12. Once the story is focused, broaden the perspective. A story focused on our cellist can raise a much larger question — why are orchestra players willing to take huge financial risks? A story on the Pennsylvania lumber industry is good. A story that relates the industry to missed opportunities and undeveloped potential is better.

13. Draw conclusions and interpret what you have seen and learned. If the most powerful banker in town has a pencil-thin moustache and dresses in hand-painted Niagara Falls ties, white bucks and loud sports jackets, provide the reader with those details. If his taste in clothes seems more befitting a used car salesman, say so.

14. Use literary techniques — foreshadowing, symbolism, imagery, suspense, dialogue, juxtaposition, anecdotes.

15. Do an outline in advance when possible. This helps you plot the flow of the story and enables you to see where the above literary techniques might be effective.

16. You are writing for an audience that presumably is more literate, better educated, younger, wealthier and otherwise more sophisticated than the general newspaper audience. Do not write down to them.

17. Save your notes in case material must be added.

18. Experiment with style. There is no right formula.

Length

SUGGESTED length for a cover story — 80 to 100 inches. Suggested length for an inside story — 40 to 60 inches.

Remuneration

PAY RATES: Between $100 and $400 for a free-lance story. Settle on a price before proceeding. For stories done on speculation, no kill fee will be paid should the story be unsuitable for use. For stories assigned by the editor, a previously agreed upon kill fee will be paid if the story is unsuitable.

PLAYBOY

<u>WRITER'S GUIDELINES -- NONFICTION</u>

PLAYBOY regularly features nonfiction articles on a wide range
of topics--sports, politics, music, topical humor, personality
profiles, business and finance, science and technology--and
other topics that have some bearing on our readers' lifestyles.
You can best determine what we're looking for by becoming familiar
with the nonfiction we are currently publishing and evaluating
our tastes and judgment. We have a six-month lead time, so timing
is very important.

<u>A brief query or proposal</u> that outlines your idea, explains why
it's right for PLAYBOY and tells us something about yourself will
get the most prompt and thorough attention. Submissions should be
accompanied by a self-addressed, stamped envelope (SASE). Illegible
and/or handwritten copy will be returned unread. Nonfiction queries
should be sent to the attention of the Articles Editor.

The average length for nonfiction pieces is 4,000 - 5,000 words.
Minimum payment for that length is $3,000. PLAYBOY buys first North
American serial rights only--no second serial rights are considered.

Lastly, PLAYBOY does not consider simultaneous submissions.

PLAYBOY MAGAZINE/THE PLAYBOY BUILDING/919 NORTH MICHIGAN AVENUE/CHICAGO ILLINOIS 60611/312 PL 1-8000

PLAYGIRL magazine is interested in articles and fiction that appeal
to the active, modern women between the age of 20 and 35 who likes
the no-nonsense approach to understanding the current world around her.

Our purpose is to inform while we entertain:

  *Writing should be humorous and informal, but well-structured
   and grammatical.

  *Articles each month fall under categories of information, sex/
   relationships and trends. Length is 2500 to 3500 words. All
   facts and statements must be documented. Examples of information
   pieces that were published in 1979 are the guide to birth control
   and how to fight depression. Sex/relationship features were
   a discussion of erotic dreams and bedroom etiquette. Trend
   pieces, for example, included women successful in business and
   whether or not marriage is popular. Non-fiction submissions
   MUST be preceded by a query letter outlining your idea and
   the intended story treatment. We will let you know if we're
   interested in seeing a manuscript. Adress all query letters
   to the Nonfiction Editor.

  *Fiction should be approximately 2500 words. Interpersonal
   relationships and erotic romance are preferred topics. Fiction
   manuscripts must be accompanied by a SASE or submissions will
   not be returned. Address fiction to Fiction Editor. Allow
   six weeks for a response.

  *Interviews with well-known and current personalities are
   accepted, but send a query letter FIRST to the Editor.

  *We accept cartoon submissions.

PLAYGIRL is always growing and changing, for we feel growth is necessary
for enlightment. The very best way to see what our magazine is interested
in, as far as workable topics which we want to present to our readers, is
by picking up a current issue on the newsstand. We think you'll get the
idea just by seeing our latest product.

                                        --the Editors

POPULAR COMPUTING

AUTHOR'S GUIDE

Popular Computing is a monthly consumer magazine for the personal computer enthusiast. Our readers are affluent, well-educated and interested in issues that affect their use of personal computers. In many cases, our readers also write for the magazine. Topics of particular interest include unusual or noteworthy problem-solving applications, programming tips that make your personal computer a more valuable tool or reviews of hardware and software products.

First Steps

Before sending a final manuscript, please send us a detailed article proposal that includes a statement of what the article is about, an outline of the complete manuscript and a brief of your background. Using this approach saves you unnecessary work and gives both of us a sound basis for coordinating the best possible article on the subject. Send your proposal to Popular Computing, 70 Main St., Peterborough, N.H. 03458 and include the words "Article Proposal" on the outside of the envelope. After we receive your proposal, it will be reviewed by the editorial staff and you should expect to receive a decision from us within six weeks. Make sure to keep a copy of whatever materials you send and call about the status of your proposal if you have not heard from us in the allotted time period. If your proposal concerns a product review, contact Beverly Cronin (software editor) or Dennis Allen (hardware editor) for specific review guidelines.

Acceptance

If a proposal sounds interesting and applicable to the readership of Popular Computing, we will contact you to discuss your article idea more fully. This step may involve discussions of story angle, length, and scope. Other considerations will be the deadline, scheduled issue and payment rate for accepted material. When we receive the finished article, a final decision will be reached regarding the acceptance of the manuscript for publication.

Format

All submitted articles must be double-spaced on 8½ × 11 inch paper and printed either by a letter-quality or high-quality dot matrix printer. Tables and figures should be clearly executed and labelled appropriately. Listings should either be printed on a letter-quality printer or provisions made to submit them electronically. Please remember to format program listings so that the paper break does not chop part of a line. Photographs should be as professional as possible and color is preferable over black and white. We prefer to work with color slides and black & white prints. Include captions for all materials included with the manuscript. Please submit two copies of the manuscript for editing.

Style

Above all else, your writing should be clear and informative. Your audience is already interested in personal computers and remains eager to learn more. When you talk to these readers, tell them what you are going to talk about and then do it. Write in the active voice and involve your reader in the article. Try to avoid peppering your text with too much jargon, but don't be afraid to use it if necessary. Don't waste your time or your reader's by treating the topic too lightly or too ponderously. Focus on the one major point you want to make and guide the reader to additional material through lists of reference and other sources. Use subheads to organize your work and to help the reader move easily through the text.

Final Word

Some of the best information about the use of personal computers comes from those who use them. Don't think that your idea will not be interesting and informative. Let us know about it.

Framework for Software Reviews

This is not a required organization, nor are any of the items mandatory. Please use it as a stimulus for questions to be asked and answered about a given product. Also realize that the background material you provide must be somewhat abbreviated.

One final note: The review is supposed to be interesting reading for casual readers as well as those actually in the market for this type of product.

I. Select Audience
   A. What does the program do; what's it for?
   B.   Who is it for; any expertise needed?
II. Background
   A. Is this a new type of program or application, a refinement, an attempt to overthrow an existing standard?
   B. Briefly explain the terms and concepts used in discussing this kind of program.
   C. Give the criterion to be used for judgments about the program.
III. Review
   A. Highlights that make this package unique.
   B. Description of important features.
   C. "Human factors": Is it practical and easy to use? Are menus and help commands provided? Good printed instructions?
   D. Limitations of the program (data storage capacity, etc.).
   E. How well does the program use the computer's intrinsic capabilities. (For example, if the computer has graphics capabilities, does the program use them? If special function keys are available, are they used?).
IV. Sample use: Give the reader a clear idea of what's involved in setting up and daily use of the program.
V. Conclusions
   A. Does it accomplish its purpose for the target audience?
   B. Is it a good value (price competitive)?

At a Glance format, software

Name: [name of product under review]
Type: [generic description]
Manufacturer: [name, address, and phone number of original maker or primary vendor]
Price: [manufacturer's suggested retail]
Format: [distribution medium (5¼ inch disk, 8 inch disk, cassette)]
Computer: [System name and minimum equipment requirements. This includes minimum RAM and required peripherals but does not include firmware. For example, don't go into details of Applesoft BASIC, Apple II Plus, DOS 3.3, etc. Instead, just say Apple II with 48K bytes of RAM (or whatever).]
Documentation: [books, audio tapes, etc.]
Audience: [who might be interested and able to benefit]

224 West 57th Street • New York, N.Y. 10019 • 212 262-5700

EDITORIAL GUIDELINES

We are always in the market for good freelance articles, and invite your queries. Because our magazine is divided into departments according to subject matter, your editorial queries should be directed to the departmental editor in charge of your area of interest. The editors are listed at the end of this guide.

Since we do not print fiction, please don't submit any articles of fiction. Because of the workload of editors, queries are best handled by a short paragraph and perhaps a photo or drawing via mail.

We print about 100 editorial pages each month. Therefore, we go through a lot of material. So before you submit a query, do a little homework. Check with the Guide to Periodical Literature and/or our own indexes to editorial features. Chances are, we've already published an article similar to the one you are about to propose. Don't waste your time unless you are ready to give us something new that we haven't run before.

Our typical reader is male, about 37 years old, married with a couple of kids, owns his own home and several cars, makes a good salary, and probably works in a technically oriented profession. Keep this in mind before proposing articles.

Submission Format

All articles must be submitted to us typewritten, double spaced on one side of the page only. All manuscripts must include a self-addressed, stamped envelope with sufficient return postage in the event we do not accept your submission.

All articles must be accompanied by well-lit, clear, black and white photos or rough artwork that we can use to produce finished art for publication. Photos should be either 5x7 or 8x10 in size, glossy finish. If we like an idea, we may also ask you to supply color photos. These should be 35mm or larger transparencies. We pay anywhere from $15 for a reader hint to $1000 and more for major features. We pay on acceptance and purchase all rights.

Here is some specific information from each of our areas of editorial interest.

- 2 -

Automotive

We're usually looking for articles on how a car owner can better
maintain and/or repair his own car. These are specific how-to
articles with step-by-step information and photos. We also like
articles on how car owners who do their own work can improve
their own shops, make new and unusual tools and equipment which
will help in their do-it-yourself projects, or extend the life
of their cars.

We also occasionally publish driving-oriented articles that help
readers handle specific kinds of driving conditions and/or
emergencies.

We do all our own road testing and conduct our own owner surveys.
So please don't query us about submitting driving reports on
specific models, or what it's like owning a specific car.

Home and Shop

We buy how-to-do-it articles on home improvement, home maintenance,
energy-saving techniques, shop and craft projects. These must
be well illustrated with photos and drawings. Finished drawings
suitable for publication are not necessary. Rough, but accurate,
pencil drawings are adequate for artist's copy. Topnotch photos
are a must, the drawings preferably done in pencil and the photos
shot during construction of the project as well as after construction.
Photos should be taken with a background that is not cluttered or
distracting from the main action.

Science/Technology

We are interested in both long and short pieces that cover the
latest developments in science, technology, industry and discovery.
We stress the newsworthy here. An old subject can be interesting
if new facts have recently come to light. Accuracy is paramount.
Check your facts and sources before submitting queries.

As a general rule, we are not interested in machines or inventions
applicable to a very limited field or industry; ordinary industrial
processes; informative material without a news angle, such as found
in textbooks or encyclopedias; items that deal with accidents or
freaks of nature.

In any article query, you should be specific as to what makes
the development new, different, better, cheaper, or interesting.

Outdoors/Boating

We publish articles on new equipment in the boating and outdoors
areas. Also, articles on how to maintain and/or repair boats,
boat engines, camping equipment, motorcycles, recreational vehicles,
etc.

- 3 -

We are also interested in articles covering new types of outdoor recreational devices, such as paraplanes, balloons, all-terrain vehicles, campers, etc. Also, articles on how to make your own recreational devices that can be enjoyed out of doors. Testing of new boats, RVs or outdoor gear is conducted by our own staff.

Electronics/Photography

We publish articles on new types of equipment in the audio, video, computer, photographic and optical fields, but most of these are done by our staff. Freelance purchases are usually articles on how to make interesting electronic projects that make life better for the user. Also, we buy step-by-step how-to features on repairing and maintaining audio, video, computer and other electronic and photographic equipment.

We also publish technique articles such as how to take trick photos, new developing techniques, how to use specific software for computers, how to hook up stereo equipment and telephones in the home, etc. Check some back issues for specific areas of our coverage.

Aviation

We publish articles on ultralight aircraft, homebuilt aircraft, new commercial aircraft, new combat aircraft, etc. Also, we are interested in restoration projects on older collectible aircraft and other hands-on type articles that involve planes.

General Interest Articles

We occasionally publish general interest articles. We look for pieces with strong science, exploration or adventure emphasis. We also publish hints that make a reader's life easier and/or more enjoyable.

Departmental Editors

If your query doesn't fit into any of the departments, send it to the executive editor.

```
        Science/Technology............Dennis Eskow

        Aviation......................Sheldon Gallager

        Outdoors/Boating..............Ray Hill

        Automotive....................Wade Hoyt

        Home and Shop.................Penny Spangler

        Electronics/Photography.......Stephen Gray

        Executive Editor..............Joe Oldham
```

Popular Photography

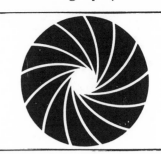

ONE PARK AVENUE
NEW YORK, NEW YORK
10016

(212) 503-3700

Suggestions for Contributors

Contributions of photographs are welcome, and all are carefully reviewed for possible use in POPULAR PHOTOGRAPHY and the PHOTOGRAPHY ANNUAL. Submissions should be addressed to the Picture Department and may be noted as entries for a particular publication; otherwise we will consider them for any appropriate use.

Edit your own work and submit the best, rather than a great number of pictures. Black and white or color prints should be at least 8x10, transparencies may be 35-mm or larger. YOU MUST HAVE A MODEL RELEASE AVAILABLE ON REQUEST FOR ANY PHOTOGRAPHS TAKEN IN THE U.S. THAT INCLUDE RECOGNIZABLE INDIVIDUALS.

Mailing: You should protect your work by careful packaging, preferably using a printing paper box or cardboard mailer larger than your prints so that they arrive undamaged. We cannot be responsible for their safe return, but we will make every effort to handle and return them with care. YOUR NAME AND ADDRESS MUST BE CLEARLY MARKED ON EVERY ITEM to prevent loss. A stamped, self-addressed envelope MUST be enclosed with the submission. If you are visiting the New York area or live close by, you may call for an appointment to present your work in person. Appointments are held on mornings during the week, except for Mondays and Fridays. Please try to call us a week in advance.

Under our new system, we will make slide dupes of any color slides and Polaroids of any black and white prints which are of interest to us. All originals will be returned to you within 3-5 weeks, along with a note telling you which pictures we are considering. We will keep the copies on file until we decide to use them, at which time we will ask you to send us the originals for reproduction.

Deadlines for Submissions:

All POPULAR PHOTOGRAPHY monthly issues are compiled six months in advance of cover date and the deadline for the PHOTOGRAPHY ANNUAL is presently November 1, but please check with us in the fall for any updates in scheduling.

Popular Photography

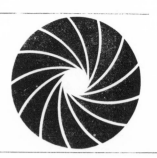

ONE PARK AVENUE
NEW YORK, NEW YORK
10016

(212) 725-3777

We are primarily interested in articles on new or unusual phases of photography which we have not covered previously or in recent years. We do not want general articles on photography which could just as easily be written by our staff. Manuscripts should be carefully prepared, technically accurate, and slanted toward the interest and comprehension of the amateur photographer. Naturally, we reserve the right to rewrite, edit, or revise any material we purchase.

MANUSCRIPTS should be accompanied by illustrations such as attractive photographs to support the text or how-to-do-it pictures (particularly when equipment is to be constructed or a process is involved).

We also welcome queries concerning any ideas for stories. These should consist of a brief, one-page outline of the proposed story plus a few pictures to show what type of illustration is available.

The rate of payment depends upon the importance of the feature, quality of the photographs, and our presentation of it. Generally, we pay by page-rate, meaning the number of pages that the story takes originally in the display part of the magazine. This does not include continued material in the back of the book, so the length of any story in words is generally not consideration in payment. Usually, payment for a black-and-white page is $125 per page; for a color page it is $200 per page. Manuscripts should not exceed 2,000 words, and fewer are preferred.

PICTURES should be of high quality, possessing human and photographic interest. We are especially interested in pictures which are unusual, dramatic, or which involve some new photographic technique. Black-and-white or color prints submitted should be no larger than 11x14 in., preferably 8x10 in. Transparencies may be of any size, including 35-mm. Color transparencies and prints will also be considered for covers and special features. Prices for pictures will vary according to our use of them.

CARTOONS AND SPOT DRAWINGS may be submitted initially in rough form. Those accepted should be finished, ink line-drawings.

All written material should be typed double-spaced on paper separate from the accompanying letter. The sender's name and address should be clearly written on the back of each picture, on the mount of each transparency, and on the first and last pages of all written material, including the accompanying letter.

When pertinent, technical data should accompany all pictures, including the camera used, lens, film, shutter speed, aperture, lighting, and any other points of special interest on how the picture was made.

Material sent to us should be carefully wrapped or packaged to avoid damage. We assume no responsibility for its safe return, but we will make every effort to handle and return it with care.

ALL MATERIAL SENT IN (whether manuscripts, photographs, or transparencies) MUST BE ACCOMPANIED BY A STAMPED, SELF-ADDRESSED RETURN ENVELOPE. SEND ALL MATERIAL TO THE ABOVE ADDRESS.

380 MADISON AVENUE, NEW YORK, N.Y. 10017, TELEPHONE: (212) 687-3000

WRITING FOR POPULAR SCIENCE
Guidelines for Contributors

"...Popular Science has always been a demanding forum. Its editors are not ready to accept unconfirmed facts and figures, vague statements, hunches, or guesswork. Contributors really have to do their homework. They also have to explain things in simple terms--not easy when it comes to the sophisticated concepts I had to wrestle with, such as inertial navigation systems, the interior structure of the sun, or the eerie aspects of future interstellar spaceflight at relativistic speeds (sorry, that's too technical: I guess I should have said at velocities close to the speed of light). Science is one of the most essential activities of our time. Popular Science fulfills a vital function by translating it from the secret vernacular of its high priests into language every intelligent citizen can understand."

--Wernher von Braun, 1972

For more than a century, since 1872, Popular Science has been devoted to exploring and explaining to a nontechnical but knowledgeable readership the technical world around us. We call Popular Science the "what's new" magazine because of its special focus: new developments in science and technology, new products, imaginative activities that spring out of those new devolopments and new products. The articles we publish reflect those three aspects of our focus:

*Science and technology. Under that general heading, we cover a vast range of subjects: aerospace, physics, energy, transportation, communication, to name just a few. We cover the technologies involved in health and medicine, although we do not cover the life sciences as such.

*Consumer information. We give our readers detailed and expert information on new cars and accessories, new electronic equipment (heavy on computers, hi-fi, and TV), new tools for the home-workshopper or Saturday mechanic, new products for home improvement, and, in general, the kinds of products that catch the interest of the intellectually curious reader with a pocketbook to buy them.

*Reader activities. Here we tell our readers how to use those new products and technologies to tune his car, to improve his home, to find new uses for his computer, and to enjoy his leisure.

PUBLISHED BY TIMES MIRROR MAGAZINES, INC.

Popular Science articles are intensely journalistic. They are up to the minute in information and accuracy. They reflect, in quotes and in anecdotes, the fact that the writer has interviewed the proper experts and informants, and has visited the sites and labs necessary to both a full understanding of his subject and a full feeling for its color and flavor.

It is the writer's job to convey not only basic information but also a sense of reality. He must take the reader on a vicarious trip and let him see, feel, touch, and smell the things he did in handling a new product, or visiting a lab, or building a project. Lively quotes, anecdotes, stories, descriptions, narrations, first-person reactions--all are part of a well-written Popular Science article. They all help to show the reader what the writer saw, instead of telling him.

We expect our authors to deliver a complete package, including illustrative material. Writers must consider gathering photographs and drawings as important as gathering information for their text. Our own artists will make the finished drawings, but we expect the writer to supply the art "scrap"--the basic material. The writer is also expected to submit suitable captions with his illustrative material. Popular Science editors frequently cut and rewrite heavily. We try to send the edited article to the original author for his approval and possible correction; sometimes this is not possible.

Many Popular Science articles are three or four pages long, but many are only a page long, or even a picture-and-caption long. Contributors should be as alert to the possibility of selling us short features as they are to major articles.

Writers should check Readers' Guide before sending queries, to avoid suggesting a topic that we have recently covered. If we have covered a subject recently, but the writer thinks he has something new or different to offer, he should make that difference clear. If a similar piece has appeared in another publication, the writer should tell us how his proposed piece differs from that.

We respond promptly to queries. We pay expenses (but require that they be approved in advance by us). We pay promptly on acceptance.

The Editors

National Trust for Historic Preservation

1785 MASSACHUSETTS AVENUE, N.W.   WASHINGTON, D.C. 20036   (202) 673-4000

WRITER'S GUIDELINES FOR PRESERVATION NEWS

PN is the monthly newspaper of the National Trust for
Historic Preservation. We use freelance pieces only
occasionally. Nonetheless we welcome your suggestions.

TOPICS: Our bread-and-butter is conflict. A shopping mall
developer wants to level a historic Main Street, but locals
are organized to counter any demolition. A city council
weighs a proposal to purchase or demolish a historic
Roosevelt-era public housing project, but Black citizens
oppose such a plan. We expect these stories to be
well-researched, reflecting interviews with those on both
sides of the issue. We think the facts of the issue should
speak for themselves and advise writers to shy away from
bias -- even if they are rabid preservationists themselves.

Another area is features about people. That could be a
profile of a local activist whose single-minded zeal
convinced a city to save its heritage, or of a developer who
has turned away from new construction to redo old buildings,
or the first "urban pioneer" to experiment with loft-living
in a mid-sized city.

We are interested in lively, concise writing. We are
not interested in memoirs, coverage of parties or parades,
or profiles of individuals who have restored their dream
houses (try Historic Preservation's "Open House"
column for the latter).

PAY: Not great. 15-20 cents a word for stories that top out
at 1,000 words. Our average is in the 750 word range,
meaning you will glean no more that $100-$150 for most
pieces. Payment on publication.

STILL INTERESTED? Send us a query letter of no more than
one typewritten page proposing the story you would like to
do. Explain why you are qualified to write about this
subject. Do not send a completed manuscript.
We have never seen an unsolicited manuscript
that we've liked. Address queries to Michael Leccese or
Arnold Berke, Preservation News.

 **EAST/WEST NETWORK**

5900 Wilshire Boulevard
Los Angeles, California 90036
Telephone: (213) 937-5810

GUIDE TO PUBLICATIONS

PACIFIC SOUTHWEST AIRLINES *PSA Magazine*

Al Austin, editor
Coverage: Primarily California, plus Las Vegas, Reno, Phoenix, Tucson, Albuquerque, Seattle, Spokane and Portland

Format: Feature Articles (personalities/Q&A, environment/conservation, sports, arts, business); calendar listings; business trends; regular columns (restaurants, saloons, show business, finance, sports, health).

---

also publishes:

PSA magazine, published for Pacific Southwest Airlines, is a lively, regional periodical focusing primarily on California but with rotating editorial coverage of Arizona, New Mexico, Oregon, Nevada and Washington as well. PSA employs a flamboyant, highly visual style in its mix of stories: serious, in-depth investigations of regional issues; comprehensive reports on business trends; lighthearted satire; penetrating personality profiles and interviews; articles dealing with fashion, leisure, the arts and much more. The magazine also features numerous monthly service columns, many of them tied to key PSA cities.

REPUBLIC AIRLINES Republic Scene

Jerry Lazar, editor
Coverage: National

Format: Editorial emphasis is on contemporary popular culture, business and sports--for the Midwestern executive who savors success at home, at work and at play. Regular departments include Technology, Sports, Media, Business, On the Go (travel trends), Americana, Health, Lifestyle.

OZARK AIRLINES *Ozark*

Laura Dean Bennett, editor
Coverage: Midwest

Format: Midwestern focus with some national; feature articles (personalities, fashion, sports, arts, business, food). Accent on the good life in the Midwest with each issue having a central theme.

WESTERN AIRLINES *Western's World*

Ed Dwyer, editor
Coverage: Primarily west of the Rockies, plus New York, Alaska, Hawaii and Mexico

Format: Editorial celebrates and investigates innovative business ventures and businesspeople and trends generated in the West that affect national lifestyles. In addition, "Portfolio" presents the recreational treasures of the West and "Datelines" provide trenchant monthly briefs on business and pleasure developments in specific destinations.

SOUTHWEST AIRLINES *Southwest Monthly*

Gabrielle Cosgriff, editor
Coverage: Primarily Texas and the Southwest

Format: Edited for Southwest's sophisticated passengers, the magazine employs superior writing and graphics to explore the business, arts and lifestyles of the most progressive region in America. Forward looking and forward thinking, yet evoking a sense of place and romance of region, it is an informed and influential voice in the market it serves.

LOS ANGELES OFFICE:
Editorial Director, John Johns

FROM THE NEW YORK OFFICE

34 East 51st Street
New York, New York 10022
(212) 888-5900

UNITED AIRLINES *United*

Tom O'Neil, editor
Coverage: Major U.S. cities, Japan and Hong Kong

Format: Executive lifestyle features; business-related features, regular columns (travel, sports, driving, personal finance); art portfolios; High level new products of interest to executives. Travel for the business person and for offbeat vacationing.

EASTERN AIRLINES *Review*

Don Dewey, editor
Coverage: Primarily east of the Rockies

Format: Selected reprints from magazines, plus art and entertainment events listings across the Eastern Airlines system.

US AIR *USAir*

Richard Busch, editor
Coverage: Primarily east of the Rockies

Format: General interest covering a wide variety of subjects; travel, business, sports, personal finance, personal health, nature, the sciences, the arts, food, photography. Edited to appeal to the affluent, well-educated frequent traveler.

PAN AM *Clipper*

Richard Kagan, editor
Coverage: Worldwide

Format: General interest stories on travel, the arts, science and technology, business, sports, food and beverages, fashion, adventure, humor. Designed and edited to appeal to the sophisticated business and pleasure traveler on Pan Am's domestic and international routes. Articles are urbane in tone, designed for an affluent audience.

All magazines include at least one destination travel feature each month. These are usually scheduled a year in advance.

No news items; no PR on personnel changes; no lisitings for calendar of events unless within deadline; no poetry, no fiction; no puzzles, games, quizzes; no cartoons; no airline-related material.

All magazines publish on the first of each month. Deadlines for feature material are ninety days prior to publication; deadlines for events listings are seventy-five days prior to publication.

5900 Wilshire Boulevard
Los Angeles, California 90036
Telephone: (213) 937-5810

WRITER'S TIP SHEET

1. Always query first, to save your time and the editor's.
   Phone calls are difficult due to an editor's tight
   production schedule. A letter allows time for valid
   decision making.

2. Include with your typewritten query, which suggests
   your topic, an outline of what you will cover in the
   article; tentative title; a description of any
   graphic material (photos or illustrations) you will
   supply with the finished manuscript.

3. It is sometimes helpful to include copies or excerpts
   of your previous work. Even though an editor may
   reject your query, he may be able to match you up with
   future assignments.

Graphic notes:

1. Each transparency or color slide should have your name
   and address on it.

2. All photos should have captions attached or listed on
   a separate sheet.

FINALLY--ALL QUERIES AND MANUSCRIPTS MUST BE ACCOMPANIED BY
THE APPROPRIATE SELF-ADDRESSED STAMPED ENVELOPE, OR THEY CANNOT
BE RETURNED.

SAMPLE COPIES OF ANY EAST/WEST NETWORK PUBLICATION ARE $2.00 EACH

psychology today

We seek authoritative articles, about timely subjects, based on solid research. Most of our articles are prepared by psychologists or other behavioral or social scientists who have done research in the fields they are writing about, but informed journalism is also acceptable.

Psychology Today's primary purpose is to provide the interested nonspecialist with accurate, readable information about behavior and society. Articles should include enough methodological information to help the reader understand how the researchers have arrived at their findings and conclusions. Technical and specialized words should be avoided unless more common words are not adequate equivalents. When technical language is necessary, it should be defined carefully for the nonexpert reader. Our usual article length is approximately 3,000 words, but longer and shorter pieces are fine when the length suits the subject.

Please address all manuscripts and queries to the Article Editor. Accepted manuscripts are edited by the staff and returned to the author for comments and approval before publication. The author should retain a copy of the original manuscript.

1200 Seventeenth St., NW. Washington. D.C. 20036 (202) 955-7800

American Psychological Association

Writing for the Public Relations Journal

In 1982, the Publications Committee and Board of PRSA adopted a policy statement for the Public Relations Journal, establishing as its mission reaching all public relations professionals, regardless of specialty and whether or not they are members of PRSA, with the goal of positioning it as "the preeminent journal" for the profession. Inherent in that statement was a belief that these readers would be primarily professionals in levels 3 and 4.

In putting together a magazine that will best serve these readers' needs, the key word to consider is mix. It is the mix of articles -- in terms of subject matter, length, style, graphic presentation -- that really determines how the magazine is read, who reads it, how much time they spend on its pages, which advertisements they see. This is particularly important with an audience as diverse as the members of PRSA, who not only are spread across nine geographic districts but who now fill up 15 special-interest sections.

To serve these needs, we've done some reconfiguring of the Journal and developed a format that breaks down into the four basic categories -- Features, Workshop, Briefings, and Departments -- that are clearly identifiable on our newly designed table of contents and were described in detail in the April issue in my "Inside Track" column.

Articles in PRJ come from a variety of sources. Many originate as unsolicited manuscripts submitted to us by PRSA members. Many are assigned, either to public relations professionals or to journalists, after article suggestions arise from editorial meetings, conversations with public relations professionals, or even the daily newspaper. And some are staff-written.

We encourage unsolicited submissions to PRJ, but suggest that potential contributors use the following guidelines:

1) Look carefully at recent issues of PRJ to see how it is structured and written and to get a sense of what we are looking for. Consider placements in PRJ the same way you'd consider placements in any other magazine.

2) Tailor your suggestion to a particular section or department of the magazine, and couch it in terms of a particular angle.

3) Remember that our mission is to reach professionals in levels 3 and 4. Before you pitch an idea to us, ask yourself if you would read this piece if it appeared in PRJ. Remember also that many of your readers will be public relations professionals with specialties other than your own -- therefore, define your terms.

4) While PRJ is published by PRSA, it is not simply an association magazine. Guidelines adopted by the Publications Committee and the Board in 1982 state that it is a magazine for all public relations professionals, regardless of their membership status. In fact, some 25 percent of our subscribers are not -- yet -- members. Therefore, we cover PRSA matters when they are newsworthy, just as we'd cover any other professional developments, and not simply because we are connected to PRSA.

5) Send us a query letter outlining what your proposal is. Feature article and department suggestions should be sent to me. Workshop suggestions should be sent to associate editor Josephine Curran, who edits that section. Briefings suggestions should be sent to assistant editor Celia Kuperszmid Lehrman, who edits Briefings.

6) If we give you the go-ahead, we'll also target an issue in which we hope to use your piece. This target date may change as circumstances demand.

7) Typically, we find that most manuscripts require some revisions, and sometimes those revisions are extensive. In assigning due dates, we generally take revision time into account.

8) We will usually take care of finding photographs or art to illustrate your piece, but we appreciate any input you can give.

Specific guidelines about manuscript preparation, due dates, copyright, etc. are available by writing to me at Public Relations Journal, 845 Third Avenue, New York, NY 10022.

Michael Winkleman
editor, Public Relations Journal

Public Relations Journal
Editorial Guidelines - Part Two

All articles must be cleanly typed, double-spaced. An additional xerox copy would be helpful, but not mandatory; please keep at least one copy for yourself to facilitate telephone changes. Please make sure any handwritten changes are legible.

Any photographs you supply should be black and white glossy prints, unless we advise you otherwise. Please do not submit books or other publications as sources of art due to problems of reproduction and permission. Reproduction fees, if any, will be paid by the magazine, but permission must be gotten by author and submitted with manuscript.

Final editing of material is at the discretion of the editor. However, all substantive changes will be cleared with authors before manuscript goes to typesetting. No author corrections are allowed in galleys. The magazine reserves the right to make necessary changes in galleys to accommodate layout when and if necessary.

Deadlines are important. All manuscripts, illustrations, credits, and captions are due by the date indicated, unless specifically discussed with the editor prior to that time. The editor reserves the right to kill any piece that is not submitted on time.

Writers are responsible for accuracy of fact and correct spelling of names and places. We do not have the resources to check all this information, so please be careful.

Public Relations Journal will be happy to send out five complimentary copies of the issues in which your article appears. However, for us to do this you must provide us with the names, addresses, and zip codes cleanly typed on standard, white, self-adhesive labels. These labels must be given to us at the time the article is due. After that time, comp copies will be provided for you in bulk at your expense. However, copies are limited, so don't wait too long.

All art will be returned to authors unless it is clearly labeled with names, addresses, and zip codes. If you've sent us comp copy labels, a duplicate set would be helpful for returning art.

Unless other arrangements are made prior to publication, the Public Relations Society of America retains the copyright to all material published in the Public Relations Journal.

Radio-Electronics

200 Park Avenue South/New York, N.Y. 10003/(212) 777-6400

A GERNSBACK PUBLICATION

Dear Author:

If you've got a story centered around electronics, I'd like to get the chance to read it, and consider it for purchase and use in RADIO-ELECTRONICS.

What type of article is RADIO-ELECTRONICS looking for? The type we've always sought - first-rate stories covering communications, computers, test equipment, TV, stereo, and virtually every other electronics subject. We want construction, tutorial and how-to articles. If they are timely, too, their appeal and chance of acceptance is further enhanced.

<u>Construction</u> articles should show readers how to build electronic gadgets and projects. The devices built must be of <u>practical</u> use in the field of electronics, in hobby pursuits, around the house or car. Cost of parts is important. The cost of assembling a project should be justified by what it does. Also, if a similar device is commercially available, then the assembly cost should be less. We use construction stories at different levels - some for neophytes and some for those who have the training to carry out complex building instructions. In general, easier projects take preference, although a premium goes to the story that tells how to build some complex project very easily.

<u>General report</u>-type features attract good attention among readers. The prime requirement is authenticity. A poorly researched article can lose its author some respect among our editors, as well as the sale. Make sure of your facts, and make them complete. Our editors should not have to do your research job. If you aren't in a position to research thoroughly and document the facts, you shouldn't write the story in the first place. Be thorough and accurate.

<u>How to do it</u> features are one of the most interesting articles you can write. Show a reader ten new ways to use his scope, sweep generator, or an easy way to make PC boards, and you'll have a friend for life. Include methods that haven't been tried before or are not common knowledge.

Troubleshooting manuscripts are not easy to handle properly. The author needs to be experienced. Nothing falls apart so completely as a troubleshooting article written by someone who knows little about it. A few good professional writers can do this type of story in collaboration with an expert troubleshooter, but they always check and recheck every stage of the writing with the expert. Technical inaccuracies quickly ruin chances for acceptance.

Construction manuscripts need special care. Photographs are a must and the focus must be perfect for good reproduction. If your project is simple, then perhaps you can show your parts layout with a tracing-paper overlay on a photograph of the unit. Include debugging information: How long did it take to get the device working? To build it? The reader may have some of the same difficulties.

Include calibration and adjustment instructions. Where special equipment is required, be specific. Do not say merely "5,000 ohm relay" if contact spacing or armature tension is critical. Give type and number and tell why it is chosen and how to adjust it. Failure to do this may mean some reader can't make the project work and will blame the magazine or author. Place critical voltages on schematics; these help the constructor check his equipment.

Send a complete list of parts, with brands and type numbers. Make sure the list agrees with the identification codes given in the text and on schematics. Avoid hard-to-get items or those that are one-of-a-kind. There should be two sources for every part. Where values are not critical, say so and give approximate tolerances. Also include a table listing the specifications of your project.

Do not dismantle equipment or make changes after sending us your manuscript. If the article is accepted, we usually find it necessary to examine the device.

New technology and the theory behind new devices are always valuable and make for interesting reading. If you're inside on some new semiconductor device, you can put together an excellent article on how it works and what it can be used for.

<u>Finish the job</u>. Don't send half-done manuscripts. "Photos to come" or "material to be added here" are flags of incompleteness. We can't judge the manuscript without seeing all of it. Don't expect R-E editors to find material for you. It's your manuscript; take pride in doing the whole job.

<u>Mechanics</u>. The best-written articles are useless if we can't get them into the magazine. An article on high-voltage sources might be well-nigh perfect; but if it requires five TV-receiver schematics it will not be printed because the drawings alone would take up too much space in the magazine. Other unprintable tricks (like charts that include figures) lead to rejection of otherwise excellent articles. Stories with no illustrations, or those without enough text to hold the illustrations together, show poor preparation and are not acceptable.

Use standard 8½" x 11" typewriter paper. Type on one side only. Double-space between lines. You must type your name and address in the top left corner of the first page; some authors use a rubber stamp to put their name and address on the back of each succeeding page. Also include the telephone number where you can be reached during the day in case our editors have a question that requires immediate attention.

Mail the manuscript flat, with cardboard stiffeners. Include a self-addressed envelope and return postage. <u>Save a carbon of your manuscript until you see it in print</u>. It is often necessary for us to ask questions about it. And, the post office has been known to lose things. Do not send Xerox copies of the manuscript or the illustrations. Send the original and keep the copy for your own files.

<u>Illustrations</u>. If any of your illustrations are smaller than 8" x 10", fasten them to standard-size sheets; a 2" x 3" piece of paper can be lost too easily, especially if we're not looking for it.

Put an asterisk or the figure number in the margin of your text when you refer to an illustration or figure. Try to scatter illustrations throughout the story so they're not all bunched. If you have page-layout ideas for your article, include them with the manuscript.

Diagrams must be <u>clearly</u> drawn in pencil or ink, but need not be finished artwork, as all art is redrawn to RADIO-ELECTRONICS style. Draw them on separate pages. Use standard-size paper or sheets that can be folded to standard size. Drawings <u>must be accurate</u>. Check each one carefully--it is almost impossible for our editors to catch some errors as we may consider them part of your design.

Photographs should be 8" x 10" glossy prints, in good focus all over. All details should be easy to see - not hidden in dark areas or "whited out" in overexposed or too-bright areas. Don't mark on prints; you simply spoil them for reproduction. If you need to identify components, put a piece of tracing paper over the print and mark the identification lightly on it, or else send an extra print.

<u>Rates of payment</u>. Our payment calculations are more complex than a simple page rate, since we consider such variables as reader interest, illustrations vs. text, charts and tables, photography, how much editing our staff will have to do, accuracy of research and originality of approach.

The rate thus determined varies from $150 to $350. Manuscripts that need practically no editing, that hit precisely the slant we want and do it completely, that are written in the easy-reading style we now strive for in RADIO-ELECTRONICS, and that are thoughtfully and imaginatively illustrated - these command an even higher rate.

<u>Our staff members</u> are trained in writing, researching, and editing. As you are developing a story, we will gladly work with you. After we buy your manuscript, your help is often needed to track down odd part numbers, fill gaps in your story, check a doubtful connection on a schematic, etc. We take every step and precaution to make sure your article is authoritative, easy-to-read, and interesting.

We'll look forward to reviewing your manuscripts.

Sincerely,

Art Kleiman
Managing Editor

NATIONAL WILDLIFE FEDERATION

1412 Sixteenth Street, N.W., Washington, D.C. 20036-2266   (202) 797-6800

RANGER RICK WRITERS' GUIDELINES

SUBJECT SELECTION

o   Our audience ranges from ages six to twelve, though we aim the reading level of most materials at nine-year-olds or fourth graders.

o   Fiction and non-fiction articles may be written on any aspect of nature, outdoor adventure and discovery, pets, science, conservation, or related subjects. To find out what subjects have been covered recently, consult our annual indexes. These are available in many libraries or are free upon request from our editorial offices.

o   The National Wildlife Federation (NWF) discourages the keeping of wildlife as pets, so the keeping of such pets should not be featured in your copy.

o   Human qualities are attributed to animals only in our regular feature, "Adventures of Ranger Rick," which is staff written.

o   Avoid the stereotyping of any group. For instance, girls can enjoy nature and the outdoors as much as boys can, and mothers can be just as knowledgeable as fathers.

o   The only way you can successfully write for Ranger Rick is to know the kinds of subjects and approaches we like. And the only way you can do that is to read the magazine. Recent issues can be found in most libraries or are available free upon request.

SUBMITTING MATERIALS

o   Send us a query outlining your intended subject, along with a lead or sample paragraph. Any special qualifications you may have to write on that subject would be worth mentioning. Please do not query by phone.

o   List all your reference sources when submitting your finished work, unless of course you are an expert in the field. We strongly recommend that you consult with experts in the field when developing your material and that one of them read the finished manuscript for accuracy before you submit it to us.

o   All submissions are made on speculation unless other arrangements have been made. Manuscripts are considered carefully and will be returned or accepted within one to two months. Our planning schedule is 10 months prior to the cover date. Please do not submit your manuscript to other magazines simultaneously.

(continued on back)

PAYMENTS

o Payments range up to $350 for a full-length feature (about 900 words), depending on quality. Poetry is paid for at about $3 a line.

o Upon acceptance of a manuscript, a transfer of rights form will be sent to you. The NWF prefers to buy all world rights. However, in some cases rights are negotiable. Payment checks will be processed after we receive the signed transfer of rights form.

o It is not necessary that illustrations or photographs accompany your material. If we do use photographs you've included with your copy, these will be paid for separately at current market rates.

The NWF can take no responsibility for unsolicited submissions. However, we make every effort to return such materials if accompanied by a self-addressed, stamped envelope.

Direct all correspondence to The Editors, RANGER RICK, 1412 16th St. NW, Washington, DC 20036. We appreciate your interest.

                              The Editors
                              RANGER RICK

How to Write for Reader's Digest

Reader's Digest, headquartered in
Pleasantville, N.Y., 45 minutes north of Manhattan, has
been published monthly since February 1922. From
that first issue, founders DeWitt Wallace and
Lila Acheson Wallace built a mass-interest magazine that
is now bought by 18 million people in the United States
and nearly 31 million around the world—reaching
more than 100 million readers every month.

What is the market for original material at The Digest? Roughly half the 30-odd articles we publish every month are reprinted from magazines, newspapers, books and other sources. The remaining 15 or so articles are original—most of them assigned, some submitted on speculation. While many of these are written by regular contributors—on salary or on contract—we're always looking for new talent and for offbeat subjects that help give our magazine variety, freshness and originality.

Payment, on acceptance, is $3000, plus reasonable expenses. For a "Drama in Real Life" or "Unforgettable Character," we pay $3500. This rate covers all worldwide periodical rights—including condensation, adaptation, compilation and anthology rights—for all forms of print and electronic publishing media. Reader's Digest also reserves the right of first refusal on all remaining rights. For assigned articles that don't work out, our kill fee is $500.

There's one other important market: fillers and short department items. We pay up to $300 for true, unpublished stories used in our departments; for original material that runs as a filler, we pay $20 per Reader's Digest, two-column line, with a minimum payment of $50. To the first contributor of an item we use from TV, radio or a published source, we pay $35. For more on this market, check the front of the magazine, where we solicit reader contributions each month.

How should an original article be proposed to The Digest? Don't send us unsolicited manuscripts. We no longer read them. Just send a letter to The Digest, briefly describing the article you'd like to do and, if you're new to us, listing your writing credits. If the idea sounds right for us, we'll check our article index, our assignment list and our inventory of original and reprint material for overlaps. If there are none, we'll ask to see a manuscript on speculation or, if the idea is assignable, we'll request a detailed outline—not a formal A-B-C outline, but a structured, reasonably polished piece of writing that sells not only the article but also you-the-writer and what you bring to your subject. In three or four double-spaced pages, give us a lead that could sit on top of your finished article, and show us where you plan to go from there. Above all, we want a sharp, crisp focus and viewpoint.

Here is how Patricia Skalka opened a proposal about a flood that threatened Fort Wayne, Ind., and how Fort Wayne's children helped save the city:

"I can't feel my fingers anymore," the young girl sobbed.

"Don't stop. Don't stop," the others cried. With hands bloody, backs sore and eyes bloodshot from exhaustion, they continued to pass bag after bag of heavy sand down the line. Nearby someone told a joke. In the distance, a rhythmic chant began.

The lines of volunteers knew the words from days of marching with school bands and cheering school teams to victory, from evenings spent sitting around Scout camp fires. "One-two. Sound off. Three-four. Once more . . ." Now in the eerie dark, rain-soaked from head to foot and mired ankle-deep in mud, they joined in the chant.

Along a 32-mile network of water-logged earthen dams, they sang.

They sang to keep going, to keep the sand bags moving. They sang for themselves, for their city. They sang to protect the lives and homes of total strangers. They sang because it is the nature of youth to face danger with bravado, innocence and good spirit. They sang to win one of the country's most awesome battles against the forces of nature.

This is the story of Fort Wayne, Ind., and last month's "Great Flood," a disaster of such proportions that it literally threatened to destroy the city. Nearly one third of Fort Wayne's populace fought to save the city from the flood waters that poured over the banks of the St. Mary, St. Joseph and Maumee Rivers. Of the estimated 50,000 volunteers who joined in the effort, 30,000 were students. Some were as young as eight years old. Some were in college. Most of them were teenagers. When it was all over, their valor reduced Fort Wayne's mayor to tears and brought them credit for saving the city.

How soon, after assignment, does The Digest expect to see a completed manuscript? We seldom set deadlines, because our magazine is geared toward articles of lasting, rather than passing or topical, interest. Such material can usually run anytime. But as a rule, writers deliver two to three months after assignment.

How long should a manuscript run? Only as long as it takes to tell your story. The average manuscript length on straight, reportorial journalism is 3000 to 3500 words. Some manuscripts run much longer, some shorter. Only after an article is purchased and scheduled do we start thinking about its final length in the magazine. So don't try to write to The Digest length—almost certainly, you'd exclude some top-notch material. Leave the condensation to us. This is a meticulous process in which article length is reduced by a third to a half or more—while preserving the style, flavor and integrity of the original manuscript and, more often than not, heightening the effect. The author, of course, reviews the edited version before publication.

How does a writer get his previously published material reprinted in The Digest? If your article has appeared in a major American magazine or newspaper, the chances are it's already been considered. In our search for article pickups, fillers and department items, our reading staff screens more than 140 publications each month, along with 2000 books a year. If in doubt, simply submit tear sheets of your article. For reprinted articles, we pay $900 per Reader's Digest page for world periodical rights. This is usually split 50-50 between the original publication and the writer.

What kinds of articles is The Digest looking for? The best advice: read and study the magazine. You'll find our subject matter as varied as all human experience. Here are some titles from a single typical issue: "Beirut Under Siege," "Why Our Weather Is Going Wild," "Help Keep Your Teen-Age Driver Alive," "Are You a Man or a Wimp?", "The Real 'Lessons of Vietnam,'" "The Day Jessica Was Born," "Troubled Waters for Our

Coast Guard," "Dancing Ground of the Sun," "Top Secret: Is There Sex in Russia?", "Trapped in a Sunken Ship," "New Ways to Buy and Sell Houses," "From Cuba With Hate: The Crime Wave Castro Sent to America."

The common thread that weaves through all these articles is reader involvement. When we deal with major concerns—child abuse, government waste, Mideast tensions, breast cancer—we want a constructive approach that goes beyond the problem itself and points the way toward solution or hope. In the same way, we want profiles that go beyond merely "interesting" or "successful" people; we want to celebrate those who inspire by their example.

"Chi Chi Rodriguez: Golf's Ace with Heart" was typical. Here's how Jolee Edmondson opened her article:

It was another tournament town, another cardboard hotel room, another evening spent staring at the too blue, too orange TV images atop the Formica-covered bureau. Juan "Chi Chi" Rodriguez, vying for the lead at the 1967 Texas Open in San Antonio, was practicing putts on the carpet and thinking about the birdies that had got away that afternoon.

The drone of the evening news suddenly riveted his attention: a reporter was interviewing a distraught woman whose home in Illinois had been destroyed by a tornado. All she had left were the clothes she had on. Rodriguez was so moved that he made a pact with himself. If he bagged the trophy the following day, he would send the tornado relief fund $5000. The next day he won— and so did the tornado victims.

A prime article category is the personal happening or awakening. In "Lure of the Winter Beach," Jean George stumbled onto one of nature's many magical surprises and had an experience everyone can readily share and appreciate. She opened her article this way:

After a storm several winters ago, a friend asked me to check on her Long Island beach house. So one bright, windy day I bundled against the cold and drove out to the edge of the Atlantic Ocean. I imagined a dreary scene—an abandoned cottage set among pines, stirred by mournful winds.

But the instant I climbed from my car my senses came awake. The air smelled clean as I looked out on a brilliant waterscape. The sea was a violet-blue, the sky turquoise, and the beach, which last summer had sloped gently, was now steep, scooped-out and luminous. Crabs scurried for burrows and gulls spiraled down on them, like paper airplanes against the sky. At the water's edge, empty shells that whisper when summer waves turn them now made shrill, whistling sounds.

What does The Digest look for in writing? Clarity. Straight, simple sentences in simple, direct language. We also want the writer to *show* us, through solid example or anecdote—not just tell us, through general statements without anything to back them up. The best writing evokes an emotion and gets the reader to experience what the writer experienced—whether shock, affection, amusement.

When he wrote his hard-hitting article on "Auto Theft Turns Pro," Thomas R. Brooks combined fact, viewpoint, emotion and anecdote in a deceptively simple, straightforward lead:

Every 28 seconds, somewhere in the United States, a car is stolen. That's 1.1 million vehicles a year. If your turn is next, chances are you will never get your car back. If you do, it possibly will have been stripped for parts. When Connecticut police showed a West Hartford owner his new Buick Riviera— minus fenders, hood, doors and wheels—he wept.

Above all, in the writing we publish, The Digest demands accuracy—down to the smallest detail. Our team of 83 researchers scattered through 19 cities around the world scrutinizes every line of type, checking every fact and examining every opinion. For an average issue, they will check 3500 facts with 1500 sources.

So watch your accuracy. There's nothing worse than having an article fall apart in our research checking because an author was a little careless with his reporting. We make this commitment routinely, as it guarantees that the millions of readers who believe something simply because they saw it in Reader's Digest have not misplaced their trust.

THE EDITORS
Reader's Digest
Pleasantville, N.Y. (10570)

REDBOOK

224 WEST 57TH ST.
NEW YORK, N.Y. 10019

(212) 262-8284

WRITER'S GUIDELINES FOR NONFICTION

Redbook addresses young mothers between the ages of 25 and 44. About half of Redbook's readers work outside the home and have children under 18.

The articles in Redbook entertain, guide and inspire our readers. A significant percentage of the pieces stress "how-to," the ways a woman can solve the problems in her everyday life. Writers are advised to read at least the last six issues of the magazine (available in most libraries) to get a better understanding of what we're looking for.

We prefer to see queries, rather than completed manuscripts. Please enclose a sample or two of your writing as well as a stamped, self-addressed envelope. Send queries to: Articles Department, Redbook Magazine, 224 West 57th Street, New York, NY 10019.

It is not our policy to provide complimentary issues.

THE HEARST CORPORATION

REDBOOK'S FICTION GUIDELINES

Redbook welcomes unsolicited short story manuscripts. Address
submissions to:

Fiction Department
Redbook Magazine
224 West 57th Street
New York, New York 10019

Redbook publishes about forty short stories a year. Our fiction has
received such prestigious honors as the National Magazine Award for
fiction (twice winners). Several selections have appeared in the
O. Henry Award Prize Collections and The Best American Short Stories.

The editors describe their target reader as a young woman in her
twenties or early thirties, married or formerly married, with young
children, most likely employed outside the home. Because the Redbook
reader is a bright, well-informed woman whose interests are varied,
she is not solely concerned with fiction that reflects her own life,
although most of our stories are about young women and deal with
topics of specific interest to women: courtship, marriage, parenthood,
in-laws, career situations, money problems, etc. Redbook assumes the
reader would also enjoy an off-beat, ground-breaking story--and so
there is occasional room in our pages for humor, horror, and fantasy.
Highly oblique or symbolic stories that come to no conclusion and
stories with obviously contrived plots are not right for Redbook.

No covering letter is necessary. If you do wish to send a letter,
include only your fiction credits. The story will be judged on its
own merits. Only those stories accompanied by self-addressed stamped
envelopes large enough for the return of the manuscript will be
returned--if you do not send SASE with your submission, you will not
hear from Redbook unless the editors are interested in buying the
story. The reply time is usually 8-10 weeks. We receive approximately 35,000 submissions a year; every care is taken in the handling of
submissions but Redbook is not responsible for the receipt or the
condition of manuscripts. In the interest of protecting the original
copy, authors may submit a legible photocopy of the story. Any story
submitted to Redbook should not be offered to another magazine for
consideration until after Redbook has declined it.

Redbook publishes two categories of short stories. Short shorts are
nine manuscript pages or less. (All submissions should be typed d
double space between the lines.) The rate for an unsolicited short
short is $850. Short stories are over nine pages, preferably under
twenty-five. Fifteen pages is considered an average length at Redbook.
The short story price range for a first purchase is $1,000 to $1,500,
depending on a variety of factors. Redbook buys first North American
serial rights and pays on acceptance. Most stories are scheduled within a year of purchase. Prior to publication, short story galleys are
sent to the author. Our contract gives us the final say on all editing
decisions but every effort is made to accommodate the author's wishes.

Redbook does not consider unsolicited poetry and no longer reads
unsolicited novel manuscripts, as condensed novels are no longer
a regular feature of the magazine.

REPUBLIC AIRLINES Republic Scene

Jerry Lazar, editor
Coverage: National

Format: Editorial emphasis is on contemporary popular culture, business and
           sports--for the Midwestern executive who savors success at home, at
           work and at play. Regular departments include Technology, Sports,
           Media, Business, On the Go (travel trends), Americana, Health, Lifestyle.

Republic Scene magazine is for accomplishment-oriented businesspeople who savor success--
      at work, at home, at play. Like Republic Airlines' route system, the publication
      is national in scope but focuses primarily on the airlines major hub cities:
      Minneapolis/St. Paul, Memphis and Detroit. Its subject matter tends toward the
      highbrow, with an emphasis on the finer things in life. From profiles of
      innovative businesspeople and exceptional athletes to articles on entertainment
      trends and fashion, the editorial menu is designed to appeal to today's inquisi-
      tive and acquisitive business traveler. Every issue features a "Day in the
      City" businessperson's guide to a major Republic destination, plus an appealing
      and exciting mix of topical featurettes on popular culture, food and travel
      trends, health and fitness tips, sports and business reportage, and even the
      latest word in personal grooming and home/office design. In sum, a contemporary
      outlook on American achievement.

For further information, see PSA Magazine.

The Rotarian

EDITORIAL
REQUIREMENTS

1600 RIDGE AVENUE
EVANSTON, ILLINOIS 60201 U.S.A.

THE ROTARIAN is the official publication of Rotary International, a world fellowship of nearly one million business and professional men united in the ideal of "Service Above Self." Thus, *THE ROTARIAN* is one of the most international magazines in the world in terms of publisher, purpose, and audience. We have more than 480,000 readers in 157 countries and geographical regions. Our readers are active men: doers, thinkers, community leaders. They and their wives and children, who also read *THE ROTARIAN*, make up a most influential audience.

"Service Above Self" is Rotary's synonym for "betterment"—betterment of business and professional ethics, of community life, of international understanding and goodwill, and of the individual in his relationship to society. The contents of Rotary's official magazine reflect these aims.

A chief purpose of Rotary's official magazine is the reporting of Rotary organizational news. However, most of this information comes through Rotary channels and is staff-written. The field for freelance articles is in the general-interest category. These run the gamut from inspirational and "how-to" art of living articles, to such significant concerns as management, disarmament, world hunger, world health, education, the environment, and business management and ethics.

Generally, *THE ROTARIAN* publishes articles of 1,500 words or less which will in some way help Rotarians help other people. An article may increase a reader's understanding of world affairs, thereby making him a better world citizen. It may educate him in civic matters, thus helping him to improve his town. It may help him to become a better employer, a better parent, or a better human being.

Criticism and exposes are out of our line. We do carry debates and symposiums, but we are careful to show more than one point of view. We do not print articles with direct political or religious slants, but we do present arguments for high standards in politics and discussion of moral and ethical problems. In short, the rationale of the organization is one of hope and encouragement and belief in the power of individuals talking and working together to make a better world.

Specifically, we stress Rotary's four "Avenues of Service":

1. Advancement of international understanding, goodwill and peace, and discussion of international issues. The United Nations, European unity, Pan-American relations, international assistance programs, world trade—all are topics we cover occasionally. We have presented Pérez de Cuéllar on "The

U.N.—Not Strong Enough," Seymour Topping on "Journey Between Two Chinas," and "Charting a New Global Economy" by World Bank President A.W. Clausen. We have devoted the editorial contents of special issues to topics such as nuclear arms, drug abuse, and world literacy.

2. Better Vocational Relationships. Articles in this category encourage higher standards in business and the professions, and explore new ideas in management and business technology. Our article, "Honesty, Ethics, and Human Freedom," took a hard look at the spectrum of human conduct, questioning whether honesty has become unfashionable. Features often deal with career counseling for young people, vocational education for high school dropouts, better employee—employer relations, business and professional ethics.

3. Better Community Life. Such articles make readers aware of community problems and suggest answers and solutions. We run articles on city planning, crime prevention, pollution control, alternative energy resources, and new educational methods. Since many of our readers live in small towns and small cities, we accent subjects of concern to such communities. We are particularly interested in descriptions of community improvements in countries outside the U.S.A. THE ROTARIAN is an international magazine.

4. Better Human Relationships. Rotary is interested in improving the human condition and in promoting good will among all of the world's people. We have presented special issues which focused on mental health, illness, and old age, among others. We tell about institutions that help the physically, mentally, and socially disabled. Since Rotary activities furnish us with a wealth of such material, we have little need for freelance submissions on these subjects. When we do accept freelance articles about community projects, we like them to have some Rotary connection—either with a Rotary club or an individual Rotarian.

Each year we publish several culture- and travel-related articles about the places and events surrounding the site of our annual convention.

THE ROTARIAN has a companion magazine published in Spanish called REVISTA ROTARIA. Thus, we are interested in Rotary and general interest stories from and about Latin America.

Because our editorial space is limited, we welcome queries in almost all instances. However, all submissions—brief notes, detailed outlines, full-length manuscripts—are read by our editors. (Again, it's worth remembering that our editors reject the vast majority of manuscripts and queries we receive because they are too "U.S." in subject matter and viewpoint.) We buy no fiction. We do buy occasional humor pieces and short poems of all types and forms. We use some cartoons in each issue. We pay on acceptance and our rates depend on the value of the material to us.

Photography and illustrations. Our articles are supported by photos and artwork, and we like authors to include photos with their manuscripts. We use both black-and-white and color in the body of the magazine. Our covers run in four-color. We prefer vertical shots in most cases. The key words for the freelance photographer to keep in mind are internationality and variety. Our covers usually have a connection with the contents of the magazine and range from fine art reproductions to contemporary art posters, glittering urban street scenes to tranquil rusticity. And we feature people in infinite variety. But consistently, year after year, our greatest need is for the identifying face or landscape, one that says unmistakably, "This is Japan . . . or Minnesota . . . or Brazil . . . or France . . . or Sierra Leone . . ." or any of the other countries and geographical regions to which our magazine travels each month.

We look forward to your query. We ask that a self-addressed envelope with sufficient return postage accompany all submissions.

—The Editors
THE ROTARIAN
1600 Ridge Avenue
Evanston, IL 60201
U.S.A.

Runner's World
Magazine Company, Inc.

Dear Writer:

As you may know from having read the magazine, we're recognized as the definitive running publication. Our editorial range allows us to write for world-class competitors as well as those just getting into running for fitness and/or sport. In order to maintain our position as the leader, we need well-researched articles aimed at an audience quite sophisticated in its knowledge of running.

To save time and trouble and allow us to plan for articles aimed at specific issues, we urge writers to query us with ideas. If you plunge right into a subject, failing to query us first, you may find that we've already assigned that topic, and your work has gone to waste.

We do encourage usolicited pieces for three of our regular columns. Guest Spot and Runner's Forum items should be no more than 600 words; payment is $50 for Guest Spot and for Runner's Forum $25. Running Shorts, humorous items that appear on our subscriber protective cover, should be 200 words or less; we pay $10 each. All contributions should be accompanied by the usual self-addressed, stamped envelope.

On the matter of preparing copy, type the story double-spaced on one side of unlined, non-erasable bond. Never use onion-skinned paper, as it smears when touched. Number your pages in the upper right corner. Deal with your subject in straightforward English. A simple story, simply told, is always best.

Our staff covers major running events, so we have no need for race stories. We don't use poetry or fiction, nor do we publish stories on "How I Found Running and It Saved My Life"; runners who read the magazine already know the joys of running, and don't have to be won over. In most cases, first-person stories are discouraged. Again, query us first on a major story.

Runner's World buys first rights with one right of reuse, unlimited promotional reuses, and the right to reprint. Contracts are used. Payment varies according to how the story is used in the magazine. The author is encouraged to make proposals for securing professional photographic coverage on any story submitted.

Send queries and column submissions to Runner's World, c/o Jim Harmon, managing editor. We look forward to hearing from you, and usually answer queries in four to six weeks.

Cordially,

James Harmon
Managing Editor

1400 Stierlin Road, Mountain View, CA 94043 (415) 965-8777

Writers' and Photographers' Guidelines

Writers

Editorial intent

Sacramento magazine is edited for the affluent and informed Sacramentan. Content covers a broad range of topics, from issue-oriented and investigative pieces to profiles to service articles such as fashion and dining out, under the assumption that our readers' tastes are similarly varied. We are looking for in-depth, thoroughly researched, sophisticated material that accurately portrays Sacramento and its environs. We are not simply a city booster magazine.

Features

Concentrate on the topical and unusual. Subjects that have been exhausted by the newspapers are generally not appropriate unless a fresh angle can be offered. Profiles of well-known and/or interesting local people and issue-analysis articles are welcome, as are in-depth, information-oriented articles. All stories *must* have a strong Sacramento peg. Length: 1,500–3,000 words. No fiction or poetry. Selected humor on an occasional basis.

Capital Assets is a bi-monthly publication appearing as a magazine within the magazine. It focuses on all aspects of the local business community with business-oriented features, profiles and notes. Any material for this section should be submitted a minimum of 12 weeks in advance of each issue.

Departments

Regular departments include Politics, Notables (short product reviews), Dining Out, and Street Talk (a man-in-the-street interview). Generally, these are written by staff members or regular columnists. Departments which run irregularly include The Arts, Media, The Law, Profiles, Consumer, Sports, and Home and Garden. Length: 850–1,750 words.

City Lights is a collection of interesting and unusual people, places and behind-the-scenes news items. Keep away from run-of-the-mill retail businesses, products and self-serving public relations efforts. These short pieces are an excellent way for a new author to start writing for the magazine. Length: 75–250 words.

Submissions

Query first; no phone queries, please. All material considered on speculation. S.A.S.E. required. Keep copies. Allow 4–6 weeks for response. Send seasonal material six months in advance. Check past issues for style and subject treatment. Do not send photocopies. Send all submissions c/o Managing Editor, *Sacramento* magazine, P.O. Box 2424, Sacramento, California 95811. We work approximately two months in advance, though feature articles are scheduled 3 to 12 months ahead of publication date.

Format

All manuscripts must be typed, double-spaced, with the author's name, address and social security number in the upper left on the first page, and the final word count in the upper right. Name and story title should appear at top left of each succeeding page.

Rights and Payment

Jonsson Communications Corporation purchases all rights through a standard contract agreement. We pay on acceptance within our regular 30-day billing period.

Photographers

Sacramento magazine focuses on the city of Sacramento and its environs, covering a range of topics from hard-hitting investigative pieces to service articles. Photography complements these stories.

Most work is done on assignment. We will consider, however, on a strictly speculation basis, ideas for photographic essays or photographic stories. Query first, with samples of your work.

We buy both color and black-and-white photographs to illustrate features, departments and City Lights. Color photographs should be 35mm or larger in format. We prefer transparencies to color negatives and prints. Black-and-white prints should be 5"x7" or larger and have a glossy or smooth-matte finish. All photographs must include caption information, identifications and credits.

Jonsson Communications Corporation buys all rights to assigned photographs produced on an hourly, half-day, whole-day or flat-rate basis. Rates are negotiable on the basis of the photographer's experience and abilities.

THE JOURNAL OF
BIG GAME HUNTING

safari

OFFICIAL PUBLICATION OF SAFARI CLUB INTERNATIONAL

5151 E. BROADWAY, TUCSON, AZ 85711, (602) 745-9109

EDITORIAL GUIDELINES

Safari was founded in 1971 as the official publication of
Safari Club International. Both are headquartered in Tucson,
Arizona. The magazine is bi-monthly, focused on big game,
and includes regular columns about SCI's chapter activities
and affiliated organizations as well as comment by officers.
Circulation is about 10,000.

Content

The magazine's scope of interest is:

- outdoor recreation, with special emphasis on
  hunting. Hunting material from anywhere in the
  world is welcome. The only proviso is that it
  should focus primarily on big game rather than
  small game, birds, or fishing.

- current and historical hunting and conservation.

- background on particular species.

- ethnic and traditional hunts of particular regions.

- the philosophy and heritage of hunting.

- conservation material and environmental affairs
  relevant to big game or hunters.

Contributors should avoid sending simple hunting narratives
that do not contain certain new approaches. No fiction or
poetry is used.

Feature stories generally run to about 2,000 - 2,500 words.
They must be informative, accurate and designed to appeal
to sportsmen, sportswomen and others who enjoy the out-of-
doors. The rate for full-length features with illustrations
is $200.00, upon publication. For shorter stories, or
material contributed on a non-professional basis by members,
an honorarium of $25.00 will be paid. We do not buy brief
news items, but we do welcome them and will include bylines.

Manuscripts should be typewritten, double-spaced and accompanied
by stamped, self-addressed envelopes. Queries about story/or
picture possibilities are appreciated, but not essential.

Editorial Guidelines
Page Two

Manuscript preparation:

1. All manuscripts must be typewritten on standard 8½x11 white typing paper; manuscripts should be double-spaced, with at least 1½" margin at left, and 1" margin at right.

2. Title page should include writer's name, address and telephone number in the upper left hand corner. Title should begin halfway down the first page, followed by text. Following pages should include writer's last name at upper left, and page number at upper right, followed by text.

3. Do not use script or other fancy type for namuscript. Pica type preferred, but elite is acceptable if clean and sharp. Computer-generated type acceptable, but if dot matrix be sure it is easily readable, with good pressure on well-inked ribbon.

4. Whether you use a typewriter or print wheel, make sure keys are clean so that type is easily readable.

5. Please double-check all proper names (people, places, etc) for spelling before submitting manuscript.

Photos:

1. If submitting color slides, use plastic sheets which hold 20 slides; do not send loose, unprotected slides. Also make sure your name is on each slide, stamped or in ink.

2. If submitting color prints or black and white prints, make sure your name is stamped or written on back. Put photos in separate envelope -- DO NOT staple or attach with paper clip.

3. We prefer color slides; they should be sharp and well-exposed. Prints are acceptable; if color, they should be printed glossy rather than matte; if from 35 mm. they should be at least double sized, and preferably 5x7 or even larger; black and whites should be at least 5x7, and preferably 8x10.

4. We prefer to see as large a selection of photos as possible; we will return all photos to author after the article is printed.

5. All photos, whether slides or prints, MUST be captioned; we prefer having the captions on a separate sheet, numbered to correspond with the slides or prints. Captions need not be in narrative form, but all essential information should be included.

Editorial Guidelines
Page Three

General:

Include stamped and self-addressed envelope with each manuscript; we cannot be responsible for unsolicited manuscripts or photos.

Do NOT staple together pages of manuscript.

Use at least one sheet of cardboard to protect photos from bending.

Send manuscripts and photos by first class mail; affix proper amount of postage and mark envelope "First Class"; if photos are included, stamp or print "Photos--Do Not Bend" on envelope.

Payment:

Safari pays $150.00 for covers, up to $100.00 for inside color, and $30.00 for inside black and white.

34 Commercial Wharf
Boston, Massachusetts 02110
(617) 227-0888

SPECIFICATIONS FOR ARTICLES AND PHOTOGRAPHS
IN SAIL MAGAZINE

SAIL magazine is written and edited for everyone who sails--aboard a one-design
boat or an offshore racer, a daysailer or an auxiliary cruiser. The articles
in the front and back concentrate on the techniques of sailing and on technical
aspects of hull and rig design and construction, while the feature section emphasizes the joys and rewards of sailing--often in a practical and instructive
way. In short, we are a special-interest magazine in a field where our readers
are hungry for more knowledge of their chosen sport.

ARTICLES:

1. Length: 1,500-3,500 words.

2. Form: Typed, double-spaced with wide margins. Author's name and address
    should be on each page.

3. Payment: Variable; paid on publication.

4. Subject: We look for unique ways of viewing sailing. Skim through old
    issues of SAIL for ideas about the types of articles we publish. Always
    remember that SAIL is a sailing magazine. Stay away from gloomy articles
    detailing all the things that went wrong on your boat. Think construc-
    tively and write about how to avoid certain problems.

    Features--You should focus on a theme or choose some aspect of sailing and
    discuss a personal attitude or new philosophical approach to the subject.
    Notice that we have certain issues devoted to special themes. For instance,
    the March issue has frequently featured chartering, and the January or
    February issue the Southern Ocean Racing Conference. (These are not defi-
    nite or fixed topics but will give you an idea of our schedule.)

    Stay away from pieces that chronicle your journey in the day-by-day style
    of a logbook. These are generally dull and uninteresting. Select specific
    actions or events (preferably sailing events, not shorebound activities),
    and build your article around them. Emphasize the sailing.

How-to, Technical--These should be clear, concise articles directed to the intelligent layman. They should discuss systems or techniques for navigation, sail trim, or seamanship that have worked well for you. Technical articles should describe successful methods of approaching projects or concepts of sailing, not bemoan unsuccessful ways. Deal with one subject in detail, rather than trying to cover superficially a wide range of topics.

Side Features--These short articles (1,000 to 1,500 words max.) run the gamut from vignettes of daysailing, cruising, and racing life, at home or abroad, straight or humorous, to accounts of maritime history, astronomy, marine life, cooking aboard, nautical lore, fishing, etc., to miscellaneous how-to pieces about boat owning, building, and outfitting. How-to pieces should be specific and instructive. These short features must be sharply focused on a single theme of broad interest to sailors and, if appropriate, should be illustrated by anecdotes from your personal experience.

News--We usually assign news reporting in advance. Query SAIL at least one month prior to the event you are interested in covering. News reporting must be accurate and clear. Regatta reports should include a copy of the official score sheet and the names, home cities, and final scores of the top 10 finishers. Be sure to describe the number and type of boats competing, the weather, and the general racing action. Advance queries about nonracing events are always welcome.

5. Queries: We strongly suggest that potential writers query SAIL about specific ideas. Although we cannot make a final decision without seeing a piece, we can tell you whether or not your idea is appropriate for SAIL.

6. Time: Remember that SAIL operates on a long lead time. For instance, we need to see a Christmas article by late summer for it to meet our schedule.

We attempt to read, consider, and reply to your article within 60 days.

7. Return: Please include a self-addressed stamped envelope so that we can return your manuscript if we find it does not meet or editorial needs.

PHOTOGRAPHS INSIDE THE MAGAZINE

1. Form: All photographs and slides should have the photographer's name and address on them.

Color--Original 35mm (Kodachrome K-25 or K-64) or larger slide transparencies. Negatives with prints are acceptable, but not recommended.

Black and white--Glossy prints, with negatives if possible.

2. General requirements: sharp focus, good variety of close-up and overall shots (depending on the subject).

    Color--Evenly lit, good saturation in warm colors.

    Black and white--Good contrast, full range of grays, good blacks.

3. Subject: Generally, SAIL does not publish photographic essays without accompanying articles. Photos should parallel the writing and tell a visual story. Photos can depict people and boats, boats sailing, or illustrate design and mechanism features.

4. Time: Photographs for inside the magazine are considered with their accompanying manuscripts. We attempt to reply within 60 days.

COVER PHOTOGRAPHS

1. Form: All photographs and slides should have the photographer's name and address on them.

    Color only--35mm Kodachrome or larger slide transparencies. Negatives with prints are also acceptable, but not recommended.

2. General requirements: Vertical in format. Good-quality color. Sharp focus. Strong composition.

3. Subject: SAIL covers feature people and boats acting together. They should be conceptually clear, so the reader can discern the mood and context immediately. Good SAIL covers are usually, but not always, action shots. Good cruising shots are always desirable.

4. Time: We attempt to reply within 60 days after considering your picture and its suitability for the cover of SAIL.

SAIL reserves the right to reproduce its existing covers and layouts (including photography and art) for incidental magazine promotional uses, i.e., circulation and advertising sales.

San Francisco Focus

The Magazine for the San Francisco Bay Area
500 Eighth Street
San Francisco, California 94103

■ 415/553-2119

TO ALL WOULD-BE CONTRIBUTORS

WHO WE ARE

SAN FRANCISCO FOCUS is the major city magazine for the metropolitan Bay Area. Our role is to cover the issues, personalities and events of our region and to try to capture the characteristics that make the Bay Area a unique place to live. In fact, arrogant or no, we want to put out a magazine that people HAVE to read in order to get the most out of living and working here. Our readers are up-scale, highly literate and live throughout the Bay Area.

WHAT WE'RE LOOKING FOR

1) Strong, punchy service features: Forget about the ten best restaurants, we've got that covered. But tell us about other goods and services that affect and enhance our reader's lives. How to's, best bookstores, parks, piano bars, medical care, etc. Or you tell us.

2) Hard-hitting issue oriented/investigative features: Check our May issue piece on the shooting of Bay Area Chinese-American journalist Henry Liu. The issues should be of Bay Area import, rather than of interest to one small community.

3) Local color pieces: Slices of Bay Area life that capture the pace, the specialness of living here. Also included in this category would be "the real story behind the story." Things the Chronicle and Examiner didn't tell you . . .

4) Strong profiles of local personalities: Celebrities, of course, but also special, local individuals who are doing something of real significance.

5) Short news items, chatty gossip tidbits, oddities: We're starting a new, front-of-the-book "Intelligencer"-type section. We want scoops, outrageous quotes, hints of scandal and nefarious goings on. This might be a good place to break into the magazine if you haven't been widely published before.

CAVEAT

As we have grown, so have our standards risen. A great idea does not necessarily become a great story. You must be able to prove that you can handle the assignment, or that you're the right person for the story. If you can't you'll be asked to work on spec..

RATES

There's quite a range here. Shorts of 50 to 500 words pay from $25 to $100. Departments and features, of 1500 to 3000 words, pay between $300 and $750. If you've got a blockbuster story, we'll talk.

HOW TO

Don't call us. Query in writing only, please. Enclose a representative selection of your published work. Address queries to: Amy Rennert, Articles Editor. Or, for news shorts, query Warren Sharpe, Senior Editor.

The Saturday Evening Post
· S O C I E T Y ·

GUIDELINES FOR WRITERS

The Post buys fiction, nonfiction, humor, poetry, cartoons, illustrations and photography. Payment ranges from $15 for Post Scripts and fillers to $1,500 for assigned articles by name writers.

The magazine reports within 6 to 8 weeks. You should query first, enclosing a self-addressed stamped envelope. Submissions must include a self-addressed stamped envelope in order to be returned.

Stories and articles should be people-oriented. Fiction with action, well-woven plot and strong characterization is a Post tradition. Our readers want mysteries, suspense stories, romance and adventure.

Sports articles, pieces on the arts, government, education, travel, religion, history, family life, animals, science, archeology, anthropology -- all are welcome. We like for the subject to tell his own story wherever possible instead of an author writing about the subject.

Length may be 500 to 4,000 words with 2,000 the average. An article with its own photographs and illustrations stands a better chance than one without.

We are looking for humor. We like positive stories. We like to think most of our readers have already been to the place you are writing about--twice. Your angle must be fresh and your research thorough.

Division of the Benjamin Franklin Literary & Medical Society
1100 Waterway Boulevard • Indianapolis, Indiana 46202 • (317)636-8881 • Telex 27-440

Saturday Review

WRITER'S GUIDELINES

Saturday Review is a national magazine that deals with features on theatre, music and records, dance, film, architecture, and art. Each issue contains a special section reviewing the most important recently published books.

We are interested in all aspects of contemporary life and culture including profiles and politics as they relate to those areas. We are not interested in unsolicited fiction or poetry. As a rule, articles should be no longer than 3,000 words.

All queries and manuscripts should be addressed to our Washington, D.C. office:

> Saturday Review
> 214 Massachusetts Avenue NE
> Suite 460
> Washington, D.C. 20002

If you feel that you have a strong, appropriate idea for the Saturday Review, please send a detailed query or manuscript, along with any samples of your writing from other publications and a curriculum vitae. Unpublished writers will be considered only on the basis of a complete manuscript. We cannot respond to queries or return materials unless you enclose a self-addressed, fully stamped envelope. If you want a sample copy of the magazine, enclose $2.50 and a magazine-size SASE.

Thank you for your interest in Saturday Review.

Sincerely,

Frank Gannon
Editor

GUIDELINES FOR SUBMISSION OF ARTICLE PROPOSALS

Savvy reports on business and financial topics to an audience of highly trained professional and managerial women. A query letter or concise statement of intent should be accompanied by clips or a similar indication of qualifications. We will be glad to consider completed articles on speculation; multiple submissions or previously published material will not be considered.

In addition to feature articles, we publish regular departments and columns as follows:

Think Tank: Profiles of women who solved a particular professional problem or expanded their business in an innovative way.

Houseguest: Home entertaining from the inside: interviews with high-profile women over breakfast, lunch or dinner.

Brief Encounters: Essays on aspects of personal rather than professional life. Humorous treatment is acceptable.

New Waves: Fresh ideas from what's new in neon to the latest in plastic surgery techniques.

Body & Soul: Quick takes on fitness topics.

Health: Issues and recent developments in the field of medicine.

Behavior: Psychologically and socially-oriented topics pertinent to our audience.

Queries should be addressed to Wendy Reid Crisp, Editor. Please enclose a stamped, self-addressed envelope and allow six weeks for reply. We do not handle any unsolicited material by telephone. Written rather than telephone queries are advised. Strong familiarity with Savvy is essential. We cannot provide sample copies.

THREE PARK AVENUE, NEW YORK, NEW YORK 10016
(212) 340-9200

WRITER'S GUIDELINES

1. Savvy strives for a tone that is insider, anecdotal, smart. Our readers are intelligent and quick to let us know when they feel patronized. You are addressing an audience of career-minded women in their late twenties and thirties. Hence, information should be presented in a clear, lively and sophisticated fashion.

2. We want real women quoted at all times, and prefer that their real names be used, except in very unusual or confidential circumstances. All subjects must be suitably identified: e.g., Mary Anne Wilson, 32, the executive vice president for product development of the InCar Division of the NorthAmerican subsidiary of Piedmont Plastics.

3. We require a cross-section of women to be presented: geographically, ethnically, professionally. No single source stories will be accepted. Quote as few men as possible, particularly as "experts." There is hardly a field that does not have at least one, if not several women experts and we expect them to be quoted when necessary in an effort to avoid a patriarchal tone. A man should be used as a source only when there is no woman available: The President of the United States, Chairman of General Motors, and the Pope.

4. Use details and specifics everywhere, all the time. Don't tell us, "She turned the company around," by "using just plain good sense." Tell us exactly what she did. If you can't get a variety of sources and details: names, dates, actions, failures, results, dollar figures, etc., call and we'll regroup. No specifics, no story. We require accurate, detailed business reporting.

5. We are serious about deadlines. If you cannot meet a deadline, call your editor immediately. If your story is more than four days late, your payment will be delayed accordingly.

6. Include the names and phone numbers of all your sources--both on the record and in background-- when you send the story. All fact-checking material (see list attached) must be included with the final draft or the manuscript cannot be cleared for payment.

THREE PARK AVENUE, NEW YORK, NEW YORK 10016
(212) 340-9200

EXPENSE GUIDELINES

Savvy will pay for:

1. Reasonable telephone expenses.
2. Travel, when approved in advance.
3. Gas/tolls/cab fare.
4. Tape transcriptions, when approved in advance.

Savvy will not pay for:

1. Supplies (typewriter ribbon, diskettes, cassettes, copying fees).
2. Meals with sources, unless approved in advance.
3. Federal Express or Express Mail or any other fast mail service used to get a manuscript here by deadline. The only exception is if Savvy has requested revisions or additions that need to be returned faster than regular mail permits.

THREE PARK AVENUE, NEW YORK, NEW YORK 10016
(212) 340-9200

        SELF is a monthly magazine for women
that publishes articles with an emphasis on
self-development and health of body and mind.
We publish no poetry or fiction articles,
except in excerpt form from new books.
We appreciate query letters rather than
complete manuscripts. We pay on acceptance
of material, and our rates are competitive
with current market scale.

        If you do send a manuscript, please
enclose a stamped, self-addressed envelope
to ensure its safe return. We are not
responsible for unsolicited material

        With many thanks for your interest.

                                Sincerely,

AUTHOR'S GUIDELINES

We are pleased you are writing an article for us, and we would like to give you some guidelines to facilitate our fact-checking efforts.

Because so many women rely on us for information, we try to do everything possible to make sure we are accurate and up-to-date. Although your job is done when we've bought your manuscript, ours is just beginning.

Every fact in your story will be checked by our research department. We like to confirm quotes and facts so that, after the story has appeared, we do not get frantic telephone calls or nasty letters saying, "I never said that," or "You missed my point." Ultimately, this service protects you and your sources, as well as the magazine. You might also find that if you preface the interview by saying that someone will call to confirm the quotes, people are less nervous about speaking on the record.

When you submit your article, please provide your backup material. (If you want any or all of your backup material returned after our fact-checking is complete, let your editor know.)

Keep in mind that <u>every</u> verifiable statement, even something that comes under the heading of "common knowledge," must be checked.

Backup should include the following:

*A manuscript keyed for research. You may do this on your original or a copy. One system that seems to work well for both writers and researchers is to number each piece of your backup (journal articles, photocopies of textbook pages, etc.) and write that number in the margin next to where the information appears. For books or long articles, please indicate page numbers as well.

*A list of authorities interviewed and/or quoted, their telephone numbers and addresses. (Quoted authorities will be sent a copy of the magazine in which the article appears.) Tell your sources that they will be called by our research department and their quotes checked. For this reason, it is not necessary to send sources copies of your complete manuscript. In fact, we discourage this practice. If the authority insists, please tell your editor who has copies of the manuscript.

*When making photocopies of articles and book pages, be sure to photocopy (or write on the copy) the journal name, volume and page number or, in the case of books, title, author and publisher.

Thank you very much for helping us maintain a high standard of accuracy and reliability.

Seventeen

MAGAZINE 850 THIRD AVENUE, NEW YORK, N.Y. 10022 (212) 759-8100

WRITER'S GUIDELINES FOR NONFICTION

Seventeen accepts articles on subjects of interest to teenagers. Writers who are not familiar with the magazine or who have not read it recently are advised to go through a year's worth of back issues (most libraries carry Seventeen) to learn more about what the magazine publishes. Desired length varies from 800 words for short features and monthly columns to 2,500 words for a major article.

Seventeen gives assignments (guarantees a fee) only to writers who have been published in the magazine or whose professional work is known to the editors. Thus, writers whose work has not appeared in Seventeen should include a list of their credits and tear sheets of published articles. Writers who have had no articles, or only a few articles published, will be asked to write on speculation (no guarantee of payment).

Allow three weeks for consideration of a query or a manuscript. Seasonal material should be submitted at least six months in advance. Work that is purchased is paid for on acceptance. Rates vary depending on placement in the magazine, quality, and length. Photographs or artwork are paid for after they are scheduled for a particular issue.

Send article ideas or manuscripts to the Executive Editor or the Articles Editor. No phone calls, please. All letters and manuscripts should be accompanied by a stamped, self-addressed return envelope sufficiently large to hold all of the submitted material. Correspondence should carry the writer's name, address, and telephone number with area code.

It is not our policy to give complimentary issues.

TRIANGLE COMMUNICATIONS INC.

Dear Writer:

Thank you for your inquiry. In order to write for SHAPE
magazine, we require the following:

- Please keep queries to two paragraphs.

- Please send us clips of your previous work.

- Check our magazine to follow our style. All
  articles are written in a very personalized style.

- We prefer specific topics, tight ideas.

- We like valid and easy to understand sidebars -
  graphics, charts and quizzes to supplement the
  article.

- We don't use writers as experts. The article will
  either carry the byline of the expert alone or
  both the expert and the writer.

- All first articles are written on speculation
  only - even if we assign them to you.

- Payment will be sent upon publication.

We appreciate your interest in SHAPE and look forward to
receiving your article.

Sincerely,

Christine MacIntyre
Editor-in-Chief

21100 Erwin Street
Woodland Hills
California 91367
(818) 884-6800

SIERRA

530 BUSH STREET, SAN FRANCISCO, CA 94108   [415] 981-8634

EDITORIAL GUIDELINES

Sierra is a general-interest magazine that publishes articles, photographs and art on environmental topics. Sierra's readers are environmentally sophisticated and may have been politically active in environmental campaigns. They favor the preservation of wilderness, our National Parks and other natural areas, social responsibility, holistic thinking, controlled growth, sound urban planning, energy conservation, and similar values. They tend to look askance at uncontrolled development, dangerous or unhealthy technologies, and other unsound environmental practices. They are generally well-educated and well-read. Many of them have travelled extensively, and most have hiked, climbed, ridden bikes, canoed or been active outdoors in some way.

Sierra publishes tightly written pieces about issues and places currently important to environmentalists. We do not publish articles of a strictly local interest; articles on local conservation battles will be considered only if they affect larger problems. We often publish articles on the Club's conservation priorities, a list of which can be obtained from the Conservation Department. In adventure or travel pieces, we prefer stories about low-technology, low-impact, energy-efficient travel that offers maximum contact with the natural world, combined with a sense of excitement and discovery. Backpacking, climbing, canoeing, hiking, sailing, and biking are the usual modes of travel. Danger, while providing a certain suspense and thrill, is not necessary; dangerous situations should be acknowledged as the result of conscious choices or of mistakes. We rarely publish fiction or poetry; both genres are best pursued elsewhere. We are interested in book reviews of important and timely books, and in articles about the natural world written by or for children up to sixteen years old.

We encourage you to submit queries or story ideas before writing an article. We appreciate receiving clips from authors who have not yet published with us. Manuscripts should be double-spaced at 43 characters to a line. Please include a stamped, self-addressed envelope if you would like material returned. Maximum length should be 2,500 words, but shorter articles are welcomed. If photos are available, they either should be mentioned or should accompany the manuscript--we use 35mm or larger transparencies or B&W glossy prints. We recommend sending photos registered mail; we return all photos that way. Sierra pays on acceptance. Send all queries and manuscripts to James Keough, Editor.

11/84

SIGNATURE

EDITORIAL GUIDELINES

Signature publishes 6-10 major features in each issue of the magazine, plus 8-12 front-of-the-book columns. The magazine's focus is the art of living well in the broadest sense—travel, dining, sports, art, music, acquisitions, fitness, etc. It is targeted toward successful business people, executives and professionals who are affluent, well-traveled and about age 40.

Articles are literary and journalistic in style and avoid the service-oriented "how-to" approach. Major articles run about 2,000 words in length; columns 1,300. Payment on acceptance begins at $700.

Queries should be in writing and should state concisely the article's concept and premise. Include a few recently published clips and a self-addressed stamped envelope. Responses may be delayed considerably if a self-addressed stamped envelope is not included. Do not include photographs or slides; we cannot guarantee their safe return.

For a sample copy of the magazine, send a check for $2, payable to *Signature*, with your request, to Barbara Tirone, Signature, 641 Lexington Avenue, N.Y., N.Y. 10022. Annual subscription rate is $19.95.

641 Lexington Avenue, New York, N.Y. 10022 (212) 888-9450

1985
EDITORIAL
GUIDELINES

DELTA AIR LINES INFLIGHT MAGAZINE

HALSEY PUBLISHING CO.

PUBLISHERS OF INFLIGHT AND CORPORATE MAGAZINES
12955 BISCAYNE BOULEVARD, NORTH MIAMI, FLORIDA 33181

GENERAL OPERATING POLICIES:

The typical Delta passenger is an affluent, professional/managerial businessperson who resides in an urban area of the Northeast, Southeast, or Midwest. Given these demographics, *SKY* may best be described as a general-interest magazine with a primary editorial focus on business and industry, as well as finance and management. These guidelines, and the magazine itself, reflect that basic editorial direction.

In addition, *SKY* publishes what can only be accurately described as "substantive good news." This positive editorial orientation precludes any coverage of topics dealing with such areas as disease, disaster, sex, crime, politics, or other controversial aspects of contemporary life. In short, *SKY* discusses solutions – not problems.

Other submissions which *will not* be considered under any circumstances include: poetry, fiction, light humor, excerpted materials, cartoons, jokes, restaurant/hotel/events listings, previously published articles, religious or first-person/experiential stories.

Experience has shown us that credibility, consistency and quality are best achieved and maintained by working with a regular group of independent professionals. *SKY* therefore relies heavily on its contributing editors and frequent contributors for material, most of which is conceived and developed by Halsey's professional staff; then refined and written by our independent associates in the field. Virtually all formatted (preplanned) editorial content and most expansion material is developed through this method.

The publisher reserves the right to edit or condense a story, and also to augment a story with additional pertinent copy or photographs. All articles submitted to *SKY* or assigned by its editors must be original and, as law provides, may not be reprinted after publication in *SKY* without the express written permission of the publisher and the contributor.

AREAS OF COVERAGE:

In order of priority, general areas of feature coverage comprising the editorial mix in a typical issue of *SKY* are as follows:

Business & Finance: Industry in general; the economy; management/manufacturing techniques and methods; corporate trends and investments.

Lifestyle: Leisure, architecture, recreation, personal health and appearance, and entertaining. (No fashion queries accepted.)

Sports & Recreation: Professional sports according to season; major amateur and collegiate events; individual sports activities and fitness.

Cultural & Entertainment: Film, theatre, music, TV, art and dance. (No reviews.)

Consumer & Personal: Contemporary trends, personal finance, how-tos.

High Technology: Computer technology, space travel, telecommunications and information processing, general scientific research and development.

Collectibles: Varietal items as seen from both a hobby/collecting and investment-oriented approach.

Leadership Profile Series: Almost exclusively focused on leading national and multinational CEOs; subjects approved by the airline at least 12 months in advance. No queries or MS accepted in this category.

Travel: Primary destination features written for *SKY* are predetermined by Delta management at least 12 months in advance.

Standard Columns & Departments: A group of regular writers provides *SKY* with material for its standard columns and departments, which include a management/business column, crossword and puzzle page, and human behavior/psychology article. From time to time, these contributors are replaced; those interested in being considered for these assignments on an ongoing basis should provide the Editor with a résumé, samples of work and professional credentials where applicable.

Expansion Stories: While the departments identified above are represented in *SKY* by assignments made according to formats determined 8-12 months in advance of publication, Halsey does maintain a catalog of stories to be on hand for expansion purposes. These stories, which are fully prepared in mechanical form and held for use when and if additional advertising pages necessitate expanding editorial content, fall into the same general categories as the standard departments. They should be timeless; not written so as to restrict use to any particular month or time of year; and consist of text/photo packages. Typically, *SKY* uses from 12-20 such articles in a calendar year.

TERMS AND PAYMENT:

SKY pays immediately prior to publication, concurrent with final clearance of the magazine by the airline. Payment varies according to several factors, and naturally is higher for text/photo packages, but in general, compensation for assigned stories ranges from $300 to $500. Compensation for expansion stories is based on the amount of editorial space allocated, and is generally less than compensation for assignments. Kill fees of from 1/3 to 100% are paid when cancellation of a completed assignment occurs through no fault of the writer.

SKY buys first North American rights only; and as a courtesy to contributors, extracts no fee for processing reprint/republication requests from writers, photographers and artists.

All photography and illustrations in *SKY* are full color. Most photography is provided by a stock photo house, as well as specific sources/contacts which writers are instructed to provide at the time of submission of an assigned manuscript. Artwork is prepared by independent illustrators with whom *SKY* works on a regular basis, as well as by Halsey's own highly creative in-house studio staff. Photographers and artists wishing to offer their services to *SKY* should contact the Art Director, Lynn David Lerner.

INVOICES:

Contributors should submit their invoices to the Editor, noting the article by title and the issue to which it pertains; and invoices should accompany assigned material when submitted. In the case of expansion stories, contributors will be notified if and when such a piece will be used, and thereafter, should invoice Halsey as above.

Long-distance telephone expenses are reimbursed, and certain other expenses may be approved for reimbursement, as well. However, prior approval by the Editor is necessary, and receipts or copies of bills must be provided for bookkeeping purposes.

DEADLINES:

SKY is distributed aboard Delta's aircraft at the beginning of each month. Copy is usually due 60 days before the date of distribution, on or about the 25th of the 2nd month preceding issue date.

The critical importance of deadlines cannot be overemphasized, and with our early assignment system (usually providing 30 days working time prior to deadline), there should be no excuse for broken deadlines. However, if at any time a problem arises which might lead to a broken deadline, contributors should notify the Editor *immediately.*

Contributors must be absolutely certain that all material provided is accurate and up to date. Facts, figures, people and places should be verified before submission. Substantiation may be required occasionally.

SUBMISSION OF QUERIES:

Although *SKY* employs a format development system which provides for preplanning of content 8-10 months in advance, queries are invited, in keeping with the departments and standards described in the guidelines. Queries should be submitted to the Editor, in the following format:

> Working Title
> General Concept (100 words or less)
> Approximate length of story
> Description of accompanying visual components

When submitting queries, projected publication dates and deadlines should be kept in mind, unless the query pertains to an expansion story.

SUBMISSION OF MANUSCRIPTS:

When submitting manuscripts, including assignments, the cover or title page should identify the story, by working title; the author, with bio if requested; the address and telephone number of the author; the issue for which the story has been assigned, if an assignment; and the estimated length of the story, in number of total words.

Manuscripts should be typed, double-spaced, on plain white paper, and contributors are urged to retain a copy for their files. Once accepted, manuscripts will not be returned.

Photographs must be accompanied by cutlines of an explanatory and informative nature, and should be original slides or transparencies sized 35mm, 2¼", or 4" x 5". Photographs should always be protected in plastic sheets or sleeves, and mailed with cardboard backings.

Submit all queries, materials, manuscripts, etc, to:

> Lidia de Leon
> Editor, Delta *SKY*
> Halsey Publishing Co.
> 12955 Biscayne Boulevard
> North Miami, Florida 33181

Unsolicited manuscripts and queries *will not be returned* unless accompanied by a self-addressed, stamped envelope to ensure a response and/or return of materials. Publisher accepts no responsibility under other circumstances.

Patience on the part of those submitting materials for consideration is appreciated. Due to the heavy volume of material received, it is generally not possible to lend proper attention to material as quickly as we would like, and 30-60 days is, therefore, our average response time.

January, 1984

SKY PUBLISHING CORPORATION
49 Bay State Road
Cambridge, Massachusetts 02238-1290
Phone: (617) 864-7360

SKY & TELESCOPE AUTHOR'S GUIDE

Sky & Telescope aims to provide amateurs and other general readers with clear, interesting, and reliable information about astronomy. It also serves as an interdisciplinary medium of communication for the worldwide amateur and professional astronomical communities.

Feature articles summarizing important new advances or topical problems in astronomical research and space exploration are welcome, as are descriptions of important new instrumentation or facilities, historical topics of general appeal, advances in astronomical education, and programs deserving wide public support. As a prospective author you are urged to write to Sky & Telescope's editor, giving a description and outline of your proposed article; this will be reviewed by the editorial board to determine its suitability for the magazine and also to check that no prior commitments for a similar article exist.

The length of a feature article is typically equivalent to 8-16 double-spaced typewritten pages. Manuscripts should be typed on one side of each sheet only, and each page should bear the author's name and a page number. Since articles are by-lined, please indicate how you wish your name to be presented and also your institutional affiliation (if any). Also include a short autobiographical description. Be sure to keep copies of your manuscript to guard against loss in the mail or other mishap (we promptly acknowledge receipt of manuscripts). The best way to judge the suitability of material and how to present it is to review a number of issues, since our editing style is fairly consistent.

Illustrations generally represent about half of the space occupied by a feature article. Photographs, drawings, or other illustrations should be originals. We use both black-and-white and color. When possible, send along negatives with black-and-white prints, as we can often get a better result from a print specially made in our darkroom. Color transparencies should be originals (not duplicates); note that we take special care to prevent damage to film in our possession. We obtain equally excellent reproduction from color negatives, as our color lab produces prints optimized for the printing process. Kodak Kodacolor II is particularly good for this, but Vericolor II works well, too. All negatives and transparencies are returned after the article is published. We can prepare line drawings as well as developed art from accurate sketches, though we prefer to have the author to supply us with drafted line work when possible (lettering and other labels are usually redone to conform to our adopted type style).

Text galleys are normally sent for author approval. Upon an article's publication, the author is sent copies of the issue in which it appears. Since reprints are very expensive (especially if color is involved), we offer as an alternative a special bulk rate to authors for extra copies of the magazine (currently $1.40 domestic, $1.65 foreign). If you anticipate ordering more than about 50 copies, we should be informed at the time galleys are OK'd. If you are interested in a quotation for reprints, that is a good time to let us know (in a separate letter).

Payment for feature articles is sent upon receipt of approved galleys. Currently we pay 10-20 cents per word, depending on numerous factors. We also pay for the one-time use of paintings, cartoons, and cover illustrations. Payment for book reviews is at the same rate, less the retail value of the book (which you keep). Other contributions do not normally receive honorariums, though nominal remuneration is available for out-of-pocket expenses. Ordinarily we require an assignment of copyright, on forms we provide.

Finally, remember that Sky & Telescope is a widely read and respected publication, and we encourage you to consider us for the broad distribution of your results and ideas to interested readers the world over. Feature articles are indexed in *Astronomy and Astrophysics Abstracts, Astronomy and Astrophysics Monthly Index, Book Review Index, IBR, IBZ, Monthly Periodical Index, Science Citation Index-Abridged Edition, The Magazine Index,* and *The Readers' Guide to Periodical Literature.*

(over)

SKY & TELESCOPE DEPARTMENTS

Contributions from our readers make the magazine live! The departments offer a means of communicating with the astronomical community at large. Letters to the Editor provides a forum for comment and elaboration on feature articles, certain kinds of announcements, and brief statements not appropriate for inclusion elsewhere in the magazine. News Notes welcomes suggestions from astronomers concerning research that should be highlighted. The submission of preprints (including illustrations) is encouraged.

The three departments where amateur astronomers come into their own are Amateur Astronomers, Gleanings for ATM's, and Observer's Page. The first provides news of club meetings and activites, plus other information that doesn't fall naturally into the other two departments. We especially appreciate receiving club bulletins and newsletters.

Gleanings is the place for amateur opticians and mechanics to publish descriptions of their telescopes, observing accessories, and optical techniques. Practically every important kind of telescope built by amateurs has been premiered and thoroughly described in these pages. Observer's Page with its lavish use of laser-generated color separations is the natural place to submit your fine photographs for our frequent highlights and roundups. Articles on how to observe and photograph are welcome here. Meteor observing, Sun, Moon, planets, double stars, deep-sky objects — all are featured, and our readers want to know how you observe them and what your results are.

To submit materials for the departments, follow the suggestions above for manuscripts and illustrations. It helps if material, including letters, is typed so we don't misread the content. We try, of course, to publish items as promptly as possible. However, there is often a backlog of deserving material awaiting publication, which may mean a delay in yours seeing print.

One last important point: Material submitted to us (other than news releases or the like) should not be submitted elsewhere unless we are unable to use it. Magazines prefer their contents to be unique; also, there are not enough pages available to publish all that is worthwhile. If you have any specific questions not answered by this guide, please do not hesitate to call or write.

The Editors

Smithsonian
Magazine | *900 Jefferson Drive, S.W. • Washington, D.C. 20560 • (202) 357-1612*

WRITER'S GUIDELINES

Thank you for inquiring about submitting articles to SMITHSONIAN Magazine. We prefer a written proposal of one or two pages as a preliminary query. The proposal should convince us that we should cover the subject, offer descriptive information on how you, the writer, would treat the subject and offer us an opportunity to judge your writing ability. Background information and writing credentials or samples are helpful.

All unsolicited proposals are sent on a speculative basis and a reply should be forthcoming within six weeks. Please include a self-addressed stamped envelope. Our fees are negotiable. If we decide to commission an article we will pay one-third of the fee in advance with the balance paid on acceptance of the manuscript. If the article is found unsuitable the advance payment serves as a kill fee.

SMITHSONIAN is buying First North American Serial Rights only. The length of our articles ranges from a 750 word humor column to a 4,000 word full-length feature. We consider focussed subjects that fall within the general range of Smithsonian Institution interests such as cultural history, physical science, art and natural history. We are always looking for the off-beat subjects and profiles that fall within our interest areas. We do not consider fiction, poetry, travel features, political and news events, or previously published articles. We have a two-month lead time.

It is important to keep in mind that illustrations play a role in our decision-making process. If you have photographs or illustrations, please include a selection of them with your submission. In general, 35 mm. color transparencies or black-and-white prints are perfectly acceptable. Photographs published in the magazine are usually obtained through assignments, stock agencies or specialized sources. No photo library is maintained and photographs should be submitted only to accompany a specific article proposal.

Rates for color and black-and-white photographs: $350 for a full page, $500 for the cover. The day rate is $300 and photographers will be paid whichever fee is higher, the day rate or the space rate.

Copies of the magazine may be obtained by sending $2.00 per copy and your request to the above address marked to the attention of the subscription office. With only 12 issues a year it is difficult to place an article in SMITHSONIAN but be assured that all proposals are considered.

I appreciate your interest in SMITHSONIAN.

Marlane A. Liddell
Articles Editor
SMITHSONIAN

254 West 31st Street, New York, N.Y. 10001, (212) 947-6300

GUIDELINES

Nonfiction: "Articles only directly about daytime and nighttime personalities or soap operas." Interview (no telephone interviews); nostalgia; photo features (must be recent); profiles; special interest features: health, beauty, with soap opera personalities and industry news, with a strong interest in nighttime soaps. "We are a 'newsy' magazine - not gossipy. No poorly written writing that talks down to the audience." Buys 2-3 mss/issue. Query with clips of previously published work. Length: 1,000-2,000 words. Pays $200 and up.

OMEGA GROUP, LTD.

P.O. BOX 693, BOULDER, CO 80306   (303) 449-3750   TELEX 450 129

SOLDIER OF FORTUNE
SURVIVE
SOF EXCHANGE
SOF CONVENTION

EDITORIAL CONTRIBUTIONS

THE MAGAZINE

Soldier of Fortune Magazine is an adventure publication written expressly for an active audience interested in going and doing. We specialize in first-person reporting from battlegrounds around the world with emphasis on current military weapons development, military/political affairs and history as well as tactics and techniques.

FEATURE ARTICLES

Soldier of Fortune Magazine publishes well-written, action-packed feature articles describing professional adventure world-wide. Succinct accounts of experiences should be thoroughly researched and include information on how the reader can undertake similar activities. Style and approach may vary, but should be aimed at an informed, intelligent, well-traveled audience.

All manuscripts are edited as necessary to conform to our style and standard of expression. Bibliographies or bibliographical notes should be used where applicable.

We take a strong stand on political issues such as maintenance of a strong national defense, the dangers of communism and the right to keep and bear arms.

Features with an active "I was there" slant are favored. Interviews, personality profiles, historical pieces, light essays, commentaries, guest editorials and humorous pieces related to professional adventure are also considered.

Seasonal material should be submitted at least six months in advance. Authors are requested to send a query letter or story outline when proposing a story idea. Phone queries are also considered. Please include a SASE or sufficient postage to cover the return of all material. *Soldier of Fortune* is not responsible for unsolicited manuscripts.

Feature articles range from 1,500 to 3,500 words. Writing should be original and accurate. We will consider reprints and excerpts from books or other publications. Manuscripts should be typed and triple-spaced. Enclose a brief biography which includes positions, experience or education that will establish your authority on the subject.

PHOTOGRAPHY

Soldier of Fortune publishes color and black & white photographs. For color, only transparencies are acceptable, in either 35mm, 2¼ or 4x5 formats. For black & white, glossy prints are preferred, accompanied by negatives when possible. 5x7 black & white prints are the minimum size accepted. Appropriate line-art illustrations will also be considered, along with technical diagrams. All artwork *must* be submitted camera-ready. All photographs and art (including color) submitted with an article are considered integral to the editorial package - no separate payment is made. Color photographs and art submitted on their own accord for use either as inside or cover illustration will be negotiated separately, on a scale from $50 to $300.

Photographs should be submitted in clear plastic sheets, properly keyed to accompanying caption material. All subject matter within each photo should be properly identified. Please include full return postage with each submission. *Soldier of Fortune* assumes no responsibility for unsolicited material.

PAYMENT SCALE

Editorial rates range from $200 to $1,000, including photographs and/or illustrations, for feature and column material. Payment is made upon publication. Cover photographs and solicited material are negotiable. Payment for "I Was There" and "It Happened To Me" is $50.00

Soldier of Fortune retains First World Rights to accepted manuscripts and photographs. Acceptance by *Soldier of Fortune* conveys all rights for subsequent reproduction and use of any published material for educational purposes.

Dale A. Dye
Executive Editor

SOUTHWEST AIRLINES *Southwest Monthly*

Gabrielle Cosgriff, editor

Coverage: Primarily Texas and the Southwest

Format: Edited for Southwest's sophisticated passengers, the magazine employs
           superior writing and graphics to explore the business, arts and life-
           styles of the most progressive region in America. Forward looking and
           forward thinking, yet evoking a sense of place and romance of region,
           it is an informed and influential voice in the market it serves.

Southwest Monthly celebrates and reflects the qualities that characterize Southwest
    Airlines. It is innovative, lively and friendly, and committed to excellence.
    We have the good fortune to represent the most vital, dynamic region of the
    United States, and our stories will deal with every aspect of living and doing
    business in the Southwest. We reach almost a million readers a month, readers
    who are intelligent and curious. We aim to entertain, inform and stimulate them
    on a number of levels. Not only will we provide information on what is happening
    in fields as diverse as business, communications, lifestyle, leisure, education,
    politics and the arts, we will also address these subjects philosophically. We
    will be on the cutting edge (to quote one of our departments) of the Southwestern
    experience.

For further information, see PSA Magazine.

Editorial Department

The writers and photographers who consistently sell material
to Sports Afield in today's highly competitive market have
one quality in common: they know the magazine. They study
Sport Afield thoroughly every month and know what's run and
what hasn't.

The mere recounting of a successful hunting or fishing trip
(me-and-Joe material, as it is called) is not what our
readers prefer. They like entertaining and well written
outdoor articles, nature profiles, some fiction, personal
adventures, new places to hunt and fish, etc. Features run
anywhere from 1500 to 3000 words and must be backed up by
fully captioned color transparencies.

Top-notch photographs are very important to your chances of
selling to Sports Afield--pictures that help tell the story
as well as highly dramatic shots. 35mm Kodachrome 64 transparencies are preferred--originals, not dupes.

We also buy short filler material with a strong how-to flavor
for the Almanac section. Other areas we cover in this
department include natural history and conservation, shorts,
humor, fishing, hunting, camping tips and useful outdoor
information.

In addition to our monthly magazine, Sports Afield publishes
several outdoor annuals with all new how-to material. These
yearly publications (FISHING, BASS, HUNTING, DEER) use black-
and-white photographs only.

All material sent to us should include a self-addressed return
envelope and sufficient return postage. Manuscripts should be
addressed to Editors, Sports Afield, 250 W. 55 St., New York,
NY 10019. Please include your social security number and a
daytime telephone number.

Thank you for thinking of Sports Afield.

                                        Sincerely,

250 West 55th Street, New York, New York 10019
Sports Afield is a publication of Hearst Magazines, a division of The Hearst Corporation

Sports Illustrated

TIME & LIFE BUILDING
NEW YORK, N. Y. 10020
212 JU 6-1212

ARTICLES REQUIREMENTS

ADVANCE TEXT:

This is text that closes two weeks before the current issue of the magazine. All stories must be appropriate for national publication, although some stories may appear in editorial space that accompanies regional advertising, which differs slightly in the East, West, Midwest and South, and some stories may appear in editorial space that accompanies select advertising in 870,000 copies. The designations "regional" and "select" refer only to advertising, not copy. These pieces are generally done on speculation and it is best to query in writing first. Short stories that run in the front of the magazine should be either 350 or 750 words long, for which we pay $750 on acceptance. Longer stories, from 900 words to 2500 words, pay $1250 on acceptance. Our categories include:

ART TALK: analysis of sporting art or art exhibits
FIRST PERSON: first person accounts of unusual sporting events
FOOTLOOSE: sports-oriented travel pieces, but not travelogues
HOT STOVE: off-season analysis of and information on any sport
NOSTALGIA/REMINISCENCE: first person accounts of past sporting events
ON DECK: profiles of up-and-coming young athletes
ON THE SCENE: descriptions of unusual or offbeat sporting events
PERSPECTIVE: opinions about sports-related incidents or subjects
REPLAY: short pieces on particularly memorable pre-1970 plays
SHOPWALK: analysis of one-of-a-kind sporting equipment
SIDELINE: general sports observations, interviews or service pieces
SPORTS Rx: what's new in sports medicine
SPOTLIGHT: profiles of excellent athletes in less well-covered sports
STATS: points or positions based on notable, newsworthy numbers
UPDATE: what are they doing now? follow-ups on former athletes
VIEWPOINT: editorial views on a particular subject
YESTERDAY: recreations of sporting scenes, pre-1954 when Sports Illustrated was started. Many of these famous events have already been covered.

NATIONAL LONG TEXT:

Most of the long text is staff-written and the staff has complete control over deadline news stories. This is one area not open to free-lance writers due to our fast-closing procedure. We are happy to read other stories submitted on speculation. Articles should have some connection with sport and be about a major personality or event. It should be remembered that articles must have a broad appeal so that they can be judged in accordance with SI's editorial standards. The fee for long text pieces starts at $1750.

All articles, queries, outlines, etc., for ADVANCE TEXT should be addressed to Margaret Sieck, Senior Editor. For NATIONAL LONG TEXT, they should be sent to William Oscar Johnson, Articles Editor. Both are at the above address. A response takes about four weeks, provided a stamped return envelope is enclosed. Please do not submit photos or artwork with text. We cannot be responsible for illustrative material. Put your name on your manuscript and keep a copy.

7/86

SUNDAY WOMAN

235 EAST 45TH STREET, NEW YORK, N.Y. 10017 212-682-5600

WRITER'S GUIDELINES FOR SUNDAY WOMAN

SUNDAY WOMAN is a weekly newspaper supplement which runs in more than 60 markets in the United States and Canada with an estimated circulation of 4 million.

SUNDAY WOMAN features solid, reportorial articles on topics affecting women, their families, lifestyles, relationships, careers, health, money and business. We look for fascinating success stories about women in business and female entrepreneurs.

1,500 - 2,000 words.

National focus.

No poetry, fiction or essays.

No pet or travel pieces, please!

First-person stories - reprints only - for Outlook column which features poignant/amusing stories.

Payment upon acceptance.

First North American rights purchased.

Happy to consider previously published material.

Include cover letter with address, phone number and Social Security number; not responsible for manuscripts submitted without stamped, self-addressed envelope.

For first-time submission of story ideas, please include samples of your writing (Xeroxes only) and SASE

Manuscripts must be typed and double-spaced.

For copies of SUNDAY WOMAN, send a separate letter with an 8 x 10 SASE.

No phone calls, please. (Don't call me, I'll call you.)

Merry Clark
Editor

SUNSHINE

MAGAZINE GUIDELINES

SUNSHINE is a weekly color magazine published with the Sunday edition of the *News/Sun-Sentinel*, a Tribune Company newspaper which circulates throughout Broward and Palm Beach Counties in South Florida. Major cities in this area include Fort Lauderdale, Hollywood, Hallandale, Plantation, Coral Springs, Boca Raton, Pompano Beach and West Palm Beach. The circulation averages 260,000, reaching nearly 600,000 readers.

The magazine accepts the work of freelance writers, photographers and artists. Most of our current contributors are established in their fields. However, we are always seeking new contributors and fresh ideas which can result in publishable features.

WHAT DO WE BUY?

Generally, anything that would interest an intelligent adult reader living on South Florida's famous "Gold Coast." We live and work in one of the nation's fastest growing regions (we have more new people coming to live here than any other area of Florida; 30 percent have been here five years or less). Because of our sub-tropical climate and the affluence that tourism has brought to our area, *Sunshine* readers are "leisure active" consumers who spend a high percentage of their incomes in spare-time pursuits, which include boating (Fort Lauderdale is one of the world's yachting capitals) and shopping (people here do more shopping in a month than most regions in the country do in three).

For the half of our population that works, the Gold Coast offers opportunities as diverse as filmmaking and high technology. For example, the IBM Personal Computer is manufactured in Boca Raton — just one of 20 major high-tech installations in our area.

We like stories that shed light on what makes life in South Florida unique: Profiles, Florida and Caribbean lifestyles, guides (recent offerings have included guides to salad bars, happy hours, health spas, bakeries, and tropical bird shops), offbeat sports and personal essays. Major stories run an average of 2,000-3,000 words (occasionally 4,000 if the subject-matter warrants it), but we're also in the market for shorter (1,000-1,500) personal essays and "think" pieces.

WHAT DO WE PAY?

All fees are negotiable, but as a general guide, our rates for accepted articles range from 20 to 25 cents per word up to $750, occasionally higher. Photo rates are also negotiable: Up to $200 for covers, up to $150 per page for inside color and up to $75 per page for inside black-and-white. We pay up to $500 for cover or doubletruck color illustrations, up to $400 per page for inside color, and up to $300 for inside black-and-white. Payment is made within 30 days of acceptance.

HOW TO BREAK IN

Send us an idea, or better yet, several ideas. Include a telephone number. We will contact you within four weeks (usually less) if we're interested. Articles or proposals that are totally unsuitable are returned with a form letter, usually within two weeks.

WHERE TO WRITE

Each story idea should be outlined in 100-200 words in which you tell us what you intend to write about, and why you are qualified. If you wish, you may include the lead to the story, to give us a better idea of your approach and writing style. Include a summary of previous writing experience and publishing credits. Address letters to:

The Editor
SUNSHINE MAGAZINE
P.O. Box 14430
101 North New River Drive East
Fort Lauderdale, FL 33302

Sylvia Porter's Personal Finance Magazine Company   380 Lexington Avenue, New York, NY 10017 • (212) 557-9100

Sylvia Porter's Personal Finance Magazine provides comprehensive coverage of subjects which affect people's pocketbooks -- and the quality of their lives.

In each issue we offer important information on budgeting, saving, investing, real estate, insurance, health care, taxes, and much more.

Our readers -- John and Mary Consumer -- are not interested in economic philosophy. They need to be prepared to meet changing economic conditions effectively. They want to know how to enrich their lives by spending, saving, and investing their money wisely.

They need to have the tools -- encouragement and information -- to stand up for their rights. They're people who are productive and busy, and need this information presented quickly, personally, and in a lively, interesting manner.

Freelancers should send a cover letter with original ideas or slants about personal finance articles they'd like to do for us, accompanied by clippings of previously published work. Our response time on queries is two to five weeks. Unsolicited manuscripts will be returned unread.

We buy all rights, and pay on acceptance. Rates are negotiable, and will be discussed with the author at the time of the assignment. We don't publish reprints or accept simultaneous submissions. If, after completion, a commissioned story is rejected, a kill fee of 20 percent of the agreed-upon price is paid to the author.

We also accept outside material for "Tips from Readers," which features short (250 words or less) items on saving, investing, earning, planning, spending, and other areas of personal finance. We pay $25 for each submission accepted. (Clippings of previously published work need not accompany submissions to this section.)

Manuscripts submitted to SPPFM must be neatly typed on bond paper, double-spaced on one side of the sheet only, with one-inch margins. The title page should include your name and address, and the number of words in the story. Enclose a cover letter.

Thank you for your interest in the magazine.

                                                        The Editors

FOR THE COLLEGE-MINDED WOMAN

TeenAge Magazine Writers' Guidelines

TeenAge **is a national news and entertainment magazine written for 14- to 19-year-old college-minded young women.** Our student interns do the majority of the writing, but we accept a few well-written manuscripts from freelancers of any age. Articles should address teenagers in a mature way and contain material relevant to young people concerned with today's issues and trends. The editors strongly recommend that you read a copy of *TeenAge*, which you can obtain by sending us a check or money order for $1.50 plus $.65 for postage and handling. All manuscripts must be typed, double-spaced, on one side of the page. Sorry, but manuscripts submitted without self-addressed, stamped envelopes will not be returned.

Features: We publish features on serious, service-oriented topics as they relate to teenagers on a national level, and interviews with famous people, including movie and TV stars, musicians, and sport figures. We also use profiles of teenagers who are exceptionally unique, talented, or resourceful. We run some fashion and beauty features. Features should be between 1,500 and 2,000 words; profiles between 400 and 1,500 words. Payment of $100 to $1,000 is arranged on an individual basis. *TeenAge* pays 30 to 45 days after publication. Address submissions to Attn: Features Editor.

Columns: Mind and Body, College, Careers, Money, and Wheels. As the columns are short, topics should be narrow and specific. As with all of our editorial, the topics addressed must be of interest to college-minded teenagers. Columns are generally 1,000 words. *TeenAge* will pay $100 to $300. Send column submissions to Attn: Associate Editor.

Frontlines: Our Frontlines column is a forum in which students express an opinion on a political, social, or personal problems that confronts young people today. We will only publish essays written by students aged 21 or younger. The editorials should be logical and to the point--the best Frontlines are the ones that cover one **specific** topic. Frontlines are 350 to 400 words in length. We pay $50. Address submissions to Attn: Frontlines.

Fiction: *TeenAge* publishes original short stories. **We do not accept any poetry or juvenile romances.** Fiction should be between 1,500 and 3,000 words. Payment is arranged on an individual basis. Address fiction submissions to Attn: Fiction Editor.

Insanity: We are looking for short, humorous items taken from previously published materials. Please send only the clip, the name of the source, and the date--we'll do the rest. We pay $25 for each clip we use. Address Insanity submissions to Attn: Insanity.

Original Cartoons: We accept cartoons on any subject, but funny gags that appeal to teenagers receive top priority. Cartoons should be drawn with black ink on 8 1/2" X 11" paper, with captions typed at the bottom of the page, and sent in a 9" x 12" manila envelope. Print your name, address, and telephone number on the back of each cartoon. Include a 9" x 12" SASE to insure a safe return. We pay up to $150 for each original cartoon we use. Address cartoons to Attn: Cartoon Editor.

A Footnote: We do our own fact-checking, therefore, we must see all factual information that the author used in writing the article, including names and phone numbers of sources and previously published material.

Editorial Office: 175 Middlesex Turnpike, Bedford, MA 01730 617-271-0330
Advertising Office: 928 Broadway, Room 303, New York, NY 10010 212-505-5350

FOR THE COLLEGE-MINDED WOMAN

Thank you for your interest in *TeenAge* (formerly *Highwire*). We have read your recent submission and have decided that it does not fit into our present editorial needs. However, we continue to look for material geared toward motivated, involved young women, and hope you will keep us in mind if you have other ideas suitable for *TeenAge*.

We have enclosed along with your submission, a copy of our writers' guidelines for your information. If you wish to receive a sample copy, please send a check for $1.50, and we will be happy to send you one. **We urge you to acquaint yourself with *TeenAge*'s editorial content before sending more queries.**

Again, thank you, and sorry about this form letter. We're unable to reply individually to everyone, but we do read all the submissions. Please try again.

Sincerely,

Good Luck!

The Editors

Editorial Office: 175 Middlesex Turnpike, Bedford, MA 01730 617-271-0330
Advertising Office: 928 Broadway, Room 303, New York, NY 10010 212-505-5350

TEXAS MONTHLY GUIDELINES FOR WRITERS

Stories must appeal to an educated Texas audience. We like solidly researched reporting that uncovers issues of public concern, reveals offbeat and previously unreported topics, or uses a novel approach to familiar topics. Any issue of the magazine would be a helpful guide. We use no fiction, poetry, or cartoons.

Submitting the Story Idea or Manuscript

All materials should be mailed to Gregory Curtis, Editor, TEXAS MONTHLY, P.O. Box 1569, Austin, Texas 78767.

A letter of inquiry should precede submission of the manuscript. The letter should provide a good sample of the style of the proposed article, indicate a perspective, and list material to be covered. A brief outline showing the direction and approach of the proposed article should accompany the letter. A self-addressed, stamped envelope should be included with all queries and all manuscripts.

Acceptance

All material should be considered submitted on speculation until formally accepted. By accepting an article, we make no commitment to a publishing date.

When your manuscript arrives in our office you will be notified. A formal answer will be sent to you within six to eight weeks. If your manuscript is accepted, an editor will be assigned to you.

Preparation of Copy

All manuscripts must be typed and double-spaced. The author should retain a copy of the manuscript. On the cover page of the manuscript the author should include his or her name, mailing address, and telephone number where editors may call during the working day. Include a SASE large enough to contain the manuscript.

Editing

The editor's job is to make the magazine as readable and unimpeachable as possible. We consult with the author about editorial changes whenever possible. The author has the option to withdraw a story if agreement on points of editing cannot be reached.

Your editor will continue to work with you until the manuscript reaches its finished form. You will be contacted by a copy editor and fact checker assigned to your story. Be prepared to submit any notes, tapes, and documents to the Research Editor. During the production process you will receive a set of galleys of your story.

(over)

Payment

Payment for a story is made on acceptance. The fee is negotiated and agreed upon when the writer is notified that the manuscript has been accepted. A written agreement must be signed before payment is made.

Length

There are two categories of manuscripts: Features and Departments. Please designate in which category you think your proposed article fits.

Features are generally 2500 to 8000 words in length.

Departments are generally 2500 words or less. They include Art, Architecture, Food, Education, Business, Politics, Theater, Classical Music, and Texana.

Reporter

While Reporter has regular staff writers, TEXAS MONTHLY welcomes ideas and tips for stories. Topics should be newsworthy and handled with a new slant. Pay scale for tips used is $20 to $50.

Photography and Art Work

Photography and art work for articles appearing in TEXAS MONTHLY are assigned by the art director.

* * *

National Reporter Publications, Inc.
15115 S. 76 E. Ave., Bixby, Ok. 74008
(918) 366-4441

WRITER'S GUIDELINES: TOTAL FITNESS

    TOTAL FITNESS is a bimonthly magazine with editorial focus
on exercise and how to use it to slim, trim, firm and shape your
figure and maintain your fitness. We seek to provide information
and inspiration to the average woman trying to put fitness into
her life-style.

    Our audience is female, 28 to 55 years old, upper middle
class. They care about health and exercise, may belong to some
type of health club but may or may not be actively involved in
pursuing fitness through exercise.

    Examples of typical articles for TOTAL FITNESS: Exercises
for overall fitness; exercises to help develop shapely legs; a
guide to choosing aerobic dance shoes; and tips on how to start
and stay with an exercise program.

    Payment is upon acceptance.   We prefer two- to three-
paragraph queries instead of finished manuscripts. Response time
is four to six weeks. Minimum payment $.10 per word.   Word
length 1,500 to 2,500 words. State availability of photos.

    Send queries to: Anne H. Thomas
                      Managing Editor
                      TOTAL FITNESS
                      15115 S. 76th E. Ave.
                      Bixby, OK 74008

Trailer Life
Editorial Guidelines

HOBBY/ACTIVITY STORIES

RVers' hobbies run the gamut, but enthusiasts are particularly interested in fishing, rockhounding, hiking, spelunking, photography and other outdoor activities that are conveniently pursued via RV. Photos and copy should depict enthusiasts actually participating in the activity–plus one or two photos showing the RV used in connection with it. Payment for hobby and/or activity features ranges from $100 to $300.

Again, either color slides or black-and-white prints, or a combination of the two, are appropriate for illustrating hobby pieces.

NEWS ITEMS

TL keeps readers apprised of legislative, industrial and financial news that affects them as RV owners and camping enthusiasts via the monthly *Newswire* department. Items submitted for publication must be brief and concise (no more than 150 words), and the source of the information must be clearly stated. *Newswire* payments range from $25 to $100.

COLUMNS

All regular columns such as *You Can't Miss It* are monthly features written by staff columnists.

PHOTO REQUIREMENTS

Specific suggestions on photographs are included throughout this guide. In addition, we would like to emphasize that quality photography is very important, especially for travel articles. Please keep "lead" photos in mind, something suitable for either a full page or double spread. It should depict the topic, and preferably include an RV,  people or activity. Attempt to shoot at different F-stops (different exposures of the same scene). Also, it should be noted that we cannot consider duplicate slides for publication. We prefer Kodachrome 64 film for 35mm photography, but welcome Ektachrome Professional film as well, although it requires more care in protection from exposure to heat. Maximum visual impact is desired in all photographs, and a very important ingredient is dramatic lighting. Be sure to number each photo or slide to correspond to accompanying caption sheet, and label each photo or slide with your name for proper photo credit and to ensure their return after publication or rejection of article.

Payment for photographs is included in the payment for an article. Color transparencies submitted alone or solicited alone are purchased at the following rates (subject to negotiation): $50 to $75 for use of the photo on less than half a page, $100 to $150 for one page, $150 to $250 for a spread, $200 to $300 for cover photos. Black-and-white prints are purchased for $25 to $100 each, depending on use.

SUBMISSION OF MATERIALS

Please enclose a stamped, self-addressed envelope with all manuscripts and photos/slides submitted to: Editor, *Trailer Life*, 29901 Agoura Road, Agoura, California 91301. Acknowledgement is usually made within one week and acceptance/rejection letters are sent within six weeks.

Trailer Life's readers are avid adventurers, eager to explore every facet of their world, via the comfort of their recreational vehicles (RVs). Whatever type of RV they own–whether a luxurious Class A motorhome or a modest van conversion, a 30-foot fifth-wheel trailer or a folding camping trailer–Trailer Life readers view their

RVs as a way to see the world their way. And it is our privilege to help them achieve that goal while they enjoy their unique lifestyle to the fullest.

In addition to describing specific destinations and suggesting en-route attractions and activities, we offer readers the ways and means of improving their comforts and conveniences. TL regularly carries how-to and do-it-yourself articles, tips for cooking, fishing and traveling with children and/or pets, helpful hints about traveling full-time (more and more people are retiring to roam), special methods of getting the most out of their present RVs, plus test reports to aid them in selecting a new model.

If you are unfamiliar with the magazine, begin by carefully examining a current issue, not only for the type of material we publish, but also for length, general approach and pictorial illustration. A word of caution: All material submitted for publication must be guaranteed exclusive to TL. (The article should not have appeared elsewhere, nor have been submitted simultaneously to another publisher.) We buy First North American Rights.

All manuscripts must be typewritten, double-spaced, on one side of paper only. The author's name, address, telephone and Social Security numbers should be on the first page, and we prefer that copy start about halfway down the first page. Pages should be numbered and identified at the top. TL editors reserve the right to edit copy as necessary, to condense, expand or otherwise revise as space or style requires, but will make every effort to retain the author's original meaning.

TRAVEL FEATURES

Although the majority of our readers travel throughout the contiguous United States, many also tour Canada and Mexico, and a few ship their RVs to distant ports to see other parts of the world. Virtually any place where automobiles are found, RVs can also be driven. We've published several around-the-world tour reports–all of which demonstrate that Trailer Life readers are adventurous. Travel features are therefore the bulk of our free-lance material. These vary from 1,000 to 3,000 words in length

All travel articles must be illustrated with quality photographs, preferably color slides. The broader the selection, the better. In addition to showing countryside and points of interest covered by the article, a few of these slides must also include RVs. A surprising number of manuscripts are returned due to lack of inclusion of RVs in at least one or two of the photographs or slides. The RV connection is *always* required. We work mostly with 35mm slides, preferably Kodachrome 64, but 2¼ x 2¼- format transparencies taken with a quality camera are also welcome. To ensure photo credit, the photographer's name should appear on each slide submitted. If photographs or artwork by someone other than the author are enclosed with a manuscript, TL assumes that person's permission has been obtained. Although reasonable care is taken of unsolicited material, we are not responsible for it, nor will we guarantee return of manuscripts for which sufficient postage and a self-addressed return envelope are not provided. Also, each photo or slide should be numbered with an accompanying caption sheet detailing its contents. Occasionally we purchase additional photos or slides to supplement the manuscript. Therefore, we will review color transparencies or lists of geographic areas covered by your photo files for possible future reference. For more specific data regarding photos, please see *Photo Requirements* section.

Travel articles also should be accompanied by a map of the area, showing routes described in the story. Staff artists will redraw the map for publication, but to do so accurately, they need a clear road map with major points of interest indicated.

Payment for travel articles ranges from $200 for *Super Sites* to $350 for full-length features accompanied by top-quality photographs or transparencies.

HOW-TO ARTICLES AND TECHNICAL FEATURES

Many RVers are do-it-yourself enthusiasts who are interested in making modifications to their rigs or customizing them for additional comfort and convenience. Typical examples of projects appropriate for TL are fold-away tables, magazine racks, tool boxes and storage cabinets. One black and white photo or sketch may be sufficient to illustrate the project or a dozen may be required, depending on scope of the article. If sketches are necessary, please furnish all the dimensions so that staff artists can draw them accurately. Also, try to estimate the cost of each project.

Most major technical articles are staff written, or are written by free-lance authors working on assignment after discussion with editors about specific content and approach of the article. We would welcome your suggestions regarding major technical articles. Examples include articles on 12-volt and 120-volt electrical systems, proper tire loading and inflation, improvement of self-containment, battery use and maintenance, fuel economy improvement and repair/maintenance of water systems.

Black-and-white 8 x 10 glossy prints are preferred but smaller prints will be considered. Include the negatives, if possible. Converting slides to black-and-white prints is expensive and, more importantly, the quality suffers in the process, so whenever possible, please provide black-and-white prints.

Payment for how-to and technical articles ranges from

$125 to $200 for one-page, do-it-yourself articles to $400 or more for full-length features requiring research and/ or testing.

HUMAN INTEREST STORIES

People are also an important subject to RVers because the camping fraternity is a very social one, and camaraderie is one of the inherent bonuses of camping. Individual RVers can be worthy of personality profiles if they are unique in some respect; perhaps they have a very unusual hobby or maybe they have a one-of-a-kind RV they built themselves. Movie stars, sports figures and other celebrities, of course, are always of special interest to our readers, if they are genuine RV enthusiasts.

Human interest articles can be illustrated either with color slides or black-and-white prints, but if at all possible, submit both. This allows your manuscript to be considered for publication either way. If prints are sharp, small ones will be considered, but 8 x 10 glossy prints are preferred. Major personality profiles or people pieces run as long as 2,000 words in length; shorter items, such as those appearing in the *People on the Move* department, may be only 100 to 500 words long. The latter carries only black-and-white photos, usually one per item. Topics suitable for *People on the Move* also include RV club rallies and other special events of interest to RVers, plus RV-related anecdotes.

Payment for human interest stories ranges from $50 for *People on the Move* items to $375 for full-length features.

TRAVEL& LEISURE

GUIDELINES FOR WRITERS

Please familiarize yourself with the magazine. Note the various sections and the service orientation. Also note that we allow each writer his or her individual style.

Our readers are not armchair travelers. They expect to be able to make use of the information presented in any article. Our readers should be able to follow in the writer's footsteps. All places discussed should therefore be open to the public, and all information up to date and correct.

Nearly all middle-of-the-book feature articles are conceived by the staff and are assigned to writers who have previously worked for the magazine.

We rarely buy unsolicited manuscripts. We prefer a three or four-paragraph query letter explaining the main thesis of the article, together with supporting facts, and your credentials. We want to be convinced that the article and author are right for us.

If an idea is accepted, you will received an assignment letter/contract explaining the assignment in detail. A statement of expense policy will accompany the assignment letter. Under no circumstances is an assignment from Travel & Leisure to be used to attempt to obtain complimentary services from hotels, transportation companies, national tourist offices, etc.

Fees, length of article and deadline will be included in the assignment letter. Our fees are competitive with leading national magazines.

1120 AVENUE OF THE AMERICAS
NEW YORK, NY 10036
(212) 382-5600

AN AMERICAN EXPRESS COMPANY

TRAVEL BUILDING • FLORAL PARK, N.Y. 11001 • 516 352-9700   *Office of the Editor*

ARTICLE AND PHOTO REQUIREMENTS

We are happy to review queries of new or established writers, but ask that you follow the following recommendations closely.

Please send us queries, not finished articles, since the odds that we will return a manuscript unread increases geometrically with the number of unsolicited manuscripts received. Potential contributors should send recently published clips along with their query.

Any writer who has not worked for us since 1981 must be willing to work on speculation, i.e., without an assignment or contract. After a writer has his/her first article accepted, future articles will be assigned. We prefer to see queries about places you have already been to, save your dream trips for dream land.

Given the proper direction, contributors are expected to write to our specifications and to rewrite an article when so directed. Those submitting articles on speculation have the option of not reworking the piece. Those on assignment however, are expected to work within our guidelines and refusal to tailor an article to our needs will nullify a contract. Payment for articles is made upon acceptance.

One last note, we purchase only first North American rights; thus WE DO NOT ACCEPT SIMULTANEOUS SUBMISSIONS.

FEATURES: Feature articles of 1,600 to 1,800 words must deal with foreign or domestic travel destinations, off-the-beaten-path or well-known, but with a new twist or update. Copy must be lively, entertaining, informative and serviceable and should include information on both daytime and evening activities, if applicable. The readers should feel as if they are actually there. They must also be able to duplicate the trip, but more importantly they must want to. Text may be written in the author's most comfortable style: use of anecdotes OK in moderation. Honest, critical evaluations are most important: no guide book rehashing. A resource box containing hard facts (where to write for further information, how to get there, etc.) must accompany all stories. Sidebars (a mini-article relating to the article) of no more than 500 words are acceptable. Features should be accompanied by a varied selection or sources of transparencies (see photo). Payment is $400.

FEATURETTES: Small towns or cities as well as museums, markets, shopping sites, art galleries and similar subjects of special interest will be considered as featurettes (800 to 1,300 words). Special aspects of a major destination--Savannah's Historical Inns, Milwaukee's Ethnic Festivals, etc.--are also suitable for submission. Payment is $250 and up.

HERE & THERE: Any unique topic that can be covered succinctly, with one piece of black and white art, that is travel related and deserves special recognition (i.e., the film studio where "Das Boot" was made, the Football Halls of Fame, the Texas Chili Cook-Off) and can be covered in 575 words will be considered for Here & There. Pieces must be written very tightly, and must really jump out and grab you. When querying for this section please send suggested lead and indicate "Here & There" in your cover letter. Payment is $150.

-OVER-

ARTICLE REQUIREMENTS

SERVICE PIECES: These are usually written by a staff member. Query us <u>only</u> on topics on which you are an <u>established</u> expert. Please, no photography, food or medical queries since we have columnists for those topics.

PHOTOGRAPHY: Although we welcome photography submitted with an article (or, if none is available, suggestions as to where appropriate transparencies may be obtained) we rarely make photo assignments. To fulfill our stock needs we contact competent photographers for the submission of appropriate stock photos. Those who wish to be considered as photographic contributors to the magazine should submit a sampling of 40-60 transparencies to the Managing Editor. Submit all transparencies in vinyl sheets and include sufficient postage for their return (registered or certified mail is recommended). Also include a stock list of the states of the USA and the countries or areas of the world of which you have coverage. Payment for photography is made upon publication. Rates are: 1/4 page or smaller - $75; 1/2 page - $100; 3/4 page - $125; full page - $150; two page spread - $200; cover - $400; black and white, any size - $25 (color converted to black and white will be payed at the $25 rate).

SAMPLE COPIES: Sample copies for writers are available for $1.00. Please enclose a check or money order when requesting a sample copy.

All material submitted within these guidelines is considered by one or more of our editors. Unfortunately, the volume of manuscripts and correspondence received makes individual replies impossible. Include sufficient postage if you wish to have materials returned. Please do not call to pitch us on an idea, and do not requery us on something we have rejected unless so directed. Finally, read the magazine and check the Readers Guide to Periodical Literature (available in most libraries)--we do not like to see queries on topics we have recently covered.

NOTICE TO AUTHORS

Tropical Fish Hobbyist considers submitted manuscripts concerned with all aspects of the popular aquarium hobby and submissions of a more scientific nature dealing with fishes, reptiles and amphians available and of interest to the hobbyist. Manuscripts must be typewritten and double-spaced on standard letter-sized stationary and vary between 500 and 2,500 words. Titles should be as brief as possible and clearly indicate the subject. The author's name and address should appear on the last page of the submitted work and a stamped, self-addressed envelope should be included where possible to facilitate the return of unaccepted articles. Tropical Fish Hobbyist reserves the right to edit all accepted manuscripts to conform with the magazine's format and style.

All manuscripts submitted to TFH should be sent to John R. Quinn, Assistant Editor, Tropical Fish Hobbyist, 211 West Sylvania Avenue, Neptune City, New Jersey 07753.

34 East 51st Street
New York, New York 10022
Telephone: (212) 888-5900

UNITED MAGAZINE

EDITORIAL GUIDELINES

We publish the following types of articles:

--travel pieces that relate to United Airlines' destination map.

--profiles of interesting and successful Americans who have distinguished
  themselves through their achievements, leadership, or creativity. We are
  particularly looking for people with a dimension that differentiates them
  from their peers. We are always looking for couples, both of whom are
  career-oriented, and especially interested in women making their way in
  the world.

--upscale lifestyle and trend pieces that relate to food, art, architecture,
  fashion, theater, entertainment, products, etc.

--first person essays about current phenomena, trends.

We put a premium on the visual presentation of our profile subjects. We
expect our articles to establish right from the beginning the importance of
the subject and why we expect him or her to command the attention of the
reader. We expect to hear the voice of the subject, but do not use an excess
of quotes.

We prefer a written query of one page or less. All queries and manuscripts
must be accompanied by a self-addressed, stamped envelope or they cannot be
returned.

Please include one or two copies of recently published work. Even though an
editor may reject your article idea, he or she may be able to match you up
with future assignments.

For further information, see PSA Magazine.

HALSEY PUBLISHING CO.
USAir MAGAZINE

GUIDELINES FOR AUTHORS AND PHOTOGRAPHERS

We are looking for outstanding ideas and/or manuscripts on most general-interest subjects including business, sports, nature, the arts, science/technology, food, Americana, education, health, personal finance, humor, and any others that are appropriate for a wide audience. Since USAir is a domestic carrier (except for Toronto and Montreal), please keep travel-related story suggestions focused on the United States.

Articles should be crisply written, lively, informative, and positive in approach; we avoid subjects that are extremely controversial. To make the magazine as visually appealing as possible, we pay special attention to articles that can be illustrated with striking photographs or artwork. Articles range in length roughly between 1,500 and 4,000 words, for which we pay $400 to $1,000. We buy first rights, and pay on acceptance.

When writing a query letter, please keep it succinct, but explain what the story is about, its relevance to a wide audience in the 1980s, the main points you would cover, and the length you have in mind. Clips of previously published articles will help convince us that you can write. Because of the volume of queries and manuscripts we receive each month (about 500), those submitted without a self-addressed, stamped envelope cannot be answered or returned.

We give occasional assignments to photographers for which we pay $300 per day. Most of our photography comes from stock. Full-page rates are $150 for black-and-white, and $250 for color, payable upon publication.

--The Editors

VANITY FAIR

Thank you for your letter requesting Vanity Fair's writer's guidelines. We do not have any guidelines as such, but we do make the following requests:

(1) All submissions must be accompanied by a stamped, self-addressed envelope. Submissions will not be returned without an envelope.

(2) Do not send transparencies, photographs, or other valuable material.

We make every effort to read all unsolicited submissions, but Vanity Fair cannot be responsible for such material.

Again, many thanks for your interest in Vanity Fair.

The Editors

The Condé Nast Publications Inc.   350 Madison Avenue, New York, New York 10017   (212) 880-8800

Published by the State of Vermont, Development Agency,

VERMONT LIFE MAGAZINE *with Business, Subscription and*

Editorial Offices at **61 Elm Street, Montpelier, Vermont** *05602. Phone (802) 828-3241*

SPECIFICATION SHEET

Vermont Life is interested in any article, query, story idea, photograph or photo essay that has to do with Vermont. As the state magazine, we are most favorably impressed with pieces that present positive aspects of life within the state's borders. We have no rules, however, about avoiding controversy when the presentation of the controversial subject can illustrate some aspect of Vermont's unique character.

With most ideas, we prefer queries first.

Articles are seldom planned for inclusion in Vermont Life before they have been accepted and received in this office. We often work as much as a year in advance in preparing articles for publication and we would appreciate it if contributors so noted.

Our text rates range between $100 and $500 depending on the length and research involved in preparing the manuscript. Most articles run approximately 1800 words and the average fee is $250. We pay by the word - 20 cents per word. We buy first North American Serial Rights to the article or photo (more detailed info is in the assignment contract) and will refer print queries back to the contributor.

We use original color transparencies (ideally 25 Kodachrome 35 mm) and black and white in equal amounts. We also accept 2¼ X 2¼ and 4 X 5 color. We do not accept color prints. We have darkroom capabilities or will accept contact sheets and prints in black and white.

In each issue of the magazine, a number of pages are set aside for purely scenic photography, ranging from landscapes to activities in a Vermont setting. Submissions to this section can be made in late June for winter, late September for spring, late December for summer, and late March for autumn. These dates are generally applicable for the planning of the issues mentioned. Submissions for our calendars should be made by early December, 1985 for the 1987 calendar and early November, 1986 for the 1988 calendar.

Slides are returned by Certified Mail only if appropriate postage is included. We take no responsibility for unsolicited materials. Slides not accepted will be returned in your SASE as soon as a decision is made, generally 1-3 months. For slides accepted for the magazines or calendars, we will pay 1st class postage for their separate return.

Photographs selected for the scenic section are bought for one time use only for $75. Occasionally we will seek permission for a second use in the calendars, and there is an additional remuneration.

The photographic rate is $200 per day, on assignment. We pay for scenics on publication and assignments on acceptance. Payment for a front cover is $200 and a back cover is $150.

We generally avoid non-photographic illustrations and we routinely eschew poetry.

<u>Writer's Guidelines for</u>
<u>VIBRANT LIFE Magazine</u>

What Type of Articles Do We Want?

The editors of VIBRANT LIFE are looking for practical articles promoting a happier home, better health, and a more fulfilled life. We especially like human-interest stories, articles on the family, inspirational pieces, features on the latest breakthroughs in medicine, health, and nutrition, interviews with leading personalities on the home and health, seasonal material, some humorous pieces--if written in a readable style that appeals to the typical man/woman on the street. Articles presenting a happy, healthy outlook on life are particularly welcome--especially if written in a Christian context.

SPECIFIC AREAS OF INTEREST ARE OUTLINED BELOW

<u>CHILDREN:</u> Articles on raising happy, healthy children written from the point of view of what parents can do. Also advice on coping with teen-agers, et cetera.

<u>EXERCISE:</u> Practical advice applicable to the typical man/woman in America today who wants to add exercise to his/her life.

<u>HEALTH:</u> All aspects of health--physical, mental, emotional and spiritual--well researched pieces, relying on quotes from authorities in the field under discussion (unless written by an authority--i.e. doctor, pediatrician, nutritionist, et cetera). We are <u>not</u> interested in articles primarily focused on one or more diseases.

<u>HOME:</u> Managing your home for a happier family, managing your budget, problems of working mothers.

<u>HOW TO:</u> How to save time, how to get out of debt, how to improve yourself, how to have a more rewarding life, how to overcome bad or unhealthful habits, et cetera.

<u>HUMOR:</u> Light tongue-in-cheek pieces on subjects related to the family, home, and health--if done in good taste (i.e. no off-color material).

<u>HUMAN-INTEREST:</u> Stories of real people who have passed through a crisis in their life to victory, especially because of a strong faith in God.

<u>INFORMATIONAL:</u> Home and family safety, consumer fraud, new research in medical/ health field, labor saving or money saving articles.

<u>INSPIRATIONAL:</u> Short articles that help build one's faith in God.

<u>INTERVIEWS:</u> With someone knowledgeable in marriage, family, or health areas.

<u>MARRIAGE:</u> How to communicate with your mate, reaffirmation of vows, articles

Writer's Guidelines for
VIBRANT LIFE Magazine
What Type of Articles Do We Want
Page 2

based on marriage authorities that present practical ways to a better, stronger marriage.

NUTRITION: Articles showing the reader how to have better nutrition, less junk food, more healthful meals, et cetera are always welcome. But articles must not rely on the use of meat or fish, since the magazine promotes the vegetarian life-style (see Vegetarian Diet below).

POETRY: We use little or no poetry and do not recommend this market for poetry submissions.

SELF IMPROVEMENT: Articles on how to take hold of your life and become a better you (i.e. how to break a bad habit, how to quit procrastinating, et cetera).

SEASONAL: Especially with a spiritual, inspirational slant. We are always seeking short pieces relevant to the major holidays of the year: i.e. New Year's Day, Mother's Day, Father's Day, Independence Day, Thanksgiving Day, Christmas, et cetera. (However, seasonal material must be submitted 6 months in advance of the month in which it would appear.)

VEGETARIAN DIET: All aspects of vegetarianism are suitable for VIBRANT LIFE, especially articles that help the reader to prepare healthful meals for a family using vegetarian principles. (Regarding vegetarianism, VIBRANT LIFE promotes a lacto-ovo-vegetarian position, which permits the use of dairy products.)

NOTE: Please keep in mind that our primary target audience is the 20- to 50-year old, husband, wife, or parent. If your article is aimed for a different age group, it should be reslanted to fit our target readership.

Writer's Guidelines

for Contributors

to VIBRANT LIFE Magazine

PHILOSOPHY: VIBRANT LIFE is a general audience, bimonthly Christian magazine presenting articles that promote a happier home, better health, and a more ful- filled life.

STYLE: VIBRANT LIFE is published for the typical man/woman on the street. There- fore articles must be written in an informal, interesting, easy-to-read style. Avoid medical or religious jargon. We stress readability and prefer the person- oriented approach (i.e. What can this do for me? How can it help me, or my family to live happier, or healthier?)

MANUSCRIPTS: Articles should focus on one topic and stay with that subject to the end. Short articles (3 to 5 typewritten pages, double-spaced) are always in demand, but regular length manuscript (6 to 10 typed pages, double-spaced) are standard. (Manuscript length should range from 750 words to 2,800 words maximum.) Manuscripts over 10 typed pages are simply too long for our publication and must be condensed before submitting to our offices. Please double-space everything, including quotes, references, et cetera.

Do not use easy-erase paper or thin paper. Send either original manuscripts or good, clear photocopies of your original. (For your own protection against mail loss, you should keep a copy of what you send in your own files.)

SASE: Be sure to include a self-addressed, stamped envelope large enough for the return of your manuscript, if unacceptable. (Articles without a SASE will not be returned and after a period of six months will be discarded.)

ARTICLE QUERIES: We prefer to see finished manuscripts, rather than article queries.

RELIABILITY: Information must be reliable, no faddism. Articles should repre- sent the latest findings on the subject, and if scientific in nature should be properly documented. (References to other lay journals are generally not accept- able.) If your manuscript contains material that needs footnote documentation, please keep them to a minimum and use the following format:

REFERENCES:

1. J. D. Lyons, Nielson Television 1978 (Northbrook, Ill.: A. C. Nielsen Co., 1978).

2. A. R. Somers, "Violence, Television, and the Health of the American Youth," New England Journal of Medicine,, 1976, 294, 811-817.

3. M. C. Long, "Television: Help or Hindrance to Health Education," Health Education, 1978, 9.

SUGGESTIONS FOR CONTRIBUTORS
Page 2

PAYMENT: Payment is based on quality of expression, accurate use of up-to-date research findings, depth, and relevance of content. Payment for short articles ranges from $75 to $125 and for feature articles from $150 to $350. Payment is made upon acceptance. We purchase first North American Serial Rights or reprint rights.

PREVIOUSLY PUBLISHED ARTICLES: We will look at previously published articles by the writer, if the writer has sold only one-time rights or has written permission to sell the article elsewhere without a reprint credit. But the articles must fit into our list of topics needed. (See "What Type of Articles Do We Want?")

PHOTOGRAPHS: Only photos that illustrate a submitted article will be considered. We prefer 35mm color slides, not prints. (Black and white glossy prints should be 5" x 7" or larger.) Please enclose a self-addressed, stamped envelope for return of slides (or prints).

CARTOONS: We use 10 to 15 cartoons a year and will consider only those that are well drawn, marriage, family, or health oriented, and on the conservative side. Payment is $50 to $100 per cartoon accepted.

NOTE: The earliest any newly-purchased article could appear in our magazine is six months, and longer than that is generally the rule, as we try to plan one year in advance. The author automatically receives 3 complimentary copies of a published article; therefore, please do not inquire as to when an article will appear. If you have a change of address before your article is published, please notify us, so that you will be sure to receive your complimentary copies, and to save us the time and expense of mailing them to an incorrect address.

EDITORIAL OFFICE ADDRESS:

VIBRANT LIFE
55 West Oak Ridge Drive
Hagerstown, Maryland 21740

460 West 34th Street, New York, N.Y. 10001•(212) 947-6500

VIDEO Magazine's Writer's Guidelines:

        We're frequently asked by beginning freelancers for
a copy of our guidelines. No such thing really exists here
at VIDEO Magazine. We like to consider our book a buff-
oriented consumer magazine (or special interest, if you
will) edited with the highest journalistic standards. Too
often writers wonder "what we're looking for." The best
way to answer that question is to read the magazine
thoroughly for a few months before you hit the typewriter.

        We demand only two things; good writing and original
ideas. The best way to get into VIDEO is with a thorough
well-researched query. A recent, slick credential helps,
but it's not necessary. Usually, we can tell in 300 words
whether you can write. We realize these two thin paragraphs
are not very revelatory, and perhaps even cliched, but it's
the best we can do.

REESE COMMUNICATIONS INCORPORATED, Publishers of VIDEO Magazine and ELECTRONIC GAMES Magazine

VIDEO TIMES

<u>KEYNOTE REVIEW GUIDELINES</u>

Keynote reviews vary in length anywhere between 250 to 500 words, depending on the importance of the video, its subject, content, and length. A keynote review should discuss what the tape is about, what its intentions are, and how well it fulfills its goals. When reviewing a film, discuss the plot only briefly, concentrate on the style, the acting, the film work, and any insights that a reader would find interesting about the film. Never give away the ending. Be critical, examine the good points as well as the bad, but don't be overly critical; we're looking for balanced, objective, well-written reviews.

Go easy on the made-for video tapes; these are the people without the big Hollywood dollars who are trying to make inroads in the video field. When reviewing an instruction tape, don't be too critical of the production values or set design, concentrate on whether it does what it purports to do. Is it informative? Is it helpful? Are there other tapes of the same nature that are more successful?

Always double space reviews. Begin the piece with a filmography (tape name, year made, whether in B/W or color, director's name, cast, releasing company's name, MPAA rating, and price). Always call a character in a film by the character's name, not the actors', identify the actor in parentheses. Check your facts; don't make claims we can't verify. Check your spelling and grammar also. Use straightforward, down-to-earth writing. We appreciate creativity and flair, but not at the expense of easy understanding. Put yourself in the reader's place and answer any questions the reader might have. Feel free to have some fun with the review...entertainment is what our magazine is about. <u>PLEASE</u> <u>PLEASE</u> put an <u>ACCURATE WORD COUNT</u> on your piece and give the tape a star rating between one and four. Four equals excellent. One equals poor.

3841 West Oakton Street, Skokie, Illinois 60076, (312) 676-3470, TELEX #280084 PIL SKO

SALES OFFICE 225 West 34th Street, Suite 806, New York, New York 10122, (212) 564-7006

VIDEO TIMES

POPCORN GUIDELINES

Popcorn is the section of Video Times that is probably
the most fun to read. It is made up of short, snappy
tidbits about films, actors, and the movie world.

Popcorn pieces should run between 50 and 150 words and
should end with a bang. The focus should be on names
and films that are easily recognizable and of interest
to a mass audience.   Films should be available on video.

Popcorn is also a highly visual section of Video Times--
it would be helpful if the piece lent itself to interesting photographs.

3841 West Oakton Street, Skokie, Illinois 60076, (312) 676-3470, TELEX #280084 PIL SKO

SALES OFFICE 225 West 34th Street, Suite 806, New York, New York 10122, (212) 564-7006

VIDEO TIMES

Actors Article Guidelines

Actors is a 1300-word feature that takes a look at a particular contemporary actor or actress. The writer should obtain a personal interview with the subject of this piece if at all possible. Background information on the actor's start in films, his or her struggles, insights, thoughts on acting, favorite films, etc. are of interest to our readers. A hardy sprinkling of quotes is preferred. Be sure to discuss the actor's films that are available on videotape, concentrating on the most recent release and on any that are high points in the actor's career. If you can obtain still photos of the subject, it would be much appreciated. Keep your writing style light, informative, and straight-forward.

3841 West Oakton Street, Skokie, Illinois 60076, (312) 676-3470, TELEX #280084 PIL SKO

SALES OFFICE 225 West 34th Street, Suite 806, New York, New York 10122, (212) 564-7006

VIDEO TIMES

Cover Story Guidelines

The Video Times cover story runs approximately 3000 words.
It is an in-depth look at a particular aspect of video.
The piece should focus on a video-related subject that is
of interest to the general VCR-owning public. Ours is a
very broad readership; we want to cover subjects that will
be of interest to a large number of people. The writing,
therefore, should be down-to-earth, lively, and informative.
Our readers want to know about video--the more exciting
and fun you can make it, the better.

We expect well-organized, grammatically correct writing with
as few misspellings as possible. We also expect all writers
to double check anything stated as fact and to be sure that
all opinions are well-informed. All copy should be double-
spaced and typewritten. A fairly comprehensive outline is
required prior to the acceptance of a piece.

Any first mention of a particular tape should include its
manufacturer and, if possible, its price in parenthesis.
Any mention of a particular actor in a role should include
the character name of that actor.

3841 West Oakton Street, Skokie, Illinois 60076, (312) 676-3470, TELEX #280084 PIL SKO

SALES OFFICE 225 West 34th Street, Suite 806, New York, New York 10122, (212) 564-7006

2nd Take Guidelines

2nd Take is a look at a number of videos that may have been
overlooked in the past. It runs about 1000 words and is
often centered around a particular genre, such as detective
films, action films, or films that spoof other films--the
categories are limitless. A maximum of nine films should
be discussed--the minimum number being six.

Keep the writing lively and entertaining; be sure it is
comprehensible to the general public. Always double space
your articles and include both the actor's name and the
characters' names when discussing a film. Include the name
of the company releasing the tape, the price (if you know
it) in parentheses after the first mention. Avoid giving
away the endings of any films. Check your facts; don't
make statements we can't verify or state an opinion that
isn't well-informed. Have fun with the piece. Chances
are, if you do, the reader will also.

3841 West Oakton Street, Skokie, Illinois 60076, (312) 676-3470, TELEX #280084 PIL SKO

SALES OFFICE 225 West 34th Street, Suite 806, New York, New York 10122, (212) 564-7006

Vista USA *The Magazine of EXXON Travel Club*

Mailing Address: Box 161, Convent Station, New Jersey 07961

Thanks for inquiring about VISTA/USA.

VISTA is the magazine of Exxon Travel Club, and it is distributed quarterly to about 900,000 club members throughout most of the U.S.

Material submitted to VISTA should generally relate to travel. We buy feature articles on North America, Hawaii, Mexico and the Caribbean that appeal to a national audience. We also publish a few articles on hobby-related topics. The emphasis is on Americana, but if a travel or geographic angle can be worked in, so much the better. Most of these are 1,000-2,000 words, although length may vary based on the importance of the subject. Rates for full-length features start at $600, payable on acceptance. Please enclose a self-addressed, stamped envelope when submitting stories or queries.

VISTA issues are planned more than a year in advance, so send in article ideas early (15 to 18 months ahead of time). When querying VISTA, tell us something about the approach you would take in writing about an area. Don't just ask if we would like a piece on Boston, the Rockies, Texas fairs, etc. Point out what you feel is significant about an area or subject. One-page narrative outlines that give a feel for the topic and your writing style are preferred.

Because VISTA is a quarterly magazine with only about 30 editorial pages per issue, we must be very selective in choosing articles. We are looking for readable pieces with good writing that will interest armchair travelers as much as readers who may want to visit the areas you write about. Articles should have definite themes and should give our readers an insight into the character and flavor of an area or topic. Stories about personal experiences must impart a sense of drama and excitement or have a strong human-interest angle. Stories about areas should communicate a strong sense of what it feels like to be there. Good use of anecdotes and quotes should be included. Do not submit articles about automobile trips. Stories should not be organized to follow a specific route on the map. Nor should they be mere rundowns on what there is to see and do in an area. Points of interest and things to do should be worked into the text in a way that illustrates your theme.

If you have any further questions, please feel free to write us. We are interested in any ideas you may have for VISTA articles.

Patrick Sarver
Editor

Notes to Washingtonian Writers

What Kind of Magazine Is This?

The Washingtonian is a city magazine—it focuses almost exclusively on the Washington metropolitan area. The magazine was started in October 1965, and its circulation in 1985 was over 135,000.

Our readers are concentrated in the District; Montgomery, Prince George's, and Anne Arundel counties in Maryland; and Arlington, Fairfax, and Prince William counties and the city of Alexandria in Virginia. Average household income of subscribers is over $84,000 a year; median age is 40; seven out of ten have finished college. It is an active, educated, affluent audience—our readers travel, read, dine out, go to plays, entertain, read, earn, and spend more than the average Washingtonian.

Thus, our readers are not a "mass" audience in the same sense as the *Washington Post's* 750,000 subscribers. The implication for the writer is that you do not have to write down to the proverbial "Kansas City milkman" or anyone else. You do have to write clearly, directly, and intelligently. Our readers recognize underreporting, overwriting, preaching, unclear thinking, and pseudo-sophistication when they see it.

What Kind of Writers Are We Looking For?

Freelancers come in all ages and types and backgrounds. Some make their living as writers; others are lawyers or housewives or professors or government officials.

More important than journalism experience is knowing a subject and being able to write clearly about it.

If you have something to say and can communicate your knowledge and interest to our readers, we want to hear from you.

What Kind of Articles Are We Looking For?

We are very open-minded—as long as the article idea is interesting and relates to the Washington area.

If we have not worked with you before, send us a written query about your article idea. Tell us who you are and what kind of article you propose to write. We'll try to let you know promptly if the idea has possibilities. If your article is already written, mail it to us or drop it off. We'll respond as soon as possible. If you want your article returned, include a stamped, self-addressed envelope.

The types of articles we publish include service pieces (How to Buy Antiques, Summer Pleasures, Guide to Fitness); profiles of people (Marion Barry, Sandra Day O'Connor, Willard Scott, William Webster); investigative articles (Air Florida Crash, Emergency Medical Care, Lie Detectors); rating pieces (Maryland vs. Virginia, Rating the Liberal Establishment, Ten Worst-Dressed Men); institutional profiles (Catholic Archdiocese, *Washington Times*, Marriott Corporation); first-person articles (What Am I Doing in Jail? Diary of a High School Senior); stories that cut across the grain of conventional thinking (Buildings We Should Blow Up; Are Lawyers Becoming Public Enemy Number One?); articles that tell the reader how Washington got to be the way it is; light or satirical pieces (send the completed manuscript, not the idea, because in this case execution is everything); and fiction that tells the reader how a part of Washington works or reveals something particular about the character or mood or people of Washington.

Subjects of articles include the federal government, local government, sports, business, education, medicine, fashion, environment, how to make money, how to spend money, real estate, performing arts, visual arts, travel, health, nightlife, hobbies, self-improvement, places to go, things to do, and more. Again, we are interested in almost anything as long as it relates to Washington.

We don't like puff pieces or what are called "isn't-it-interesting" pieces. There should be an idea behind the story. We don't run articles on people, places, or businesses just because they're there.

In general, we try to help our readers understand Washington better, to help our readers live better, and to make Washington a better place to live.

What Makes a Good Washingtonian Article?

A magazine article is different from a newspaper story. Newspaper stories start with the most important facts, are written in short paragraphs with a lot of transitions, and usually can be cut from the bottom up. A magazine article should have more shape—it usually is divided into sections that are like the chapters of a short book.

The introductory section is very important—it captures the reader's interest and sets the tone for the article. Anecdotes are often used to draw the reader into the subject matter; the writer starts with specific descriptions and then moves into a general explanation. The introductory section should foreshadow what the article is about without trying to summarize it—you want to make the reader curious. Each succeeding section develops the subject. Evaluations, recommendations, and conclusions come in the closing section.

We think there are three qualities to a good magazine article: Most basic are thorough research and reporting, and a writing style that is appropriate to the material. But what separates the very good from the adequate is the writer's ability to fit his material together and to give it meaning and focus. Newspaper reporters ask who, what, when, where, and why?

The most important question a magazine writer asks is, "What does it all mean?"

Also remember that a magazine writer is usually more subjective than a newspaper reporter; try to relate directly to the reader.

And because *The Washingtonian* is a monthly and has a six-week lead time, keep in mind that our articles should have a long-term perspective that makes them as readable several months from now as they are today.

Deadlines and Other Specifics

The magazine is published about the 28th of each month. The October issue, for example, is on the newsstands and reaches subscribers about September 28. We need completed manuscripts six weeks before publication. Thus, an article for the October issue should be submitted by August 10.

Include your name, address, and telephone number on the first page of the manuscript. We prefer 8½- by 11-inch paper, with copy typed and double-spaced, and with a margin of at least an inch. Copy does not have to be perfectly typed, but it should be easily readable.

The length of articles varies. We don't like to specify a length—we'd like each piece to run at its optimum length. Capital Comments range from 50 to 600 words. Most front- and back-of-the-book pieces run 1,500 to 3,000 words. Center-of-the-book pieces are usually 2,000 to 7,000 words, but some run as long as 20,000 words. When in doubt, ask us about it.

Our regular payment is 20 to 40 cents a word, depending on the length of the article, the amount of research, the number of interviews, and how much work we have to do on it. We pay one-third upon acceptance of the manuscript and the remaining two-thirds on publication. Again, if you have doubts or questions, talk to us. We normally don't pay expenses, but sometimes do when an unusual amount of travel or luncheon interviews or long-distance calls are involved: Talk to us first.

Basically, we buy first North American rights. After the article is published, the author is free to sell it to any other publication; in such cases, we will arrange for a transfer of copyright. The Los Angeles Times Syndicate sells second rights to our articles to other publications—usually to large newspapers. When that happens, we share 50-50 the second-rights payment with the author.

Some Generalities

First, we hope our writers are readers of the magazine. It is the best way to get a feel for what we are trying to do and how your article might fit in.

Before you start an article for us, we'll want to talk with you about your research, your interviews, the kinds of questions you are going to try to answer, the way the article will be organized. We may have suggestions on where to find background information and appropriate people to talk with.

For major articles, you probably will want to check the *Reader's Guide to Periodical Literature* to see what already has been written on the subject. You may want to look at clips in the Washingtoniana room of the Martin Luther King Library or at the National Geographic library. The Library of Congress is a very good resource.

As your research and interviews continue, don't hesitate to call us if there is some question about the direction you are taking. After you have finished gathering material, it's usually a good idea to talk to us before you start writing. Many writers find it best to organize their material into a rough outline and to go over it with us before they start writing.

Suggestions on Style

We have no rules on writing style. The style should come naturally from the writer and the material. In *The Elements of Style*, William Strunk made these suggestions:

1) Be specific, concrete, definite.
2) Use the active rather than the passive voice.
3) Put the statements in positive form.
4) Write with nouns and verbs.
5) Don't overstate.
6) Avoid the use of qualifiers.
7) Don't explain too much.
8) Avoid fancy words.
9) Be clear.

In his essay "Politics and the English Language," George Orwell pointed to these sins of bad writing: "Staleness of imagery . . . lack of precision . . . the concrete melts into the abstract . . . a lack of simple verbs." Some of Orwell's suggestions:

1) Never use a metaphor, simile, or other figure of speech that you are used to seeing in print.
2) Never use a long word where a short one will do.
3) If it is possible to cut a word out, always cut it out.
4) Never use the passive where you can use the active.
5) Never use a foreign phrase, a scientific word, or jargon word if you can think of an everyday English equivalent.
6) Break any of these rules sooner than say anything outright barbarous.

One last word: Speak to the reader as an intelligent friend. The best style is clear, honest, and direct. We like sophisticated ideas and simple language, not the reverse. And don't forget the favorite question of the late *New Yorker* editor Harold Ross: "What the hell do you mean?"

—JACK LIMPERT

THE WASHINGTONIAN
1828 L Street, NW, Washington, DC 20036. 202-296-3600

WEIGHT WATCHERS MAGAZINE
360 Lexington Ave., New York, NY 10017   (212) 370-0644

Dear Writer:

Thank you for your query concerning editorial requirements.

We are a weight-control magazine, devoted to weight loss and related fields, including food, food preparation, health, nutrition, exercise, fitness, the psychology of weight loss, and weight maintenance. We are not interested in fiction, poetry, beauty and fashion articles (they're staff written), or recipes (they're handled by our food department).

We are interested in general health and medical pieces; nutrition pieces based on documented research results; fitness pieces on types of exercise that don't require special skills, special equipment, or extensive financial costs; and weight-loss stories that have an interesting angle. We seldom use humor in the magazine.

Feature articles should run 1,200 to 1,500 words. Payment varies, ranging from $250 to $500, depending upon the piece, with a 25 percent kill fee for assignments that are unusable. First submissions are always on speculation. We buy first North American rights. We do not use previously published material.

If you feel you have something suitable for Weight Watchers Magazine, send a detailed query letter, outlining your idea, your qualifications for writing the article, and, if possible, a list of sources you plan to use. DO NOT SEND FULL-LENGTH MANUSCRIPTS. And please, no phone calls. Include previous published samples of your writing and a self-addressed, stamped envelope. Replies are generally within four to six weeks. Send your query to: Cheryl Solimini, Senior Editor.

Unfortunately, we cannot send sample copies of the magazine. If you would like one, please send $1.75 (to cover cost of the magazine, postage, and handling) and we'll be happy to forward one to you.

The publisher assumes no responsibility for unsolicited manuscripts.

Thank you again for your interest.

THE WESTERN HORSEMAN

 Since 1936, the World's Leading Horse Publication

3850 NORTH NEVADA AVENUE

COLORADO SPRINGS, COLORADO 80933

Area Code 303 • 633-5524

EDITORIAL GUIDELINES

We appreciate your interest in our magazine, and hope the following editorial guidelines will help you select and write a story we can publish.

We're a general interest horse magazine, but our emphasis is on Western riding and Western lifestyles involving horses. We publish articles on ranching, rodeo, individual horses and owners, trainers and various horse training techniques, equine health care, horse gear and Western apparel, and Western historical stories that have a strong horse angle.

Much of our material is staff written, but we do use free lance material regularly. And we always have a need for good, in-depth stories on horse training and equine health care, plus the relatively short, handy hints for horsemen that appear under the title, "Here's How."

We like to see training stories in which the reader can learn, step-by-step, how to teach a horse one particular movement or manner. Examples from stories we've used in the past include: how to teach a horse to stay ground-tied; how to teach a horse to change leads on command; how to teach a horse to load into a trailer. Maybe there is a horse trainer you know who has an especially effective program for starting colts, or correcting bad habits in an older horse.

A lot of our health care stories are written by veterinarians, but we've also had many related articles written by others who have either interviewed horse practitioners on specific subjects, or written from knowledgeable, first-hand experience on some phase of horse care. Examples: how to properly wrap a horse's legs; how to care for the horse that is "on the road" a lot, being trailered to rodeos or horse shows; how to care for an injured horse while waiting for the veterinarian to arrive. Maybe there is a respected trainer on the race track who would agree to an interview on how he conditions horses.

The "Here's How" category may consist of only one or two paragraphs, or more if necessary, along with one or more photos. It may take up a partial column of space in the magazine, or maybe two columns or even a full page, if warranted. These hints can cover the entire spectrum, and past examples

include: "horse-proof" corral gate latches, emergency equipment repair, and a tip on how to safely remove a halter from a horse that might turn and kick as he is being freed.

There is no set length on any story or article--use however many words, or few words, it takes to write it. But a rule of thumb for feature articles is 1,500 words; if available, your manuscript should be accompanied by black-and-white and/or color transparencies.

In consideration for our free lance contributors, we pay for material on acceptance, rather than on publication. There is no set fee scale; we will notify you regarding payment after we've reviewed your work. We do give careful consideration to every manuscript that is submitted; those we accept are purchased for first-time rights, and may not be submitted to another publication until after they have appeared in our magazine.

Sample copies of the magazine are available at newsstands, libraries, or from us at $1.75 each.

Thanks again for thinking of us, and best wishes to you.

WESTERN AIRLINES *Western's World*

Ed Dwyer, editor

Coverage: Primarily west of the Rockies, plus New York, Alaska, Hawaii and Mexico

Format: Editorial celebrates and investigates innovative business ventures and
            businesspeople and trends generated in the West that affect national
            lifestyles. In addition, "Portfolio" presents the recreational treasures
            of the West and "Datelines" provide trenchant monthly briefs on business
            and pleasure developments in specific destinations.

Western's World celebrates the romance and adventure of accomplishment in the American
      West. It does so by focusing in its features ("Innovators," "Perspectives,"
      "Western Living"...) on the people and enterprises that make "Winning the West"
      an exciting, ongoing story. In its "Datelines" from around the route system,.
      Western's World guides its readers in discovering the fine foods, memorable
      scenery, unsurpassable outdoor activities and vast opportunities of the West,
      Alaska, Hawaii and Mexico. To sum up, Western's World mixes business and
      pleasure in a provocative and entertaining fashion designed to appeal to the
      mover and shaker <u>and</u> the vacationer.

For further information, see PSA Magazine.

MAILING: P.O. BOX 2890 TERMINAL ANNEX • LOS ANGELES, CALIFORNIA 90051

FACT SHEET TO PROSPECTIVE PHOTOGRAPHERS FOR WESTWAYS

WESTWAYS is a regional magazine, which includes all states west of the Rocky mountains, Alaska and Hawaii, as well as Mexico and western Canada.

Except for extraordinary instances, photographs appearing in WESTWAYS are provided by the authors with their submissions or are assigned either to the Automobile Club's staff photographers or professional photographers we work with on a regular basis. These photographers are long-time contributors familiar with our particular needs or requirements.

However, we do not rule out the off-beat, the one-in-a-thousand shot, the humorous, whimsical or just simply 'beautiful!' photographs that come along. We prefer color transparencies — black and white is considered only if the subject warrants it artistically.

We purchase one-time publication rights and must know if the photographs have been published previously, by whom and when. We pay $50 for each photograph published. Payment is made upon publication.

We maintain a reference file of photographers who can provide stock photographs. If you are interested, we suggest sending a detailed list of subject matter you have available.

Thank you for your interest in WESTWAYS.

EDITORIAL OFFICES: 2601 S. FIGUEROA ST. • LOS ANGELES, CALIFORNIA (213) 741-4760

NICHOLAS J. KOCKLER
Publisher

MARY ANN FISHER
Managing Editor

GEORGE T. MILLER
Associate Publisher

MAILING: P.O. BOX 2890 TERMINAL ANNEX • LOS ANGELES, CALIFORNIA 90051

FACT SHEET TO PROSPECTIVE FREE-LANCE WRITERS

WESTWAYS is a regional magazine, which includes all states west of the Rocky Mountains, Alaska and Hawaii, as well as Mexico and western Canada.

We are interested in receiving queries or suggestions pertaining to: 1) modern activities in the West, 2) outdoor recreation and travel, 3) Western history, 4) profile pieces on interesting, unusual people or places and 5) world travel. We are always looking for humor and off-beat articles that defy categorizing. The majority of articles, unless otherwise specified by the managing editor, should not exceed 1,500 words.

WESTWAYS is planned 3 to 4 months in advance and no story is purchased without a specific issue in mind. If a suggested story is seasonal, the lead time required is at least four months; e.g. August for Christmas, December for spring or Easter, etc. You must indicate if photographs are available if you do not submit them with your manuscript. We require color transparencies (35mm or larger) for most articles, and black-and-white glossies for historical articles.

Free-lancers new to WESTWAYS are paid approximately twenty cents a word for the copy we use. Our purchase includes the first publication rights and the right to publicize the story if we deem appropriate.

First-time submissions should include background about the writer and names of publications where articles have been published. Please include a stamped, self-addressed envelope with your queries and manuscripts.

Thank you for your interest in WESTWAYS.

EDITORIAL OFFICES: 2601 S. FIGUEROA ST. • LOS ANGELES, CALIFORNIA (213) 741-4760

NICHOLAS J. KOCKLER
Publisher

MARY ANN FISHER
Managing Editor

GEORGE T. MILLER
Associate Publisher

The Westways Writer

Winter 1985
Written by Mark Donnelly
Designed by Madeleine Herold

By Way of Introduction

As stated in the Fall issue of TWW, Andrea Paymar has moved to London and I've taken her place on the newsletter. Naturally, I'll be putting my own ideas and style into each issue, but I'm sure there will be some similarities to what Andi wrote. And certain standard elements will remain the same. Any suggestions you have on what should be included in the newsletter are welcomed.

The Personal Approach:

This won't be a place to teach people how to write. That's something you must come to on your own. However, there are some things that we are looking for at WESTWAYS in terms of writing style. A piece submitted to the magazine should be inspiring, interesting, creative. A good travel piece should encourage a reader to want to visit the locale. Take the personal approach. By this I don't mean writing in the first person, but rather, take your own approach to a place you've been to. What was it that really excited you during your stay?

Painting with Words:

We receive so many stories in the "If it's Tuesday it must be Belgium" style-- galloping surveys of what to do and see in Montana, India or wherever that never really capture the spirit of a region. We're looking for stories that give readers a feel for a place, that paint a picture. Have good photographs, yes, but don't rely on these to provide your visual images. Your words should be doing this. That way, photos and text work together in harmony. The reader should come away feeling that he or she has gone on the trip with you-- the old armchair traveler.

Accuracy:

The same ingredients of excitement and personal angle go for historic and profile pieces too. Anything you submit should come from the heart as well as the mind. And show this sense in your query letter. You should convince us that your topic is interesting, that you are capable of writing about it in clear, accurate language. Accuracy is a major concern. Know your facts and be precise in the text. Carry this accuracy over to information supplied with your top-quality photographs.

Caption Information:

Provide complete caption information: Give us who, what, when, where, why. We'll put the information into glowing prose, but we can't make it up! Including the information upon submission will save valuable time and make our jobs much easier.

Story Ideas:

I have a few suggestions on how to come up with interesting stories. Read. Stay up on newspapers, magazines, books (both fiction and nonfiction). These are invaluable sources for ideas. And specifically, you should know what's already been done. Your story on backpacking in the Sierras should have a different slant than what's just been done in National Geographic. The value of looking at other magazines, specifically travel if you're submitting to this market, is getting a feeling for a publication's style. What flies at WESTWAYS? What flies at Travel-Holiday?

And be an observer. Be open to the world around you. Notice people, their clothes, their expressions. Observe streets, cars, whatever is going on, whether at home or in a new spot. This observing is the material for your stories, be they fiction or nonfiction. Take mental notes or jot things down. Use your own style on this.

Business as Usual

1. WESTWAYS, published monthly by the Automobile Club of Southern California, welcomes articles about Southern California, states west of the Rocky Mountains, Mexico, Hawaii, western Canada, Alaska and world travel.
2. QUERY or send a complete manuscript with accompanying transparencies ...and an SASE.
3. ON SPEC...is the modus operandi of WESTWAYS.
4. 1500 words is the maximum manuscript length, unless otherwise specified by the editor.
Exceptions are Wit & Wisdom (750-1000 words) and Around

the Southland (1000 words).
5.   CONTRACTS...are for purchase of first rights. Manuscripts are paid for thirty days prior to scheduled publication month; photos, upon publication.
6.   A PICTURE IS WORTH...$50 (35mm color slides or color transparencies).   Black and white photos are acceptable if the subject requires them and are worth $25.

Scheduled

General Interest/ Western Travel

Boise, Idaho
Sundance Cruise/Alaska
Flights of Fancy
(Paul MacCready's latest
  design)
Easter Bunnies
Dashiell Hammett Literary
  Tour
The Banning Museum in
  Wilmington
Wyoming

World Travel

Scandinavia
Great Britain
Germany

Recommended Books

Writing From the Inside Out by Charlotte Edwards ($9.95, Writer's Digest Books).   Using your emotions and experiences in your writing.

Writer's Guide to Southern California by Maggie Kleinman, $8.95.   L.A. Writer.   1984.   Lists of Writers' Organizations, workshops, literary magazines, bookshops, research sources/facilities in the area.   Plus

observations on the S.C. literary scene.   Available in selected bookstores and by mail order from L.A. Writer, P.O. Box 1183, Culver City, 90232-1183. Telephone orders: (213) 837-1196.

The Write Stuff for Westways

Western and world travel (focusing on unique events, culture, the unconventional)
The Northwest
Montana
Jackson Hole, Wyoming
Photo Essays
Recommended winter vacation spots
(warm and cold weather)
Profiles of interesting people & places in the West
Humor pieces

Workshops

San Diego Writers/Editors Guild Third Annual Writers Conference.   Rosarito Beach Hotel, Rosarito Beach, Baja, Mexico.   April 19-21.   All types of writing forms, ranging from plays to magazine articles, plus the business side of publishing. For further information call Betty Smith (619) 449-0968 or leave message at (619) 223-5235.

Travel Writing Seminar University of California Santa Barbara.   Sat. and Sun., May 18 and 19, 9 A.M. to 4 P.M. (805) 961-3695.

Writing Seminars Santa Monica College "Thirteen Ways to Get Published" Sat., March 9, 9 A.M. to 1 P.M. $25.

"How to Sell 75% of Your Freelance Writing" Sat. April 20, 9 A.M. to 1 P.M. $40.   Santa Monica College. Make checks payable to Santa Monica College, Community Services, 1900 Pico Blvd., S.M. 90405. Phone (213) 452-9214.

Westways Staff

Mary Ann Fisher...........
              Editor
Carol Byers...............
            Staff Editor
Mark Donnelly.............
            Staff Editor
Penelope Grenoble.........
            Staff Editor
John Skinner..............
            Staff Editor
Angela Spikes.............
          Editorial Assistant
Vincent Corso.............
      Executive Art Director/
        Production Manager
Paul Miyamoto.............
            Design Director
Judith Lynch..............
        Production Coordinator
Madeleine Herold..........
            Staff Artist

The Next Issue

of TWW will be published in Spring of 1985.

Write to us at:
Post Office Box 2890
Terminal Annex
Los Angeles, CA 90051

Phone us at (213) 741-7460

Many thanks to Madeleine Herold, staff artist at Westways and designer of The Westways Writer, for all her work.   She's heading back to Boston.   We'll miss her.

HARRIS PUBLICATIONS, INC.
1115 BROADWAY NEW YORK, N.Y. 10010 (212) 807-7100

WRITER'S GUIDELINES FOR WOMAN MAGAZINE

1. Our primary need from freelancers is for short humor pieces (no more than 600 words) and for personal experience articles. We are also continually searching for subjects to feature in our Bravo Woman column.

2. All articles are requested on speculation.

3. Articles should not exceed 1500 words unless otherwise noted (see 4).

4. WOMAN IN THE NEWS and LET'S PUT OUR HEADS TOGETHER articles: maximum 500 words.

5. All purchased material is subject to editing before publication.

6. Please do not submit poetry or fiction. We do not publish either.

7. We DO NOT have a kill fee.

8. We purchase <u>one-time, North American printing rights.</u>

9. Our pay scale ranges from $15 to $125.

10. Submissions should be accompanied by a stamped, self-addressed envelope.

Woman's World is a national general interest magazine for working women and homemakers between 18 and 60. Articles are dramatic, human interest, informative. Sections include:

INTRO: Runs gamut of other sections, including IN Real Life, Families and Turning Point. Features best dramatic, touching, or light people-oriented human interest story. Photos crucial; needs subject's total cooperation. 800-1000 words.

POP PSYCH: General interest topic, somewhat controversial. Story discusses issue, pro & con, and should leave reader thinking about his/her opinion on subject. Can you survive your husband's affair? Are you a pushover? 800-1000 words.

REPORT: Probing, investigative news features with statistics and national scope. Cites authorities. Ten best and worst jobs of the future; Divorce over 60-the new problem.

IN REAL LIFE: Adventure, drama or emotional real-life stories. Can be told first person; with dramatic quotes and anecdotes. My 5 missing days; She returned from the living dead. 1000-1200 words.

FAMILIES: An unusual family--what they do, how they deal with problems; work together; lead unique lifestyle. A family of street musicians; Life together without father. 1000-1200 words.

WOMEN & CRIME: True stories of women convicted of a crime; unusual twist. If possible, sympathetic toward her. Scofflaw!; She stole money for love. 1000-1200 words.

TURNING POINT: Dramatic, first person account of an experience that changes a woman's life. Jilted-how could a love so right go so wrong?; "I'm a wheelchair mother".

BETWEEN YOU & ME: Essays on self-improvement; first or third person with humorous and/or poignant flavor -- Send me to my room-please!; A son's first love. 600 words.

Send queries to:

Janel Bladow
Articles Editor
Woman's World
201-569-0006 ext. 68

310 TOWN & COUNTRY VILLAGE, PALO ALTO, CA 94301
TELEPHONE: (415) 321-5102

WRITERS' GUIDELINES

Women's Sports and Fitness is a monthly publication devoted to women's sports, fitness and health. The average reader is between 20 and 30 and participates in two or more sports. We buy material from freelancers for the following:

DEPARTMENTS:

End Zone: This is our column of opinion. It can be political, personal, humorous or controversial, but it must be specific, well focused, substantiated and less than 1,500 words. End Zone pays $75.00.
Sports Pages: This section contains short profiles of collegiate and high school athletes, as well as women of any age who show promise in the sports world, and sports-related news items. Payment is $75-100. Send queries to Sports Pages Editor.

FEATURES:

Personality Profiles: We're looking for in-depth portraits of women who have achieved extraordinary results in their field, as well as of lesser-known women who would be an inspiration to our readers because of unusual accomplishments. **Coverage of sporting events**: Most of this text is staff-written because of fast closings but we will look at materials on spec. **Off-beat and recreational sports and adventure**: Stories that inform and encourage involvement in active living (e.g., backpacking, aerobic dancing, windsurfing). **Non-sports authoritative articles**: We're looking for articles on fitness, nutrition and sports-related issues. Subjects we've covered in the past include osteoporosis, vegetarianism, steroids and stretching exercises. **Strong personal reminiscences** will be considered as will **sports-related fiction**.

These articles are usually done on speculation although it is a good idea to query first. We pay approximately $200-$500 upon publication. Features range in length from 1,500 to 3,500 words.

QUERIES:

Queries should be in writing. Letter should be at least a page or two long. In addition to describing what will be included in the story, let us know why our readers will sit up and take notice. Articles must have a broad appeal so that they can be enjoyed by readers without a special knowledge of the subject or personality. Photography submissions may help sell your idea although we can assume no responsibility for art. Please send copies of previously published clips with your query. **Manuscripts**: It's best to read a few recent issues of the magazine to determine what we're looking for. Back copies can be purchased for $2; one-year subscriptions for $12.

Address all queries and manuscripts to our Queries Editor at the above address. Be sure to include an SASE or work will not be returned. Response time is generally six to eight weeks.

The official publication of the Women's Sports Foundation

MODERN HANDCRAFT, INC.

4251 PENNSYLVANIA AVENUE • KANSAS CITY, MISSOURI 64111 • 816/531-5730

WORKBENCH MAGAZINE

EDITORIAL REQUIREMENTS

WORKBENCH is a do-it-yourself woodworking, home improvement and home maintenance publication. We desire stories in these categories from all parts of the country and from both professional and amateur writers. Writing style is not important as articles may be rewritten to give them the WORKBENCH "slant."

We want do-it-yourself articles that show how average people are using ingenuity to modernize their homes, improve their lifestyle and to reduce energy consumption. We like stories that provide facts on reliable, inexpensive energy alternatives, and that will show our readers how they can incorporate these changes into their homes. We particularly want stories on maintenance and improvement of manufactured housing, including mobile homes. Stories should be detailed enough so our readers can duplicate the project, possibly with modifications to suit their own needs or situations.

Our woodworking projects range from simple toys and other easy projects for the beginning woodworker to copies of museum furniture pieces for the expert craftsman, which many of our readers are. We currently have a need for contemporary, practical home furnishings that would appeal to the woodworker with average skills. We are known for our accurate, detailed drawings of our projects, so submissions should include working drawings (pencil is acceptable) that are complete and accurately dimensioned. Blueprints are not required as all artwork is redrawn to fit a particular space. We want the step-by-step instructions, facts, and a materials list, if appropriate.

We stress good, sharp photography. The quality of the photography submitted with the story may mean the difference between acceptance and rejection. Black and white photos should be glossy, 4 x 5 or larger. If in doubt about the quality of the prints, send us the negatives. We can print those needed and then return the negatives. Color transparencies, 2-1/4 x 2-1/4 or larger, are desired, but sharp 35 mm slides will be considered. We prefer black and white "in progress" photos, but color photography of the finished project is encouraged. Instant color prints (Kodak, Polaroid) are not acceptable.

Generally, we do not make a decision to buy based on a query. We want to look at the complete package – story, photos and drawings. Payment is on acceptance and we report within two to four weeks. Our basic rate is $125 per published page. Payment is higher for regular contributors of quality material and lower for articles where we must provide photos or make working drawings. An additional payment is made for the use of color photography.

We ask that our contributors obtain several issues of our magazine and read them cover to cover to get a basic idea of our editorial approach. We will provide one free sample copy. Additional back issues are available for $2.00 each. We work six months ahead, buy for a year ahead, sometimes longer. For return of rejected manuscripts, enclose a stamped, self addressed envelope.

The Editors

MODERN HANDCRAFT, INC.

4251 PENNSYLVANIA AVENUE • KANSAS CITY, MISSOURI 64111 • 816/531-5730

WORKBENCH MAGAZINE

Beginning January 1, 1984, the Internal Revenue Code requires recipients of certain payments, to furnish their Social Security Number or Taxpayer Identification Number (TIN), as appropriate, to payors required to report such payments to the IRS. Failure to provide the correct taxpayer identification number to us may subject certain payments, that may be due to you, to withholding tax at a 20 percent rate, until this information is received.

Please fill in the appropriate blanks, and return this form along with your first manuscript submission to WORKBENCH.

Name: _____

Address: _____

_____

_____

Social Security
or Taxpayer
Identification Number: _____

_____ Sole Proprietorship

_____ Partnership

_____ Corporation

Signature:_____   Date:_____

WORKING MOTHER

Thank you for your interest in WORKING MOTHER. The magazine is looking for articles (about 1,500 to 2,000 words in length) that help women in their task of juggling job, home and family. We like humorous pieces and articles which sensibly solve or illuminate a problem unique to our readers. Topics that particularly interest us include: time, home and money management, health, family relationships, single parenthood and job-related issues. Pieces dealing with food, beauty, and fashion are usually staff-written.

If you submit a manuscript it should be typewritten, double-spaced and accompanied by a self-addressed, stamped envelope large enough to contain the manuscript. Manuscripts must be submitted on speculation at the author's risk. (We will not be responsible for lost material.) We prefer receiving proposals for pieces, rather than completed work. Then, if we find the subject suitable, we can discuss the best way to handle the material.

We occasionally publish short stories (around 3,000 words in length) which are entertaining or enlightening, whose characters have experiences similar to those our readers might have. We prefer receiving manuscripts rather than proposals for fiction and humor pieces.

All manuscript and queries should be addressed to the Editorial Department, WORKING MOTHER MAGAZINE, 230 Park Avenue, New York, N.Y. 10169.

A Division of The McCall Publishing Company

WORKING
WOMAN

342 Madison Avenue, New York, NY 10173 (212) 309-9800

Dear Writer:

Thank you for your interest in <u>Working Woman</u>. For the best idea of the kind of material we use, we suggest you check several recent issues of the magazine. Generally, our editorial requirements are as follows:

We accept non-fiction freelance articles and some humor pieces (no fillers) on all aspects of working women's private and professional lives. We also use pieces on various career fields (these should be broad in scope, well researched and include interviews with established women in the field). Our readers are career-oriented and already involved in their careers, well beyond deciding whether or not to have one.

Feature articles run about 2,500 words. Column lengths range from 1,500 to 2,500 words. Rates vary. Payment is made upon acceptance of the article for publication.

Health, finance, legal, political and entertainment columns are written by assigned writers who appreciate reader response and comment.

Queries and manuscripts should be sent to the attention of Julia Kagan, articles editor, and should be accompanied by a self-addressed, stamped envelope. Please include samples of your work with queries. We prefer to have a completed manuscript submitted to us on speculation.

All queries and manuscripts must be typed on 8½" x 11" white paper and must be double spaced. Please submit original and keep a copy for yourself. Replies to unsolicited material take from three to six weeks.

Sincerely,

The Editors

Guidelines for Writer's Digest Writers

9933 ALLIANCE ROAD
CINCINNATI, OHIO 45242
TEL. 513-984-0717

General Focus

Writer's Digest is a monthly handbook for writers who want to write better and sell more. Every word we publish must inform, instruct or inspire the freelancer. Our readers want specific ideas and tips that will help them succeed—and success to our readers means getting into print.

Yet, that doesn't mean that we don't have a little fun in WD. Our style is informal and personal. We try to entertain as well as instruct. We try to speak with the voice of a compassionate colleague, a friend as well as a teacher. And though we don't shy away from explaining the difficulties of getting published today, all of our articles share a certain optimism. WD is infused with a belief in anyone's potential to succeed as a writer.

You can best understand our philosophy by being intimately familiar with *Writer's Digest*. We are a monthly publication with a circulation of approximately 200,000. Our readers are of all ages and are scattered throughout the US, Canada and several other countries. Each year we buy about 60 major articles and scores of shorter items; our annual *Writer's Yearbook* and associated publications use an additional 30-50 manuscripts. Yet, we do not publish fiction or scripts.

To obtain sample issues of Writer's Digest, send $2.50 per copy to the Circulation Secretary, Writer's Digest, 9933 Alliance Rd., Cincinnati, Ohio 45242. An index of each year's contents is published in the December issue.

How to Submit

Writer's Digest editors prefer queries, not unsolicited manuscripts. Queries allow us to review your article ideas and to suggest how to tailor them for our audience before you begin writing. Queries also save you time and energy should we reject your idea.

Queries should include a thorough outline that introduces your article proposal and highlights each of the points you intend to make. Your query should discuss how the article will benefit our readers and why you are the appropriate writer to discuss the topic. Although we welcome the work of new writers, we respect success and believe the selling writer can instruct our reader better and establish more credibility than the writer with a good idea but no sales.

Please submit only one query at a time, and allow us 4-6 weeks to review your proposal; ideas that spark our interest are routed to other editors for review. Queries to *Writer's Digest* are also considered for *Writer's Yearbook* and associated publications. There is no need to query these publications separately.

If we like your proposal, we may either assign you to do the article or ask to see it on speculation ("on spec"). We often work on spec with authors who are new to us or whose ideas are not as clearly developed as we would like. It's also possible that we'll ask to see a more detailed query before we make a decision.

In certain cases, we do prefer complete manuscripts. These include short items and poetry for The Writing Life department, Tip Sheet items, and Chronicle articles. Submit only typed manuscripts, double-spaced, on 8½x11 white bond paper, one side only. No erasable paper, please. Legible photocopies are preferred (always keep copies of manuscripts you submit for publication). We'll look at good-quality dot-matrix printed manuscripts, but we prefer letter quality. Each submission must include your name, address and daytime telephone number.

No simultaneous submissions, please.

All submissions *must* include SASE—self-addressed, stamped envelope. We are not responsible for queries and manuscripts unaccompanied by SASE.

We do not accept unsolicited electronic submissions. Unsolicited electronic submissions accompanied by SASE will be returned unread; others will be discarded. However, tell us in your query if you have the capability to submit assigned work on disk or by modem.

Finally, we expect writers to double-check all facts included in their stories. Writers working on assignment or submitting unsolicited manuscripts are required to submit documentation to support the information included in their stories. Such documentation includes photocopies of title pages and mastheads indicating proper titles and spellings for all books and magazines mentioned in a piece. If you quote more than a sentence from another writer's work, we require a photocopy of the material as it appeared originally. If you interview editors or other writers, provide us with a telephone number for each source.

Photos and Artwork

If you are submitting a profile or interview, photos may be useful—or even required. Hold all photos until we have an acceptable manuscript, but do let us know the availability of photos when you write your query. (More on interview photos later).

We use cartoons, but they must be well drawn to merit consideration here. A clever gagline alone won't do. Send finished cartoons, only, in batches of ten or more. We prefer single panels, either with or without gaglines. The theme is the writing life—we want cartoons that deal with writers and the trials of writing and selling their work. Also, cartoons about writing from a historical standpoint (past works), language use, and other literary themes. Original artwork is returned after publication.

We do not accept unsolicited illustrations.

Payment and General Terms

We usually pay 10-20¢ per word, on acceptance, for manuscripts, and buy first North American serial rights, one-time use only. Poetry earns $10-$30, depending on length. Cartoons bring $50-$90. Contributors copies are sent to writers and artists whose work appears in that issue. (Should we want to reprint anything we've purchased from you, we will pay you 25% of the original purchase price for reprint rights for each use.)

What We Want—Long Stuff

Freelance submissions are accepted for nearly all sections of the magazine. The exceptions are: our regular columns, bylined department sections, and the New York, The West and The Markets reports.

How-to articles are our mainstay: how to write better, market successfully, recycle and resell manuscripts, maintain records . . . and more. These articles present a common problem or goal, offer the appropriate solution, and give an example of how that solution has worked. Articles generally run 2,000-3,000 words, though cover stories often run longer. We also look for pieces that can cover a topic completely in 1,000 words or fewer. Actual length will be discussed when the article is assigned.

Topics for features vary widely. Categories that we seek material for include writers' opportunities and money-making ideas; the business of writing; reference sources; writers' tools, equipment and supplies (however, we are not interested in material on word processing, which is covered by one of our columnists and seldom appears elsewhere in the magazine); writing discipline; language use; quizzes; personal experiences (but only if they teach a lesson or prove a point); marketing mechanics; and three types that will be covered more fully below: writing techniques, profiles/interviews and market reports.

In general, don't shy away from the word *I* in your articles. The first-person perspective is important to establishing your credibility. But don't overdo it. We want instructive articles, not "and then I wrote" essays. Round out your experiences with those of other writers and with information from editors, when appropriate.

We use a friendly, informal—but not lackadaisical or cutesy—style. We demand lively writing. Use anecdotes, examples, samples and quotes to strengthen the message of the article. We like lively headlines, and our articles are sprinkled with subheads at appropriate places to help readers locate particular sections when returning to the article. Writers who use lively headlines and subheads in their manuscripts demonstrate their familiarity with our style.

Writing Technique Articles. This brand of how-to article is most important to *Writer's Digest.* These pieces highlight an often misunderstood or poorly utilized writing method and detail how to use it precisely, appropriately and successfully. We are always hungry for these articles. Examples include how to write an effective lead, how to use dialogue to establish character, how to brighten your prose, how to use suspense effectively.

Articles may cover fiction, nonfiction, poetry or scriptwriting techniques, but must be accessible to all writers and offer advice that can be applied directly or indirectly to all forms of writing.

How a particular piece is structured depends on the complexity of the subject, but every piece will need to:

- Define the technique and its importance. Draw broad lines of application to other forms of writing.
- Outline how to use the technique. The best explanations break the technique down into distinct parts and deal with each part individually. When appropriate, use a step-by-step explanation.
- Give examples of its usage. A vital part of your article; give us more than you think necessary—and then add two more. Illustrate every point with examples—either from your own writing or from well-known works. On major points, readers can benefit from "right" and "wrong" or "before" and "after" examples, showing writing before the technique is applied or when it is used inappropriately, followed by the corrected version.
- If appropriate, give readers tips on incorporating the technique into their writing. For example, an article on using anecdotes gave tips on how to collect anecdotes to use.

As with all how-to articles, instruction is the key to making the article work. Analyze your own writing to determine what gives it power, what makes it successful. Then give our readers a thorough guide to using that technique powerfully and successfully, too.

Interviews and Profiles. Major interviews, using the Q&A format, should be with authors of stature; those currently in the news or on the bestseller lists. Length ranges from 2,500 to 4,000 words; we occasionally use longer pieces as the subject warrants. Narrative-style profiles of major writers usually run 2,500-3,000 words. We also use short profiles (about 1,000 words or fewer) of lesser-known authors who can inspire and give advice to our readers.

Lively quotes and anecdotes and solid information are as essential for profiles and interviews as other WD articles.

Even more essential is an understanding of the major elements of a WD interview or profile. These articles must be directed at the working writer; pieces rewritten from general interest magazines or book-review tabloids are not acceptable. For that reason, we require a detailed query for all interviews.

These are the major elements of a WD interview or profile (in order of importance):

- The writer's product. What the writer produces and why it is different and noteworthy; why it succeeds. (Writing samples often help, but they cannot tell the full story.) How the writer developed this trait and refined it. What the writer thinks of his work. What needs the writer thinks he is fulfilling. What brings power to his work. The conscious process of putting words on paper.
- Advice to other writers. What can other writers learn from the author and his work, his career? What problems can the writer steer readers around? What techniques can he instruct them in? What shortcuts can the writer suggest? What solutions to common problems can the writer recommend?
- The road to success. Failures and handicaps the writer has overcome, and how they were overcome. When the writer first realized he could succeed at the typewriter. The first break, and where it led. The rewards and the costs of success.
- How the writer works. Work habits, including number of hours per day and his timetable. The physical act of writing—does the writer use pencil, pen, typewriter or word processor? Where does the writer work? How does the writer discipline himself?

Unlike other WD articles, photos are essential to the interview/profile. Photos should concentrate on the subject's face and upper body. We like a good selection of shots that show gestures and capture the character of the subject. We prefer shots in which the subject is looking directly into the camera—though not awkwardly so. We also like to see a few middle-distance shots that show the subject in his/her work area, at the typewriter, or interacting with others who are pertinent to the story. If there's something special about the writer's environment, give us a long shot of the writer in this atmosphere. Natural lighting is best—avoid shadows, etc. If you cannot provide these photos yourself, provide us with a source for them.

Market reports. This an evolving category, so you'll want to study current issues to determine the exact treatment of such articles.

In general, market reports highlight general article or book styles and offer instruction on how any writer might break into this lucrative area. Examples might be writing the true-life drama, or the as-told-to article or book. A market report may also identify a particular market, such as writing for trade publications or writing a cookbook, but the market must be large and diverse; we aren't interested in pieces that spotlight highly specialized markets that can embrace only a few writers. Paint with a large brush in market reports; we're more likely to publish an article on writing expertly about health and fitness than an article on writing for the health and fitness market. There's a difference. If you don't understand that difference, don't attempt to write market reports.

In writing the market report, you'll want to cover several essential elements. This isn't a formula—only a checklist. Remember, anecdotes, specific examples and quotes are important here, too.

- Establish the market. It must be current and have a growing need for manuscripts. Quote editors. Emphasize specific sales and payments, either your own or other writers'.
- Describe the market. Detail the differences from and similarities to other markets and types of writing. Give an idea of who's interested in these types of articles so readers will know if this is a market that appeals to them.
- Explain how to find ideas for the market. What kinds of topics and treatments does the market use most? Point out how writers can generate ideas that are salable. Provide tips on matching ideas to publications.
- Explain how to write for the market. Detail the process of turning ideas into salable stories. What are the special requirements of writing for this market or writing this type of article or book? Point out common pitfalls and how to avoid them.

What We Want—Short Stuff

The Writing Life. This section uses brief, lively items that are offbeat or on-the-mark glimpses of the traits, transgressions and follies peculiar to writers and their life. This section is always fun and light, but instructional tips that also entertain are welcome. Length is 50-500 words—and here, shorter is better. We don't buy jokes, but we do buy short bits of humor (anecdotes, ironies, quotes and puns). Submit items on separate sheets of paper, please.

Poetry. We use no more than two poems an issue, so competition is severe. And we have very definite needs. Poetry is used only in The Writing Life department, so short, light verse is preferred. Serious verse is acceptable, but stands less chance of acceptance. Whether it's light or serious, all poetry must focus on writers—their joys, despairs, strategies and relationships to the world. Length rarely exceeds 20 lines.

Tip Sheet. This is our newest section, so you'll want to look at recent issues to see how it's developing. This department offers short (1,000 words, tops), instructional bits of information that help writers live, write and market more successfully. Possible topics might be advice on manuscript problems, business concerns, language stumbling blocks, and tax questions; suggestions on new ways to make money as a writer; and reports on more efficient office procedures.

My First Sale. An "occasional" department, these articles are first-person accounts of how a writer broke into print. These pieces, which are about 1,000 words long, should use a narrative, anecdotal style to tell a tale that is both inspirational and instructional. Query first, telling us what solid lesson your story would offer other new writers.

Chronicle. These are first-person accounts of writing successes, failures, incidents, problems and insights. They should be, as the name suggests, open, honest accounts—told either humorously or dramatically—as if you were sharing a few pages of your journal. A narrative style and a message that all readers can share are musts. Length is 1,500 words, maximum.

A Few Final Thoughts

WD editors will respond to all submissions or correspondence if SASE is included. We cannot be responsible for submissions that do not include SASE.

WD's editors answer specific questions about writing and marketing in the Tip Sheet department. Personal responses to such questions are generally not possible, although we do try to steer correspondents to sources that might be helpful and instructive. Also, please be generous in the time you allow us to answer—our first priority is to produce a magazine each month.

WD's editors appreciate hearing of your experiences marketing articles. We cannot, however, act as a writer's editor, evaluator or agent. We do, on occasion, intercede on a writer's behalf, but only after that writer has exhausted all other avenues. Address new market tips and other information to Markets Editor at the above address.

We don't purchase newspaper clippings.

WD sponsors an annual writing competition. Entries are accepted in four categories—Fiction, Nonfiction, Poetry and Scripts. Submission deadline is May 31; winners are announced annually in the October issue of WD. For rules and other information, write to WD Writing Competition, 9933 Alliance Rd., Cincinnati 45242. Include SASE.

WDS

20 rules for good writing

1. Prefer the plain word to the fancy.
2. Prefer the familiar word to the unfamiliar.
3. Prefer the Saxon word to the Romance.
4. Prefer nouns and verbs to adjectives and adverbs.
5. Prefer picture nouns and action verbs.
6. Never use a long word when a short one will do as well.
7. Master the simple declarative sentence.
8. Prefer the simple sentence to the complicated.
9. Vary your sentence length.
10. Put the words you want to emphasize at the beginning or end of your sentence.
11. Use the active voice.
12. Put statements in a positive form.
13. Use short paragraphs.
14. Cut needless words, sentences, and paragraphs.
15. Use plain, conversational language. Write like you talk.
16. Avoid imitation. Write in your natural style.
17. Write clearly.
18. Avoid gobbledygook and jargon.
19. Write to be understood, not to impress.
20. Revise and rewrite. Improvement is always possible.

WDS

young miss

RE: WRITER'S GUIDELINES 1985-86

Dear Writer:

Thank you for your interest in Young Miss magazine.

We are a national magazine for teenage girls ages 12 to 19. They're bright, enthusiastic, inquisitive. Our goal is to guide them--in effect, to be a "second best friend"--through the many exciting, yet often rough, aspects of adolescence. To that end, we have an interesting range of monthly columns: "What's the Problem?" (psychological issues), "Keeping Fit" (exercise, general health, and medical topics), "Dear Julia" (questions about sexual matters), and "Heroes & Heroines" (teen celebrities), to name just a few of the columns written by the staff. We also publish several major articles and one to two short stories each month.

While most of YM's columns and all our fashion/beauty copy are staff written, we purchase articles (1,500 to 2,500 words) on numerous topics of concern to teens. For example:

Personal growth: How to be a better friend, the pros and cons of popularity, coping with a "perfect" sister, and so forth.

Emotional dilemmas: Such as getting along with stepparents, overcoming shyness, understanding "the blues," coping with moving away, etc.

Boy/girl relationships: The abc's of blind dating, whether or not to go steady, getting "him" to notice you, being "just friends" with a guy, and so on.

As for "filler" articles (750 to 1,000 words), we are interested in humor and unusual or instructive personal experiences (both of which should be written in first-person style), offbeat how-tos, and quizzes on topics such as those listed above.

All articles should be lively, informative (but not academic in tone), and based upon thorough interviews with appropriate experts (psychologists, school counselors, physicians, etc.). They should also strongly represent teenagers' feelings and be illustrated with anecdotes and quotes accordingly.

Payment begins at $75 for filler articles and $250 for full-length features but varies according to the length and type of article. Please query us in writing; we prefer that to telephone calls and unsolicited manuscripts.

One request: Please familiarize yourself with Young Miss before submitting any material. Check your library for back issues or send us a check or money order for $2.00 plus a 10 X 13" SASE, and we'll send you a copy.

Sincerely,

The Editors

685 THIRD AVENUE, NEW YORK, N.Y. 10017 (212) 878-8700
TELEX-147129 TWX-710 581 2511

Magazines That Accept Freelance Contributions
But Have No Writer's Guidelines

The Atlantic
8 Arlington Street
Boston, Massachusetts 02116

Avril Cornell, Assistant to the Editor: "*The Atlantic* is always interested in poetry, fiction, and articles of the highest quality. A general familiarity with what we have published in the past is the best guide to our needs and preferences."

Boating
One Park Avenue
New York, New York 10016

Roy Attaway, Editor: "We are in need of technically correct stories written about modern production of fiberglass powerboats. We don't do sailboats at all, nor do we pay much attention to older wooden boats. As for payment, this will vary anywhere from $350–$1,000, depending on the article, and how badly we want it. We also prefer tack-sharp Kodachrome 35mm transparencies. We do not like Ektachrome, because it is too blue. I would suggest that any writer wanting to write for us should send a query letter first. . . ."

Boy's Life
Magazine Division
Boy Scouts of America
1325 Walnut Hill
Irving, Texas 75038-3096

Estelle Rutherford, Assistant to the Editor: "We no longer have printed guidelines for prospective contributors. We have determined that no condensed set of suggestions or single copy is adequate guidance for writers interested in our market. The best guide is the study of at least a year's worth of published material supported by a working knowledge of the program of the Boy Scouts of America."

California Magazine
11601 Wilshire Blvd.
Los Angeles, California 90025

Helene Goldsen, Assistant to the Managing Editor: ". . . We generally tell writers to thoroughly read *California Magazine* to become familiar with our style and our tone. Though we don't often assign freelance pieces, we do welcome all specific written queries. We would prefer not to receive whole manuscripts. All queries should include a SASE."

Columbia Journalism Review
700 Journalism Building
Columbia University
New York, New York 10027

Gloria Cooper, Managing Editor: ". . . the *Review*'s operations are too informal, and too low-budget, for formalized guidelines. We normally respond to . . . requests from authors by suggesting that they look at the magazine itself."

Commentary
105 East 56 Street
New York, New York 10022

Marion Magid, Managing Editor: "*Commentary* has no specific guidelines beyond the usual requirements of a legibly-typed manuscript accompanied by a stamped, self-addressed envelope.

"We publish articles on subjects of literary, political, and social interest, and we also publish fiction, but we do not publish poetry, art work, photographs, or any other illustrative material. Our book reviews run to 1,500 words or thereabouts, and our articles start at about 2,000 words."

Country Life
King's Reach Tower
Stamford Street
London SE1 9LS
England

Geoffrey Lee, Executive Editor: "We do not issue any guidelines to our authors . . . We merely ask our authors to study the magazine before submitting material."

The Family Handyman
1999 Shepard Road
St. Paul, Minnesota 55116

The Editors: "We no longer issue guidelines but suggest that you study the . . . recent issues of *TFH* to familiarize yourself with our writing style and story requirements."

Food & Wine
American Express Publishing Corporation
1120 Avenue of the Americas
New York, New York 10036

The Editors: "We do not have formal guidelines for writers at this time. However, if you have some current culinary or beverage *ideas*, as opposed to topics (avocados, Spain, fondue), you're welcome to submit developed proposals for consideration. Please address your queries to: Warren Picower, Managing Editor, *Food & Wine*, 1120 Avenue of the Americas—9th floor, New York, New York 10036.

"*Food & Wine* seeks to provide its readers with thorough, accurate information on dining and entertaining at home, as well as in restaurants, locally and abroad. The magazine tries to supply this kind of complete information in every feature article, comprehensively but concisely.

"The cost for a mailed copy of *Food & Wine* is $2.00, should you wish to receive one."

House & Garden
Condé Nast Publications, Inc.
350 Madison Avenue
New York, New York 10017

Jerome H. Denner, Managing Editor: ". . . *House & Garden* has no printed author's guidelines.

"We do not encourage unsolicited manuscripts and our policy is to return them unread.

"We do accept and read inquiries, but it is very rare indeed that one is followed up.

"Almost all of our material is done on assignment and by writers we use regularly or experts in a particular field."

Inside Sports
1020 Church Street
Evanston, Illinois 60201

Michael Herbert, Editor: "If you're writing about professional sports and have unique inside information, inside access to professional sports, and you are an outstanding writer, then we would be interested in your freelance contributions. We're not looking for first time writers; we are looking for professional sports journalists. Ninety-five percent of *Inside Sports* is freelance written."

Life
Time & Life Building
Rockefeller Center
New York, New York 10020

Dean Valentine, Articles Editor: "To be bluntly honest and thus helpful to your readers, *Life* is not exactly a target of opportunity for freelancers.

"The majority of articles in the magazine are staff-prepared. The only regular exceptions are one 2,500 word "American Address" column in the front and one long 4,000 to 7,000-word so-called text piece in the back. These outside contributions tend to come from a small group of regulars, many of them Time, Inc. veterans.

"Theoretically, a freelancer would have a shot if he or she offered unique access to a much sought-after subject. I say, theoretically, because I can't cite a specific example. Writers who do submit such ideas should enclose clips that give evidence of their experience and prose style.

"I'm sorry to be so discouraging, but these are the realities."

Modern Photography
825 Seventh Avenue
New York, New York 10019

Julia Scully, Editor: "We have no Writer's Guidelines as such, as we are mostly staff-written, using freelance writers only for highly specialized or technical subjects."

Opera News
Metropolitan Opera Guild
1865 Broadway (at 61st Street)
New York, New York 10023

Dennis McGovern, Production Associate: "The vast majority of our articles are either written by staff or assigned to writers who have been with the magazine for years. This is the fiftieth anniversary of the Metropolitan Opera Guild, publisher of *Opera News* and there has been a publication in one form or another since the beginning.

"Query letters are replied to as time permits and over the transom submissions are read when time permits but not encouraged. A query letter is always preferable.

"In the area of reviews, new writers might be given an opportunity to write for the magazine should there be an operatic event of sufficient importance taking place in their area.

". . . chances for new writers are not very common in *Opera News*."

PC
Ziff-Davis Publishing Company
One Park Avenue
New York, New York 10016

David Baker, Editorial Assistant: "We do not have any formal guidelines to offer prospective writers, but suggest they keep reading the magazine to develop a feeling for our general tone, content, and audience.

"As a special-interest consumer magazine, *PC* Magazine has a well-defined editorial focus. As a result, our article assignments are made months in advance and unsolicited manuscripts rarely fit into our editorial schedule. We do welcome specific, detailed proposals, however."

People
Time & Life Building
Rockefeller Center
New York, New York 10020

Hal Wingo, Assistant Managing Editor, says that his magazine does consider freelance material. "We accept suggestions of 3 or 4 paragraphs that would be relevant to the particular sections of the magazine. We are always happy to take suggestions about achievers in special fields."

Personal Computing
Hayden Publishing Company, Inc.
10 Mulholland Drive
Hasbrouck Heights, New Jersey 07604

The Editors: "As a matter of policy, all reviews are staff written. However, we will be happy to consider queries for feature articles or 'People in Computing' profiles.

"We do not publish editorial calendars, and therefore, are unable to supply you with one."

Playbill
71 Vanderbilt Avenue
New York, New York 10169

Louis Botto, Senior Editor: "Unfortunately, we do not have any [writer's guidelines]. Much of our material is staff-written. We also have a group of free-lancers who have been writing for us for years. Therefore, we are not really looking for unsolicited manuscripts.

"The Editor-in-Chief prefers to receive article ideas by mail, addressed to her: Joan Alleman. We mainly publish articles on current Broadway shows, their start, authors, directors, etc. We do not publish fiction and rarely use verse or cartoons. That's about it."

Science Digest
1775 Broadway
New York, New York 10019

Frances Bishop, Editorial Assistant: ". . . we will accept SHORT query letters.

"It has been my observation during over a year of reading and referring unsolicited material—both mss and queries—that only about 3–5 were deemed worthy of publication."

Scientific American
415 Madison Avenue
New York, New York 10017

Linda Hertz, Senior Educational Assistant: "We do not have a style sheet or 'author's guide.' If someone would like to write an article on our behalf, he or she need only give us an outline on what he or she has in mind."

Skiing Magazine
Ziff-Davis Company
One Park Avenue
New York, New York 10016

Alfred Greenberg, Editor-in-Chief: "We do not issue general guidelines. Each assignment is accompanied by a letter of specific instructions."

Stereo Review
Ziff-Davis Publishing Company
One Park Avenue
New York, New York 10016

William Livingstone, Editor-in-Chief: "We do use a lot of freelance writers, but they are audio specialists and

people we know who have established a reputation for music . . . people with a real understanding of music. We are not a market for someone who just wants to be a writer. Their inexperience shows."

Success!
342 Madison Avenue
New York, New York 10173

Grace Dowling, Assistant to the Editor: "*Success!* magazine accepts freelance contributions. *Success!* does not have formal guidelines. We think the best guideline is to read the magazine."

Tennis
495 Westport Avenue
Post Office Box 5350
Norwalk, Connecticut 06856

Shepherd Campbell, Editor: "We feel that the best way to get an idea of what we're looking for in articles is to scan a couple of issues of our magazine.

"We accept, on speculation, tennis-related articles of most any length—but preferably not longer than 3500 words. We pay on publication, and will make every effort to return any manuscript that we feel does not fit into our editorial plans.

"Please send your story to the attention of the 'Articles Editor' and enclose a stamped, self-addressed envelope.

"Thank you for your interest in *Tennis* magazine and we'll look forward to receiving your manuscript."

TV Guide
Radnor, Pennsylvania 19088

Andrew Mills, Assistant Managing Editor: "Yes, we do accept freelance contributions. When I receive a request for writer's guidelines, my response is 'Read the magazine, because what we print is a good indication of what you should be writing'."

Vegetarian Times
P.O. Box 570
Oak Park, Illinois 60303

Paul Obis, Editor: "If it were only that easy! An editor always has to keep an open mind and a publication must reflect societal changes.

"Several pages would be required for us to detail the kinds of things we look for in an article and even then it would be subject to numerous revisions and clarifications.

"Our magazine is hard to break into because of the specialty of our audience and because of our committment to quality.

"I feel the only way a person can really understand our magazine is to read it. For this reason, we don't publish guidelines."

Vogue
Condé Nast Publications, Inc.
350 Madison Avenue
New York, New York 10017

Amy Gross, Features Editor: "*Vogue* does not publish editorial guidelines. Our suggestion is that the writer become acquainted with *Vogue*'s content and style and select material accordingly."

The Writer
120 Boylston Street
Boston, Massachusetts 02116

Sylvia K. Burack, Editor-in-Chief: "*The Writer* is a limited market for free-lance material. Though we make no assignments (everything is submitted on speculation), we read all manuscripts submitted, respond promptly, and pay on acceptance for articles we accept. Articles should be about 2000 words long, approximately 8 pages, double-spaced."

Woman's Day
1515 Broadway
New York, New York 10026

Rebecca Greer, Articles Editor, says that although her magazine does not have formal guidelines, it does accept freelance contributions. Says Greer, "Read the magazine. Few do this judging [from] the inappropriateness of the material we receive. A new writer has to come to me with a new idea. Writers should look for material on local stories about real people who have done something remarkable—something our readers would relate to, be inspired by, or want to emulate."

Yachting
Box 1200
5 River Road
Cos Cob, Connecticut 06807

Deborah Meisels, Associate Editor: "We accept freelance contributions. We prefer fewer than 2,500 words, narrative in style, and accompanied by good transparencies." Ms. Meisels also reminds us that social security numbers are needed these days for payment. Meisels continues, "If authors would include these, much time would be saved in the payment process."

Index